THE YEAR OF
EATING
DANGEROUSLY

ALSO BY TOM PARKER BOWLES

E Is for Eating: An Alphabet of Greed

THE YEAR OF EATING DANGEROUSLY

A GLOBAL ADVENTURE IN SEARCH OF CULINARY EXTREMES

TOM PARKER BOWLES

ST. MARTIN'S PRESS 🙴 NEW YORK

www.stmartins.com

Library of Congress Cataloging-in-Publication Data

Parker Bowles, Tom.
    The year of eating dangerously : a global adventure in search of culinary extremes / Tom Parker Bowles.—1st U.S. ed.
        p. cm.
    ISBN-13: 978-0-312-37378-8
    ISBN-10: 0-312-37378-3
    1. Food. 2. Cookery, International. 3. Food habits.
4. Parker Bowles, Tom—Travel. I. Title.

TX355.P25 2007
641—dc22

                                                          2007020484

First published in Great Britain by Ebury Press, an imprint of Ebury Publishing

First U.S. Edition: September 2007

10 9 8 7 6 5 4 3 2 1

to Sara

Contents

ACKNOWLEDGMENTS

I would like to thank the following for all of their help, advice, and support. Without their help, this book would not have even got off the ground.

Guido Agnello, Riccardo Agnello, Antonio Baucina, Hermione Del Bono, Luca Del Bono, Andrew Parker Bowles, Rose Parker Bowles, Duca Enrico Paterno Castello, Johnson Chang, Tony Chiu, Horace Cook, Richard Cook, Camilla Cornwall, Dave DeWitt, Lucy Gormanston, Geordie Greig, Gerard Grieve, Eddie Hart, Sam Hart, Jeongdo Hong, Mrs. Hong, Jake Irwin, Riccardo Lanza, Giada Laudicina, Sebastian Lee, Lucky, Ellen Nelson, Sam and Sang Norman, Leoluca Orlando, Dana de Patto, RB Quinn, The Dowager Viscountess Rothermere, Ivan Scholte, John Shen, David and Lucy Tang, Ed Victor, Joe Warwick, Rob Waugh, Colin Westal.

My agent Grainne Fox for her endless patience, support, and inspiration.

Hannah McDonald for her honesty, input, and exemplary editing. And for gently nudging my rather lumpen prose into something a little more readable.

Sarah Bennie and Ed Griffiths for their publicity magic, and Fi and the marketing team for their polished savvy. And everyone else at Ebury.

Thanks also to everyone at St. Martin's Press in the United States, especially Michelle Richter, Ellis Trevor, and my wonderful editor Elizabeth Beier.

And thank you to Lee Schrager and Ben Elliot for their hard work helping to launch the book stateside.

INTRODUCTION

My love affair with America was, for the first twelve years of my life, a far-off, unrequited crush. I gazed longingly at this mythical land from afar, my youthful passion fuelled by a ceaseless flow of movies, television, and comics. It mattered little that the farthest west I'd ever been was Cornwall, at the toe of Britain's isle, because the accent of my imagination was firmly American. Anything that glided over the Atlantic, from Indiana Jones, Archie, and Ronald Reagan to Lifesavers and Tab Clear, seemed impossibly glamorous in comparison to the seeming drabness of my own world. But my infatuation with American food overwhelmed any other concern. While we were draped in the dull brown and orange livery of Sainsbury's—a glum, plodding existence—America seemed glossily alive and dynamic. Not for them variety packs of ready salted crisps or bulk loads of PG Tips; America had Fritos and iced tea. It had cherry slushies, all frozen and tingling. We had Sainsbury's orange squash. America was a land filled with McDonald's, Burger King, and Dairy Queen, bright, pristine, and filled to the gills with glorious burgers. We had the dull suburban yawn that was Wimpy, with its sad meat patties and second-rate, watery milk shakes. America had Willy Wonka candy, Twinkies, Baby Ruth, M&M's, Reese's Pieces, Hershey's Kisses, and a million other exciting, slick sweets that were made all the more desirable by their appearance on the big screen. All we got was a Terry's Chocolate Orange. And because of this imagined world, America became an edible Emerald City, a culinary Kubla Khan where hot dogs paved the streets and Kool-Aid flowed from taps. A place where Chuck Norris took it in turns with Arnie to keep the peace, while Corey Haim kept the well-coiffed vampires at bay. This was my culinary mecca, not the familiar landscapes of home, or France, Spain, or Italy. And the sooner I could get there, the sooner I could start my edible American Dream.

It's not that my own life was dull or unhappy. Anything, but, in fact. I grew up in a big house in the country, with a farm attached. My family has always been great eaters and food a source of joy and celebration rather than just fuel to get by. Actually, we're all pretty damned greedy, full stop. My father was, and still is, a keen gardener. When I was a child, he'd bring in hauls of knobbly Pink Fir Apple potatoes, tiny broad beans nestled in their furry pods. Then plump, fiery radishes, endless varieties of lettuce, curly kale, prickly artichokes, and mammoth cauliflowers. There were plums and apples and pears in autumn, picked straight off the tree. And figs as warm and seductive as a Sicilian breeze. This was local, seasonal fresh food way before the concept became trendy. I assumed that everyone's father had large kitchen gardens and chickens pecking about the lawn. My sister and I used to collect fresh eggs from the hen-house every morning (very softly, so as to avoid the broody hen's angry beak). They were warm to the touch, with a brilliant yellow yolk. At Easter, my father would swap the brown speckled eggs for chocolate ones, covered in a sugar shell so realistic that even the birds were fooled. We all had favorite birds, including one called Whitey who was convinced he was human. He'd strut into the kitchen and chase the dogs. Sadly, he fell victim to Mr. Fox, who ripped off his head along with six of his favorite ladies. So we respected the various animals that milled about the farm but were under no illusions as to their purpose. The link between beast and plate was always made clear, in very unsentimental terms; all the creatures on the farm were for milking or eating, save Humphrey, an overweight and irritable sheep who had escaped the abattoir though pure strength of character. Cruelty to any beast was unthinkable and still remains one of the most important lessons I learned; if we eat meat, we must ensure it was raised in the most humane way possible.

It was only my mother who cooked, although we had various lovely (and generally wide) ladies in to help occasionally. My father could hardly boil a kettle, let alone fry an egg (he's improved now, stretching to Dover sole, kippers, and steak). He would grow, raise, or buy the ingredients and my mother would cook them. Thankfully, she was a master of simplicity. She made no secret of hating pastry and cakes and the other, more empirical side of British cuisine. But show her a flappingly fresh Dover sole or a piece of well-hung beef and she'd produce perfection every time. The average time between being dug up and appearing on the plate was about thirty minutes so the flavors were clean, pure, and sharp. This sort of pared-down cooking only works when the ingredients were of the very highest quality...which they were. Summer nights were filled with the aforementioned sole and sauté potatoes, say, with a handful of rosemary from the bush outside the kitchen ("always pick from the highest branches, as those dogs," warned my father, "just love to piss on the base"). Freshly podded peas with roast chicken (perfectly burnished, with the "essential lemon up its ass"), freshly boiled prawns with mayonnaise and blushing pink wild salmon with buttery new potatoes. Then summer puddings pregnant with tart berries and gooseberry fools, homemade, with just the right amount of tart to make the lips pucker. Winters meant hearty, soul-sustaining stews and braises and roasts and buttery potted shrimps (always from Mr. Baxter in Morecombe Bay) and the very tenderest of calves' liver. Pudding was treacle sponge or treacle tart and I never remember a hungry or unhappy meal. These first eight years of my upbringing were blissful in every sense. But then, out of nowhere, came the sucker punch that would change my happy, privileged world forever...five years of prep school.

This particularly British institution sees eight-year-old boys packed off for five years of education away from home. As sad as I was to leave my parents and sister, I wasn't unduly worried by the whole thing. I had friends from my previous school to meet up with and the whole thing seemed more adventure than trial. But it was there, cosseted behind high walls just outside Oxford, that I learned the true meaning of disgust. The food was institutional slop of the lowest form, the sort of bland, unthinking crap that gave British cuisine such a filthy reputation. Within two days, I'd moved from belly-filling bliss to hellish gastronomic torment. Breakfast consisted of scummy, pallid flaps of tired bacon, cooked days in advance. God only knows the state of the wretched pig that produced this sorry dross but you can guarantee he wasn't a happy porker. Then fried egg with the consistency of ice hockey pucks and imbued with a faint, sinister, fishy tang. There was fried bread sodden with cheap grease that would slip down your throat and taint the palate for days to come; and highly suspect sausages that almost certainly contained the ear lobes and assholes and other assorted detritus of the abattoir floor. Even the toast was either burned to ashes or raw and soggy.

Lunch was equally depraved, usually mince, gray, gloomy, and gristle filled. A few despondent boiled potatoes, complete with mouldy black eye, stared up, begging the horror to end. Sometimes, these wretched specimens would be given a very cursory mashing (i.e., they were broken up with a fork) and put on top of the mince. This was dubbed Cottage Pie. Sometimes they added a tinned tomato and a handful of musty oregano and named it Bolognese (if I hailed from Bologna, I'd sue the bastards for libel). Or slip in a few uncooked sheets of lasagne and christen it—yup, you've guessed it—lasagne. When it came to mince, my school's kitchen creativity knew no bounds. Liver was particularly horrific, tough, pungent, and riddled with chewy veins. Of course, the plate had to be cleaned before you could move from the hard wooden bench. You had to swallow vast lumps with a torrent of water, or stash it in your pocket to throw away later. Even the birds turned up their nose at this organ. I can go on and on: fish pie that was all uncooked flour and sharp bones, salt-lick gammon steaks with a cloyingly sweet pineapple ring perched daintily on top. And a chicken casserole that resembled the contents of a vomitorium. Sunday lunch was decidedly the worst, in that this fine symbol of the pleasures of British life was reduced to gutter level, the holy made profane. There was no way you could tell the paltry, processed and limp slices of beef from the pork and lamb in flavor. Everything was just a slight variation on beige. For a young boy raised with a true love of food, Sunday lunch at school was torture. All I remember is hunger, a gaping emptiness that followed me about like Banquo's ghost. Of course, I knew nothing of true hunger, but those five years laid the base for a greed and obsession with good food that would shape the rest of my life (as well as the ever-increasing curve of my belly).

One of my favorite places to escape was the library, with its sombre air of enforced tranquillity. I'd find a distant corner and drool over Time-Life Guides to America. Filled with picture-perfect American families, all bright eyes and white grin, I'd stare transfixed at their impossibly juicy hamburgers, devoured in gleaming white, pristine kitchens. There were tables groaning with scarlet crayfish, as alien to me as the tyrannosaurus rex. I knew how to eat a crawdaddy way before I actually got around to trying one. A detailed diagram made every last detail clear. The next page would have bare-chested Rhode Islanders digging into a clambake, right down to sucking the empty skulls. I sat for hours devouring these images, mouth agape, living vicariously through the musty photos of an old Time-Life tome. This was gastroporn in its purest form, with me the desperate, but oh-so-willing, voyeur. By the age of eleven, I was backward in most things, but entirely conversant on the matter of Coke's fiasco with New Coke. I could hardly add, yet I knew that M&M's had royally screwed up in not getting their product into *ET* (the role went to Reese's Pieces instead). I probably knew more about American fast food, candy, and soft drink that I did about the kings and queens of England. In fact, I *know* I did. But my first experience of real America—rather than my long-held fantasy—came at age twelve, when we spent a summer in the Bahamas. As we touched down in Miami and climbed onto the monorail to change terminals, my heart threatened to rip through my chest with heady excitement. I was actually here, two feet placed in the Cinnabon-scented Promised Land. So while the Bahamas had suitably limpid seas and powdery beaches, it was the artificial chill of the supermarket that held the most appeal. Here, at last, was American consumerism in full flow (although we weren't strictly in the country), my movies' visions made real. This was a place where the grocery store aisles were crammed with Cap'n Crunch and Fruit Loops and Pop Tarts. Then Oscar Meyer bacon and Squeezy Cheeses, Clamato, Beefmato, Cherry SevenUP, root beer, and Frito Lay's. How could anyone be unhappy in a country with such choice, so many "free gifts" and "special offers" screaming out from every pack? My father, no slouch when it came to shopping himself, had to drag me out and onto the beaches. "We're surrounded by sea and all you want to do is wander those freezing aisles." He couldn't have been more right.

It was six years before I got back to the states, and this time I was ready for third base and beyond. After that first, subzero kiss of the Bahamian hypermarket, I was ready for full consummation. Aged eighteen, this was my first taste of real freedom. It was 1993, school was out forever, and two old friends and I aimed to drive and Greyhound our way through the West and Southwest. At first, the endless small towns and strip malls provided an education in real fast food. Hot dogs at Dairy Queen, sliders at White Castle, and all-you-can-eat pizza at Domino's. But even a trio of ravenous junk food addicts began to struggle after the fifteenth Jack in the Box of the week, and began to crave real food. As much as we revelled in those burgers, I wanted a taste of Time-Life America, all those clams and crawfish. The one advantage of bussing through the likes of Barstow and Indian Springs, Rockspring and Rawlins was a view of the real America, not just of the stoning vistas and ever-changing views, but the endless uniformity of super edible brands. In parts of the country, one town was near identical to the next, only a road sign to tell them apart. In Wyoming, we found margaritas made in old petrol cans and buffalo wings in the Silver Dollar (they didn't card us there). Santa Fe was my first taste of a burrito, then Albuquerque for mountains of crispy bacon and eggs over easy. The waitress called us "honey" and had a pencil stuck behind her ear. There were freshly boiled crabs in San Francisco and dinner at The Ivy in LA. We flew back, seeing ourselves as real men now. Our parents, pleased as they were to see us, quietly disagreed.

But it was my first visit to New York that sealed the relationship. A few rocky moments in the West (sleeping outdoors in bear country, for one) did nothing to quell my love but New York blew my mind and belly, too; all I ever do in that city is eat, or think about where to eat next. A cheeky dog on the way to breakfast, usually eggs and bacon. Then dim sum in Chinatown or a brace of lobster rolls at Mary's Fish Camp. If there's room, perhaps a bite of pure burger perfection at The Corner Bistro (if I'm uptown, JG Mellon is just as good). Maybe a sleep before a quick run to Gray's Papaya for hotdog and juice (for health reasons, of course), then a kip. Then dinner, maybe a steak and salad frisée at Les Halles, or buttery o-toro at Blue Ribbon sushi. No evening is complete without a late-night stop off to Union Square's Coffee Shop and some chilli cheese fries. For me, New York is the greatest eating city of them all. By this time, I was writing a food column for *Tatler* magazine, being paid to eat. More excuse, then, to slope over the bridge for a charred Peter Luger Porterhouse or back to Ray's on Prince for thin crust pizzas so fine that I'd run off, join a cult, and drink gallons of Kool-Aid for just one more bite. New York is my sort of city, a place where the glutton is seen as gourmand, the troughing pig as discerning auteur. The moment I'm in under that tunnel or cross over that bridge, I feel that all is well in the world.

But it wasn't just America that had designs on my heart. I had traveled around India and Thailand, developing a taste for the sour and salty, the hot and pungent. Each different area had its own cuisine, its own table d'hote to be discovered and devoured. Thai food became an addiction, the heat and fragrance driving my taste insane with sultry, exotic new sensations. And I had started to cook properly, too, first British and Italian, then anything I could lay my hands on. But America was still sacred and every new visit offered some new and delicious revelation. I discovered Calvin Trillin and A. J. Liebling, two masters of elegant, greedy prose. While Liebling concerned himself with Paris (his *Between Meals* is a collection of unparalleled passion, libido, elegance, and gustatory joy), Trillin went in search of the true American flavors. It was Trillin who taught me about buffalo wings, Cincinnati chilli, and the true home of real "que" (Arthur Bryant's Barbeque, of course). Not that your Carolinians, Texans, and various other Southerners would agree. I loved Trillin for his well-honed, clean prose and his inquisitive delight in all things edible. I must have read his Tummy Trilogy over a dozen times now, and each time, it seems to improve. My first brush with barbeque was in Virgil's, just off Times Square in New York. When I admitted this to a true Q head, he laughed me out of town. "You go to New York for Que. Jesus, that's so wrong. I'd keep that dark little tale secret if I were you." But a few sessions judging at The Jack Daniel's Invitational Barbeque Competition in Lynchburg, Tennessee, soon taught me the difference between Boston Butt and Baby Back ribs, wet rubs and dry.

Barbeque is a top ten food (alongside caviar, Joe's Stone Crab, roast beef, Pho soup, cheeseburgers, potted shrimps, a proper meat ragu sauce, prawn dim sum, decent smoked salmon, chilli, and o-toro sashimi... wait, that's eleven. And I've hardly started. Tomorrow's list is guaranteed to be different) and near impossible to get over here. I crave its smoky allure and miss it like a parent misses his child. It's *that* bad.

In Britain, as a result of foot and mouth and BSE and avian flu and every other damned disaster that has erupted in the past few years, we've started to look more closely at where our food comes from, how it's produced, and how far it needs to travel. Thanks to the likes of Jamie Oliver and Nigella Lawson, food has become headline news, something to be discussed, argued about, and improved. And not a moment too soon, as obesity levels are rising and the long-term cost of cheap, processed foods ruinous. Although the organic movement moves from strength to strength, I worry that the big corporations just see organic branded goods as a way to make bigger margins. We should care about organic as a sustainable system of farming, not because it's this week's new trend. I've met scores of brilliant farmers who refuse to turn organic (it might cost too much, take too long, or just seem unnecessary) yet their produce is among the best in the country, as they farm using old-fashioned methods. Intensive farming is at the heart of all our problems, not non-organic food. Food miles are another huge issue. How "green" are organic French beans, jetted half the way across the globe from Africa? Good, healthy food comes from sensible, humane farming practices—a respect for the soil and the environment. Local food, too, is all very well in spring, summer, and autumn but life could get a little dreary in winter without lemons, oranges, and olive oil. So pragmatism is important, too. There is no easy solution to any of these food questions, but we should never stop searching. Food not only keeps us alive but is tightly entwined with politics, economics, health, and happiness. In Britain, we're once more starting to relish our national produce, to rediscover regional specialties, be they Melton Mowbray Pork pies or West Country cheddar. For me, simplicity and a respect for ingredients are fundamental for good food; a perfectly hung piece of steak with crisp chips with fluffy insides, say. Or a slow cooked stew or chilli. And it's my love of the regional cuisine of all countries (for there is no national cuisine, just a collective of regions) that remains constant. As much as I respect the Kellers, Towers, and Trotters, my love is of the regional: the clambakes, boudin stalls, crawfish boils, breakfast burritos, and frozen custard. Give me a napkin and a pile of boiled blue crab over silver cutlery and three Michelin stars any day. A good oyster Po' boy is a thing of true beauty, and for me, more attractive than the creamy flourishes of New'awlins Creole cookery. I like unshowy kitchen knowledge, accomplished technique, and quality of ingredients, not over-embellished flummery (though an evening with Blummenthal or Adria can delight and dazzle the palate, too). Give me Goode's smoked link and brisket over a whole river's worth of foams and reductions. And that philosophy, I hope, permeates the book.

The Year of Eating Dangerously is not so much about picaresque derring-do (although there's a little of that, albeit rather windy), but a fascination with the world's diverse cuisines. And why one man's insect is another man's garni. I wanted to sample everything, however gruesome, to try and establish some kind of culinary context. Very rarely did the taste repel on my travels. More often than not, it was the *idea* of the insect, dog, or snake that put me off. It was my brain shutting down before I had the chance to reason. Strip away our preconceptions and everything's just another source of food. British food—the real, artisanly produced stuff—is in rude health at the moment. You might laugh, but Britain's raw materials are among the best in the world, some of our chefs and producers, too—these are passionate people dedicated to quality and flavor, not to making a quick buck. For those of you who see the UK as a culinary joke, think again. We're a food nation on the up. But this is not the time or place for patriotic war cries. This is a book about food in its every guise. Although the title might sound a little sensationalist, I hope that my love of all cuisines shines through, from the high altar of Roubochon and Blummenthal and Ramsey to the pure incendiary joy of Prince's Hot Chicken restaurant in Nashville, Tennessee. I went looking, not just for bizarre food, but to see if local food cultures were standing up in the face of ever-more homogenized fast food and processed pap. Even though two chapters are set in America, I have many years of research in the U.S. left to do—I want to crack Dungeness crab and catch shrimp off the Gulf Coast. I want rainbow trout in the Rockies, chilli cook-offs in Texas, and the chilli harvest in New Mexico. Kansas City is a must, if only to bring to life Trillin's immortal words on the subject. I want a genuine Philly cheese steak sandwich (not a flaccid Vegas knock off), and a proper New England clambake. And that's just the beginning. Despite my lifelong love affair, I'm only really getting to know America now. As for America's most dangerous food? No hesitation there, it's got to be those anonymous service station sandwiches that clog up the chilla cabinet like ghostly moans. That flap of lurid cheese, the over-sweetened bread, and the slimy, processed ham from God knows where. They're usually called something like "Happy Snack," when they're actually anything but. In a whole year of eating dangerously, in a country blessed with a truly glorious regional and modern cuisine, this symbol to the cheap, the mass-produced, joyless, mediocre, and unthinking was by far the most frightening thing of all. This is a book about a love of good food, and a fascination with other cultures. Far from being some gloating, narrow-minded rant about the strange food of foreign countries, I see this as a love story about all things edible. And, at the very least, I hope it makes you hungry.

THE YEAR OF
EATING
DANGEROUSLY

CHAPTER 1

ELVERS

It started with a pea. Nothing exotic or bloody or rancid, just your everyday, deep-frozen common garden pea. The unfortunate vegetable was being pushed from one side of the plate to the other.

'It touched the sausages, I swear. I can't eat them now. Please, get it away.'

Had this been a four-year-old child, the reaction would be understandable. But for a 34-year-old male, it was downright bizarre. I quizzed my friend further on the matter.

'I just can't bear them. Even the thought of those repellent little balls makes me ill. A sheep's eyeball is nothing in comparison.'

Here was a perfectly reasonable, intelligent human reduced to a quivering wreck by the sight of a harmless legume. The more I looked into this extreme food aversion, the more surprised I became. Another friend, Dougie, fiercely bright and fearless in the face of most foods, has a problem with bananas.

'How do I feel about bananas?' he told me, his face turning puce with rage. 'Imagine you were incarcerated in the toughest jail in America for a crime you didn't commit and ended up being serially raped by the muscle-bound prison daddy. A few years later you're walking down the street, a free man, when, suddenly, you spot the rapist standing on a corner, chatting with a bunch of mates. The trauma you'd experience at that moment, the mixture of abject terror and psychotic hatred – that's how I feel when I look at a display in a supermarket and see a banana.'

Then there are the legions of folk who won't touch liver or beet-root or swede, because they had bad experiences at school or because they don't like the texture or 'feel funny' about them.

I started to think about the relativity of dangerous foods, how one man's pea is another's tripe. The thought of eating insects in the West is, on the whole, greeted by shrieks of disgusted laughter. Yet in South East Asia, they're an entirely normal source of protein, like a chicken breast or a rasher of bacon. It's our perception of different foods, of offal or blood or unusual beasts, that's usually the biggest obstacle to trying new things, not the taste itself.

I began to widen the parameters of my search for dangerous food. All food is potentially dangerous if not treated or handled or stored properly. It rots, grows mould, degrades and poisons. The advance-ment of civilisation could be seen as a battle to remove the danger from what we eat, to cook, preserve, can, irradiate and freeze. In the West, the supermarkets get more powerful every year, offering their vision of tasteless perfection. And despite our food renaissance, the sale of ready meals rises steadily each year. A Big Mac and large fries is far more dangerous to your health than dog stew or snake soup. Yet it's the idea of the latter two that disgusts us, rather than the taste itself.

The more I thought about the concept of dangerous food, the more difficult I found it to get to its heart. The puffer fish or fugu contains deadly poison, so there is a chance of being killed by your lunch. Catching the baby eels, or elvers, involves a shady, nocturnal world of cash, pitched battles and the occasional shotgun. Fishing for

2

percebas, or the goose-necked barnacle, is highly perilous, a few men against the might of the Atlantic. Super hot sauces burn, raw tripe revolts. The list goes on.

So I decided to set out on a journey to find out what dangerous food really meant. Some people are driven by passion, some ambition … I live by the whim of my belly. Even my dreams are crammed with snowy-white crab claws, succulent, smoky barbeque and vast ribs of bloody British beef. To describe me as being bitten by the food bug is somewhat of an understatement. Mauled and savaged more like, and left for dead.

There are, of course, downsides to this largely benevolent gastro-dictatorship. Moods darken when meals are missed. Cheap, mass-produced, flavourless pap makes me rage like Lear on the heath. And I often have to go hungry rather than submit my body to the bland indignity of a supermarket ready meal. But I'm far from a food snob. I'm just as happy chewing on a plate of Buffalo wings as I am with truffle-studded sweetbreads. A rich, unctuous steak and kidney pudding is as exciting as quivering o-Toro sashimi. Crisply battered fish and chips vies with osietra caviar in the fish stakes while a perfect cheeseburger is a thing of exquisite beauty.

Then there's the issue of 'eating dangerously'. Some might see this as some chest-thumping quest to prove my virility, a masochistic voyage of endless ego-fluffing. In the beginning, I had visions of swooping into Iraq, riding shotgun with the British army's dawn patrol before stopping off for a lunch of fresh grilled Tigris fish. Or getting rowdy in Kabul with a grizzle of mercenaries, loosing off AKs while feasting on sheep. If I were very lucky, I might even get a beach barbeque in Somalia. Then I realised the howling crassness of such a thought, cheap thrills and even cheaper copy. Talking of feasts and fancies while others lay dying around me.

But even in the altogether less risky parts of the world, I still bore a problem that I couldn't ignore – me. I'm not a six foot two, achingly cool New York chef who'll devour anything in his sight. As much as I want to be Anthony Bourdain, it ain't going to happen. I'm a rather windy, five foot eleven and a half toff. Unlike the great Hugh Fearnley Whittingstall, I would balk at chewing on placenta or pig's bollocks.

Much of what I planned to eat or do appalled me, but I suppose that was part of the fun. But I wanted to start off near to home, and somewhere which wouldn't involve eating cat meat sashimi or porcupine brain. And the first stage of my journey saw me venturing just 100 miles to the south-west, to the exotic wilds of Gloucester.

It is Joe who starts it all off. The editor of a national restaurant magazine, he is to be one of my companions on the hunt for elvers. An angelic mop of curly hair does little to hide a world-weary, sardonic humour.

'The Elvers have landed,' comes the Belfast whisper. 'And this time it's for real.' Thank Christ for that. There is no time to linger, so I stumble around my flat, frantically throwing clothes, notebooks and waterproof everythings into a bag in preparation for my trip down the M40. It is mid-May, and I have been waiting a month and a half for a confirmed call to action. But every time my Gloucestershire adventure seems ready to roll, Mother Nature throws another hissy fit, conjuring up yet more torrential rain or cloudless skies. Irritating at the best of times but downright excruciating when you're awaiting the perfect conditions for the fishing of elvers, or baby eels. I begin to fear that I will never make it, thwarted by the elements and sent reeling by the cruel right hook of fate.

My Lear-like pout against nature is all forgotten, though, as I pick up Joe and we crawl west through the fumes and fury of rush hour traffic. Hungry, and with our only prospect of sustenance the unspeakable horrors of the petrol station chilla-cabinet, I begin to dream of a vast plateful of elvers, freshly plucked from the river and fried in pools of glimmering bacon fat. With this delectable image infusing my imagination, not even the pious glare of endless speed cameras can dull my excitement. This is the life, I think, as grey concrete turns, gradually, into winding lanes, over-priced antique shops and luscious green vistas.

So enraptured am I by the brilliant glory of British spring, at this moment gambolling past my windscreen, that I begin to sing a cele-bratory tune. Joe is less enamoured by my tuneful rendition of 'The Sun Has Got His Hat On' and asks me politely to cease and desist. If you can call 'shut the fuck up' polite. We drive on in silence, only to realise that I have taken a wrong turn somewhere near Bibury and led us on a rather lengthy diversion through the deepest Cotswolds. But even this entirely usual occurrence – I must learn that a gut-instinct for a rural short cut does not necessarily make a map redundant – does little to blunt my jolly swagger and a few hours later than planned, we arrive in Newnham, a chocolate-box-pretty town a few miles outside Gloucester. There, we were to meet up with Horace Cook, a legendary elder statesmen of the elver scene and a fount of knowledge on all things black and slippery.

As we wait for him to turn up, thoughts turn to a pint of local cider. Two gulps later, and we are ready to take part in a great old English tradition, one as popular now as it was 200 years back. But whereas once the spoils of the fishing were devoured within hours of catching, today's haul is far too valuable for mere eating.

As near back as 50 years ago, the elver was a much-loved regional speciality. A recipe from a Mr Smith, 'late of Fisher's Tudor House, Gloucester, and The Plough Inn, Cheltenham' in Florence White's

Good Things in England, instructs that 'A plateful makes a complete meal for a working man.'

For a few months from the end of February until the end of May, millions of elvers or 'glass eels' would swarm up waterways from the sea in search of the perfect habitation. It was such a popular occasion that huge celebrations called 'eel fares' (probably where the word elvers came from) were held alongside the banks of English rivers, where you could dip your net into the water and haul it out filled with writing bounty.

I found a notice board on the Internet, dedicated to Gloucester life and found 'Nobby' talking about his youth.

When I was a boy, we used to catch them by the tub load at Weinlodes (I know I spelt it wrong). Elver net with 12 ft pole, net with 4 ft x 3 ft backboard. Into the galvanised tub and then 'whomp' them by the pillowcase full. Ears peeled for the sound of 'Floodho!!!' coming from down stream. At which point you, your mates, the net, the elvers and the Tilly lamp would career up the bank. Next morning, taking them round the White City, ringing the bell and shouting, 'Helvahs, Helvahs,' and selling them by the pint. I still remember when the first Elver Station appeared. One wonders what the Elverers of the old days would feel of their prize going to become a dish for the Japanese.

He's not quite right about the elvers becoming a dish for the Japanese (they are mainly eaten as adult eels and bought small to breed) but it was very much a part of local life. And so numerous were these translucent, noodle-like wrigglers that the excess catch was used for pig feed and fertiliser. Now, only the most extravagant working man would consider a few pounds for his tea. And the fairs have crumbled into the mists of history. Those cheery visions of bucolic bank-side parties, which sound about as threatening as a National Trust tea doily, have been replaced by something altogether more perilous. Because this particular stretch of Severn riverbank – the one I am to visit tonight – is no *Wind in the Willows* idyll. Judging by the stories that I've heard for the last few months, certain areas seemed more like downtown Baghdad than a comfy place to plop a net.

The change in elver fishing image, from regional treat to multi-million pound industry, has been slow but inevitable. The main problem is that while the worldwide demand for eels is ever growing (especially from those eel-obsessed Japanese), the numbers of elvers is in freefall. If scientists had perfected the farming of baby eels, this wouldn't be a problem. Just grow a few more and, before you can say 'smoked eel with horseradish', you've solved the problem.

But the eel, as I am to find out, is the most mysterious of fish and not given to such facile solutions. Despite years of experimentation and laboratory high-jinks, scientists have not found a way to hatch eels from their larval stage. So every single farmed eel in the world (and the demand for eel way outstrips the rivers' natural stocks) must be grown from a wild-caught elver, which puts one hell of a bounty on their translucent little heads.

Last year, elver prices reached a high of £400 cash, per kilo. Seeing that anyone – in theory – can pitch up and try his luck, there's a lot of money to be made for seemingly little effort, most of it beyond the taxman's sticky mitts. Throw in a fast-running river and a couple of pints of beer and this piscine gold rush starts to look a little hairy. Add a gaggle of ex-SAS soldiers, brought in to protect some particularly lucrative spots, an Anglo-Sino face-off and an entire armoury of shotguns, flick-knives and four by twos and the whole thing looks downright suicidal. That's not to say that there aren't plenty of law-abiding, tax-paying fishermen operating completely above board. There are. It's just the others one has to worry about.

'It can get a little rough out there,' warns Joe, as we nurse our pints and wait for Horace. 'And the river bank can become a very dangerous place to be at night. Especially,' he adds with a twinkle in his eye, 'for a nosy toff like you.'

I assure him that I can handle myself and that he doesn't want to see me when angry.

'Ooh, it's Pooter with attitude,' he roars, eyes watery with mirth. 'I'm cacking my pants. And I'm sure all those big lads out there tonight will be too.'

I stare deep into my diminishing pint, worrying about the evening ahead. Forget *The Old Man and the Sea* ... this promises to be *The Wild Bunch* on the banks of the Severn.

Little known outside the West of England, the Severn elver run marks the ultimate stage of a stunning natural exodus, where millions of young eels wriggle from the salt waters of the Atlantic up into the fresh of the Severn. Their ultimate aim is to find the perfect muddy patch of river, a place to call home for the next few years. But they have to battle upstream first and do so using the power of the Severn Bore, a tide that occurs one to three days after full and new moons. These miniature tidal waves can move at speeds of up to 21 km per hour, reaching heights of up to three metres, big and fast enough to surf on. I've seen the pictures.

Nowadays, their numbers are diminished, and you have to look very hard to spot them. A hundred years back, it was an entirely different story. In 1902, these miniature, writhing serpents, about two inches long, were so numerous that they even made it up the Thames. According to C.J. Cornish in his *Naturalist on the Thames*, they 'came up in such tens of millions that they made a black margin to the river on either side by the bank, where they swam because the current was there weakest'. Theodora Fitzgibbon describes the ascending hordes as looking like 'a mass of jelly swimming in the water', adding that 'they should only be eaten when they are transparent and plump, never when the skin has darkened'.

And it was their abundance and excellent flavour that endeared them to generations of locals. This was free, seasonal food at its finest. 'Severn Eels are good eating,' enthuses Geoffrey Grigson in *The Shell Country Book*.

> They can be bought by the pint in Gloucestershire, the elver-fisherman's headquarters, in the market and at fish mongers, about Easter time when the elvers crowd up the Severn on the spring tides. There are various ways of preparing them – with beaten-up eggs; dusted with flour and fried in oil or deep fat; boiled in a cloth to make an elver loaf, which is then sliced and fried.

'Local consultations are advisable,' he finishes ominously. The first time I came across cooked elvers was in a London restaurant. I was fascinated by this ruinously expensive pile of threads (£25 for a side plate's worth) and they arrived at the table, sizzling in a terracotta dish. They were cooked in the Spanish style, which meant chilli and garlic and I'll never forget that first taste; their texture is superb, soft but faintly crunchy. And their flavour is subtle and elusive, just tempered by a whisper of the sea. Ever since that fateful mouthful, I not only wanted more but wanted to find out more. A huge delicacy in Spain, they're almost ignored in England. Here, people would balk at paying such astronomical prices for little more than a bowlful of worms. And as I am later to find out, the vast majority of Gloucester elvers are whisked off to foreign climes for breeding.

Nowadays, the Spanish style of eating anguillas is the best known. But the British have many a traditional recipe for them too. The 'Gloucester style' involves their being washed in plenty of salted water (like adult eels, they are coated in a slimy mucus) – Jane Grigson recommends using a pillowcase so you can wash them, then squeeze out the moisture – before frying up a couple of slices of bacon until crisp. The bacon is removed from the pan, the elvers thrown in and cooked until opaque. You mix in a beaten egg, cook for a few moments more before pouring it all on the bacon and eating with a splash of vinegar. A near-perfect, porky piscine breakfast. If you wanted elver cake, you'd add herbs and onion juice to the mixture, before turning them into a dish, pressing down and cooling until hard set.

Regional variations abounded – in Keynsham, for example, they were put into a shortcrust pastry with herbs and salt and pepper, similar to a Cornish pasty. In those days, there were more elvers available than could have possibly been eaten and no one, save the odd greedy gastronome, paid the slightest attention to them outside of the area. But the world's appetite for eel, along with rising levels of river pollution and the artificial filling in of homely, muddy streams, meant that this seasonal pleasure changed from free treat to lavishly expensive treasure.

As Paul Richardson writes in *Cornucopia*, 'I was partaking here of a dead delicacy, a piece of culinary archaeology that will never again form part of our national cuisine …' But unlike other lost, regional culinary specialities such as Hindle Wakes or Singing Hinnies, elvers have not disappeared thanks to the influx of fast food, ready-meals and

Turkey Twizzlers. The reason we no longer partake boils down to nothing more than cold-blooded market economics.

The eel, for the most part, has a wretched reputation. Dark, slippery and faintly sinister, it squirms around the black depths of our imagination, a noxious combination of wily snake and slimy beast. Sliding along the riverbed in the dead of night, it fixes its prey with jaundiced eye and malevolent glare. 'The eel is a mysterious animal, unpleasantly like a snake and like a snake scaleless,' thunders P. Morton Shand in his *Book of Food*. But like anyone who has taken more than a moment to consider this incredible creature, he has a grudging respect, calling them 'intelligently slippery' and says that 'all those of the most aristocratic lineage or leanings, make their way to the Severn in preference to any other river, British or foreign'.

I'm not entirely sure how he came to this conclusion (aside tasting every species in the world, a task not entirely unbelievable for this gruff gourmet), but would certainly agree that Severn eels are superlative. But it's their life cycle which is the most fantastic, mysterious and mind-boggling of all. We live in an age where technology and science is so far advanced that we can clone indignant-looking sheep and send microscopic robots swimming around our blood vessels. Yet when it comes to finding out about the eel, we know next to nothing. There's probably more information on the make-up of Mars, which is 34 million miles away from our planet, than the life cycle of the eel.

We have one of the most fascinating, exotic creatures in the world wriggling around our steams and rivers, yet we pay it no heed because it looks all wrong. We're often too busy looking off into the distance to see the true beauty that is right at our side. The eel is one of our national treasures, every bit as mighty as the golden eagle or wily as the fox. It's just as remarkable and perfectly evolved as the Great White Shark or humpback whale. But the eel just isn't sexy enough to capture our hearts and minds. Just as some people won't eat rabbit because they had a fluffy bunny as a childhood pet, so the majority of British refuse to even contemplate eel because it wriggles most disconcertingly. The scientists, though, have long appreciated its charms but despite all their efforts, next to nothing is known of this mysterious fish.

What we do know of their lives makes compelling reading. The average eel's epic journey across the globe makes the combined voyages of Cook, Raleigh and Columbus look like a paddle across a puddle. Even the heroic trials of the salmon, fighting its way upriver, is nothing in comparison to these tenacious wonders. It was only recently that we came to learn even the basic facts of the fish's life. And over thousands of years, some of the greatest of all minds were applied to finding out their origins. Pliny the Elder reckoned that they reproduced by rubbing their bodies against the rocks, and the skin that came off transformed into baby eels, while Aristotle saw them as springing from the mud. In *Nature in Britain*, a 1936 collection of natural musings, E.G. Boulenger reflects on its origins.

Little more than 30 years ago the eel's origin was largely wrapped in mystery, and until the beginning of the last century the creature's early history was the subject of the most fantastic and extravagant conjectures. Eels were by many considered to be 'spontaneously generated' from mud and slime, or to develop from horse hairs, a legend no doubt arising from the fact that eels are often found in waters which horses habitually ford, or enter for drinking purpose ... as late as 1862 a Mr Caircross published a theory to the effect that the silver eel was the offspring of a small beetle.

The reality is hardly less fantastical.

It all starts – or ends depending on how you look at it – in the Sargasso Sea. The name sounds wild and romantic, a place of sultry passions and torrid affairs. But far from being some tropical, inland sea complete with dusky maidens and limpid swell, it's actually a huge and remote area of the Atlantic ocean somewhere between Bermuda and the Azores. Two million square miles of warm, exceptionally clear water, the sea is not actually fixed but floats about as freely as the weed that riddles its surface. 'It is one of the emptiest, least-known parts of the world, and it is vast,' writes Richard Schweid in *Consider the Eel*. 'Strangest of all, perhaps, are the thick mats of sargassum (the Portuguese word *sargaço* means seaweed) seaweed that appears floating on the surface of the sea, then disappears, hundreds of miles from shore.'

This mysterious area is also at the heart of the Bermuda Triangle, that patch of sea that's said to swallow boats and aeroplanes without a trace. The perfect base, then, for the enigmatic eel.

Scientists are convinced that this still, desolate sea is the cradle of life for all the eels that populate the Eastern rivers of North America and the rivers of Eastern and Western Europe. The only problem is that they have no proof; no adult has ever been seen swimming, reproducing or dying. Not even a wriggle, despite exhaustive research and endless surveillance. In fact, no adult eel has ever been seen there alive. In 2006, this crucial ritual of life and death has yet to be observed by human eyes. The only concrete evidence comes from two adult eels found dead in the bellies of other fish cruising the Sargasso Sea.

Despite this paucity of information, it is generally agreed that the eels hatch in the sea as larvae and spend the next three years drifting across the ocean towards European rivers in the form of leptocephali (the American eels, *anguilla rostrata*, tend to take around a year), shaped like small oval leafs. As you'd imagine, they make easy snacks for the fish below and birds on top as they're utterly defenceless in their epic float. After this mammoth ordeal, their bodies start to grow and develop as they approach shore. And by the time they reach the brackish, coastal waters (where salt and fresh meet), they have become, in the words of Tom Fort in *The Book of Eels*, 'an animated aquatic toothpick', or elver.

Despite having spent the best part of three years as a floating fancy for any passing pair of jaws, their determination to get up river is more heroic still. E.G. Boulenger is unstinting in his respect.

> Those which arrive at our and other European shores invade practically every body of fresh water promising the means of livelihood. No river, ditch or canal is guaranteed to escape their notice. The growing eel is voracity personified, and having exhausted the resources of a given lake or stream, travels over-land under cover of night, or in flood time, and so discovers new worlds to conquer ...'

There are tales of the elvers climbing weir walls and dams, using the bodies of their dead relatives to scale the heights. Another danger is added to the natural roster of hungry pike and perch, peckish voles and wily water rats – now they must avoid the wide nets of eager fishermen too. Instinct kicks in for those few that do make it, and they look for the perfect place to lay their pointed heads. The male doesn't usually travel far upriver, seeming to prefer spending time in the brackish water. Some never even enter the fresh water, but as we know so little, no one is certain. But the female goes further and once the perfect des res has been found, they tend not to stray much from the area, settling in like happy home-owners.

Summer nights are spent hunting mainly live snacks such as crayfish, insect larvae and small fish (contrary to popular opinion, the eel prefers fresh food to rotten), and winters are spent tucked up below a thick blanket of mud. The eels might spend up to 20 years writhing through the river's waters, and making a fairly nice, middle-class life for themselves. Then, and no one knows quite how or why, they react to some primeval call back to the place of their birth and start the journey back downstream.

In preparation for the voyage home, they start feasting on all and sundry, stocking up for the miles of swimming ahead. Their colour changes from a greenish muddy-yellow (yellow eels) to a darker, white-bellied prime (known as silver eels – thanks to their fat reserves they make the very best for eating and smoking). When they hit the estuarine waters, they rest before the final push. Their bodies are now about 28 per cent fat and from that moment on, nothing will ever pass their lips again. Their pupils expand and turn blue, all the better for seeing through the deep, murky Atlantic waters. Their body adapts, too, to the huge pressure they'll encounter in the depths of the ocean. Once back to weedy square one, the females produce eggs for the males to fertilise and then they all die.

The whole life-cycle has a beautiful poetry to it, and you cannot but admire the single-minded survival skills of this highly evolved, tenacious creature. Their end, too, has a melancholy satisfaction, dying in the depth of the Sargasso Sea, their life's mission achieved. I bow to nothing in my admiration for the eel. And as international jetsetters, these fish make Odysseus look like a stay-at-home slouch.

One key biological fact, and another string to the fish's mysterious bow, is that the eel has never been successfully bred in captivity. Nor have they ever been known to reproduce anywhere outside the Sargasso Sea (although no one has ever seen them do it there either). Endless attempts have been made – and some have even succeeded in hatching the eggs – but every time, they wither and die before reaching a decent size. So they're caught as elvers and fattened up to a decent size in farms. Without the wild elver, the worldwide eel market would collapse.

During the last twenty years, the number of European eels in the wild has fallen by more than 90 per cent. A number of reasons are offered, including over-fishing and water pollution, but there's little doubt that the wild population is in terminal decline. In the Sixties and Seventies, there was not much call for elvers, save for a local market. It was a cheap, local food – used when plentiful and not too ruinous if numbers were low. But as Tom Fort explains,

> Gradually more potent forces came to bear. Consumer demand
> for the adult eel was buoyant, and the pioneers of fish farming
> began to get interested in it … At the same time, as Japan
> became the most dynamic economy on the planet, the appetite
> of its people for kabayaki expanded way beyond the capacity of
> its own eel farmers to satisfy it.

A central part of Japanese cuisine, eel is a summer speciality that's grilled over glowing charcoal and brushed with a teriyaki sauce. The taste is almost decadent in its richness, sweet and soft, yet never over-whelming. Having pretty much decimated their own anguilla japonica stocks (which they prefer to the European or American eels because they believe it is fatter with a finer flavour), they began to import elvers from across the globe to feed their appetite.

China is a massive market, too, for eel farms as there is more space than in Japan and costs are lower. They entered the British elver market, happy to offer huge prices for Severn elvers with little worry for the consequences of flooding the market with excess cash.

'Men of oriental appearance with bulging pockets were encountered on riverbanks at the dead of night in the depths of winter,' continues Fort, 'offering incredible sums of money to anyone who would sell them glass eels.' It might all sound a little fantastic, this Chinese invasion of western Gloucestershire. But as I found out later that night, the stories and whispers were all too real.

For a night on the river, there are no better companions than Horace and Rich Cook, a father and son who know as much about the elver industry as anyone alive. Horace is the godfather of commercial elvering and his son Richard, or Rich, is the man behind the redoubtable Severn and Wye smokehouse in Minsterworth. Both grew up in the area and are well known and respected by everyone we speak to. Neither are big men (although Rich looks like he would know his way around a punch or two) yet exude a powerful, primal authority.

All this talk of violence and aggro was making me a little nervy.

'Stop being a pussy,' spat back Joe when I told him of my fears. So much for mutual support.

It's all well and good writing about riverside pitched battles from the safety of my London desk but when it came to actually getting down to the front line, I was less than keen. Woefully unfit and highly ineffective in any remotely threatening situation, I'd stand little chance against suspicious, broad-shouldered fishermen. But for all his bluster, I knew that Joe wouldn't go down to the river alone. Horace and Rich were not only our guides, they were to be our protectors too.

The fifth member of our night's sport was the hirsute Dai Francis, bear-like gourmand countryman, complete with an endless knowledge on all things rural and edible. He's also the much-lauded supplier of finest dairy products to the country's best restaurants. As we wait for

Horace in the local pub, a swarthy gent in the corner takes one look at our table, pulls down his cap and scuttles out of the door. I look to Dai, wondering if something's amiss.

'I recognise that fellow,' he muses into his glass. 'I don't owe him any money. But by the way he leapt out of here, he might owe me.'

He lapses again into a contemplative silence. We're shaken from our apple-based reverie a few moments later, when the pub suddenly seems to rise from its cosy slumber. A chorus of 'Evenin' Horace' erupts from around the room and the subject of this salutation strolls towards us. Small, ruddy-cheeked and with a merry glint in his eye, Horace manages to look both boyish and wise. Dressed in thick tweed trousers, heavy brown shoes and olive green gilet, he must be about 65 but exudes the healthy vitality of a man 30 years his junior. In comparison, I look like a sallow city ghoul. After introducing himself with a steely shake (my lily-white, writer's soft hand seems to disappear within a palm that has really known hard work), he looks at Dai.

'There's some fine old sea-trout up in the lake, Dai. Fancy going up tomorrow to have a go?'

Dai looks up from his pint, his eyes mist over and he can hardly contain his excitement. 'I'm already dreaming of how I'll cook that fat 18-pounder that I know is aching for my hook. I'm going to smoke the bugger to perfection. I'll get him, just you wait.'

Horace has more pressing matters in mind. 'Right lads,' he smiles, looking us up and down. 'Let's stop the drinking and get off to dinner.' I nod dumbly and we pile into his jeep.

Within moments we're hurtling around the countryside at breakneck speed. Forget the threat of being battered into a cold murky river by an irate elver fisherman, I think as we fly full pelt – and in the middle of the road – around another blind corner ... I'm off to meet my maker before we even start. I try to make banal conversation but this dries up along with my tongue. I can hardly get a squeak out.

Seemingly sensing my fear, Horace twists round in his seat – his eyes, to my increasing horror, fixed on me rather than the road.

'You're not of a nervous disposition are you?' he shouts with a cackle.

I'm too busy grasping the smooth plastic handle to come up with a normal reply but Horace hoots and drives on.

As woods and glades whip past at lightning speed, Horace gives a running commentary on the blurred view. 'Chestnut woods there, see ... to the right, an old fishing lodge ... more chestnuts over there ...this is Blaisdon, home of the great Blaisdon plum ... and look at that beautiful oak wood over there.'

Then all of a sudden, we screech to a halt on the brow of a hill and alight beside a patch of bluebells. They cover the ground like a soft cashmere blanket. As my heart slips back out of my mouth and into its rightful slot, I begin to take in the view. The Severn Estuary stretches before us, wide and flat, the landscape peppered with tiny steeples and spires. Roads scar the landscape but don't detract from its quintessentially British rural beauty. Even the industrial black pylons look somehow majestic in the soft evening haze. All around, the air is thick with spring; the cluck of a pheasant and the baa of a sheep mix with the twitter of unseen birds. In the far distance, I can just catch the endless drone of the M4. Even this sounds lyrical rather than jarring when surrounded by such unselfconscious harmony.

The gaping mouth of the Severn looks muddy down in the right-hand distance, a mass of sandbanks and glittering channels. But in a few hours' time, the spring tide will smother the flats, pushing upriver and bringing up with it millions of those elusive elvers. Inspired by my surroundings, I start to compare the sinuous curves of the river to those of the eel and am in mid-poetic flow when I'm interrupted by Joe.

'You'd better stay off the local cider mate. It's making you naff.'

I take one last look at this fast-fading vista and climb back into the jeep, ready for a ten-minute white-knuckle ride en route to dinner.

The Red Hart Inn is small and snug, overflowing with guest ales and warmed by roaring fires. It's known as a stop-off for elver fisherman on their journey out but all I see are two sturdy, leather-clad bikers and their adoring ladies.

'Don't mind them,' says Horace, noticing me shrink back into the depths of my chair. 'They're good lads. Like a bit of elvering too.'

Great, I think, not only plank-wielding nutters but a chapter of the local Hell's Angels too. The arrival of the food temporarily takes my mind off the upcoming night's adventures and Horace fills me in.

'The elvers ride in on the Severn Bore,' he says between mouthfuls of freshly grilled sardines. 'The higher the tide, the further they get upstream. You never fish in the day, as they don't swim near the sides of the river. And they prefer to travel by night anyway, under the cover of darkness. The blacker, the better.'

He pauses for a sip of water. 'Fewer about this year too. All this heavy rain means that they don't show in the river.' I realise why the weather conditions are so important. Get it wrong, and you catch nothing.

Horace is also a master of understatement. As I tuck into a second Otter Head beer, I start asking about peril on the banks.

He smiles. 'Yup, sometimes there's a spot of aggro. The fishermen can get a little over-excited and some poor bugger ends up in the river.' Coming from Horace, it sounds like nothing more than a case of boyish high-spirits.

At this point, Rich comes in. Of average height and solidly built, he's softly spoken and a little more reserved than his father.

'Everything's changed now,' he says as he settles down at our table. 'It used to be the right of the poor to access the elvers. And historically, fishermen never paid to fish the river. It was just local people, farmers and the like, who came to fish. Then, the council started to auction off parts of the land, good tumps [spots where you fish from]. So I bought Gloucester Tip, Pete Wood, Woody Bough and a few others. I kept them for about three years, and then took the council on. I told them that anyone who lives within two miles of the river – on the Wye, it's within one mile – has the prescriptive right to fish the river.'

Although both Rich and his father have made good money from elvering, they leave you in no doubt where their loyalties lie. He orders a steak and kidney pie, waves a greeting to the owner and goes on.

'But this takes no account of human greed, so we set up an association. You pay a small sum and, in joining, you adhere to certain guidelines. You look after the land, make sure that it's left in good condition. Then the money raised from the subscription is used to employ police or security to kick out any rogue fishermen. The landowners are happy and the fishermen too.'

A self-regulating society and one that seemed to work.

'In the old days, they were fished in pillowcases, because it didn't matter if the elver was alive or dead. When I started, I just dealt with dead elvers, sent off to Spain to eat. £2 per kilo dead, and only £3 for live. But it soon changed and now live is crucial for breeding purposes. You've got people coming in from across the country, and even from China, looking to make a quick bob. A few years back, you used to be able to leave a stick at your tump, go to the pub for a few hours and come back to it without anyone jumping in. Now, it's got to the point where some people had to hire ex-SAS blokes to protect their patch. Only problem was that the soldiers decided they liked it, so moved in and took it. You're not going to argue with the might of the regiment, are you?'

Theoretically, any person can stump up the £65 needed for a season's licence but the reality is rather less rosy.

'Turn up as a newcomer,' adds Dai, 'and you'll be pushed out pretty quickly.' Still, even those who are well known to the elvering community decide to save themselves a few extra bob by avoiding detection.

'It works out about £1 per night, so it's relatively cheap,' sighs Rich, 'but still they prefer to live in fear of being caught by the bailiffs every single night. Anyway, drink up, it's time to get going.'

It's about 9.30 and my fears seem to have dissipated thanks to a couple of pints and a fine dinner. The bore's coming down at about ten tonight, and outside it's pitch black and the air has a vicious bite. Horace has gone back home, to check on the elver stock kept there. I look back longingly at the soft, warm light spilling out of the pub windows. Every time the door opens and shuts, I catch a bewitching aroma of just-cooked pies, pipe tobacco and a whiff of bitter.

I suddenly feel like Bilbo Baggins leaving the cosy charms of Hobbiton and striding forth into uncharted lands. Even Joe is quiet and pensive. For a moment, I consider giving the whole night a miss. Horace, however, seemed to sense my momentary quiver, and hurries me into the car.

As we drive through the night, we pass a few paths down to the river. Pointing one out, Dai warns, 'We're not going down there – it can get a little rough.'

By now, my previous fear has been replaced by an alcohol-fuelled bravado and I've turned from wimp to real man. Goddammit, I think, I want rough. The flash of the switchblade, the sound of fist on flesh, the crunch of wood on skull. I imagine myself parrying blows from enraged fishermen, karate kicking them into the river as they fall upon me, weapons in hand. We pull up alongside an old mill, sitting at the point where the river hits a stream.

'It's a great place to be,' says Horace, 'as the elvers pour into the stream to escape from the ebb flow of the river. They like the fresh water and tend to stick up against it.' As we get out, I spot two men armed with nets, taking it in turns to wobble along the specially constructed duckboard which sits astride the stream. When one stops for a swig of cider and a rest, the other takes over.

'Evening Horace, evening Rich. Tide's just crept past. It's an 8.2 [metres]. Help yourself to drinks.' Suitably armed with a bottle of cider, I look around. It's a beautiful old building, converted into a house. And this fishing spot is unbeatable, like dropping a line out of your bedroom window.

'How come you get the best spot?' asks Joe.

'Because it's my bloody house,' answers Tone, our Italian-born, avuncular host. In the far distance, beyond the stream and out on the banks of the river, I see the ghostly glow of five headlamps. They rise and fall with the movement of the net, but are too far away to make out any human detail. The sight sends a shiver streaking down my spine, as if I were watching criminals from afar, desperately trying to bury a body. The fishermen are entirely innocent but the imagination starts getting a little over-excited under the influence of booze, cold and a whiff of danger.

'Do you want to have a go?' asks Tone and I leap at the chance (literally, and nearly land in the river). The net is large and rectangular, with a long handle and thin gauze. It looks similar to the hood of an old-fashioned pram and once it is in my hands, surprisingly heavy. I clamber onto the boards and follow the instructions. You dip the net into the water and sweep it along the mouth of the stream. At the end, you lift the net and pour the contents into a bucket sitting at the side. It's hard work and some skill is obviously needed, as I manage to haul a grand total of one wriggling little strand of rice noodle-like elver. I pick it up and look more closely. A black lateral line runs from head to back, while two tiny full-stop eyes focus on getting back into the water.

A hearty laugh erupts at the sight of my haul and Joe takes over. His luck is no better. He squints at the contents of the net. 'Mine's dead,' he moans.

'At the price they get, give him the bloody kiss of life,' replies Tone.

Even dead, the elvers fetch £100 per kilo but these occasionally make their way into the pan.

'Do you ever eat your elvers?' I ask.

'Only when we get the dead 'uns,' says Tone as he takes the net and sensible fishing is resumed. It's a slow, solitary and overwhelmingly quiet business. The fishermen are as economical with their words as they are with the movement of their nets. Like all fishing, though, it seems therapeutic, lulled by the gentle swish of the net and an occasional unseen splash. In moments, Tone has hauled in at least a dozen.

'In the good old days, 30 or 40 years ago,' says Horace, 'you'd catch a pot full in five minutes. That's 50 pounds' worth. There was hardly any demand for them and I'd take them to the village in a jar in exchange for a feed.'

Horace and Dai start reminiscing about the days when the water was alive with elvers. Things are rather different now.

'On the best night this season, we caught between a quarter and a half kilo,' says Tone. I ask Horace why he thinks elver numbers are dropping.

He pauses for a moment. 'There are fluctuations in different years,' he says slowly and carefully. It's a subject he's obviously pondered at length. 'But the peaks are no longer as high as they were. Many of the places they used to migrate to have been filled in by the government. They paid us to fill in the pools to stop the cattle drinking dirty water. It was the time of the TB threat. I think they'll be incentivising us to look after them soon. The wild eel is now becoming an endangered species. We've destroyed their natural habitats, and all they want is a deep, dirty spot with lots of mud.'

Just as I'm starting to make myself comfortable, it's time to move on again. I drain the flaccid dregs of the bottle and climb back into the jeep. This time, we stop in an upmarket housing estate. It's now about 11 and the security-lit facades of these spanking modern mansions seem at odds with this age-old nocturnal art. A couple of other cars are parked nearby.

'Fishermen,' nods Rich and we set off through the prissily landscaped paths and lawns, passing an ugly man-made lake and on until we reach a gate. A few metres away, I catch the flickering dance of a fire, partly hidden through the thick copse. Although the rain has kept away, the air is sharp and the prospect of warmth hugely attractive.

'Watch your head,' warns Dai as we bend down and enter a vision of domestic bliss, only all laid out in the open air. The branches of a willow make a perfect shelter and the fire crackles and hisses. To my left, six beers sit in a cooler alongside a kettle and an endless supply of tea. It's a cheering sight, more Hobbit hole than late-night fishing spot. I tell Rich I could happily spend a few nights here, cooking sausages on sticks and steadily working my way through a few of those beers.

'You wouldn't think that when it's below zero and pissing down with rain,' he replies. 'It might look all cosy now but believe me, it's bloody rotten when you're soaked to the skin, waiting for the elvers to arrive.'

Two makeshift benches surround the fire and a path leads down to the river, where a solitary man is immersed in the rhythmic dipping and pouring of the elver fisherman. His headlamp reflects weakly on the water, dropping and rising in time with the net. Dave sits up in the camp, dressed in ragged jeans and thick jumper. He's one of the old bunch and nods his greeting to Rich and Horace, updating them on the nightly river gossip.

'Coppers down tonight, catching the prats without licences. Running through the bush, they were, in every direction. Scared stiff. You have to laugh.'

They nod their agreement. Dave has been fishing elvers on the river for 17 years. Like most of the local fishermen, he has a day job too. He gets off work at seven in the evening, then straight off to the river until at least four. Then home for a shower and back to work again for nine. The story of the diminishing catch is exactly the same.

'Twelve years ago, you'd easily get 18 kilos in a night. Now, you're lucky to get a kilo. There used to be four collection stations in the area, where you get your catch weighed and paid for. And a mobile unit too. But as numbers have dropped, there's just one station left in Gloucester. And all these amateurs turn up, trying to jump in where there's said to be a good catch. They never get it right though.'

At the peak, in 1999, there were a thousand fishermen per night on the river.

'It was like carnival on the bank, lights everywhere.'

Dave's story is suddenly interrupted by a frantic crashing in the bushes behind us, like a wounded buffalo charging towards us in the gloom. I jump about two foot and see Joe do the same. We turn to see a bedraggled figure stumble from the shadows.

'Evening all,' says the man, as casually as if he'd just walked into a bar.

'Alright Sean. Still on the run?' asks Rich.

'Yeah, spent most of last fucking night hidden in a ditch. Was convinced those fucking bailiffs were gonna grab me. All for the sake of a bloody licence.'

He shakes himself down and moves closer to the fire. Rich raises an eyebrow but Sean is an old-timer, well known and liked by all.

'Last night, some new fella turned up at a tump just down river,' says Sean, 'good spot and all. Just sat there and started fishing. Well, he found his head dunked in the water and we haven't seen him since. Cheeky fucker.'

'You don't fuck with the old boys,' says Rich.

I ask Sean if he has been the victim of any aggro in all his years.

He pauses to wrap up a rollie, then lights it and takes a lungful.

'Well, do you remember that bugger who turned up on your spot?' Dave nods and continues. 'So this bloke is sat at my tump, happy as Larry, and I ask him, "Who the fuck are you?" and the bastard comes back saying, "Who the fuck are you?" So I stopped and took stock. He was a big lad and I was starting to worry a bit. I couldn't back down. "You ain't fishing down here," I say. And he comes back at me, chest all puffed out, with, "Says who?" Shit, I think, but at that moment Sean appears from the bushes with a huge plank in his hand. "Says me," says Sean and whacks him into the water. That fucker never came back.'

They both collapse into fits of laughter that reverberate down the misty river. Rich then tells of the time he had a shotgun pulled on him by a man called John Kent. What did you do, I ask in naïve, tremulous excitement.

'Left him the fuck alone,' comes the retort.

I hear tales of boat chases down the river; once or twice a year, a motor boat is caught on the river, trawling for elvers with a D-shaped net. This is highly illegal and involves both police and bailiffs. But the police, for the most part, are happy to let Rich and his crew of veterans look after the river themselves. Despite a few hairy tales, peace reigns tonight on the riverbank. Step out of line, though, and you'll find yourself swimming home.

I've expected pitched fights with the clank of nets and the cry of oaths filling the night sky. And if I went wandering into someone else's tump, armed only with a net and a bad attitude, I was pretty certain that I'd find a bit of excitement. But this closed game is well regulated by the likes of Rich, who keeps order thanks to the respect he commands. Of course, there are certain spots near which I am not allowed, but a journalist waving a notebook and camera are rarely popular in any slightly sensitive situation.

I continue to thank God for the Cooks, though. Just being with them allows me to get much further into this twilight world than I ever could have done alone.

Rich tells me that the Chinese are the biggest danger at the moment. Armed with sackfuls of cash, they come down to the riverbank and try to buy the catch for hugely inflated prices. They're desperate for live elvers and will pay far more than the weighing station. It started off pleasantly enough, with Rich supplying the fisheries in China.

'But then these two blokes, David Lung and Lee Wee Chung, started giving us problems, making a fuss and querying our prices. So we stopped supplying them. Then Lung told us that if we wouldn't sell to him, then he would attempt to take us over. So he went and set up his own collecting station, trying to put ours out of business. Anyway they lasted a few years but they didn't have a fucking clue as to how to run a business like that. And sure enough, they went home with their tail between their legs. We'll never see them again.'

It seems that you have one chance in this business. Bugger it up, and you're best served staying away. In the hour or so we sit, gassing around the fire, the fishermen probably pull in about half a jam-jar's worth. But the night is still fresh and Dave will be there until sunrise. I turn to say goodbye to Sean but he has slipped off some time ago, spooked, no doubt, by the thought of bailiffs hurtling towards him from the dark. We trudge back to the cars and I wonder if the affluent residents of this inelegant gated community are at all perturbed by the ceaseless flow of track-suited, stubbled folk parking by their drives and drifting off to tumps on the river.

'It's an ancient right of the poor, and there's nothing they can do about it.' It's for the elverers to put up with the new, hideous houses and not the other way around. And from what I've seen, they have little need to worry. Every fisherman I've met so far is a million miles away from the sword-wielding lunatic of my imagination. Despite all the stories, the vast majority are honest people looking to earn a little extra legitimate cash.

Moving from the silent country lanes to the street-lit outskirts of Gloucester is a little jarring and the Elver Station is no architectural beauty. I don't know what I expected; possibly some picturesque mill with fishermen lolling about, swapping tall tales. Instead, it's located in a grim modern warehouse but it is, nevertheless, the nerve centre of the Severn Elver industry. Every elver caught comes in here to be weighed, and the fishermen paid for that weight. During the season, it's open 24 hours of the day, seven days of the week. Set up by Horace and Rich – and still bearing their UK Glass Eels name – they sold their share a few years back.

'They call me down if any trouble breaks out, but that's about it,' says Rich. He doesn't elaborate on exactly what 'trouble' might involve but knowing his gift for understatement, it probably means an all-out war. There are a multitude of tricks and scams to make the elvers seem more alive than they actually are. If they're slow and list-less, it's usually presumed that they're near death so the fisherman would get less money.

'If you piss on a bunch of moribund elvers, the thermal shock gets them wriggling and looking as if they are in the prime of their life,' says Glynn, the manager of the station, whose gruff manner conceals a bone-dry wit. 'Sugar does the same thing too. So they get 'em to you alive but they're really on the edge of death.'

I wonder how he tells if they're trying it on. 'Well, you can taste the sugar in the water. But it's a bit of a fucker if it's piss.'

He pauses, mid-explanation, to welcome a scrawny, feral-looking fisherman. He grabs the bucket, has a peer inside, then pours the contents onto the scales and notes the weight. The elvers are then transferred to tanks at the back of the room, highly oxygenated, and here they're held until the next part of their unnatural voyage abroad.

'Alright mate? Good night. Now make sure you wash the containers.'

This dialogue is repeated sporadically throughout the time I'm there, and silent men drift in and out, swapping elvers for cash and disappearing back into the gloom. These men are far closer to the elverers of my imagination. No one walks, rather slinks, lurks, slides or creeps. For the most part, conversation is sparse. While a few seem safe, and friendly even, the rest snarl if you get within four foot. I count enough tattoos, piercings and broken noses to see off an entire chapter of the Hell's Angels. Grim expressions match gaunt, beaten faces – this is the underbelly of society, British citizens on paper but in reality living below the radar. They might claim the dole but theirs is a cash economy where the softness of the suburban world has no place. The taxman is an especially hated presence.

'Let's just say that certain elements around these parts could live without their company,' observes one wag as his haul is being weighed. Once again, I thank God for Rich's steadying presence. Even the most gnarled and toxic of the visitors offer him a quiet, unspoken respect. They nod at him, he nods back. Glynn treats them all with a measured civility. It's a quiet night, being towards the end of the season. But there's a steady flow of grey-faced punters, arriving in all manner of transport.

'What amuses me,' says Dai as we're standing by the entrance chewing on a hot-dog of dubious provenance, 'is the different modes of transport going to the station. Bikes, motorbikes, prams … I've seen them all.'

The elvers are mesmerising to watch en masse, billowing and flowing like thick auburn hair in continuous waves and breaks. They huddle together under the pipes pumping oxygen into the water, hiding away from view. Rich and Glynn swap news and Rich's knowledge of every face and spot is encyclopaedic.

'A tall, scruffy lad came in the other day,' says Glynn. 'Looks like a Klingon and works on his own. Anyway, hauled in seven kilos. Never seen him before.'

Rich goes quiet for a moment, trawling through an endless gallery of rogues. 'I know the one, fishes upstream. Stuart, yup, he's an odd 'un.'

Wandering about the station, I find a tin of elvers, apparently from Spain. They're selling them at a fiver a pop which seems the bargain of the century.

'They're fake,' says Glynn, noting my surprise. 'Artificial elvers started 15 years ago, made by the same company who supplied the most real elvers in the country. They take fish like Alaskan Blue Whiting and pulp them into a paste, then shape them into elvers and paint on eyes and the lateral line with squid ink. All the big producers do three or four different ranges and the Spanish now consume over 1,000 tonnes of them per year.'

I try them and although suitably fishy, they lack the magical texture and delicate flavour of the real thing. Add enough chilli and garlic, though, and you'd be hard pressed to tell the difference.

'I reckon the Spanish hardly know the difference,' chortles Glynn.

By now, it's past two in the morning and I am beginning to flag – I feel the gritty hangover of yesterday's pints coming back to haunt me and start to dream of bed.

We leave the dribs and drabs coming in to their weighing and set off for Horace's house, about five miles outside town. It's here, in the back yard of a pretty farmhouse bought 'a while back' for £2,000, that the elvers are made ready for their final, though certainly not most arduous, journey to fisheries and farms across the globe. We're greeted by two wagging dogs, squirming with excitement at being reunited with their master, and wander into the welcome warmth of the house.

'First up, a sharpener,' declares Horace and reappears with a few mugs of black coffee, liberally dosed with a fat slug of brandy. Suitably enlivened, we wander across the yard to the holding barn. To get through the door, chains and padlocks are ceremoniously removed, and alarms punched off.

'It's all jigged up with the works,' explains Rich. 'There's over a million quid's worth of stock in here, and we're up against the best criminals out there. They've tried a few times, but never got through.'

The lines flicker on and I'm greeted by the sight of a large barn filled with 16 tanks. As it's near the end of the season, 13 stand empty but three are writhing with life.

'Once they're weighed at the station, they're brought here and quarantined in very cold water. This prevents them from losing weight between being caught and being sold. The water is conditioned too.'

Rich then points at a tank filled with the elvers. 'Those ones floating at the top,' he says, gesturing at a few dozen spiralling about by themselves on the surface, 'have mere moments to live. They've suffered tail damage or have been treated roughly during capture and they'll die soon. The French allow trawling and millions are killed like that, as it's so haphazard. They might catch many more but the quality is so much lower. Still, it doesn't seem to bother them as they freeze live and dead together and no one makes a fuss.'

As I saw in the station, the elvers seem to crowd under the oxygen pipes, ebbing and flowing as if one. I notice a pile, in the corner, of dead elvers.

'They're incredibly tidy,' says Horace, 'and move the dead fish to a special burial ground where they don't get in the way.'

How civilised, I think, watching the dead being pushed away from the living. The more you learn about these creatures, the more you respect them. Once the elvers are ready to be transported, the plug is pulled in their tank and they flow down to another section where they're sieved and sorted into boxes for the long trip ahead.

'We have our own plane for short journeys,' says Horace, 'but use commercial for long distances. We even had some BA fella in the other day, telling us how to spot a bomb. Not sure what help that is to us but we nodded throughout anyway.'

We all stand watching these precious threads, crowding the pipes or making their last few wriggles at the top of the tank before giving up and floating down to their death. With one glance, Horace can actually tell where they've been caught. To me, it's like telling the difference between grains of sand but Horace seems to breathe elvers.

'The Somerset ones from the Severn are bigger and clearer, the best of the lot. Those from the Wye are darker with a different feel.'

I take one final glance at these stunning creatures before the lights are cut and we make our way back to the car. Joe is almost asleep already. On the drive home to the B&B, I go back to dreaming about breakfast, and a plateful of elvers in the Gloucester style.

'Fat chance,' laughs Rich. 'Every single one we catch goes off for restocking and aquaculture abroad. There's simply not enough to eat. It's bacon and eggs for you. And I've got some great new smoked haddock at the smokehouse for you to try too.'

It seems entirely fitting that I won't get my elver feast. But I can't get too teary eyed over the loss of a local delicacy, as it provides a booming seasonal industry for thousands of people. Unless there is some miraculous change-around in the current pattern, elvers will never again be a Gloucestershire delicacy. In a generation's time, their taste will be as alien as that of Dodo meat. They'll still be eaten in their billions in Spain and in the finest restaurants in London. But they are now a luxury, not a seasonal staple.

We are now mere minutes away from a warm bed. The only noise in the car is Joe's gentle snores. My expectations of pitched battles were thankfully proved wrong, though this is a world to treat with respect. The danger is never far away, bubbling under the surface. We stop and clamber wearily from the car. We are home. But as I say goodnight to Rich, I realise the truly scary part of my night on the Severn – the rapidly dwindling stocks of the wild eel. Unless something is done to attempt to reverse this slide, the great and glorious eel could soon become another relic of the past.

I went looking for danger. What I have found is a whole lot more frightening.

CHAPTER 2

NEW MEXICO

I can't remember the exact point when my liking for chilli turned into a full-blown obsession. But I'm certain that my first taste was a furtive sip of a Bloody Mary, grabbed when the grown-ups had wandered in to lunch. The odd drop of Tabasco aside, my parents had (and still have) an aversion to hot food, so it certainly didn't come from the diet of my youth.

These were the Seventies and early Eighties, only 25 to 30 years back but a world away in terms of choice. Indian and Chinese restaurants were well established, but supermarkets were still a long way off stocking seven different kinds of chillies, as they do now. There was no fish sauce or galangal or nori seaweed or any of the other exotica now so easily available. Foreign foods were still impossibly exotic and played no role whatsoever in my upbringing. Chillies were virtually unheard of in our house.

In countries where chilli is an integral part of the cuisine, children are gradually weaned on these fiery fruits, starting off with a bland diet and slowly developing a taste until they're throwing fistfuls of incendiary pods into their dhal and pho with no apparent effect. But this was not the case in early-Eighties Wiltshire. For my sister and I,

Tabasco was a fun food, something to use not just as a flavouring but a miniature weapon of mass destruction. We would dare each other to shake drops on our tongues, before running around the house, fanning our mouths in fevered agony.

Quickly tiring of harming ourselves, we moved on to our parents' friends, dosing peanuts, salami and anything else edible that hung around on communal plates. We howled with laughter as an innocent handful of pre-lunch snacks transformed into a chilli-spiked minefield and unsuspecting munchers started to stutter and sweat. One day, though, we went too far. Emboldened by our previous success, we poured half a bottle into one unsuspecting man's tomato juice and scuttled under the table to await the inevitable explosion. He grabbed the glass, took a deep draught and set it back down on the table, carrying on his conversation as if nothing had happened. We cursed ourselves at the dose, promising that next time, the whole bottle would go in.

Then it happened: a deep, primal moan as the wretched fellow fell to his knees, eyes streaming and face taut with pain. We looked at each other with ashen faces, and each immediately began to blame the other for this heinous trick. As far as we were concerned, he was dead and we were on our way to a lifetime behind bars. It was only later we found out the poor man had an ulcer and the matter was put to rest with a stern telling off.

My next taste of the chilli came years later, in the heavily flocked surroundings of a Windsor tandoori house, an impossibly exciting place for a hungry boy who knew nothing of Indian food. It was like stumbling on some fantastic world, the flavours completely alien yet instantly attractive. I started low, building my way up through kormas and biriyanis until I found the Madras. It seemed painfully hot, but thrillingly glamorous too, a dish for real men. This was my first experience of real spice, so different from the instant hit of Tabasco. The chilli was slower burning, and a pint of fizzy lager did nothing to quell the pain. Gritty from an excess of stale, cheap chilli powder, I still managed to devour every bite.

My tongue swelled, my throat blazed and my forehead trembled with sweat. But despite the pain, a huge smile plastered itself across my face and I wallowed warmly in the afterglow of an endorphin rush. Everyone else around the table had a similarly proud grin. It was as if we had conquered the same mountain peak together and made an important step towards maturity. As the years passed, my tolerance and passion increased. I craved chilli at least twice a week, taking my fixes wherever I could; drunken kebabs slathered with violently fresh chilli sauce; generic Thai curries and litres of Tabasco poured over all and sundry.

At school, it was all macho posturing and pungency prowess – real men eat vindaloo and similar sort of crap. But I soon began to appreciate these diverse and versatile fruits in their every shape and size; the searing, fruity intensity of the lantern-shaped *habenero*; the sweet, unpredictable heat of the bullet-shaped *jalapeno*; the vicious, immediate burn of the Thai bird's eye that still managed to leave a floral trail as it went down the throat. And the warm, smoky glow of the *chipotle*, all brown and shrivelled up like a stag's scrotum. I carried Tabasco in my pocket at all times to guard against bland food, began to collect hot sauces and desperately pleaded with foreign restaurants to 'make it hot, like you eat it' (of course, I couldn't begin to withstand the native heat and would collapse to the ground, much like the unfortunate gentleman of all those years ago). I became a full-flown hot-head, as obsessed with the heat as much as the flavour. I began to subscribe to *Chile Pepper* magazine, and found comfort in the fact that I wasn't alone. I was just one of many freaks out there.

So the search for ultimate heat seemed the most natural next stage of my journey. I had thought about them and eaten them almost every day of my adult life, so what could be more suitable than a quest for the hottest chilli in the world. But rather than travel to the depths of Mexico or India, where I would find the farm, try the pepper, sweat and fly back home, I wanted more. And there was one event, one place, that had it all. The National Fiery Foods and Barbeque Show in Albuquerque, New Mexico, a chilli-infused Emerald City at the end of a long and winding Yellow Brick Road. For any self-respecting chilli head, this was the equivalent of a pilgrimage to Lourdes, a vast temple to heat where purveyors of rare and mean spices would gather in all their glory.

The more I read about this hallowed event, the more desperate I was to attend. I imagined this to be the ultimate gathering of chilli freaks, the sort who populated websites, used excessive exclamation marks and gave long, rambling rants about eating the hottest sauce in the world. A stately pleasure dome to all things spicy, this was my Xanadu and sitting atop it all was the Kubla Khan of capsaicin, Dave DeWitt.

Dave is not only founder of the Fiery Foods Show, and co-founder of the Chilli Institute (an international, non-profit organisation devoted to education, research and archiving information related to the chilli) but was the editor-in-chief of *Chile Pepper* magazine for ten years, the editor and publisher of *Fiery Foods* magazine and the author of over 30 books – ranging from *The Fiery Cuisines* to *Great Bowls of Fire* – on his beloved fruit. He's not known as the 'Pope of Pepper' for nothing.

The Fiery Foods Show was the chilli fiesta to beat them all. But I knew it was not a place for the faint of tongue. I was off to mingle with the big boys and if I were to have any chance of keeping up, I needed my palate fit, strong and ready for anything that might be fired my way.

In the months before I left for New Mexico, I punished my palate with a rigorous regime of endless chilli, moving from hot sauce warm-ups to fresh Scotch Bonnet sweat fests. Pastas were packed with fierce little pepperoncini, shepherd's pies perked up with a handful of chopped scuds (or mouse shit) and roast chicken dusted with Tennessee Gun Powder ('Good for sprinkling in shoes on cold days. Eats ulcers before they eat you. Frightens haemorrhoids and increases prayer life at same time … can cause internal combustion').

I worked my way through the hot sauces, starting with the mellow charms of Tabasco and moving upwards through the Scoville Scale. The fruity charms of Susie's Hot Sauce made way for the rather less subtly named 'The Beast' ('It's time to possess,' screams the blurb on the bottle, 'to destroy, to unleash its fiery fury on the taste buds of all mortal men') and right on up to the virtually inedible extremes of Endorphin Rush, a super-hot sauce that decimated any flavour in its path. I tried a full-stop-sized blob on the end of a matchstick and spent the next hour with my tongue in a pot of yoghurt. This was fierce, a whole different level of utter discomfort. It had no flavour to speak of, just a guttural roar of pure chemical heat. This sauce would ruin any food it touched and so sat in my kitchen as more of a warning than a condiment.

But if I wanted to keep face among the crème de la crème of the hot sauce world, I had to be prepared for all eventualities. By the time I was ready to go, I was in the peak of physical chilli condition, ready to challenge the great and good of the Fiery Foods World. My tongue felt asbestos-lined, raring to take on even the most leathery of palates.

This, I told myself, would be a blast. My training was completed and I was ready to go play chilli chicken with the titans of the hot food world.

For a relative newcomer to the world culinary scene, the rise of the chilli pepper has been swift and meteoric. Before 1492, they were much-loved – but very much localised – players in the South American and Caribbean culinary world (they were actually thought to have originated deep in the jungles of South America). They were certainly one of the earliest domesticated crops of the New World (around 7000 BC in Mexico) but were utterly unknown elsewhere.

Yet when Columbus almost tripped over the West Indies in 1492 in his search for India and the hugely valuable black pepper, he also happened across the fiery fruit. The variety he found was the chiltepin, a tiny, vibrant red berry of a chilli that resembled ripened black pepper. As it was spicy, he erroneously named the fruit 'pepper' and brought it back to Europe in 1493. From there, the capsicum (the genus to which all chillies belong) began its unstoppable voyage east, along Spanish and Portuguese trade routes, on the road to worldwide domination.

Within 150 years, the chilli pepper (which is a member of the Solanaceae family and related to tomatoes, aubergines and even Deadly Nightshade) was a global superstar and one of the key components in cuisines right across the Indian sub-continent and Far East. The long-held theory has the Spanish explorers actually reintroducing the chilli to Mexico and the American South West during their conquests.

But Dave DeWitt has little time for such European arrogance, arguing in *The Fiery Cuisines* that this 'smugly suggests that Europeans were more appreciative of hot foods than the primitive societies they were ravishing'. His argument, which is a sound one, runs that there were plenty of pre-Columbian chilli recipes and the fruit probably made its way up into what is now the South West of America by trading between the Pueblo Indians and the Toltecs of

Mexico. Carmel Padilla, in *The Chile Chronicles*, points out another factor in their travel north – birds.

'Birds are naturally attracted to red fruit and, unlike most other small mammals, are equipped with digestive tracts that chemically soften seed coats without damaging their potential for germination.' But as she readily admits, 'The sequence of events that compromises the history of chile [note the different American spelling] is as scattered and inexact as the seeds that pre-Colombian birds deposited upon the Americas.'

But when they did eventually begin cultivated life in New Mexico, they found the climate of warm days and cool nights very much to their liking. It was the opening of the Santa Fe Trail in 1821 that saw the chilli's move from bit part to starring role in the USA. So it seemed somehow fitting that I was off to the very state where the chilli domination was first born.

The reason for the chilli's heat is simple … the fruit simply isn't interested in being eaten by mammals. A slow journey through their digestive systems would damage the seed, making that much less likely to germinate at the other end. The birds are unaffected by the heat, as well as passing the seed through their bodies quickly with no harm done to it. This allows the seed to be effectively spread over great distances. This is a seed that not only knows where it wants to go (everywhere) but exactly how it's getting there too.

But the actual heat comes from a nasty little alkaloid called capsaicin. Without flavour and colour, capsaicin is plucky and robust, able to withstand extremes of heat and cold without losing its power. When the chemical comes crashing into contact with the pain receptors in the mouth and nose, the brain releases endorphins (natural painkillers) to fight back. Your blood vessels dilate, your heart beats more quickly and you start to sweat.

These endorphins released create a slight giddiness and euphoria, and makes the chilli rather addictive. 'Many chilli lovers exhibit distinctly druggie habits,' muses DeWitt in *The Chile Pepper Encyclopedia* (yet another of his excellent works on the subject). 'We've seen people who always travel with their stash of hot sauce [like me, cradling my precious bottle of Tabasco close to my heart], Texans who carry their tiny chilipiquin pods in silver snuffboxes, and Californians who mix chilli powder with their cocaine before snorting it. "The pink fix", it's called.'

Of all the uses of chilli there are, from folk medicine to flavourings, this particular treat strikes me as downright masochistic. But as Dave points out, 'Many of the people who like hot and spicy foods tend to be a little bit more outrageous than those who do not. They like travelling, wearing colourful clothing [!], meeting new people, and trying new things.'

Little wonder, then, that the chilli is known as culinary cocaine. Just keep it away from the inside of your nose. The heat varies hugely from species to species but a decent rule of thumb is that the smaller varieties are usually rather more hot. Yet the likes of the Asian Goat Horn can grow over five inches and still pack a fiendish punch so it's always best to proceed with caution when trying a chilli for the first time.

The capsaicin is produced by glands in the placenta (that white, central section in the middle of the fruits) and you'll find most of the power in the placental tissue and seeds. When cutting the chillies, you're advised to wear gloves. Or, at the very least, to scrub your hands afterwards. I, of course, learnt this the hard way. After chopping up God knows how many *habeneros*, I went for a pee before giving my balls an absent-minded scratch.

Moments later, I was squealing with pain, as the searing, acid-like heat caused agonising havoc across this most sensitive of areas. I spent the next few minutes with my burning member firmly dunked in a basin of ice cold water, whimpering softly and vowing never to make this mistake again.

All chilli heat is measured on the Scoville Scale, named after its rather adventurous inventor, a chemist called Walter Scoville. In 1919, this brave boffin developed a rudimentary test to gauge relative heat. Pure-ground chillies were mixed with sugar water and then tasted. This solution was increasingly diluted with the sugar water until no trace of the heat remained. And the amount of dilution needed became the final rating. One part chilli to 2000 parts water was recorded as 2000 SCU.

Nowadays, things are a little more high-tech (using High Pressure Liquid Chromatography measuring the amount of capsaicin present in parts per million then converted in Scoville) but the units remain the same. Different chillies have different SCU, with the bell pepper at the bottom with a grand total of nought. The jalapeno can range from a civilised 2000 up to a sweaty 15,000, while Tabasco sauce sits around 15,000 – a drop of this magical sauce on the tongue can cause a good deal of pain, so imagine the ferocity of the *habeneros* that can reach as high as 577,000 SCU (in the case of 'Red Savina', one of the hottest ever recorded).

Beyond that is a world of pain and insanity, of 'extract' sauces that use the pure capsaicin in bottled sauces. I have an inedible sludge called 'The Source' that weighs in at a sphincter-trembling 7.1 million SCUs. The hottest sauce in the world at the moment, Blair's 16 Million Reserve, reaches a staggering, bowel-shattering 16 million units. This would blister concrete from 100 paces so God only knows what chaos it would inflict upon the belly. It's not even a sauce, rather small white crystals that you'd have no problem calling sir. It costs $200 and you have to sign a legal disclaimer before buying it.

One of the things I am looking forward to most at the Fiery Foods Show is to find some hothead who is actually dumb enough to try a spoonful. In fact, I imagine the whole place to be full of cartoon-like characters with steam flying out of their ears. At this heat, even a river of yoghurt or a crate of bananas (both good for chilli pain, unlike water which just spreads the oil around the mouth) would do little to salve the onslaught. As I get off the plane in Albuquerque, New Mexico, I suddenly begin to worry that my months of preparation are going to be wholly and embarrassingly inadequate.

But help is to hand, in the large but perfectly formed shape of my friend Seb. A dedicated trencherman with matinée-idol good looks, he wears a couple of excess pounds with the ease of an old tweed jacket. Well over six foot, I have known him since the grey, gristly mince days of prep school and our passion for eating is mutual. We both see greed as something to be relished rather than avoided, although my wife refuses to eat with us if the food involves communal plates.

'I blink for a moment, and you two gannets have cleared the whole table,' she once sighed. 'It might be good for my waist but it's actually getting boring.'

A born gourmand, he has long been my partner in travelling to the more obscure boroughs of London in search of mouth-numbing Sichuan, quivering fresh toro sashimi or anything else that has caught our greedy little eyes. Unlike many of my more puritanical friends, he totally understands the joy of a five-hour Monday lunch. We both share a loathing of fussy eaters, the ones who mutter, 'One course should be enough for me' or 'Oooh, I might be a real devil and go for the "Death by Chocolate".' In short, a willing, experienced and very able adventurer for this particular leg of the culinary road. He's pretty handy with the hot-sauce too.

Our first dilemma hits us the moment we step off the aeroplane in Houston and onto Texan soil. Do we risk missing our onward connection to Albuquerque by nipping into the city for some barbeque? More specifically, a vast plate of brisket and ribs at Goode's BBQ. We debate the matter with all the intensity that such a momentous decision requires but it is with heavy heart that I pull rank.

'Seb, this is work, you know, not some jaunty beano tasting our way across America. I'm looking for extremes here, not givens.'

'You could have fooled me,' he grunts but admits that the brisket can wait. Instead, we comfort ourselves with a couple of chilli dogs.

'Way too sloppy,' grumbles Seb, still dreaming of the smoky meat mere miles away.

We have decided to arrive in New Mexico a few days early, to get a feel for the local food and visit Santa Fe too. 'A period of culinary acclimatisation' is the way Seb describes it. One of the joys of travelling with such an old friend is the complete lack of effort needed from day to day. Neither of us is remotely interested in churches, museums and temples so the only real arguments that occur are over our choice of dining establishments. Even these are few and far between.

New Mexico is chilli-loco, a place where the Official State Question (seriously, it was passed by the New Mexico legislature in 1996 though I could find no evidence of any other state having one) is 'Red or Green?' referring to the freshly made chilli sauces that are ubiquitous with every meal. Chillies are at the heart and soul of the state, both in the culinary and economic sense of the word with 99,000 tons of chilli being grown per year. New Mexico produces over half the hot chillies grown in the States, and the industry is valued at over $49 million. This makes it the state's number one cash crop.

Coming from the temperate, rainy climate of the UK, chillies seem exciting and glamorous, so much more thrilling than beets or Brussels sprouts. But it's a serious business, as the brusque headline of today's *Albuquerque Journal* spells out, 'Soggy soils, Weeds, Threaten Chile Crop,' news that pushes the Iraq war and various terrorist outrages off the front page. The South Western cuisine is no stranger to war itself, though, marked by the constant invasions of this desert land – Pueblo Indians, Spanish conquerors, Mexican neighbours and the relatively new influx of Anglo-Americans all have left their mark. But when it comes to ingredients, the chilli is king.

The red chilli is simply a ripened version of the green. The latter has a crisper texture and a more vegetable-like taste. 'Before they can be used,' warns Huntley Dent in *The Feast of Santa Fe*, 'green chillies must be roasted and peeled. Upon that point there is really not much compromise, I'm afraid. If you miss the roasting process and leave the chilli unpeeled, you miss the characteristic flavour and texture of South Western green chilli.' It is, he admits, a time-consuming chore: '... the prospect of charring a dozen Anaheim chillies over a gas burner [so all the skin is charred],' he warns, 'can be especially dismal.' The basic 'green' chilli sauce (of which there are thousands of variations) consists of the roasted, peeled, seeded and chopped green chillies along with onions, herbs and spices, water, stock and pieces of pork. Heat ranges from the soft and mild to the slightly more assured but this is about flavour as much as heat.

The red chillies are, according to Dent, even '... more important in Santa Fe cooking than the fresh green ones'. The fresh green are a seasonal treat while the dried red are easily available all year round. They are still a ubiquitous presence across the state, hanging in long bunches called *ristras* (harvested, red ripe chillies left to dry in the dry desert air). To us British, they might look like some sort of ghastly 'lifestyle' choice, the sort of almost edible souvenirs that cost a small fortune and show you're a well-travelled man.

But these red chillies are a culinary staple used every day in a dazzling array of dishes. You can either rip off thick chunks for stews, reconstitute them in water or grind them into a powder. They have a sweeter, richer flavour and the heat depends on how much is added. 'Red' sauce, made in much the same way as green but with ripened chillies, can be as hot or mild as you want it. Although the New Mexicans have a raging taste for chilli, the taste is more important than pure brute heat.

Santa Fe is a strange hybrid of a city, part cultural icon and part South Western Disneyland. Like the rest of New Mexico, its population is made up of Native Americans, Hispanics and whites (or 'Anglos' as they're politely known). The brown adobe buildings that dominate the centre are undeniable attractive, both soft and bold. The high desert air is crisp as freshly laundered linen and the light fantastic, even to my untrained eye. The air seemed infused with Friar's Balsam, a smell forever associated with my childhood. The centre plaza is a town planner's wet-dream, lush with perfectly manicured lawns, yet unmistakably South Western in style. In the distance, rolling hills keep a benign watch on this tiny city.

Visiting in March, we are among the only tourists tramping around town. We file past St Francis Cathedral, a monument to the city's Catholic past, and watch the Indians laying out their wares for the day ahead. They avoid eye contact as we walk past, just pointing to the assortment of turquoise jewellery before them. Just behind, Starbucks is opening for the day and the first wave of white locals stream in for their insipid morning fix. Try as I might, I can't muster even a shred of affection for the place. I know that I am supposed to like it, meant to wax lyrical about the liberal attitudes and picture-perfect adobe houses, but it leaves me cold. The stunning light and clean air have made it a haven for artists for many decades yet I can't escape a feeling of overwhelming smugness. Santa Fe exudes self-conscious pride in its heritage yet seems curiously lacking in spirit.

'It's a well-dressed fraud,' noted Seb as we pass the hundredth shop selling Native American artefacts, 'pretty but also pretty fucking dull.'

As we wander about, the initial small gasps of pleasure change slowly into a desensitised boredom, as endless worthy art shops mingle with the souvenir tat to make every single print, picture and piece of jewellery seem utterly identical. The juice bars, reiki centres, yoga classes, poetry readings and music festivals should all seem proof of a thriving arts scene, yet so relentless are they in keeping up the 'Santa Fe artistic' cliché that they start to overwhelm and grate.

After an hour or so, the place strikes me as little more than a dusty Virginia Water, a perfectly manicured theme park with real life 'injuns' and a pretty town square. All its undeniable charms – the perfect climate, the hippy ethic and easy pace – seem slightly false, as if steeped in a prissy marinade of bourgeois sensibility. For all its beauty and apparent artistic flair, the place lacks soul.

The first restaurant we eat in, a 'Navajo-themed' place called Anasazi, seems to sum up Santa Fe. Although the menu is thick with local produce, it is all too twee and pretentious. No flavour is allowed to speak for itself; ingredients are piled on with heavy hand, seemingly to show the culinary intelligence of the chef.

My first dish, 'Cinnamon chilli rubbed beef medallions with *chipotle* white cheddar mashed potatoes and mango salsa', takes longer to say than it does to eat. The cinnamon dominates everything and although its heart is in the right place, it just tries too hard. The same can be said of the 'grilled Iowa pork tenderloin with green chilli whipped sweet potatoes, red onion and currant sauce'. It ticks all the right South Western cuisine boxes (a sprinkle of Native Indian, a dollop of Mexican and a flourish of modern American cuisine) but fails to satisfy. Rather like the city itself.

The room is empty save a very young lady and an elderly man I can only presume is her 'uncle'. He doesn't draw breath for an hour, starting off on long, loud and boastful accounts of his net wealth ('Well into the seven figures, sweetie, but I wouldn't want to shock you with quite how much'), famous friends ('dear Tupac. God rest his soul') and immense power. The poor young lass does not utter so much as a syllable the whole night, save to excuse herself for the bathroom. As she totters out, he looks over to us and gives a huge wink. We smile weakly in response. As we walk home at about nine, the street is eerily deserted, as if a curfew has been put in place. The canopy of stars above dazzle but the city is dead.

But early the next morning, all seems well again. I open the curtains to see an impossibly pale blue sky – the colour of bantams' eggs – bathing the desert landscape in pin-sharp light. I stand transfixed, my eyes soothed and heart calmed. The dawn sun is as cleansing as a steaming power shower and I begin to regret being so hard on Santa Fe. How can I get any sort of intelligent feel for a city after just 24 hours? True, I stayed here for a week back in the early Nineties. But then, I was more interested in scoring dope and growing my hair (I was fresh out of public school and ready for some well-mannered rebellion).

I am torn away from gazing into this addictive light by a heavy hammering on the door.

'Breakfast,' yells Seb. 'Get your fat ass out of bed.'

As we amble down a narrow street, Seb's eye is caught by a sign in a restaurant window.

'Not responsible for too hot chilli,' it states bluntly.

'Sounds good to me,' says Seb.

Tia Sophia's doesn't look remarkable but is packed with locals, lingering over coffee and burritos, reading the local paper. Apparently, it's so popular with politicians and town officials that many a law has started its life here, over a plateful of *huevos rancheros*. And rumour has it that Tia Sophia's is the birthplace of the breakfast burrito. Fame indeed and there is little choice but to order it in all its glory, 'potatoes in a flour tortilla topped with chilli and cheese and bacon, with a fried egg'.

'You want red or green with that, honey?' asks our waitress.

I hesitate. 'Christmas please,' I reply. I have been told this is the local parlance for both red and green but am not sure. It could well be slang for some New Mexican sexual deviance. Or worse, it may not mean anything.

She just nods and, emboldened by my getting down with the locals, I order a side of green chilli stew.

'Show-off prick,' mutters Seb as I sit back with a smug smile.

When the food arrives, even Seb is rendered speechless by the pure bulk of the beast before me. The size of a sofa, my breakfast burrito is a huge unidentifiable lump smothered with fire-hydrant red chilli, shockingly yellow cheese and a thick river of mossy green chilli sauce. It weighs in around the same as a small retriever and I notice Seb eyeing it covetously between bites of his own, table-sized platter of eggs.

I take my first bite and realise that this is the great British fry-up dressed in New Mexican garb. The red chilli is mild, with a sweet hint of spice. The green chilli is far hotter but lifts up the mass of dairy and meat within. It is a feast fit for five but I am determined that not one crumb of this masterpiece is to be wasted. I alternate between shoving vast mouthfuls into my mouth and fighting off Seb's greedy advances. He doesn't favour a subtle approach, instead launching a frenzied attack when I am distracted by my coffee and making off with his plundered bounty.

'Fucking good,' is Seb's incisive view and I can only splutter my agreement.

My green chilli stew is equally gargantuan, studded with meltingly tender chunks of pork and a riot of contrasting flavours. This is our first taste of the real South West, the heavenly blending of Mexican, Native Indian and European. For the first time in Santa Fe, we waddle out of the restaurant with heaving bellies and broad smiles.

Quickly tiring of town, we decide to take the car off into the desert. We have also heard of a restaurant in Espanola, a small town a few miles north-west of Santa Fe. As the city melts away in our rearview mirror, the scenery moves into Peckinpah land, the arid scrub providing perfect contrast for his torrents of blood and redemption; isolated, craggy rock, foolhardy shrubs and distant snow-flecked hills. This is the 'big country' of Western legend, a place where men are men and wily roadrunners are pursued by dopey coyotes. The natural landscape is dotted with huge advertising boards, exhorting weary drivers to come and lose their hard-earned cash on slots and Caribbean stud poker, all with the best odds for 50 miles. Pueblos (Indian villages) flash by, some a motley assortment of run-down adobes, others replete with the trappings of casino money, huge satellite dishes and gleaming RVs.

The radio is set to 94 ROCK! FM and we drive to a medley of soft rock ballads. Just as you reach the crest of one hill, another unfolds before you and the view stretches out endlessly. Just before lunch, we decide to drive around Los Alamos, a once-secret city and birthplace of the atom bomb that destroyed Osaka. As you drive over the hill, you're met with the most incongruous of sights – a sprawling, Fifties-style town that looks more like a Lake Placid-style summer camp than a high-security nuclear city.

'It looks like that place in *Dirty Dancing*,' says Seb, surprising me with his knowledge of Eighties romantic movies, 'you know that place where Swayze and the bird get it on.'

This hitherto hidden sensitive side is only allowed to blossom for a moment. Some poor elderly soul in a battered Chevy takes a moment too long at the junction, and Seb makes his feeling clear via a prolonged hit on the horn.

Founded in 1943, Los Alamos was built expressly to build an atomic bomb before the Nazis. Secrecy was everything, with some of the sharpest and brightest brains in the country recruited and shipped in. Schoolchildren living there were forbidden from using their surnames and the scientists were banned from talking about their work at home. We drive past 'Explosives Areas' on Bikini Atoll road and the cheap housing has a decidedly military feel. You'd find it hard to believe that a weapon of such cataclysmic might could have been dreamt up in these quiet, pine-covered hills. But the Los Alamos National Laboratory is still as secretive as ever and there is little chance of getting anywhere near the core.

One man, though, fights a lonely war, doggedly camped on the front lawn of this nuclear mansion. Ed Grothus is owner of the Black Hole, a sprawling warehouse overflowing with Soviet-era Geiger counters, spent artillery shells and archaic computers with wires spilling out like disgorged guts. A few hundred metres away from the main nuclear laboratory, it's like an anarchist Office World, with tattered chairs, rusty filing cabinets, combat fatigues, radio spare parts, prop swords and car batteries. Groth is a committed anti-nuclear protestor, with a shock of white hair, burnished brown skin and two hearing aids.

'I've been here 39 years,' he hollers, whacking me on the knee to emphasise his point. 'The official line at Los Alamos is science. But that's rubbish … it's stockpile research. Now sit down, sit down, you must watch this video.'

Seb points at his watch, then his tummy. 'Lunch,' he mouths.

But it's too late and Groth fights his way through the junk, video-tape in hand, and finds a hidden VCR slot. We both grab a secondhand office chair and wait.

'It was smuggled out of the lab,' he says as the television flickers on. The video is an undercover recording of an arms seminar, with a stern lecturer going through the country's nuclear arsenal. We hear about W88 ('America's hard target killer!' says the dour suit with a hint of pride), B61s ('the burrowers … destroy bunkers with case') and the W78 intercontinental missile ('a threat to the existence of any enemy').

It's chilling stuff, especially the way the main scientist talks of these weapons with paternal pride. To him, they're babies not killers, creations to be proud of, not to fear. I doubt America's enemies agree. His cool, measured argument is that they 'provide the ultimate defence of our nation'. Groth has seen it so many times he knows it by heart, and mouths the words as he stares to gauge our reaction.

Even the usually cynical Seb is moved to comment. 'Now I'm really scared,' he says, thoughts off lunch for a moment.

'Los Alamos has a duty to the nation,' the government suit continues. 'We defend freedom on this planet … we try real hard to be the good guys.' At this point, Groth switches off the tape, eyes ablaze. 'No social responsibility, no moral responsibility. "Just doing our jobs," they say. Just like the Germans in the concentration camps. You heard about living legends. I'm going to be the world's first living pain in the ass. I'm scared to death we're all going to blow ourselves up. One bomb is too many.'

He predicts that the nuclear age (which started in Los Alamos in 1943) will end in 2013, with Washington DC destroyed in the autumn of that year. He presses more videos into our hands, telling us to go spread the word.

'You guys from England? You know Bryan Cathcart?'

'Um, no,' says Seb.

'You should do … he wrote a brilliant book on the British bomb.'

We promise to look him up and walk out into his backyard strewn with decommissioned missiles, broken fridges, lonely sinks and rusting launch devices. He lives among this wreckage of the nuclear age, preaching his gospel of a world free of nuclear weapons. He points to a large building with a CND sign on top.

'That's my own church. I say a critical mass every Sunday, turning wine into water. And now the Pope's jus died, I see an opening for myself up there.'

An old couple appear, looking dazzled by the military detritus about them. He spots them and wanders off. 'Have you seen the video,' I hear him say as Don Eduardo de Los Alamos leads the next disciples into his cluttered, single-minded and wholly admirable world.

As we get back into the car, I read his Los Alamos poem, 'composed for the 52nd anniversary of the bombing of Hiroshima and Nagasaki, Japan on August 6th and 9th, 1945'.

What cause? What reason
To Use a nuclear weapon even?
Deplore we must proposed production
More 'pits' designed for mass destruction.

'The nuclear holocaust may be imminent,' says Seb as we climb back into the car, 'but I've got to eat.'

We drive for 20 minutes and into El Paragua, a renowned old-school Mexican restaurant in Espanola, a small town crowded along two main roads. Crisp empanadas (billowy tortilla pillows) arrive with a pot of honey, chicken and cheese enchiladas, thick with green chilli; a vibrantly fresh and spicy tomato dip with fresh baked tortilla chips; Caldo Talpeno, a deeply savoury chicken stock filled with great chunks of avocado, shards of chicken and squares of tomato. The taste is fresh, honest and deeply satisfying. And a million miles removed from the greasy hell that is your average English Tex-Mex. The food is spicy and wholesome; our only regret is we don't have the space for more. But we have to return to Santa Fe, as we're leaving town the next day.

One last call is into the Chile Store, where we hope to get a final try of heat before hitting Albuquerque tomorrow. A middle-aged lady – more WI than chilli addict – welcomes us in.

When we ask about the Fiery Foods Show, she smiles. 'Jeez, there's a whole load of testosterone down there. It's the culinary equivalent of running with the bulls. Multo Macho.'

Seb and I can hardly control our childish excitement but manage to look suitably serious. I ask if she'll be attending.

'Oh God no. Been there, done that.' She shrugs indulgently. 'I'm too old for that crap now.'

We nod sagely, well aware we're fooling no one.

'One last thing,' she says as we get ready to go, 'don't get too involved in those extract sauces. They hurt.'

By the time we reach Albuquerque, the car is awash in a flood of testosterone.

'You haven't got a chance, little fellow,' gloats Seb. 'And no tears either. Tears are for pussies. You gonna get a chilli whipping from me.'

I wittily respond with allegations as to the size of his manhood and the inane, macho banter eventually burns itself out. Our old buddies at 94 ROCK! FM – 'the station that loves a good brew … and a good pork too' – are equally abuzz with excitement at the show and this morning's star guest is none other than Dave DeWitt, introduced as 'the golden calf of the hot sauce world'. Also present is Rosie McMaster, the managing director of Susie's Hot Sauce.

This potent, fruity brew is one of the highlights of a holiday in Antigua and I can hardly contain my glee that two hot sauce heroes are sharing the same mike.

'For the next three days,' screams a very excitable DJ, 'Albuquerque will be the mecca for hot-food lovers. Roll up, cause this one going to go off.'

Arriving at our hotel puts somewhat of a dampener on proceedings, a dull, monolithic block and a shrine to the utter emptiness of business travel. One look at the rusty trouser press, UHT milk sachets and postage-stamp sized pieces of soap and I'm ready to pack up and leave. Within two minutes of arriving in my identikit, grey corporate cube room, I start to fantasise about thin walls, giant cockroaches, mysterious stains, even bedbugs … anything to break the turgid monotony of freeze-dried coffee, regulation-sized towels (somewhere between a flannel and a pillowcase) and mail-order art. This is room design by proxy and portion control, a place of beverages, comestibles and hospitality suites. Its only redeeming feature lies in its close proximity to the Albuquerque Conference Centre and after dumping my bag, I wander out into the midday desert sun, ready for my first taste of The Fiery Foods 2005.

I'm hardly endearing myself to New Mexicans anywhere, but Albuquerque is a pig-ugly city, a concrete sprawl at the industrial heart of the state. Even the *Lonely Planet*, which manages to find charm in even the tiniest of villages, admits that Albuquerque was 'never considered a great beauty'. Yet its location – sprawled in the shadow of the walls of Sandia Crest – is stunning. At sunset, the cliffs take on an exquisite, rosy tinge that only serves to highlight further the general drabness of the city below.

This state must have been one hell of place before anything was built. With one of the lowest rates of personal income – and the second highest rate in the entire USA – the atmosphere at night is occasionally fractious. New Mexico has the highest violent crime rate in the country, as well as the top in burglary and aggravated assault. So the police officer's job is difficult and often dangerous, but our only taste of violence comes when we see a drunken teenage girl – no more than 16 years old and five foot tall – knocked to the ground by two cops. They wrench back her arms, tighten the cuffs and throw the little wretch into the car.

Her crime? Wobbling down the street and bumping into the wrong policeman. It is downtown, and the streets are thronged by Latinos, whites and blacks moving from club to club. The atmosphere is tense, as police crawl up and down the main strip, pouncing on inebriated revellers. We are appalled at the heavy-handedness of the police but a resident with us just shrugs it off.

'She might be carrying a gun or a knife,' he shrugs, 'and the police have to be brutal. It's the only way they keep control.'

The girl looks incapable of carrying a handbag, let alone a lethal weapon.

The main hall of the Albuquerque Conference Centre is home to the show and has over 250 different stalls arranged in eight vertical rows. At the far end of this aircraft hangar-sized room is a small demonstration stage where the likes of Dr BBQ (aka Ray Lampe) will be wowing the crowds. The first day is trade-only and as we step in, I am struck by the calm gentility of the whole thing. It could be the Chelsea Flower Show. The air is one of whispered efficiency, as storeholders from all over America – as well as China, Jamaica, South Africa, Australia and Brazil – carefully unpack their wares, ready for the three days ahead.

At first glance, I feel deflated. All this build-up, only to be confronted with what seems like a seminar of timeshare salesmen. Where are the fire-breathing clowns and the Kamikaze chilli eaters? It all looks so respectable, so calm and measured. I have always known that the trade part of the show is more important than the spectacle and all these hot-food wholesalers have travelled miles for one reason … to get their product sold in as many places as possible. But I can't help feeling a mite disappointed.

But once we begin to wander the aisles, things improve. Here, for the first time in my life, are over a thousand people who walk the hot-food walk and talk its talk. Far from being a bunch of masochistic, testosterone-stoked chilli kicks boys, all are encyclopaedic in their knowledge of their product, stressing the different flavours over all-out heat. Most are keen cooks, coming up with their own recipes for sauces, marinades and rubs. My first impression is of passionate enthusiasm and gentle professionalism. I came expecting chilli-eating contests and instead am faced with a whole bunch of connoisseurs.

One of the first stalls we stop at is Hot Shots, 'Your One Stop Supplier for Hot Sauces and BBQ Foods'. Most of the sauces are laid out on shelves, a dizzying array of colours, hyperbole and exclamation marks. The Hot Sauce humour is neither subtle nor particularly funny. Most is in a similar, frat-boy vein and usually concerns either 'hot women' or 'hot asses' in both senses of the word. Hence 'ANALize This XXX', Ass Blaster, Bayou Butt Burner, Bayou Pecker Power,

Brand New Asshole, Butt Twister, Colon Cleanser, Ditch The Bitch, Haemorrhoid Helper, Hot Bitch on the Beach, Hot Buns At The Beach, Hottest Fuckin' Sauce, No Fat Chicks! A Fat Ass Sauce, Pain is Good, Rectal Revenge, Show Your Tit, Wet Fart XXX ...

The list goes on and on, mostly in the same sniggering vein. The labels are loud and brash, the contents even more so. Marginally more funny are the up-to-the-moment political statements, ranging from the left wing – 'Love Your Country But Fear Your Government Hot Sauce' – to the Right – 'Kerry's Flip Flop Sauce (with Kerry, Clinton, & Ted Kennedy)' and 'Bomb Saddam Mad Blast'. But there is no true political ideology, just hot-sauce sellers trying to grab the attention of every potential customer.

Dave Lutes runs the company from Charlotte, North Carolina, and is a softly spoken, middle-aged man garbed in a chilli-print shirt. 'This hot-sauce business is ever-growing,' he says, making sure the Assplosion sauce is exhibited with the label facing forward. 'We're up by 25 per cent every year since 1996 ... that's 120 months without a dip, so you could definitely call it a growth business.'

His hottest sauce is the Blair's Holiday Reserve, at a terrifying 16 million SCUs. It comes in a small, limited-edition bottle, signed and sealed with Italian black, red and white resin and complete with a small skull on top. Its cost: a mere $300 (although, thanks to its rarity, the price has now doubled). He holds the bottle lovingly to the light, pointing out the pure capsaicin crystals.

'These are collectors' editions and no one would be stupid enough to eat them. Well, I hope not. We have a disclaimer to sign when you buy it, taking any responsibility away from us. It's the very hottest of the extract sauces.'

These extract sauces are at the extreme end of the heat scale, sold more as status symbols than ingredients. It all started with Dave's

Insanity Sauce, which extracted pure capsaicin from chillies then concentrated it down. Of course, all the endless disclaimers and warnings boost sales. As I told you, I have a sauce called 'The Source' (dig that pun) which has reams of mumbo-jumbo about ancient cultures and 'Are you strong enough to face the challenge?' Inside the tiny bottle is a thick, brown sludge, the merest whisper of which would have you on the floor.

In fact, many of the super-extract sauces are stronger than police-issue pepper spray. When you think what this powerful deterrent does to a human – inflaming the mucous membranes, causing closure of the eyes, coughing, gagging, shortness of breath and an acute burning sensation on the skin and inside the nose and mouth – you have to wonder about the mental state of anyone even contemplating this level.

For all my interest in finding extreme food – and eating whatever is presented – I have to draw the line at sheer physical agony and a possible spell in hospital. Yet the pleasures of this pungent pod, at less-extreme levels, are what fire the entire conference. That first hit of heat, followed (you hope) by the flavour of the chilli. It energises food without destroying the flavour and adds a zing that is absolutely addictive. Everyone here appreciates the chilli in all its forms. Without this enthusiasm, there wouldn't be a show. But the extract sauces are simply too powerful for enjoyment and although many dealers sell them, few would be foolish enough to try them out.

Mike Cates joins in the conversation, a genial Texan who has worked with Dave for six years.

'As with connoisseurs of wine and other fine foods, there are connoisseurs of hot sauce that can actually describe other actual ingredients of flavour and taste. Others are just satisfied with intense heat. Using these extract sauces to add heat to their recipes and sauces is their goal, not to forget the aspect of just showing off and enjoying ultimate heat sensations.'

I ask why he thinks hot sauce is now such big business. In the past, it was Tabasco and Crystal and that was about it.

'Well, the worldwide appeal of hotter and spicier foods is a result of baby boomers going from more bland diets of their youth and broadening their horizons through travel. Now, everyone wants hotter and hotter. Many companies started increasing heat levels with more and more pepper extracts. People are always asking and seeking hotter and hotter. The packaging on many 100 per cent food grade additive extracts, the quest to produce more Scoville units of heat, has resulted in higher concentrations of extracts. Now manufacturers are using hotter extracts to produce hotter sauces as a result. God knows where they'll stop.'

Surely no one actually eats these sauces. 'Well, I'm not sure,' says Dave. 'You get these guys shuffling in who don't look like they have enough money to buy shoes, let alone a $500 hot sauce. But they snap them up. Oh, and those tall, white-faced teenagers, too. What do they call themselves?'

'Goths?'

'Yup, that's the one. They have loads of tattoos and don't talk much. But I've heard they use it as part of their cult initiation, you know, "Eat this and you're in."'

I make a note to keep an eye out for Fields of the Nephilim T-shirts. I wave goodbye and carry on.

Seb is grilling Craig Muchow, the owner of 'The Fartless Factory', manufacturers of Fartless 16 Bean Soup.

'Does it actually work,' he asks, waving the jar about.

'Sure does, we soak the beans in yeast. No farts, I promise!'

Next door is Golden Toad, 'Saving the Planet One Tongue at a

Time'. These sauces are not so hot and their *chipotle* pepper sauce has a smoky, tangy flavour. Far removed from the excesses of Blairs and Dave's Insanity, every bottle sold means a donation towards Wildlife Conservation. Less worthy, but with even better sauces, are a bunch of hungover 30-somethings, plugging Danny Cash Hot Sauce. Danny himself has a *habenero* red Mohican and they talk about the quality of their sauce with all the passion and reverence of an 82 Petrus. They dollop a drop of Bottled Up Anger on a cracker for me and tell me to taste.

'See,' says Danny zealously, 'the sharp, Serrano-lime bite, then the garlic blast then the fierce *habenero* burn.'

The taste rolls across my tongue, not so hot to obliterate any subtlety but just enough so that you can taste each of the chilli's individual flavours. This is a hot sauce of quality.

'You coming tonight to the Chilli Head party? Eight o'clock at the Liquid Lounge. Should be a blast.' We carry on our wander through the stalls, tasting and chomping, our tongues getting fatter and fatter from the burn. After a while, the palate gives up and everything starts to taste the same. But as long as the extract sauces are avoided, it's good clean and non-extreme fun. The problem is, this particular leg of the Year of Eating Dangerously is beginning to look worryingly soft.

You can't miss Tahiti Joe's stands, as it's run by what looks like a cross between Crocodile Dundee, a German porn star and the guitarist from Status Quo. His chest is bare, save a flowery waistcoat, and a straw hat sits at a jaunty angle on his head. Underneath, straw-like hair cascades down his back. He exudes a seedy charm, accentuated by his red-lensed shades.

'You want to try the Camel's Toe,' he leers as we pass. It has the smoky taste of *chipotle* tempered by a sweet kick of mango. He starts on the pitch: 'Call it what you want, yeah, snapper, bearded clam, cooler cleavage, the pink taco, Beavage, there's nothing that tastes or smells like a camel toe.'

We nod, each trying not to catch the other's eye.

'So you guys here for all three days, yeah?'

We nod again.

'Well, you just wait. I got a camel toe model turning up in the tightest hotpants you ever saw. Don't miss it, 'cause she's hot.'

In the background, his big-haired wife stares into space, apparently unconcerned by the dribbling pervert before her.

We promise to return to check out the 'killer Camel's Toe' and move on. Our tongues now feel the size of lilos as we're assaulted by what looks and sounds like an extra from Mad Max 2. Built like a beer barrel, he appears to be the sort to know his way around a schooner or two. With shaved head and a bushy mass of beard, he looks halfway between soccer thug and stand-up comic. His black shirt is covered with chillies and he wears a plastic string of them around his neck.

'Haggis is the name,' he says, offering a pudgy but powerful hand. 'I've been giving people the shits for years,' he drawls, 'and I've only just worked out that I can get paid for it. Now try out me Redback Pleasure 'n' Pain.'

He deposits a furious red blob on the ubiquitous cracker and hands it over. It's a creeper, the first taste sharp and fruity, before the *habenero* heat rumbles in.

'This stuff'll give you a facial orgasm, ain't that right darlin',' he shouts at a pretty passer-by. She looks up briefly, then hurries on.

'You want to try a bit of this mate,' he says, accosting a middle-aged passer-by.

'No thank you very much,' comes the indignant response.

'Wanker,' hisses Haggis. 'At Horrible Haggis, the customer's always fucking wrong, got it.'

Seb asks if there are a lot of Australians here.

'Yeah. Actually, no. There is a bloody Californian Aussie over there but forget about him. You coming to the party? It's a right piss up ... Hello darling, now have you ever had a facial orgasm?'

We leave him to his banter. Despite a marked lack of chilli-eating competitions, the whole Fiery Food Show is growing on me. The super-hot sauces are there but the vast majority of sellers are uninterested in extreme heat, people who care about flavour but love the burn. Like so many other places I've visited on these travels, the thought is often so much more sensational than the reality. You build up a vision of a place in your head, colouring it with what you want to see and experience. So the initial reaction will always be a little depressing, as your imagination is replaced by cold reality. But after a quick sulk, that imagined vision is quickly forgotten and you set out to make the very best of what's actually there.

The show also appeals to my inner chilli geek, which is never far from the surface and is now given glorious, unself-conscious free range. I can sit and chat Scovilles, extracts, capsaicin creeper burn and Dave's Insanity without one stifled yawn or raised eyebrow.

Seb's tolerance, though, is lower than mine. 'Right, I can't taste anything anymore. My lips feel like Leslie fucking Ash's and I'm certain that I'm dribbling too.'

He ambles off and I try to get into work mode, interviewing hapless vendors and asking half-baked questions about their 'hottest' experience. I should have left with Seb, as my critical faculties are as shot as his. A day of tasting hot sauces is certainly fun, but after the thirtieth sample, they all start to taste the same.

My notes from the party are scrawled, spidery and next to useless.

'Salsa de assholes ... hot, keeps building, building ... tongue hurting ... ooh, *habenero* extract kick ... 4 minutes and still getting worse

... ow, please, burning ... non stop ... can't talk ... Jesus, help me ...'

They end there. And it takes Seb and me a good half hour to work out exactly what happened. The first hour passed without incident.

'Well, at least we can both remember that bit. Small bar, free beer and tequila,' he says, sipping on a cup of black coffee. 'And Haggis was pretty well-oiled from the start, so no surprises there, then.'

Although the finer details were hazy, the main event will be seared on my memory forever. It started as I chattered to John 'Cajohn' Hard, a bearded, bespectacled middle-aged man who looks more suited to the college lecture circuit than purveyor of fiery foods. The only give-away is his chilli-splashed pyjamas. His son Nathan, with goatee and mullet hairstyle favoured by German Death Metal heads, is similarly attired and they huddle in a group with their 'scientist', the man who develops their sauces. Pale, tall and with straight brown hair flowing down his back, he looks like a cross between Jesus and the BFG.

After a few minutes of idle chilli chat, the scientist pulled out a small bottle from his pocket, cradling it as if it were a lump of gold. 'You wanna try this one? It's extract, real strong. A real clean heat. It's about two million on the Scoville scale.' About the same strength as pepper spray, then.

The whole process felt deliciously illegal and underground, miles removed from the more family-orientated charms of the show. It was as if I were being offered a new, potent designer drug that promised me three hours of blinding bliss.

By now, a small group had gathered and, emboldened by a few beers, I stepped up to the challenge.

'I did try to warn you,' adds Seb, 'but you were being a lippy twat. So I just left you to suffer.'

I realise that beery bravado was the main culprit but I do remember (very vaguely) thinking what the point was in going on a search for the hottest sauces in the world if I didn't at least try a splatter. I imagine myself stepping up to the challenge, a brave knight fighting for the pride of his homeland.

'Bollocks to that,' says my ever-sensitive friend. 'You were a sweaty mess, and the whole crowd was waiting to see you go down in a blaze of unglory.'

Apparently, the braying masses whooped for joy when I took on the challenge. And the crowd grew bigger still, as at least a dozen hot-sauce maestros gathered expectantly to have a laugh at the English fool. The bottle appeared once more, named Salsa Para Pendejos.

'You know what that means?' asks Seb. 'Sauce for assholes. Very apt.'

Jesus inserted a thin straw into the bottle. He pulled it out, coated in a thick brownish goo, and passed it over. 'Lick the whole thing, man,' he said with an ominous smile.

Now it's one thing drunkenly agreeing to try a drop of this liquid fire but quite another to risk putting myself in hospital before I've finished at The Fiery Foods Show. I took the straw, touched it to my palm so there was a dot no bigger than a comma. A few in the crowd voiced their disappointment.

'Pussy,' shouted one.

'Yeah, English pussy,' shouted another.

Ignoring the heckles, I touched the tip of my tongue to the dot of sauce on my hand, probably taking no more than a quarter of the punctuation mark blob. The crowd went silent, craning their necks to get a better view.

'What are you getting?' asked Jesus, eyes glittering with excitement. At first, nothing, just a hint of sharpness. Then a slight warmth, spreading around the mouth. Nothing painful, just an all-round glow. About a minute had passed and the heat increased slightly. I detected the fresh, almost grassy taste of *jalapeno* but that soon passed.

Two minutes in and slight discomfort came rolling across the tongue, like set after set of fiery breakers.

By the third minute, the discomfort had blossomed into full blown agony, as the full power of the sauce was unleashed on my unwary mouth. It was shock and awe on the palate, a blazing holocaust so powerful that it knocked out my senses. Sweat started pouring from every orifice and tunnel vision took over. The reality of the moment had little relevance as this pyrogenous fury engulfed my brain and every iota of my being. I was overwhelmed by a heat so pure that nothing else matters, like that moment at the moment of orgasm. I lost control of my mouth and could be dribbling deep puddles on the floor, for all I knew.

For a second, I got sweet relief as my body fought back, releasing an army of endorphins. My senses sharpened to superhuman level and I saw everything in pin-clear detail – Seb asking if I was OK, the grins of the spectators, the clink of the bottles behind the bar, the murmur of early evening drinkers, the pride of Jesus's face. Then my vision blurred again behind a sheet of tears and the incandescent agony kicked back in again, fiercer than ever.

Six minutes had now passed and I was in the eye of the storm, every pain receptor in my mouth screaming, buzzing and jarring. I had no feeling in my mouth and my tongue lolled uselessly. I threw down a bottle of beer but it made about as much difference as pissing on the Great Fire of London. I'd do anything to stop this agony, pay anyone to put out my mouth. I started to feel nauseous, like the intense earaches of my youth. I grabbed the bar for support and stood, with my back to the crowd, begging the pain to calm down.

By the tenth minute, some form of normality started to return. I uttered my first words ('thucking ell') and managed a weak smile. By now, the crowd had dispersed as the entertainment had finished. My mouth and throat throbbed but my heart slowed, my tears dried and reality resumed. A strong buzz remained, the endorphins still whizzing around my bloodstream. I felt giddy, weary but jubilant.

I ask Seb what I looked like, as the whole experience, at the time, was blurred into one long scream.

'You didn't look too well at one point. Your eyes were closed, you grabbed the bar for support and didn't respond to anything. I thought we might be paying a quick trip to the local casualty.'

Apparently Cajohn wandered over afterwards, a wry smile peeking through his beard. 'Some sauce, hey?' Some sauce indeed.

Saturday afternoon sees the show opening to the general public and there's a palpable hum in the air. Giant chillies wander around the room, handing out leaflets and sweating inside their suits. I pass Dave's Hot Shots stall, where he has all the expensive, $200-plus sauces laid out hopefully. 'I'll keep an eye out for them Goths. They come in, and they won't want to be paying full whack. So I'll let them negotiate a little. But these are collector's items, you see. Their value just goes up and up.'

I wander off in search of Haggis, but his stall is empty. It's ten in the morning, with just two hours to prepare for the public onslaught.

'He's probably still in bed,' says the next door stallholder. 'Or in prison.'

The products at the show range from the very fine to the downright idiotic. 'Spepper' falls firmly in the latter category. Run by the goofy but amiable Nathan Banker from Denver, its publicity blurb describes it as

a precise GOURMET mixture of flake salt and fresh cracked pepper in the same shaker. (We know ... simple huh?) Spepper has been blended precisely to offer its user a perfect blend of Salt and Pepper everytime!!! Spepper uses BIGGER holes on its shakers so you don't have to shake whatever shaker it is you may be using for 3 minutes to get an 'iffy' amount!

Are people really so pig-lazy that they can't be bothered to shake salt first, then grind pepper? I just can't think why anyone would want to buy it, yet they seemed to be doing a roaring trade. And plaudits fill the website. Most prominent of all is one Danny Cash, also from Denver.

'I never used to salt anything. Now, I Spepper everything! It's incredibly addictive.' The Danny Cash stall is just over the way. Nathan admits it's selling OK, but he's also behind a website called The Masturbation Station.

'But hey, don't tell no one here. I'll probably be thrown out.'

I've been trying to grab a few moments with Dave DeWitt since I arrived and occasionally catch sight of this rangy figure, dressed in the obligatory chilli shirt, rushing about from stall to stall, but have never managed to speak to him. Eventually, I'm granted a few minutes just before midday. A half-halo of hair surrounds his head and his long face carries a neat moustache. His voice is a deep, soothing drawl (he has done many a commercial voiceover) and his manner relaxed. He seems a little surprised that I've come all the way from England but is more than happy to talk.

'It all started 17 years ago. I had been a show producer doing other kinds of shows. You know, custom cars, antiques, that sort of thing. Hey Chip, how's it going?' He nods to a Boss Hogg lookalike with twinkling blue eyes.

'Then I started writing about chillies – which were a passion – and launched *Chile Pepper* magazine in '82. Hi there John, all good? Great. We'll talk later. Then I realised there was no trade show for the chilli industry. Anyway, I had a magazine to promote it with and in 1988, we held a very small show with 37 exhibitors. I made $100 profit. Now we have over 250 exhibitors.'

As much as the Pope of Pepper is a passionate advocate of all forms of chilli, he's pragmatic about the show.

'It's all about business. I do it to make money. Now the business is reaching into Middle America. It's no longer confined to Louisiana and the South West. It's everywhere now.' He stops to shake a couple of hands. 'Glad you could make it. So the thing about hot and spicy foods is that they are addictive. You never hear anyone saying, "Hey, got into spicy food but now I'm bored and want to go back to bland."'

He has little time for the extremes of the extract sauces, seeing them as a liability if anything.

'Most of the extract sauces are sold as gifts and never consumed and that's fine. But soon, I'm afraid that there will be an unfortunate incident – someone with a heart condition or breathing problems – and the government will crack down, banning them all.'

DeWitt has actually banned extract tasting from the show. A few years back, a child took a huge mouthful of one of the super-hots and fainted. Of course, there will always be fools (like me) who are desperate to give a sauce a sample. But it's certainly not officially condoned. Dave Lutes agrees when I speak to him later.

'Yeah, if the government do decide to act, they'll probably not allow anything over one million Scovilles to be sold. Which will be a shame.'

There's nothing, of course, to stop you buying a sauce and sampling it on the spot. My ten minutes are up and he shakes my hand and wanders off into the crowds. I get the impression he didn't really like me. Perhaps it was the endless questions about extract sauces and he thought that I was trying to stitch him up. Or perhaps he just has little time for plummy sounding Brits. For Dave – and this is made clear in his myriad collection of excellent books – chillies are about flavour and good heat, not mindless machismo.

Chip Hearn is the portly gentleman who greeted Dave a few minutes earlier and I find his stall to talk hot sauce. Like Lutes, he has a massive range of hot sauces, from the everyday to the super-hots. He has fluffy white hair, ripples of chins and is based in Delaware. The title on his business card reads 'Sauce Innovator' and his shirt is – yup, you've guessed it – covered in chillies. He has the easy, slick patter of the professional salesman and I wait while he flogs boxes of sauces to various suppliers.

'Listen, the extract sauces are little more than a bit of fun, gimmicks and things for the shelf. They're way too hot to enjoy and destroy any flavour. The likes of Endorphin Rush and the others taste horrible and gritty, pure heat and nothing else. And that's not what hot sauce is about. It's about flavour, fruits and *habeneros*, or vinegar and *jalapenos* ... I've tried a million different kinds, all with markedly different characteristics. Some mild for dipping, others fiery as hell. But all developed in the mouth. Over 600,000 SCU, you can't really taste anything but heat.'

The majority of decent sauces (not the ten-a-penny novelty ones with garish labels and comedy names) are brewed by food lovers, and are meant for cooking. Still, that doesn't stop him having an area of his website, peppers.com, called 'I survived' with pictures of people's faces after eating the super-hot sauces. Looking through the assortment of gurns and grimaces, I suddenly realised quite how ridiculous I must have looked last night. Seb is more than happy to confirm this.

At 12.00, the doors open to the public – there's still no sign of Haggis – and a stream of devotees wander in. There are families out for an awayday, spotty chilli fanatics in tie-dyed 'Chile Head' Grateful

Dead-style T-shirts. Then a couple of waddling white men, mid-twenties and clad in over-sized sports gear. Both wear a thick chain around their neck, with a bottle of Pepto-Bismol at the end. Sales pitches fill the air, as the stallholders vie for custom.

'Before it hits the palate, just check out the bouquet,' cries one.

'Feel the heat, taste the passion,' implores another.

'It's hard to use *chipotle* and make it mild … see, a good sweet taste with a little lingering heat … can you feel the jalapeno develop across the tongue …' It goes on and on.

'I reckon the number one reason for all these people coming is free food,' says Laura Maxhado of the New Mexico Chile Co. 'Before, though, it used to be all about the heat. Now, it's about flavour. People actually want to taste the chillies.'

I leave Laura to her queues and pass Casa Fiesta Food, home of the Screaming Monkey hot sauce.

'I grew up on black pepper and Tabasco in Canada,' admits Lynn Anderst. 'And now I'm making up for it. Jeez, I got all excited when Taco Bell came to town. I was that deprived. We make all our own sauces now. Try one.'

It has a vinegar kick, followed by a full *habenero* heat. Then I spot the whole *habeneros*, dipped in chocolate and sold for a buck a piece. I hand over a dollar and look at the glossy fruit, shaped like a lantern and coming complete with a fearsome kick. After last night's experience, I am a little wary. I look for Seb, hoping to force one down him, but he has disappeared into the crowds.

'Oh go on. It's not that bad,' smiles Lynn. 'Just get it down and get it over with.'

I gulp and throw the whole thing in my mouth, crunching furiously and chewing as fast as I could. The first taste is of chocolate, then that exquisite fruitiness of the pepper. The burn starts after

30 seconds, fearsomely hot but nothing compared to the night before. After two minutes, I'm giddily light headed and after three, I'm back to muck sweat state again. This heat reaches a peak in about the fourth minute. But the intensity, although searing hot, is not a fraction of last night's torture. Although my tongue still throbs for hours to come, it seems like 'good' pain. Compared to last night, though, the pain is brief, intense and short lived. I wipe my brow and hang around the stall, watching the punters try their luck.

'We do warn people that these are hot as hell but some don't listen. One lady burst into real tears – not ones induced by the heat – but it was because she came to the show on an empty stomach.'

I watch a teenager in a Hot Head T-shirt convince his dad to try one. 'Go on, give it a go. Please.'

'No way kid. I know what these bastards do to you.' They walk on.

A middle-aged Hispanic man stops to buy one. 'Very tasty,' he says between bites. After a few seconds, his face changes. 'Oh God, my throat's going numb. Oh God, it's creeping, getting stronger and stronger.'

He rushes off to find something to cool his mouth. A couple of waddling American flesh mountains buy two each, and eat them with all the ease of a strawberry. Not even a glimpse of the famed 'habenero beads', those tiny droplets of sweat that form on the brow. Mostly, it's men who try the fruit, either showing off to their friends or girlfriends. Watching grown adults trying to pretend the heat doesn't bother them is pure comedy. Some nibble, some bite, one man even swallows it whole. They sell at least 60 in the half hour that I sit watching these contorted faces of pain.

'Man, that's hellish hot,' says one teenager to his sullen friend.

'Are you hurtin'?'

'Shit, yeah, man. Man, this shit hurts.'

His friend's face breaks into a smile. 'How much it hurtin'?'

'A lot, man, just shut the fuck up, I need some soda.'

They slouch off, their bickering disappearing into the general hubbub of the show.

Just as I'm about to leave, a sudden commotion catches my eye. I look through the crowds to see a huddle of concerned faces looking down at someone in their midst. I wriggle through and see a teenager with a face of purest pea-green, violently puking into a rubbish bag. His friends mop his brow and wipe his face while he flops about, moaning gently.

'Oh Jeez,' he murmurs, as another stomach of fiery sauce comes hurling out. Apparently, he overdosed on a super-sauce. I feel his pain. I know how bad it is going down. But coming up again, back through the mouth and spilling through the nose. That is true torture. I ask how much he ate.

'Enough,' replies a very serious friend. A stern-looking administrator storms off to find the offending vendor. Apparently he was breaking the rules by giving out extract samples. I follow in his wake and it's not too hard to spot the offender. A huge crowd of sweating loons surround his stall, all gasping, some with their tongues buried deep in small tubs of ice cream. You almost expect to hear the sizzle. He gets a verbal cease and desist, much to the disappointment of the watching masses and they move on in search of further stimulation.

My job done, I say goodbye to my new friends and make my way back to the hotel to find Seb. If the show wasn't the no-holds-barred chilli fest I was expecting, I certainly wasn't disappointed. This was, on the whole, a group of chilli fanatics who loved every aspect of this wonderful fruit. Sure, even if you forget the extracts, a lot of the sauces were strong. But this wasn't some extreme, macho bullshit where pain was good and flavour and passion irrelevant. The Fiery

Foods Show was far from being some dangerous free for all, rather a civilised celebration of the chilli pepper. Like so many other countries, cities and cultures I've visited in my Year of Eating Dangerously, the true spirit of a food can be overshadowed by the hype. But this was one thriving industry, a mass of artisan producers doing what they love best. Long may it prosper.

I call Seb and we meet for one last drink. By now, we are desperate to leave the city. We are both missing our wives and starting to get a little bored of each other. With the Fiery Foods Show all but over, there is little to keep us here. The sun is as clean and crisp as ever and we sit outside, watching the low riders cruise by. But all of a sudden, the relative calm of the afternoon is shattered by a bellow from across the street. We both look up, to see a tall man with a shock of white hair, a tangle of dirty beard, ragged shorts and mirror sunglasses shouting at us from across the street. He could be anywhere between 40 and 60 but has the look of a man who's long been tramping the road.

He waves his stick, topped with feathers, bellowing in our direction: 'Fuck Bush up the ass.'

We play typically British and look down, laughing, but desperate to be ignored. To our horror, he comes bounding over.

'I'm walking across America for peace in the Middle East.' Well-spoken, if a little frenetic, he pauses his introduction to scream, 'Fucking Republican bastards,' at a startled old couple.

'That's hardly peaceful,' says Seb.

'No, man, you don't get it. I'm a radical pacifist, man, like the Kennedys and Martin Luther King.'

'So why are you screaming at harmless people?' asks Seb. 'That's aggressive.'

He's silent for a moment, his sunglasses reflecting our quizzical faces. 'Oh yeah,' he growls and leaps over to catch up with the couple.

He stops in front of them and they cower, obviously terrified. 'Hey, sorry guys.'

They nod and move away as fast as their aged legs will carry them.

'Well that helped,' whispers Seb.

He swaggers back and peels off his T-shirt to reveal a distended belly spilling over his shorts. 'My name's Mike, Mike Oren. I started walking from San Bernardino, California, on September 21st 2004 and so far, I've walked 475 miles. I want to make it to the Statue of Liberty and I want nothing but world peace.'

With that, he leaps up onto a rubbish bin and starts screaming, 'Fuck Bush up the ass ... Republican scum.'

'Gandhi, he ain't,' says Seb.

For all his obvious eccentricities, though, he's not without charm. He gets us to sign his petition, LA to New York on foot. Then admits he's taking the bus to Santa Fe.

Seb is now in full swing. 'Bus? That's cheating. You're a fraud.'

'Hey, fuck you, man,' comes the response. 'That's off the trail, man ... I need to get laid up there.'

We continue talking – he is lucid, sober and eager for attention. But not mad. Now and again, he screams something about Bush and bum sex, occasionally apologising for swearing when a child walks past.

'Sorry, kid, ignore my language. I've been in jail a hundred times, but never in prison.'

One mother smiles and says not to worry – 'Bush is far more offensive than a mere fuck.'

By this time, word is travelling up and down the street and a small crowd gathers to watch his antics. He, of course, acts up, yodelling and throwing in a few more 'fuck Bush'es for good measure.

'Change the record,' orders Seb. 'I'm bored of Bush and butt sex. Say something new.'

'Hey, fuck you, man, Bush needs to be fucked up the ass. Stop killing the vibe.'

Some of the crowd applaud, others storm off appalled. He sees an empty chair and comes to sit down next to us. He stores his stick in the bin in front of us and sits down.

'You want to help a pacifist pilgrim ... buy him a beer.' Sure. We order a beer and as the crowds thin out, he calms down. We sit and talk about his family (his father was in the Marines) and he makes for fascinating, if occasionally deranged, company. Then a couple of police cars draw up to the kerb, disgorging four worried-looking cops. After our experiences of a few nights back – where the girl was beaten to the ground by police – we realise he is about to spend his 101st night in prison. One officer strides straight up to the table, looks him square in the eye and starts to speak.

'Excuse me, sir,' he asks nervously, 'we've had reports of a wild-looking man shaking a stick and shouting obscenities. He might be a native American.'

The stick quivers next to the cop in the dustbin, brushing his holster. As cool as can be, our friend just shakes his head. 'No idea what you're talking about. He might be up there', and points up the street. Without blinking, they move off on their search up the street.

'Gotta run boys,' Mike smiles and leaps off, grabbing his stick and pack and disappearing into downtown Albuquerque. The policemen come back, shake their heads, frustrated, then make up for it by pulling over a passing Buick, full of Latinos, for playing their music too loud. Like Ed Grothus of Los Alamos, he's another eccentric with a pacifist message. And like Grothus, a man to respect rather than fear.

* * *

I wake up on the last day to a snowstorm. The mountains, once rosy, are covered in white, like chunks of Turkish delight under a blanket of icing sugar. And I immediately fear the worst, snowed in in Albuquerque for ever. The prospect is a grim one. By now, we have both had our fill of burritos, breakfast or otherwise, and even the chilli stew, so beautiful a week back, is beginning to grate. But a brief break in the weather makes sure the plane can leave. And as we climb up into the sky, I look down at the long, winding desert roads below. Somewhere down there, Mike Oren is walking east for peace. And Dave DeWitt, too, packing up and getting ready for next year.

As for me, I have the very briefest of stopovers in England, before moving off East and into the vast land that is China. In preparation for the trip a few months back, I have gone to meet an old family friend, David. There are few men who know more about the intricacies and intricate flavours of Chinese food than David. To call him a bon viveur does him an injustice as he is the owner of three of the most beautiful private clubs in the world as well as being a concert-level pianist, philosophy teacher, restaurateur, art dealer, Honorary Consul to Cuba and board member to God knows how many Blue Chip businesses. I'm still convinced he's BA's best private customer (he denies it) and probably spends more time in the First Class lounge than he does in his own bed.

He plays the magnate to perfection, with a booming voice, flaw-less enunciation (except when he breaks into fluent, expletive-studded Cantonese, at which point he turns into the Chinese titan rather than English gent) and a huge Havana cigar is never more than a metre from his mouth. He has an explosive temper to match, a roar that literally shakes the foundation of any city he is in. Woe betide the fool who falls short of the David standard of perfection. It always passes quickly but is a terrifying sight to behold. But underneath the elegantly cut Chinese silks and sharp Savile Row suits lies one of the most kind-hearted, intelligent and generous men I've ever met. He is also one of the great cussers of our time, a man who has as many uses for 'fuck' as the Eskimos do for snow. We meet in Hakkasan, slurping over congee and soup, while he outlined my tour.

'Forget all the usual Chinese shit,' he cries with a wave of his cigar. 'If you come with me and Luce,' he gestures to his wife, who is deep in conversation with mine – neither pays the slightest bit of attention so he raises his eyebrows and carries on, 'you'll see the real fucking China. We're there for Hong Kong and a bit of Beijing, then I have friends everywhere else to take you around.'

This is no mere statement but an order. 'Anyway, if you don't speak Mandarin or Cantonese, you'll find fuck all.'

This is fine by me. The thought of the company of good friends makes the journey all the sweeter, especially if I am sure that no culinary stone will be left unturned. He orders a few more dishes to an already groaning table then launches into the basics of Chinese cuisine.

'First up, and best of fucking all, is the Cantonese food of the South. I'm Cantonese. It's the finest, the haute cuisine. Some say it's a little snobby but the Cantonese are perfectionists. Everything has to be fresh and of the ultimate quality. There's an old saying. "Live in Hangchow, marry in Sochou, dine in Canton, and die in Liuchou." The first has the greatest views, the second the most beautiful birds, Canton has the finest food and the last, the best coffin wood you can get. They get it right too.'

He pauses to light his cigar, puffing until his whole head is enveloped in a blanket of smoke. He takes the first deep draw and leans back, blowing out a thick plume.

'The Cantonese are famed for eating fucking anything. Snakes, turtles, dog, no fucker is safe. It's also the best-known style in the

West, though most of it is inedible shit. In Hong Kong, ah, Hong Kong, you'll find the greatest Cantonese food in the world. So you'll start there.'

An ashtray appears at his side. He nods his thanks then continues.

'Next, up to the Eastern school of Shanghai. They're proud of their regional food, but cook mainly with lard so it's real stodge up there, dumpling and noodles and pig fat. It's very sweet too. That's why they're all fat bastards with red faces. Good stodge though, for cold winters, I see it as the Yorkshire of China, and that's a compliment.

'Right, then Peking, or Beijing as it's now known, the Northern school. It's more refined and imperial and a culinary centre. How's that congee? Good, eh. You just wait until I get you to Victoria Seafood, my favourite restaurant in Hong Kong. Then you'll see some proper Cantonese food. No time for Sichuan and Hunan in the West, but I'll show you stuff that's even better than you'd get in those provinces. And dangerous food? I'll show you some fucking dangerous food.'

He winks and taps off his ash.

Two months later, and a mere two days after arriving back from Albuquerque, I'm back on the plane and flying off, once more, into the unknown.

CHAPTER 3

CHINA

Arriving in Hong Kong, I plunge, almost immediately, into the belly of the dragon. After just one hour in this sultry mega city, I find my dinner mere inches away from my face. And it doesn't look happy. Fixing me with his beady onyx eyes, the cobra tracks my every move, his engorged hood swaying in time to my sweaty twitch. He is so close that I can make out each individual dirty scale on his neck. Every time his tongue flickers out, I swear I catch a whiff of musty breath, like mice that have died under the floorboards and not been found for weeks.

I gulp in a mouthful of the thick, greasy air but it does little to soothe my nerves. The city's mercantile hubbub now seems a long way off as the cobra slides closer. On the whole, I try to avoid confrontations with deadly snakes. But this time, I have no one to blame but myself. If I hadn't insisted on having his gall-bladder cut out and added to the cup of rice wine before me, everything might have been fine. The snake would have slept on and I could have continued on my culinary jaunt, unimpeded by six foot of angry serpent. He is merely inches away now, deep into my discomfort zone, and the threat of a deadly dose of neuro-toxin seems all too real. I edge back a little more but a solid table blocks my escape. I flinch and it senses my fear, drawing back like a taut bow, every muscle rigid beneath its shiny skin. Then it strikes, firing a thin clear stream of venom directly towards my eyes. I have been in China just 60 minutes and this is not the best of starts.

China can be a perilous place for the squeamish or unwary eater. Perilous riverbanks and incendiary sauces are one thing, but braised donkey penis quite another. Actually, I only come across that particular speciality after I have left the country, and seen a report on Beijing's first 'penis' restaurant. The place has opened just weeks after my departure and despite an initial disappointment – julienned dog cock would have made for spectacular story-telling – I can't say I am too sorry to miss it. But what more could China offer the curious gourmet? Well, pretty much everything. The Cantonese alone are famed for eating 'anything with four legs, save a table'. Still, I usually like to take a few easy hours finding my culinary feet in any new place. After the bland indignities of airplane food, you crave an easy entry into the local cuisine, a spicy bowl of noodles or one of the more 'vanilla' cuts of a cow. I am aiming to start off slowly in every country I visit and ease myself gradually into an alien culture. From that easy starting point, I can build up, at my own pace, to the more extreme-seeming delights.

There's been no such worries in Gloucester, and New Mexico had plenty to offer a timid tummy. But the term 'extreme-seeming' lies at the heart of my whole journey. My first task is to embrace culinary relativism for all it is worth, in that one man's snake is another's steak. If I am going to enjoy any part of the next few months, I will have to set aside my Western prejudice and approach each dish with an open mind. Turning my nose up at tripe, for one, will have to become a thing of the past if I am to get any understanding of another cuisine.

Food is inherently dangerous. It rots and becomes poisonous and perilous to our health. What civilisation has done, over countless millennia, is remove that danger. From that moment where meat and fish first met fire, through to preservation via salting, drying, pickling or canning – right up until the advent of refrigeration, irradiation and climate-controlled vacuum packing – we have been locked in a battle to make food safe and longer lasting, to remove any chance of spoilage or bacteria or poison.

The supermarkets sit at the very apex of this battle, gleaming, sterile temples of uniformity, safety and conformity. The temperature is closely controlled, the produce all resembles the fruits of Eden and they all gleam and glitter in a perfect approximation of real food. Yet one taste shows they are anything but, pathetic, bland shadows of the things they once were. Good-looking, sure, but impostors all.

Part of my desire to get out and taste everything stems from a hatred of this awful homogenisation of our national palate, of the dreary ready meals loved not for flavour but convenience. My problem is not with our methods of preservation – so essential for survival in the days without electricity – but the fact that we accept the mediocre, the desperately dull, as everyday. The chance to eat one's way around the world is not to be sneered at, especially for a truly greedy bastard like myself. But to try everything with truly open palate is often easier said than done. And it does not bode well for the rest of my trip that I start the Chinese leg of my journey mere inches away from one of the world's most venomous snakes.

'They make you horny,' says Alex, David's driver, as we drive towards the Sham Shui Po area of Hong Kong to try out a snake tonic. He gives a low, rumbling chuckle. Alex is six foot five and resembles Odd Job on super-steroids. Despite his threatening appearance – shaven head, moustache and hands the size of small hams – he is endearingly gentle with a slight lisp. His appetite, though, is gargantuan and he boasts he has never left as much as a scrap on his plate.

Ever. I happily resign myself to a lengthy and gluttonous night. 'Now is not the best time for snakes,' after he climbs back into the car.

A run-in with a particularly pedantic Hong Kong traffic cop has darkened the mood a little. But at the thought of snake, harmony is restored.

'Snakes best and fattest in winter, when they are hibernating. In summer, a bit shit. And flavour not so good. But snake soup makes the body warm.'

Like so many ingredients in Chinese cooking, the snake is not just appreciated for its taste but its medicinal value too. It's Yang food, the positive and masculine half of Yin and Yang. And it promises to do wonders for your sex-life. We drive under the harbour, into Kowloon and onwards. As we get nearer, the glitzy stores and designer hotels make way for rickety buildings, old noodle shops and streets entirely filled with piles of old televisions, computers, watches and washing machines. It's the flotsam and jetsam of the microchip revolution, an electronic tide line of last week's technology.

Still, nothing is wasted here. At one stall, moribund computers are fixed on the spot by nimble-handed technicians. Wobbling towers of chunky calculators sit next door, then a jumble of broken digital watches. Amongst all this low-tech effluence, an ancient, toothless woman hawks mangoes and durians, thrusting them out and underneath the noses of passers-by. To her right is an impromptu pig stall, with a severed head hanging off a hook, its long-lashed eyes closed in what looks like blissful sleep. The windows are crowded with lacquered ducks, their heads tucked neatly beneath their wings. Noodle shops are everywhere, pouring fragrant steam out into the sticky night.

Alex strides ahead, his mobile phone swinging from its holster like a Colt 45, brushing off vendors with a sullen grunt. Suddenly, he stops outside an open-fronted room. I peer into the harsh, strip-lit place and look for some sort of sign. Alex points at the glass cabinet to the right of the entrance. It looks like a two-level food warmer, a couple of glass boxes one stacked upon the other. I assume he's showing me some type of Cantonese bun when something moves within. I draw closer then jump back.

On the top are two sleeping cobras, sleek and serene, while the bottom box contains a pair of large geckos, snacking from a china bowl filled with writhing maggots. Alex taps the box and the snakes awake and rear up angrily. One pulls himself into strike position and seethes at Alex's sausage-like digits.

'Makes 'em angry,' he chortles, 'and they taste better. The more poison, the better, more potent.' I'm not so sure. The last thing I want is a furious reptile breathing down my back so I mouth an apology as I walk past them and into the restaurant. The snakes look deeply unimpressed.

Two tabbies sleep next door on an old hostess trolley, seemingly unbothered by the 12 foot of combined killing power just inches away. The room is basic and spartan with three plastic tables and a few chairs. The right side of the wall is thick with jars and bottles, filled with every kind of pickled reptile you could imagine. Lizards of every size and snake after snake, floating gloomily in their rice wine. It was like the reptile room in the Natural History museum, except that these were for drinking not studying. Some of the bigger jars have as many as five different snakes within, all coiled together in their murky suspension.

The kitchen is at the back, part of the main room. On the left side are piles of old, identical wooden boxes lining the wall. A television sits on top, blaring out Chinese pop. The boxes are battered but sturdy. As we sit down, Alex tells me that they're filled with live snakes. This is not what I wanted to hear. I expected that the serpents would be either kept behind glass or, at least, locked away at the back. Here, they are less than a metre from me, only a flimsy wooden door between us. I try to keep my feet off the grubby tiles below but it doesn't make for comfortable seating. Behind us, an older couple are bent over a pot of soup and slurping intently.

'The old love snake, very traditional. But the young prefer McDonald's.'

I ask if traditional cuisine is dying away because of the fast food chains, checking all the while for fugitive cobras.

'Fuck no,' he splutters, seemingly contradicting himself. 'All Chinese love Chinese food. Just the young ones like eating McDonald's too. You want soup first?' asks Alex and I nod distractedly.

One of the snakes in the glass cabinet – so rudely awoken by Alex – is watching my every move and I'm doing my best to avoid his glare. Why is he paying no attention to Alex? I try to point this out, gesticulating wildly under the table.

'It was the big fella,' I attempt to tell him in a telepathic stutter, 'I'm your mate.'

The snake soup is dumped in front of me and his stare intensifies. Great, I think, not only is he convinced that I woke him up. But I'm just about to slurp down a member of his close family too. It's all going a bit too Titus Andronicus for my liking.

The soup has a gelatinous consistency, very similar to a typical hot and sour soup. Mushrooms and slices of cabbage wallow alongside long, thin strips of meat that look like bleached anchovy fillets. This is the snake flesh. It doesn't have the strongest of tastes (cheap chicken, I suppose) but it's far from disgusting. By the time I've tried my first mouthful, Alex has finished his. He sits back and burps contentedly. The soup is unremarkable, as is the snake meat. But after a few more spoonfuls, I give up.

'You want that?' says Alex, licking the last drops of his from his moustache. I shake my head and he reaches over and finishes the soup in a few pelican-like gulps. 'Now, I'm a horny motherfucker,' he announces and burps again. He barks a few more words to the owner then asks if I'm ready for the bile. Not really but this is supposed to be the star attraction of the evening. I nod.

'How many snakes?' he asks. The theory is that the more snake bile you drink, the more potent the drink is. The best is seven of China's most poisonous snakes, all mixed together in rice wine. Not only do I have no need to get that horny (if it does indeed work) but the price is astronomical, about £300. I tell Alex that just the one cobra will do for me.

'You sure?'

Absolutely. The owner, a slim, wren-like lady in her forties, Ah Shum, slips on a pair of flimsy white cotton gloves. They look as if they'd hardly stop a stinging nettle, let alone an angry cobra. Her shorts and flip-flops offer scant protection from well-aimed fangs too. She opens the door of one of the wooden boxes and hauls out a writhing length of snake. It's as if she is casually measuring out a quarter of wine gums and although her concentration is intense, there's not a glimmer of fear. To give the snake its due, it seems equally relaxed. She brings it over to me to check, and I nod nervously, putting as much distance as I can between the white-bellied serpent and my ankles. As she draws it back towards her, the snake decides it's had enough of this softly-softly approach and flares its hood, striking at the lady. She performs a neat – and spectacularly unconcerned – pirouette and the fangs snap shut on empty air.

While my hostess wrangles with the cobra, I'm trying my utmost to seem calm. This is not helped by the fact that I'm perched atop my chair, much to the amusement of the old couple next door. They stop eating their soup and cackle at the idiotic gai-jin. One of the cats opens an eye to check out what all the fuss is about. Seeing the same old scene, it stretches and falls back asleep. Alex just continues to pick at the remains of his soup. The lady then wrangles the snake and forces it into a thick white bag, head first. She feeds the entire length – a good seven foot – inch by inch until only a foot or two of tail remains.

The snake goes frantic, tossing its head about and making strange, thrusting outlines in the cloth. Ah Shum's pace quickens now, as she feels the exposed belly for the right place to make a cut, like a doctor searching for a swollen appendix. Once the spot is located, she makes a quick incision with a Stanley knife. The bag goes into overdrive, throwing shapes as if an orgy were playing out under a sheet. A thick hiss escapes and fills the room. Meanwhile, the two snakes in the glass box are both glued to the action.

I start to feel a little guilty, all this suffering for a few lines in a book.

Alex has no such qualms. He watches, transfixed, with a wide grin. 'Don't worry about the snake. It will be made into soup later anyway.'

After the cut has been made, the lady squeezes out a small, blue sac the size of a pea. Her foot is now firmly planted on the tip of the tail, so as not to be distracted by the flailing beast. With one quick flick, she separates the gall bladder from the creamy innards and lops it off. Putting this aside, she stuffs all the innards back inside the body and swabs the raw slit with alcohol. The last stage of this operation is to empty the snake into the glass box (it's a recovery chamber), where it joins the two already there. I'm wet with sweat just watching but the lady's pink T-shirt is unmarked.

With the snake safely enclosed, I risk a quick glance. It's suitably irate (as would I be with a gaping wound in my belly) and stares hatefully, hood out wide. I'm only a few inches from his face and trapped from moving back by Alex and the table. It leans back to strike and I instinctively duck. A thin stream of crystal-clear venom shoots towards my eyes but is stopped by the glass. It dribbles impotently down the side. I turn away as my warm rice wine arrives. Ah Shum makes a hole in the gall bladder and a thick, green liquid pours out, spreading around the alcohol like a lazy ink blot. She gives it a stir and then passes the cup over. 'In one,' throwing back her arm. I empty the contents down my throat. The rice wine is warm and strong but I detect a faint, bitter grassy tinge. The warmth of the alcohol surges through my body but the effects of the bile are negligible.

'No hard-on yet?' asks Alex.

Nothing but I'm still trying desperately to avoid the eye of my victim. The bill arrives and I pay $330 Hong Kong, which works out at about £20.

'More expensive than the local hookers,' whispers Alex. 'I've heard, anyway,' he adds quickly. I'm more than ready to flee the snake shop and am just getting ready to go when something brushes past my leg. I shriek and fly out into the street, overturning the table, and not stopping until safely on the other side. I look back, expecting to see cobra carnage. Instead, a startled cat perches where I once sat, perplexed as to my sudden exit. I'm not sure how I confused cat fur for cobra skin but in my heightened state of anxiety, everything felt like snake. The other human inhabitants, including Alex, are bent double with laughter, tears of mirth streaking their face. Even the three snakes, locked in their glass box, have calmed down. And from where I'm standing, I swear that the recently opened cobra is wearing a very satisfied grin.

'Right,' says Alex as we walk back towards the car (my heart is still hammering), 'let's eat.'

I thought we had but Alex dismissed the two bowls of snake soup as a 'taste'.

'I know a good fish place just around the corner.'

How convenient. The 'place' turns out to be a few seats outside a busy fish market. There are pictures of various dishes attached to the wall and Alex seems to order them all. Catherine Zeta Jones smiles down from the television above, playing second fiddle to an orangutan in a Visa advert. A pile of green crabs arrive first, fried with garlic and black beans. Alex attacks them, hewing the beast limb from limb and spitting the remains onto the street beside him. The crab is subtle and fresh and followed by a seemingly endless procession of snails, fried rice ('it must be made with yesterday's rice,' warns Alex, 'otherwise it's shit'), plump clams, tender fried octopus, sweet and sour pork and a mountain of sticky fried prawns.

'I eat at my favourite restaurant every day,' he says between bites, 'usually four times but sometimes five. It's over the harbour.'

A crab leg flies out of his mouth and onto the ever-growing mound of shells and heads beside him. This isn't Hong Kong street food but simple, seasonal seafood. The recent SARS virus has meant that all street vendors are banned. David calls this 'a fucking tragedy' and it is once again a reminder of the dangers inherent in food. The disease might not be caused by the street food, but is easily spread by it thanks to poor hygiene.

The Hong Kong government feels that the street stalls are unsafe and a prime place for the virus to spread. The mention of SARS reminds me of my ongoing quest to find the famed ortolan of France. This tiny songbird is captured, kept in the dark to keep it quiet and fattened on a diet of millet and oatmeal until it becomes little more than an exquisite lump of fat. It's then drowned in brandy, cooked and eaten whole. Once the greatest delicacy of all, it's now illegal. Still, it's seen as one of the pinnacles of French gastronomy and you're only ever supposed to eat one. At Mitterrand's final dinner, he managed two, which caused delight and controversy in equal measure.

But my attempts to find this elusive bird are being hampered by the bird flu crisis which is making its way west from Asia. Previously helpful restaurateurs clam up and leads have gone cold. Even while in China, I am in desperate email contact with a mysterious Swiss gourmand who is hoping to get some brought into Geneva. His last email ends with 'Things look a little hot at the moment. But fingers crossed. Will let you know as soon as I know.'

I am desperate for success but just have to wait and see. Bird flu is spreading fast among poultry, thanks to our reliance on the bird. Once more, food is proving to be a lot more dangerous than mere problems of taste and texture. But all this is at the back of my mind as we finish our dinner. Although the surroundings are less than salubrious, the food is fresh and boldly flavoured. I have never seen a man with appetites quite as large as Alex's, and he single-handedly consumes the contents of what looks like the entire South China Sea. My pile of carcasses looks pathetic in comparison but the unbridled joy of eating with your fingers and spitting body parts into the street makes this an uninhibited paean to the pleasure of eating. Alex worries I haven't devoured enough and orders a few more dishes just in case.

'You want to go out. The boss says I'm to show you a good time.'

But I'm exhausted and the only thing I want to do is sleep.

'Maybe we could stop at a curry fish ball place for a snack on the way home,' he offers.

I just nod, bloatedly.

* * *

'Now look here. Look ...' David waves his chopsticks at the steamer full of dim sum.

'This ... this,' he repeats for emphasis, 'is the best fucking Shanghai dumpling in the world.'

His cut-glass English accent reverberates around the gilded room. It's the evening after the snake feast and we're in Victoria Seafood, David's favourite restaurant in Hong Kong. The decoration is hideous, all over-wrought Chinese kitsch, thick red carpets and blindingly gold paint. Despite this – and being hidden away on the top floor of an unassuming high-rise by the harbour – David says it's the best Cantonese food in Hong Kong. That's some accolade.

I think back to the book I was reading that afternoon, E.N Anderson's *The Food of China*. Although a Californian professor of anthropology, his often arid prose comes alive on this particular subject, providing a useful grounding in the basics of the regional cuisine.

> Cantonese food, at its best, is probably unequalled in China and possibly the world. No other cooks insist on such absolute freshness [well, the Japanese do, for one, but you get the point] ... No other cooks control cooking temperatures so perfectly and maintain such split-second timing ... No other cooks insist on such quality in ingredients ... No other cooks draw on such a wide range of ingredients ... No other cooks can be so eclectic while maintaining the spirit of their tradition ... No other cooks excel in so many techniques ... No culture is more obsessed with food.

Fulsome praise, but many of our experiences of Cantonese food are wretched. Those sickly, deep-fried balls of gristle, flecked with fruit and artificial flavouring they call sweet and sour pork; rancid fried rice, served up from industrial trays in West End hellholes; and chop-suey, which Anderson points out actually was a Cantonese dish (tsap seui, or miscellaneous scraps) but is made still worse when served up in cheap packets and greasy boxes.

'Much of what passes for Cantonese cooking in the Western world would sicken a traditional Cantonese gourmet,' he concludes, stressing that the very best of Cantonese involves seafood, slow roasted pork and dim sum.

Before we leave Anderson for the delights of some true Cantonese food, he does clear up one point. Ever since watching *Indiana Jones and the Temple of Doom*, I've hankered after a taste of fresh live monkey brains, chilled and throbbing. Actually, that's completely untrue. I am just fascinated by this theatre of cruelty, this Grand Guignol of the dining table. Faced with such a vision, I'm not sure entirely how I would react. The sheer, wanton cruelty of this dish would overwhelm, I hope, any perverted curiosity as to its taste. But I have heard that you can find them in Hong Kong. Friends whispered of special tables, with holes at each place and a clamp to keep the poor beast in position.

'Bollocks,' cries David, 'a silly urban myth.'

And Anderson agrees. 'I have never seen anyone bring a live monkey to the table, cut its head open, and eat the brain out as strengthening food, though this is done in some places. It is a medicine rather than a food in any meaningful sense.'

Thank God for that. But now my thoughts turn to an altogether more palatable feast.

'Of course, dim sum is traditionally never eaten at dinner in China but you have to try these.'

Four plump steamed dumplings sit in their bamboo tray, and I pick one up.

'Watch your mouth,' warns David. 'It has hot stock in it. You bite a hole, suck out the liquid then eat the dumpling. Look, like this.'

I follow his lead. The soup inside is searing hot and savoury ('They make the flour dough thicker, so it keeps the soup in,' he adds between mouthfuls) and runs down my throat like molten bliss. And the dumpling itself is perfectly steamed, the ginger perking up the pork within.

The next few hours are spent deep in the Cantonese cooking school; first, a sliced, slow-cooked shoulder of pork that melts on the tongue. The burnished crackling adds crunch yet the delicacy is stunning. A plate of cabbage and fermented prawns comes sizzling to the table.

'It must be eaten red hot,' exhorts David as he digs in, his face radiating pure gustatory joy. A slight taste of rotten pungency under-pins the dish but it's well balanced. Then a whole lacquered chicken, cut into sections and served with salt and lemon juice. The meat is soft and yielding, the skin gloriously crunchy. There is a delicate, milky soup with noodles and spring onions, and a pile of freshly steamed Flower crab in a Chinese wine sauce. This is a Hong Kong classic. The meat is impossibly silken, with a sauce as poised and ethereal as Grace Kelly.

I keep going back for more and more until I am running my finger through the remnants, cleaning every last splash of my plate. No flavour overstays its welcome, every texture stimulates and teases the mouth. Even the look of these dishes is structured and elegant. Sitting back at the end, I have to admit it is the best Chinese food I have ever eaten. Despite its fearsomely gruesome reputation with snakes and dogs and the rest, real Cantonese food treats both the ingredients and preparation of them as both art and visual feast.

'Right, tomorrow, we're all off to Guilin,' announces David as he crunches the last remaining crab, 'a beautiful place an hour's flight from here. And I've another surprise planned for tomorrow night.'

David's generosity and knowledge is endless, and in just 24 hours, I have grasped the soul of Cantonese food, with its flawless ingredients and technical skill. But sometimes, I miss travelling alone, that glorious selfishness that lets you move at exactly your own pace and do whatever you please. With David, everything is perfect and every experience expressly designed to teach me something else. But at heart, I like the solitude of travel, despite missing my wife and home. I'm also pig lazy, preferring another hour in bed rather than an early call to cram in something else.

Looking back, I realise how important it was being forced to pack in as many experiences as possible as it gave me a bigger snapshot of China. And travelling with Lucy and David was like living in a fantastic, rarefied bubble of sheer luxury, where nothing was too much trouble, no question too pernickety or idiotic. It also meant I got to see a China I had little hope of gazing upon alone. After Guilin, I was to be on my own again and wasn't sure if I was dreading losing the company of good friends or looking forward to cutting my own path once more.

I had no idea what to expect of Guilin. I didn't even know where or what it was until I opened my guide book. I read that it was famed for its stunning scenery, with over 30,000 different limestone peaks and rocks, viewed by sailing down the Li river. But as we arrive that night, it feels like a study in neon lighting. The roads are lined with glowing palm trees, strip lights and garish signs, all flickering in the humid night air. The buildings are thankfully low, and I can just make out the outlines of the hills that surround the town. The bleak communist architecture looks a little ashamed by all this electric frivolity and the buildings sit, unsmiling, in their squat, utilitarian way.

By night, it's a remarkably ugly city but we are here for a natural beauty made real by daylight. Before we get to our hotel, David announces we're going down to the Li to watch some birds. Great, I think. I fucking hate watching birds. As ever, though, I get it wrong. Fishing with birds is an ancient Chinese tradition and they use the long-necked cormorants to dive into the muddy water, chase after the fish and bring them back to the surface. A small ring is tied around their neck to stop them swallowing and one bird is said to catch as many fish in a night as three fishermen (the ring is made from rice straw and tied with great care; too tight and they choke, and too flaccid and you lose the fish).

Every seventh fish, the ring is loosed and the birds get their piscine pay. If not, they're said to just bugger off for good. The men fish at night, using small, shallow canoes and a light to attract the fish. The birds are noisy and quarrelsome, endlessly bickering with colleagues and owners alike. Despite the ring, they all give it their best shot in getting the fish down their throat but the fishermen grab them and throw them into a bucket. The birds dive back into the murk for their next swoop. This stretch of the river was packed with fellow tourists, all glued to the exploits of these chattering birds.

As we leave the river and the cackle and squabble of these lippy birds, David spots a man upriver, pouring live fish into the water.

'So much for fucking authentic,' he says as we get back in the car.

The idea of eating dinner in a cave is hardly appealing, bringing back memories of school expedition days where we'd sit in some damp hole in the ground and chew gloomily on stale bread spread with Sandwich Spread (although it looked like vomit, I had a real fondness for this acrid filler) and an Orange Club. Being David, though, this is more banquet in a cavern than packed lunch in Wookey Hole.

The limestone hills around Guilin are riddled with caves of every size, but the biggest and most famous is the Reed Flute cave. Once used by bandits to hide from the authorities and, more recently, locals sheltering from the Japanese bombs, David has managed to get the place specially opened for our dinner. Inside, the air is thick and damp, and the floors slippery. The lighting is a barrage of multi-coloured spots, drowning every inch in a Technicolor flood. The modern Chinese tourist ethic seems to revolve around the use of as much wattage as possible. But as we walk into the main chamber, any chatter stops. Here, the blue lighting seems almost subtle, reflecting the glittering stalagmites with an eerie glow.

The space is cavernous and the scene resembles some fantastical ancient world, with odd rock formations hanging down, sprouting up and all around. In here, it seems as if the rock grows like a living thing, throwing up magical shapes and spires. But strangest of all is a table in the middle of the cavern, set with white linen, silver candelabra and cutlery. On a free-standing sideboard, a few bottles of Lyches Bages sit breathing the heavy air. It is as if the English country house dinner party had been transported halfway across the globe to an ancient cave in the South of China. To make matters more surreal still, a three-piece Chinese orchestra plucks away as we sit down. We eat well, from what I can remember, but faced with such an extraordinary spectacle as this, even food pales into insignificance.

This evening, though, David and Lucy are returning to Hong Kong while I am breaking off to fly north to Shanghai. As they walk through the gate, back to the familiar warmth of Hong Kong, I feel that the holiday has ended and now the real slog begins. I wander aimlessly through the terminal, feeling that for the first time I am part of the real China, the day-to-day reality behind the tourist bumph.

Of course, this is a tourist hotspot and I am far from the only Caucasian face. But while I should be chomping at the bit to get back on my own again, I just feel empty. Guilin airport is that special shade of depressing grey that only communist countries can come up with, a colour that sucks any life out of its immediate surroundings.

I flick through the macabre packets of dried lizards, snakes and sea-horses in the numerous tacky gift shops, deciding whether they are worth buying and taking home to some unsuspecting friend. But the thought of desiccated lizard parts milling around my luggage is enough to put paid to that. I toy with a bowl of greasy noodles, poke at soggy wontons and twiddle my thumbs. My China Eastern Airways flight is delayed and my Mandarin isn't up to understanding why.

Only if the word 'deall' were to be spoken would I have any idea of the reason. But as this means 'fuck', the chances of it coming up across the public address system are low. All the excitement I thought I'd feel at getting to Shanghai has long disappeared. I think of David and Lucy arriving in the comforting, bright lights of Hong Kong while I sit and stew in this dreary provincial airport. For all my earlier yearning for independence, I wish I was with them now rather than stuck in this wretched airport.

My spirits sink lower still as the plane's take-off seems more and more delayed and at one point, I consider giving up the whole stupid project to fly home to Sara. The plane finally limps in four hours late and as we lift off from Guilin, I smile for the first time in hours.

The drive from the airport to Shanghai takes you whisking through shiny new skyscrapers and huge billboards and, even in the back of a cab, you feel the city throbbing and growing beneath your feet. Skyscrapers jostle for space with the elongated super-cranes which look like dozing giraffes. Everywhere, lights flash in celebration of an ever-growing sprawl. This is a city on the move, wildly ambitious and with no intention of stopping just yet. My hotel is sat within a thrusting phallic symbol to the new China, an armour-plated vibrator placed bang smack in the middle of Pudong, the business district on the east side of the Huangpu river. Once a fishing village, Shanghai now has 17 million inhabitants and is growing.

My mood has improved considerably, especially at the thought of a decent hotel, room service, cable television and all the other modern luxuries that I should be cursing rather than missing. Some are appalled by the idea of wasting valuable 'authentic' moments in a foreign land by ordering burgers and sitting glued to BBC World. But occasionally, you need a taste of home so as to appreciate a new country all the more. I wish I could lie and shake my head in disapproval. After four hours spent in Guilin airport, Jeremy Clarkson's guttural exhortations have rarely been more welcome.

The next morning, the city throbs under a thick, dirty blanket of fog. I meet up with John Shen, a friend of David's, for a walk down the Bund. This mile-long stretch of grand old colonial buildings faces the Pudong from the other side of the river. It could be a Parisian boulevard, a street off Trafalgar Square with its heavy, stone-fronted facades and monuments to the might of Empire within. These temples to European greed once housed newspapers, customs houses and old-money banks. Taken back by the Communists for the best part of a century, they have now reverted to temples to wealth once more, only this time typified by expensive European-style boutiques and brasseries, offering gaudy cocktails to the city's new financial elite.

Everywhere you look in Shanghai, the past is acknowledged but the future embraced. Standing with my back to the Bund, the view is so futuristic that I half expect space ships to buzz between the buildings. If you saw this sight on screen, you'd dismiss it as cheap CGI. As cargo boats float down the river in their scores, the new skyline is more *Blade Runner* than communist China. I gaze over, my mouth agape, while John, well-dressed, boyish and fluent in English, tells me of the changes.

'When I was young, no one lived in the East, where you are staying. And it was only in 1998 that the Pudong area was developed.

Now look.' He stops and waves his arm around the mass of super-cranes, skyscrapers and building sites. 'Once, you could look out over the city and see nothing but a few factories and traditional houses. It was a poor area. But not any more. Now it's just an unceasing build-ing site.'

The Oriental Pearl Tower, purple Christmas tree balls impaled on a syringe, looks like a Jeff Koons-designed joke and dwarfs the build-ings around it. It, in turn, is dwarfed by the priapic might of the Jinmao Tower. It's all about bigger and better and faster and richer, and the landscape seems to change and evolve before my eyes. The traffic is thick and stifling, never advancing beyond a crawl while bicy-cles and scooters swarm about, squeezing into every possible gap. The overwhelming noise in the city is that of car horns, a constant cacoph-ony of parps, squeaks, bellows and plaintive moans. Despite the heavy traffic, there's a feeling of constant activity here, everyone rushing from one place to another with single-minded intent. Yet I am left strangely cold by the whole spectacle, little more than a mildly inter-ested observer, entirely unable to enter into the city's unceasing spirit.

John takes me to the Old Town next, the most traditional part of the city. Well, traditional if Disney had taken over and shown their view of what life in the 'good ole days' would have been like anywhere. Although the Yuyuan Gardens were originally built towards the end of the sixteenth century, they were ransacked by both the British (who used them as a base in the 1842 Opium War) and the French and have been restored since. For the Chinese, this is perfectly normal. The thing might only have been built a few years back but if it's exactly the same as it originally was, then that's the main thing. Although I fight my fellow tourists for the perfect picture of these shady crannies and pretty pavilions, the place still seems miles away from the building excess of the rest of the city.

We stop for a cup of tea in the Mid-Lake Pavilion Teahouse and breathe in the mannered charms of this newly reconstructed part of the old town, with ornate decorations and blood-red wood. The bright green surface of the pond is occasionally broken by the orange lips of the over-fed carp who patrol the waters, rendered plump by the tourists' fish food. As pretty as it all is, I want to move on and get my first taste of Shanghai food, so John takes me to a food hall where we pile our trays high with soup buns (or shanghai buns) the size of a mug, with a plastic straw poking out of the top. The soup is burning hot but fantastic, followed by tiny river shrimp fried in a sweet sauce. The hangar-sized room is packed with lunching workers, heads bent over their bowls in deadly serious conversation. This is a city which adores its food and is the home of rich, sweet cuisine. There are more fried dumplings, sweeter and heavier than in Hong Kong.

'Shanghai food is more oily than the rest of China, with some sweet in it too,' says John between bites. 'Everything is cooked in pork fat and the flavours can tend towards the sweet. For aesthetic value,' he admits, 'I prefer Cantonese. It looks nicer and is healthier. But when it comes to food craving, I love Shanghai. It's what my mother cooked, a taste of home and although traditionally heavy, the food is getting lighter nowadays.'

He produces his *pièce de résistance*, a plate of something so foul-smelling and grotesque that I instinctively shy away, my sensory glands knocked sideways by the fetid pong. It's deep-fried tofu, in greasy squares, but fermented. The bean curd is inoculated with a mould, incubated until covered with white mould then put in a bottle with rice wine, salt and water. It's left to ferment for a minimum of three months. It's seen as a great delicacy and the smell hovers somewhere between ripe Camembert, old socks and festering rubbish. The taste is barely different.

'The more it stinks, the better it is,' laughs John as he sees the horror on my face. 'But the children don't always like it. Nowadays, they love McDonald's and KFC but only when they're young. My daughter no longer likes fast food but she adored it when she was ten. She never used to like Chinese dishes but now she's 15, she loves them. I think that at a certain age, these American imports are attractive. But then you realise that you won't get true enjoyment from McDonald's.'

We're back to the same theme that I discussed with Alex, how the young Chinese see the likes of McDonald's as attractive and different but soon seem to grow out of these childish tastes. Yet looking at John chewing happily on the smelly tofu, McDonald's suddenly seems very alluring. The company likes to boast that their Big Mac tastes the same whether you're chewing in London, Berlin or Denpassar. It's that uniformity, that guarantee of the same, bland experience that makes it so damned attractive. You think it's a taste of home while in reality, it's a sham, cooked up in corporate headquarters to fool us all. Yet this power is so endearing that when faced with this reeking tofu, I crave a cheeseburger, a Big Mac, anything that doesn't have this uncomfortable, alien edge.

The moment passes quickly (and despite all my hatred of their ethos, they sure make a mean cheeseburger – not a 'cheeseburger' but a 'McDonald'scheeseburger', a product all of its own) but I suddenly see the appeal of these fast-food chains in bright relief. They offer the opposite of danger, an escape from the unpredictability of food. Corporate fast food will never be risky, and therein lies most of its appeal. We get what we think we want, even when we have no idea we want it.

* * *

As we brave the traffic to drive under the river and back to the hotel, John tells me about his typical eating day.

'We eat rice every day with different dishes,' as we sit beneath the river, marooned in a steel sea of stationary cars, 'and might eat dumpling and noodles about once per month. Mostly rice though.' A scooter with a family of three perched on top snakes it way through the traffic.

'Usually, we'd have six dishes and some soup for dinner, smaller families might have three or four dishes. But always soup.'

We move forward a few precious inches before shuddering to a halt again.

'I have congee and pickles for breakfast, but my kids might have bread or pizza. In Shanghai, congee is always made with last night's rice whereas in Beijing, they use fresh stuff.'

We hit a fluid spot and glide all of 20 metres without stopping.

'Quality is very important here in Shanghai. My father-in-law is in charge of buying the food and gets very worried that we don't eat enough. That's why people always order masses of food in restaurants with guests, to show that they are not stingy.' By now, the end of the tunnel is in sight. 'So we always have more food than we need at home.' He smiles as we reach the light. 'Tonight, I've got some friends together to come and eat at a very traditional restaurant. I'll see you about seven to pick you up. And don't eat too much this afternoon. It will be a proper feast.'

I look down at my belly. Never taut, it has now taken on a worrying wobble.

How many times have I been warned about a feast, and not paid the blindest bit of attention? I couldn't resist a bowl of noodle soup as an afternoon snack, so the edge of my hunger was dulled somewhat as we arrived at Nanling restaurant, in the downtown area of the city. Here, the roads were broader and the streets more leafy. It was in the French Concession, once home to the wilder side of old Shanghai life, the sort of carousing and brawling and gambling and loose living that made the city so famous. It was this area that gave Shanghai its 'Paris of the East' moniker, with leafy roads and French-style architecture. Although, ironically, not many of the residents were ever French.

The restaurant is over a hundred years old and specialises in the Shanghai style of cooking. It has high ceilings and is blessed with an airy, nonchalant cool. This is obviously a destination place, rather than some local eatery, though it doesn't seem like a tourist trap. I am the only white man there. We pass through the main room, which is busy as dinner is eaten early here, and troop upstairs to a private room. Already there is John's wife, all smiles and flawless English. Next to her, a famous food critic, lean with square glasses and a sombre expression. He has his telephone ear piece attached and constantly breaks off conversation to shout something into thin air. The rest of the table have their phones in front of them and although all very polite, see nothing wrong with picking it up while talking and eating. This is entirely normal.

The usual selection of cold starters appears and I do my best to rein in my greed. Most are of the one taste and smile variety anyway, so not so hard to start with; dried fish in soy sauce (intensely fishy), cold boiled chicken (rich, with fatty skin), slightly dried tofu and a pressed pork dish with lots of jelly and fat, served with a sweet vinegar dip.

'Most Chinese prefer the fat to the meat,' explains the food critic between measured bites. He looks very serious indeed and eyes me with distaste. 'I certainly prefer it,' he concludes, taking a huge bite of pork lard.

The others nod and I smile weakly, saying I'm more of a meat man. If anyone else disagrees, they don't let it show. The mannered politeness to me, their foreign guest, is touching but a little unnerving too. I wish I could break into fluent Mandarin, and argue politics, food and anything else. Instead, I sit mute, occasionally making some glib remark about the weather. Can you ever truly know a country without learning the language? I think not, and I feel like a dumb, stuffed prune, nodding like a car accessory and not having the faintest clue what is being talked about. John translates so I get the gist, but I get the feeling I'm missing the asides, the chattering of real interest. In Gloucestershire and New Mexico, I had no such problems in communications. But for the rest of my trips, things might not be so easy.

We drink a warm, caramelly rice wine, aged for 20 years, which slips down with velvety ease. A Shanghai duck appears, with less fat and crispier skin than the Beijing version. Actually, it turns out to be in the Cantonese style as the Food Critic informs us that Shanghai does not traditionally eat roast duck.

'The Cantonese like to keep the real flavour of their food in each dish, while the Sechuan prefer more spices. The Cantonese really let each flavour talk.'

As he speaks no English, John translates his every word. And this seems to suit the Food Critic, who has barely glanced at me all night. He lets pearls of wisdom drop, and we are supposed to scramble down in the dirt for our share. But the duck is a thing of golden beauty, with perfectly rendered skin, the sort of thing to which every fowl should aspire when it dies; crunchy and succulent and melting on the tongue. I go back for more and more, shards of soft meat and this heavenly skin.

'We have a lot more to come,' warns John as I stuff another lump into my mouth.

'I have a huge appetite,' I answer, forgetting any modicum of restraint. Plump river prawns tempt me next and I shovel them by the pound into my mouth, their succulent bodies crush sweetly between my teeth. The vinegar which accompanies them sharpens my taste buds as my belly begins to fill. We start talking about the differences in Chinese regional foods.

'The Cantonese will eat anything, except humans,' says John, a view I hear again and again.

'They'll probably eat those if they're in the right sauce too,' adds his wife with a smile.

I wonder what our learned foodie friend's take is on McDonald's. John is too polite to look bored by the repeated question and translates. For the first time that night, the Food Critic blesses me with his gaze. He puts down his chopsticks carefully, wipes his mouth and looks straight into my eye. He clears his throat and starts to speak, a low, learned murmur, transformed by John into English life.

'I believe fast food will influence Chinese food but it will never overtake it.' He pauses to take a sip of rice wine. 'Chinese food culture is certainly strong enough to withstand the onslaught of fast food. We grow up on Chinese food,' he proclaims, echoing John's earlier comments, 'so it will always survive. Look, many Chinese move over to Europe and some have been there for over 50 years. Yet their eating habits hardly change. Even kids of the fourth and fifth generation are still eating their national food. That is fitting testimony to our love of our national food.'

He stops speaking and picks up his chopsticks once more. The lesson is over. I still wonder, though, once the Chinese, or any other country, get a taste for the safety of fast food, that escape from doubt and danger, how much it will permeate their culture. But to everyone that I've spoken to so far, all agree that this is just a phase that children go through, like fighting with sticks and wetting their bed, before returning to the true taste of their youth.

A platter of Shanghai ham is put down, streaked with thick expanses of yellow fat, and I presume it's slow cooked in a honey sauce. It's eaten with steamed bread, thick, tender, and salty and sweet. I'm stuffed full yet am utterly aware of the onslaught still to come. I curse myself for my unthinking greed, massaging my stomach under the table to gain precious space. Individual shark fin soups appear, filled with vinegar, bean sprouts and a herb somewhere between parsley and coriander. It's gelatinous, flavoured with chicken stock and ham bones and the fibres crunch slightly like chewy noodles. They squeak between the teeth.

'If you want the best food,' admits the Food Critic, deigning to talk once more, 'you're better off in a Cantonese restaurant. This soup is traditionally Cantonese but now we all love it as it's a luxury. This isn't too bad actually.'

I feel self-conscious about clumsy chopstick work and the area around my plate looks like a pile up on a seafood highway. By now, I'm taking smaller bites and the fixed smile appears on my face. Steamed river crab, finished in oil, are a little greasy, doused with sweet sauce, a Shanghai specialty from the Yantong River. Vinegar is served alongside for sharpness.

The Food Critic seems on a roll now, his tongue loosened by the wine, and he tells me that the Cantonese did not traditionally eat crab but when the rich Shanghai folk moved there, they brought it with them where it caught on quickly.

Fried fish come next, and I chew a few. But the sea slug in brown sauce is a more taxing prospect, exactly resembling a freshly laid turd. I cut off the tiniest portion and lower it daintily into my mouth, expecting the worst. It's slightly slimy but the texture is pleasing, tender like a mushroom.

'This is a great delicacy,' says the Food Critic, 'as it needs to be cooked in many stages.' He puts a huge chunk into his mouth and chews happily.

I'm just praying for the end but still there's no respite. Deep-fried fish in a sweet and sour sauce, Shanghai dumplings the size of my fist (I can't even appreciate these beauties now) – I'm now dreading each time the door opens. As guest of (somewhat dubious) honour, I'm offered every dish first and have to take a piece and eat it as the rest watch me. There is no place for shirking. I dare not open my mouth for fear of food spilling rudely out.

But at last, with my suit trousers gasping open under the table, a simple soup arrives, then sticky rice and finally, hallelujah, a slice of watermelon. Never have I been so happy to see a slice of this boring fruit and I kiss it in celebration. The rest of the table look bemused.

'My favourite fruit,' I hastily splutter. They look unconvinced.

We finally leave, 22 courses later.

John looks at my face. 'I think you could do with a walk.'

I only manage a nod.

The next day offers more of the same. This Chinese trip has been relentless and my jeans have moved to the tighter side of uncomfortable. I realise that some people might brand me ill, sickened by the effects of compulsive overeating. What I see as a pleasure, others take as a curse. At the moment, though, my waist size is the last of my worries. I can always run it off in the hotel gym, I reckon, fully aware of my own lies. I've a lunch date with Mr Jin, David's old tutor and a Senior Fellow at Sanda University in Shanghai.

'I wanted to show you the greatest cookery style in the whole of China,' he tells me as we sit down in the Great China Flower restaurant. 'It is, of course, my cuisine, the Imperial food of North East China. It is the food of the Manchu, and you will, I believe, enjoy it.'

It's the first time I've heard anyone describe anything but Cantonese food as the finest. Once more, we are shuttered away in a private room and, once again, I resign myself to another endless feast, where my every mouthful would be scrutinised. Mr Jin is a rabid Anglophile, firing off anecdotes about Piccadilly Circus, James I and the correct way to make 'a coopa of tea'. His English is scrupulously grammatical, enunciated with 1950s BBC precision. Occasionally, he breaks into a Scottish accent which is not entirely successful.

'Now David told me how much you love tripe, so I have ordered a feast for you.'

Thanks David, I think. I usually go out of my way to avoid the stuff but have no escape here. The subtleties of the Glaswegian burr are lost on me but I'm too busy trying to force the offal down my throat. It's barely cooked and squeaks around my mouth like meaty rubber. I swallow another huge gulp of malt tea to swill it down.

'Now, how is my Scottish accent?'

'Brilliant,' I say, and smile at his wife.

'Well, have some more.' He pauses. '"I wood lik a coopa tea." That was in an Indian accent.'

Oh right. Bull thighs turn up next, huge Fred-Flintstone hunks of flesh.

'Beef is very important in the north of China, and this Imperial cuisine is very close to Mongolia, and the cuisine,' announces Mr Jin, 'as it is in Britain. Ah, roast beef and Yorkshire pudding on a Sunday. Wonderful.'

He closes his eyes for a moment in blissful recollection. I look back at the bones, and see the Genghis Khan connection. The meat is soft and succulent, slow cooked for hours.

'Now, what do you think of Shanghai food?'

I open my mouth to speak but Mr Jin has other ideas. 'I agree,' he says before I can utter a word. 'I hate it. Far too sweet.'

It certainly hasn't been the highlight of the journey though hate seems a little strong. But Mr Jin will hear nothing more of it. As usual, the courses seem set on fast-forward and I don't dare stop eating. The mouthfuls, fortunately, do get subtly smaller; hot and sour mushroom soup, cut with vinegar and hot with chillies. An ancient vegetable, 'eaten by the dinosaurs' according to Mr Jin, green and crunchy. Then, a horribly familiar smell wafts up my nose.

'Ah, smelly tofu … stinks like sheet,' say Mrs Jin, one of the first sentences she has uttered.

We all smile politely, while I blush.

'It's very delicious though,' she adds.

'Despite smelling like sheet,' laughs her delighted husband.

I push a scrap of this rotten muck around the plate and mix it with as much chilli sauce as I can. I take a tiny bite and pray I've got away with it. No one seems to notice. As a way of getting the scrutiny off my plate, I ask my standard question as to the influx of American food in China.

'Ah,' says Mr Jin, 'in China, KFC does the best business because it's the most Chinese. Children are crazy for pizza and McDonald's because it's so exotic.' He pauses to swallow a chunk of the tofu. 'Yes, delicious. But they will always revert back to Chinese food.'

I try to dodge the next 11 courses (prawn dumpling, fried dumpling with mutton and black rice, under a gauzy web of batter – there are over 40 different kinds of Mongolian dumpling – a side of slow-cooked veal, crimson, soft and fatty), taking birdlike pecks of everything, trying to limit myself. Despite getting a true taste of Chinese regional food – everything I set out to do – I'm starting to crave boiled eggs and soldiers, shepherd's pie and a plain roast chicken. Safe food, things that I can trust. It's back to the McDonald's argument again, though I crave comfort, not pure blandness, just as David craves Cantonese and John the taste of his mother's Peking food.

But I've no time to sit and wallow. This afternoon, we're off to another eating marathon, this time to a traditional village, Suzhou, 100 km north-west of Shanghai. I'm beginning to fade fast.

I never imagined that this constant eating would send me into such a decline. Just a couple of months back, while seated at my desk, this entire journey promised to be one long eating beano. Travel the cuisines of the world in search of the delectable and exotic – how hard could it be? OK, so I imagined that the odd dog steak or insect salad might be testing, but nothing I couldn't handle. I had spent ten years in the public school system, for God's sake, enough to put even the most intrepid gastropod off his food. Surely nothing I found abroad could compare to the horrors of the prep-school kitchen.

I was looking for evidence that local cuisines are still thriving around the world in the face of the fast-food revolution. And to prove to myself that what seems disgusting or alien when sitting behind my London desk is – when eaten in context – perfectly normal. With the elvers, I found an old English delicacy disappeared not for reasons of ever-dulling taste buds and lack of interest in local cuisine, but pure hard market economics. They were too expensive to consider eating. And in New Mexico, I had built up the Fiery Foods Show into some endorphin-laced carnival, when in reality, it was just a trade show filled with businessmen and enthusiasts. Yet South Western cuisine was very much alive and well.

Here in China, though, the pace is relentless. Away from David and Lucy, I seem a long way from home. And lacking a handy pair of ruby slippers, there is to be no clicking of the heels for a quick ride back to Sara. This relentless eating is threatening to take any pleasure away from food, like when, at university, I had to read all of Dickens in a week (so likely) and began to hate the master's every word.

But then I speak to my wife and realise how lucky I am for this opportunity. How the hell can I moan about this ultimate eating grand tour? I'll be back in a couple of weeks, bursting with stories with which to bore my friends and family. The pace seems tough at this very moment but really ... I am eating my way around China. Hardly a day down the mine, is it?

As we drive out of the city, I see the real Shanghai, the crumbling tenement blocks and cracked concrete where the majority of the population survive. Crammed together like rotten teeth, they offer a bleak, overcrowded view of the flip side of Shanghai life. As the new, glittering city expands, and fills with the winners of this new world, the old inhabitants – the losers – are pushed further and further out, brushed under the carpet and out of the way of the glare of the world's glossy media.

The rain now becomes so torrential that we can hardly see a metre in front of the car. The traffic thins as we leave the city but the torrents reduce us to a soggy crawl. Given the choice, I would far rather be tucked up in my hotel room with a book. But David is insistent that I try the country food of the area, and this is the best place to start.

Zhujiajiao is a small village, built on a traditional network of interconnecting canals, about an hour out of Shanghai. These villages and towns were once numerous, the water used to transport goods across the region. But the Communists filled in the majority of these waterways with concrete and only a few remain. At the moment, it's difficult to see anything through the relentless drizzle; my appetite for any type of Chinese food has reached an all-time low and my mood is darker than the clouds swirling overhead.

If I never saw another dumpling or hunk of fatty meat, it wouldn't be a moment too soon. What I wouldn't give for a shepherd's pie now, so calm and reliable, studded with peas and eaten with a spoon. Food you can trust. No threat, danger or anticipation. No worrying about eating every last morsel or swallowing without tasting, or smiling in the right place. I want to be with my wife on the sofa, pie in hand, moaning about her watching *EastEnders*. Oh Walford, I apologise for getting you wrong. You're not tawdry melodrama, but sweet normality, Monday night and early bed.

We tramp though the muddy streets towards the restaurant, down narrow, bustling streets that occasionally open up to a bridge or canal. Doors are kept open to the world and I get brief glimpses of the life within. Huge piles of cooked rice, studded with pork or sweet red bean paste, are being wrapped in lotus leaves for the high summer Dragon Boat festival tomorrow. The canals, now almost invisible because of the thick fog and rain, were once the lifelines of the village, taking away rice to sell and connecting them with other towns and villages. But even in this gloom, there's no doubting the faded beauty of the place, with its brown and white wooden houses clinging to the sides of the canal.

The food of the area is mostly taken from the nearby lakes and rivers, and is renowned throughout China. I arrive at a small restaurant, overlooking a canal, to meet up with Johnson Chang, one of David's best friends and the man behind the regeneration of many traditional villages in the area. He is immaculately dressed in Chinese silk, radiating erudition and a learned serenity. He speaks quietly, but with conviction and warmth. Also around the table are an assortment of Chinese intellectuals and artists, rather than the urban professionals of the night before; Samuel, one of the best jade dealers in Hong Kong; an architect who specialises in timber architecture; and a Hong Kong tea expert, Professor Tea. Their English is impeccable and they go out of their way to make me comfortable.

I start to relax. Well, until I see a starter of cold chicken feet. It's now too late to start moaning and I'm too exhausted even to feel disgust. Tonight, I just can't be bothered, it's too much effort. My sullen mood (hidden behind a forced grin) overrides my natural disgust for these bony morsels so I pick up a claw and strip the cool meat from the bone. The flavour is strong and the flesh gelatinous, but once you get over the physical aspect (i.e. sucking a chicken's claw), it's fine. I even go for a second. Take away the prejudice, the inbuilt Western fear of these things, and the palate becomes a blank canvas once more. If I can remember this, I'll get through the whole trip OK.

The rice wine (from the Qingpu region) is like rich, caramel-infused sherry and I pour it down. Deep-fried river fish follow, then plump river shrimp, cooked with peas. I pick now, like everyone else, not gorging but pacing. 'It's a marathon, not a sprint,' runs the mantra in my head, round and round and round until it takes up residence somewhere deep in my skull.

Dr Tea tells me about the 'maiden's' red rice wine, one you bury when your daughter is born and dig up when she becomes a woman. The problem is that Dr Tea can't remember where he buried his. Bitter gourd with bamboo shoots starts off sweet and crunchy and ends with a bitter note. But just as I'm starting to actually appreciate this feast, I smell it again – deep-fried smelly tofu, fermented silage with a greasy skin.

'It's like the armpit of a French woman,' says Dr Tea and I don't know whether this is meant as a compliment. I do my usual trick, telling everyone how I'm getting used to it before taking one tiny bite, silently gagging and moving on.

There are river snails, chopped with pork, then stuffed back in the shell, fresh and robust. A whole steamed river fish from Tiahu Lake, to the north, is soft and fragrant, a great delicacy as it cannot be bred or farmed. The food is lighter than in Shanghai, and seems fresher. White shrimp and white silver fish come next, then pork wrapped in rice stalks that gives the meat a taste of straw. There's a steamed water plant – like bamboo – stuffed with minced pork, a whole river eel, curled up in the pot and cooked with garlic, and wild turtle, cooked in a fishy broth. This is not particularly appetising, with stringy, fatty, fishy meat and the merest hint of chicken. I surreptitiously remove a chunk of pure sinew and hide it in my napkin. Turtle is an auspicious food for birthdays, as it signifies long life, as do noodles. Having tasted the turtle, I wonder whether long life is all it's cracked up to be anyway.

The sight of fresh asparagus is sweet relief. 'Welcome to the table, my tight-tipped friends,' I think, still picking turtle fat from between my teeth. They clear my palate and I'm all smiles, until more stinky tofu arrives and the stench of rotten feet and manure fills the room once more. I refuse this last course and rejoice as the fruit arrives. When dinner is good, it is awesome, fresh and cooked with a real understanding of flavour and texture.

I'm relieved to get back to Shanghai though, and with only five days to go, it's time to move up to Beijing. I am happy to get out of Shanghai too. For all its glitz and energy and mercantile glamour, it has failed to move me and I haven't connected at all. I feel like the bored outsider looking in, although this is based on just a few days' stay. It seems impersonal, and the food is a little heavy, a touch too sweet for my taste. As a city, you cannot fail to be impressed by the energy, the juxtaposition of old and new. But funnily enough, it is the staid, dusty charms of Beijing that really win my heart.

Because if Shanghai buzzes, then Beijing moves at a gentle hum. The city is sprawling and dusty, and traffic-choked, yet it has a quiet, ageless majesty that transcends the hundreds of faceless apartment blocks that ring the centre of the city. As a centre of government, it's like Washington compared to New York. Rather quieter, uptight and serious. Tiananmen Square is truly impressive, a great expanse of open space that is the biggest in the world. Where the tanks once were, portly Americans now barter over a couple of cents for images of Mao. All around, the square is flanked by serious-looking, monolithic monuments to Communism.

I'm tiring fast but know that there is little chance of escaping a day of culture and even I, the committed philistine, trail around the Forbidden City, mouth agape. Sir Roger Moore's silken commentary helps, though the siting of a Starbucks right in the centre is proof that this insipid chain is nigh but unstoppable. But after ten days of a perfect-functioning tummy, a dodgy dumpling is a burden too much. I try to feign interest in the concubines' chambers and the like, but in reality, can only think of finding the nearest loo.

Not for the first time, my day is dictated by the whims of my digestive system. It's amazing how that desperate urge destroys all other thoughts or actions. It takes over your entire being. My guide Zhangye is insistent that we get to lunch quickly, so I leave the tourist-friendly facilities of the Forbidden City behind (with their clean spaces, loo rolls and seats) and move into the sit-and-squat world of the native Beijinger. If you're used to this position, nothing could be more natural. For me, it is more of a problem. Every time I disappear from the guide's side (he has already taken a virulent dislike to me, thinking me uncaring when in fact I am just fighting with my belly), he grunts angrily upon my return. I keep pretending I have important phone calls to make, while rushing off again with another handful of paper napkins.

But lunch is decent, in between loo breaks, typical of the Northern school of heavy, hearty grub, less oily and sweet than Shanghai. Noodles and dumplings also play a major role rather than rice. The room is noisy, packed with Chinese families. One old, drunk man keeps leering over at me, lifting up his fists as if asking for a fight. Occasionally, he lunges, too close for my liking. His family pay not the blindest bit of attention, nor the guide, but combined with a dodgy ass, it isn't the most comfortable of lunches.

Soy bean juice with fried dough (a traditional northern speciality, not much liked in the south) is bitter yet the soup that follows, unstretched noodles bobbing like gnocchi in a rich broth with tomato, egg and Chinese greens, comes close to soupy perfection. It is fuel for the cold, bleak winters of the North. Cold handmade noodles, with carrots, lettuce, cucumber and beans, are also good, dipped into a glutinous soy and pork sauce. Far superior to Shanghai food, this is more my idea of fun. The Great Wall of China, though, is not. Zhangye insists that we take the hour's journey, despite my protestations that I have seen it from the air.

When we arrive (with me still in the throes of a dodgy gut), tourists throng the steps, and the section I see, while stunning from a distance snaking off into the horizon, is cheap and seems to have been recently rebuilt.

'We now climb to top,' orders the guide.

I disagree, not wanting to venture that far from the bathrooms.

'Just as good here,' I moan.

'Chairman Mao say you are not a real hero until you have climbed the Great Wall.'

Screw the murdering dictator. I need the loo.

After a brief and much-appreciated break, we leave the Great Wall behind us (well, I have seen a part of it) and are soon speeding back into Beijing.

As usual, I only have a few moments to bathe before the next adventure. Beijing eats early, the staider older sister to Shanghai, and despite the traffic, it seems calm and even provincial. Tonight, I am to sample the city's famed duck and am accompanied by the wonderful Tony Chiu, manager of David's club, to the best duck house in Beijing. Geoffrey, his smooth-skulled food guru there, also comes and both chatter excitedly on the way. I tell him about my lunch.

'Christ, I hate that bean juice. I retch when I drink it,' says Tony. 'The younger generation hate it too. But this duck is good, even for a Cantonese man like myself.'

Geoffrey nods his agreement. Li Qun is one of the oldest duck places in town, not as famous as the Da Dong Roast Duck but apparently better. It's tucked away in Pu-dong, the poor warren of backstreets. We pass houses with at least ten people crammed into a tiny room, staring at the TV and slurping noodles. Piles of camber wood sit outside the door and no one pays any attention as we pass.

The restaurant is no more than an ante-room afterthought, a courtyard covered with a grotty piece of corrugated plastic. The tables and chairs are plastic and huge freezers take up part of the room while our table is hemmed in between empty beer crates. At the back is an open kitchen where half a dozen chefs fight over one wok. There are probably 60 covers, yet everything arrives fresh and hot upon the table within minutes.

'They wind-dry the duck first, in those cabinets over there.' I thought they were walk-in freezers. 'The electric fan dries them out, for the best crispy skin.' An entire duck, burnished and golden, floats past my nose. 'Then they roast it in a kiln-like oven.'

Tony orders an entire bird, as well as hearts, tongue, gizzard and intestines. The liver arrives first, in a huge beige pile, marinated in salt and water. It's divine, as rich and creamy as foie gras and it melts on the tongue. The duck hearts swim in warm rice wine and are far more tender than I thought they would be, with a faint taste of kidney.

'Overcooked,' announces Geoffrey after a bite and Tony agrees. I thought them perfect. The intestines are deep fried with a little chilli, a touch of the offal flavour and rather gamey. At this point, they seem immensely civilised. Nothing rotten or fermented or moving, just good old duck's gizzards. Tongue is less exciting, a whole lot of texture, chewy but not soft and some nasty cartilage that cracks in the teeth. Cooked with chilli and celery, I have a gossip's worth and move on.

The duck itself is magnificent, golden and rather more fatty than usual, as is the local style. The entire body is quickly chopped up and not a morsel wasted. This is true beak-to-butt eating. The neck is superb, rich and juicy and the pancakes too. The duck eyes me mournfully from the plate, his beak removed. The duck feet in mustard sauce are served cold, wide and rubbery, like flip-flop sashimi. One is quite enough (they are not exactly small), although Tony reckons they aren't all that good. Both agree that dinner is above average and for a place that gets through about 220 ducks per night, this is praise indeed. Tony wants to know if I feel up for the night markets. 'They've got it all there – insects, snakes, the whole bunch.'

For the first time on the trip, I say no. I have one more night to go, and this grisly feast can certainly wait another day.

David and Lucy are back in Beijing for my last night and, after the past week, I almost fall at their feet with excitement.

David promises some real danger. 'What do you know about the Great Hall of the People?' he asks.

If I were Bond, I would shoot back with, 'The venue of the National People's Congress which takes up most of the West Side of Tiananmen Square. The heart and head of the Chinese communist party and the location for those famed state banquets.' Instead, I have to admit to not having a clue. David doesn't look impressed.

This vast, pillared building dominates the west side of the square and we climb up the steps in the soft evening light and realise that the government is hosting a dinner for the President of Peru next door, in a room that can hold banquets for 5,000. This building is said to be heaving with bugs and hidden cameras. This is where Mao ate his beloved Hunanese food, Thatcher tripped on the steps and Bush senior puked into an astonished President's lap. The place where heads of state sip tea and smile politely at each other.

Once inside (and past a fairly cursory security check), we wander about quite freely, posing for photographs, nosing about but well aware of being on camera. China is far more free now and people can leave the country (well, some anyway) but criticism of the government is still unacceptable. I ask what would happen if someone protested in the Square.

'He would be removed pretty sharpish,' is the response.

I hear the story about one US president, staying at a luxury hotel, who was advised to eat first as the food at the Great Hall of the People was pretty basic.

'You sure won't get lamb chops,' advised an aide.

To their amazement, though, there were perfect lamb chops at this place when he arrived. The hotel room had been bugged and the Chinese had not only heard everything, but acted on the information too.

We start off sitting in a high-ceilinged ante-room, thick with eye-wateringly bright red carpets. And sit before a wall-sized painting of the old imperial city. It is all in the worst possible taste, garish and over-stated without even a whisper of that elegance and poise for which Chinese art and architecture is famed. From a distance, everything looks just about respectable. Close up, it is plain tacky. I look for moving cameras but see nothing so concentrate on sipping the Great Wall Cabernet Sauvignon (perfectly drinkable).

A fairly lacklustre plate of cold starters arrives first (as is the tradition) while our fellow guests, stern but not severe, talk business with David, in between shouting down their phones. My infantile obsession with surveillance is given free rein here, and I look closely at flowers, soy sauce bottles, anything that might show we are being watched. The room is all marble and shag pile carpets, gold inlay and well-heeled excess. I wonder if it was like this in Chairman Mao's time. The food is distinctly average but to eat dinner in the centre of the Communist Party Parliament is deeply memorable.

'Now, for more danger, let's go to the night market. There you'll see some weird shit,' says David.

He's not wrong. About a hundred food stalls stretch down the main road at the Dong'anmen night market. Brightly lit, they offer a taste not only of every Chinese region but of the very essence of the weird, wonderful, pungent and plain ghastly.

'This is more of a tourist attraction than proper Chinese street food, and it's not all that hygienic either. Some of it's fucking disgusting.'

Each stall specialises in something different. Children wander past, merrily chewing on scorpions on a stick. The stalls are filled with seahorse satays (looking less fragile in death than life), water beetles, locusts, next door to the chicken, beef and more usual meats. I try a millipede, glazed in a sweet sauce then cooked over coals for a few moments. It's brittle to the bite, with exactly the texture you'd expect from a cooked bug, dry and bitty. I find legs in my teeth for hours afterwards. The locusts are a little burnt; not unpleasant, and good crunch. I can't see them storming the West just yet though. The vast cockroaches are far more ghoulish, with a white, soft substance in the middle, like a fondant fancy. The goo is bitter and dirty tasting and I spit it to the ground, much to the amusement of David and Lucy. They have seen all this before and are not the least bit interested in trying anything.

'It's not proper Chinese food, more novelty. Though it is eaten in some regions, just not really here in Beijing.'

I pass silk worm pupae and some kind of braised dog stand, but decide to leave both for my Korean leg towards the end of the year. Then lizard skin, deep fried and ready to eat. Long, dried squid, skinned snakes, limp and pink. Bubbling vats of offal soups sit next to offal stalls that sell chicken hearts on a stick (chewy but very edible, though I prefer the Yakitori of Japan). Starfish cook on charcoal braziers, slabs of liver reflect the street lights and tourists walk up and down with faces of disgust or delight.

We stop for pork dumpling, fresh and hot and doused in a vine-gary chilli sauce. Pork kidneys are cooked up and sprinkled with chilli powder, fresh and tinged with piss, if a little tough. After a while, we get bored of the culinary cavalcade and wander back to bed.

'So,' David says as we part for the night, 'was China as dangerous as you expected? I hope you actually got a taste of proper Chinese food too.'

I nod. China has eaten me, and my belly is close to collapse. But I've learnt to start disassociating my preconceptions of certain foods from the cold reality. If I can develop this skill, the rest of the trip will be that much more palatable. The next stage, I think, will be a whole lot more easy. All I have to do is eat some barbeque in Tennessee. How hard can that be?

CHAPTER 4

NASHVILLE

After the two-week gorge that was China, I'm looking forward to Tennessee.

I have stayed just a week at home, calming the palate with roast chicken and shepherd's pie. The further I go on this journey, the more I appreciate the warm hug of comfort food. There's no risk involved, no danger of prejudice getting in the way of my eating. Having cooked these dishes so many times – and eaten them all my life – I knew exactly what to expect. No fear, revulsion or disgust, just something that soothes my hunger. Safe food, but not bland food. These brief gaps are becoming more and more important, a time in which I can switch off and retune my palate, put the food I had eaten into perspective. Just sitting on the sofa at home with my wife and staring at the television has become a luxury. Two weeks away and the mundane has become special. All the while I am home, I keep up a cryptic dialogue with my ortolan man.

'Any news?' I type.

Nothing. Then three days later, 'Bird flu getting nearer. Contacts shaky. But still hope. Can't say more. Hold tight.'

Having communicated only via email, I have no idea what he

looks like. At the moment, he is just a terse collection of letters filling up my screen. I imagine him as the intrepid gastronome, totally unfazed by anything he encounters. The opposite of me, the sort of man who will 'sort you out' when you come over for your fix of rare songbirds, tapir's tongues and hummingbird hearts. I feel like some far-flung operative, picking up coded messages from a dead letter box in a Moscow park. At any moment, I expect Smiley to appear as I am on my way to the market and tap me on the shoulder. 'The birds have flown. Control needs you back.'

I even start to peer over my shoulder as I read his electronic missives, fearful that my every move is being watched by some all-powerful governmental organisation. As I fly over the Atlantic, though, my thoughts move from small edible birds to large, edible chunks of pig. In Tennessee, at least, I am safe from elderly spies, flabby duck's feet and nuclear-powered hot sauces. The only real peril at the moment is to my ever-expanding girth.

Over the next few days, I will be obliged to ingest an obscene quantity of flesh. Even for the dedicated trencherman, the world of American competitive barbeque can be a daunting one.

'In the real world,' notes Lolie Eric Elie in *Smokestack Lightning*, his lyrical road trip across the barbeque country of the South,

> most people don't know a brisket from a butt and feel not the least bit impoverished by their ignorance. But like Trekkies or bungee jumpers or Civil War re-enactors, competitive barbe-quers spend weekends in their own orbit. They worship their own gods, they speak their own language, and they think that the ability to distinguish a brisket from a butt is no less basic to a civilised existence than are lounge chairs and chilled beer.

So I am understandably nervous. Although I know my bastes from my butt-rubs, will I be able to detect the taint of Liquid Smoke (an artificial smoke flavouring) in a mouthful of perfectly pulled pork? Will my plummy accent stir memories of colonial tussles or one wrong black mark see me chased from the barn by the likes of Bad To The Bone Too, Let's Kick Some Ash or any of the other 48 teams competing today? Luckily, I am just about fluent in the basics of barbeque judging, thanks to spending an intensive morning with the Kansas City Barbeque Society. The KCBS is one of the pre-eminent barbeque organisations with a mission to 'celebrate, teach, preserve, and promote barbeque as a culinary technique, sport and art form'. They also preside over the official judging and like Judge Dredd, their word is the law.

Yesterday morning, I served three hours deep with 'KCBS Official Judges Certification Program'. Food theory is rarely going to get the taste buds raring but I needed all the help I could get. You score the meat on appearance, taste and tenderness, with a minimum score of 1, or disqualified, to 9 which is pure perfection, and start at 9. If the brisket tastes too tough, or the pork too dry, you take off a point.

The system seemed simple enough so I began to doze, daydreaming of setting up my own rig (Parker's Porkers), stealing in at the last moment and snatching the Grand Champion from under the nose of the old pros. I was just revelling in the cheers when I was brought back into the room with a start. A polystyrene box appeared beneath my nose, the smell of cooked pork the barnyard equivalent of smelling salts.

'What's wrong with that sample?' I was asked by one of the experts. Thirty pairs of eyes turn expectantly onto me.

All I could see was glossy brown ribs on a soft bed of red-tinged lettuce. I reckoned it was a trick question.

'Absolutely nothing,' I answered with a smug grin.

He frowned. 'Have you not been listening for the past ten minutes? This sample is illegal. Why?'

I went for the gag. 'Soliciting?'

Silence. I looked around and no one would meet my gaze, most tutting and looking away in disgust.

'No sir, the only garnish allowed is green-leaf lettuce, common curly parsley and cilantro. No toothpicks, skewers, foreign material or stuffing permitted. No foil. The contestant gets this wrong, and he gets a 1. Which means disqualification. This is very important.'

It seemed a little draconian that someone could have their two-day cooked Boston butt eliminated for the wrong kind of greenery but this was the law. And I was hardly in a position to dispute it.

The rest of the lecture was brusque but good humoured, peppered with gags against Texans, Bostonians, the government and vegans. There were also a few jokes at the expense of Memphis in May, a rival judging organisation with different rules. This event is the biggest in the barbeque circuit, a riotous celebration of booze and pig. In contrast, the Annual Jack Daniels World Championship Invitational Barbeque – known locally as 'The Jack' – was a much more austere event, not least because it was held in a 'dry' county.

The irony of the Jack Daniels Distillery is that it's set in the heart of Moore County, a dry county (where alcohol cannot be sold but can be given away). This is not lost on any of the judges. But by the end of the session, I had a half clue of what to look for. Tough brisket ('the most difficult thing to cook well,' we were warned. 'Get it wrong, and you're talking beefy chewing gum'), over-dried pork ('like chomping down on cardboard'). And we were constantly reminded to 'judge each entry on its own merits rather than comparing the six samples as a group'.

Before we were let loose on the mountain of meat, we had to sign the 'KCBS Judges Code of Conduct'. More like a legal manifesto than barbeque rules, I felt a little perturbed by its content. The part about 'I will treat table captains, other judges, contest officials, contestants and the general public with respect' seemed reasonable enough as did Rule 2, concerning the non-consumption of 'alcohol or other mind-altering substances prior to or during judging'. I had no intention of attempting 'to impose my personal taste preferences on other judges' either.

Rather more worrying was Rule 4 that asked – well, demanded – that 'I will stay silent and maintain a neutral body language while I and the others at my table are judging'. What if a rib was so exquisite that I let out an involuntary moan? Or a piece of brisket so tough that I could not stifle a retch? These vexing questions hurried around my already data-soaked brain as I wandered out of the seminar, back to Nashville, and prepared for the day ahead.

This judging lark, though, isn't as straightforward as it appears. While I have learned the basics in my seminar, there are certainly pitfalls.

'You gotta pace yourself,' warned R.B. Quinn, an old friend, fellow judge and barbeque columnist for *The Tennessean*. My lessons had finished; it was the night before the competition and we were sitting outside in his backyard, among his collection of homemade smokers. There wasn't a lot of room to move, as in addition to the cookers, there were half a dozen motorbikes in various states of mechanical undress. All contestants in The Jack use real fire as opposed to gas. And grilling was looked down upon as an inferior art. As the ribs smoked away and the corn bread baked, we debated the finer points of gas versus charcoal, dry rub versus wet mop and other subjects close to our heart. With round glasses, rumpled plaid shirt and baggy trousers, he has the look of the eternal student. The acoustic guitar that rarely strays from his hand does little to dispel the image.

But despite an encyclopaedic knowledge of the Dead, Stones and Zeppelin, R.B. is not only a master at the barbeque but a lecturer in Political Science too. He is also one of the meanest pit masters (all the cookers, whether a hole in the ground or gleaming gas machine are known by this name) in all of Tennessee, and over the past few years, we have spent many a drunken night, master and apprentice, as I learned the basics at his knee.

'Just the right amount of smoke, so it breaks down those tough fibres and gives a smoky tang,' he'd say and I would lap up every word.

And once you've tried his signature wet rub (they're basted as they cook) baby back ribs, you'll think you've died and gone to hog heaven. They usually arrived about five hours late (a perfectionism I fully understand, much to the hungry frustration of my wife and friends) but one try and you'd fall at his feet. R.B. is a high priest of 'Que' and his ribs are sweet, succulent and tinged with smoke. They slip off the bone as effortlessly as an unzipped silk dress. Emboldened by a litre or two of beer, I told him that I had no problem keeping up with the big boys and puffed out my belly in indignation.

'It's not about ego, y'all,' he told me in his soft Southern twang. 'Just plain common sense.'

My actual induction to the world of the competitive barbeque circuit is a curious mixture of the sober and surreal. Standing in an open-sided barn in the depths of rural Tennessee, my right hand is held up to God while I solemnly swear an oath to 'truth, justice, excellence in Barbeque and the American Way of Life'. My whispered incantation is echoed around the building by my fellow barbeque judges, all 61 of them. As I look around the sea of faces, I notice that some eyes are scrunched closed in patriotic concentration while others are brimming with tears.

Clearly, the 16th Annual Jack Daniels World Championship Invitational Barbeque held in Lynchburg, Tennessee, is no ordinary backyard barbie.

'Hobnob with the elite of the barbeque world, the legends of the coals, the barons of barbeque, the best of the best,' purr Rick Browne and Jack Bettridge in *Barbeque America*. You can't just pitch up, wheel out the Weber and get messy with the lighter fuel. No sir, this is a prestigious, invitation-only event, made up solely of teams who have won state barbeque championships over the past year.

Competition is fiercer than a charcoal furnace as teams battle for the title of best Boston butt or shoulder, brisket, chicken and whole hog, culminating in the crowning of Grand Champion. With a prize fund of over $20,000, there's much more than honour at stake. For the committed carnivore, this is pure piggy heaven. There is, though, the small matter of judging (and gnawing through) a small hillock of charred flesh. Ten pounds and up, more if you can handle it.

Of course, the veterans of the circuit advise taking just a small bite from each sample before moving on to the next. But thinking that I know best, I ignore any well-meant advice. Unlike the other local judges, who could wander home after The Jack, digest their meat, and pick up another pulled pork sandwich as and when they wished, my options are limited. The really good stuff is non-existent in Britain. If I am to survive the next few months on memory reserves alone, I am determined to make them as vivid, and barbeque sauce drenched, as possible.

At the first glimmer of sun, we British like to light up our barbeque, play with fire and sink a few litres of beer. The food resembles a fossilised turd and tastes unspeakable but we're so happy to be outside that we rarely care. In England, it seems, bad barbeque is expected. In America, though, barbeque is worshipped as high art. For a start, it's a noun (you go and grab some 'Que') as well as a verb.

At its heart is the slow and low cooking of meat by an indirect source. Cooking over direct heat is known as 'grilling' and looked down upon by the true Que disciples. Tough cuts of pork and beef are ideally suited to this style, as all that tough connective tissue is slowly broken down into luscious shards of gelatine. You should be able to eat pork butt with a spoon, the rib meat should fall off the bone (just as R.B. proved) and the smoke flavour permeates the whole way through.

It may sound simple, but when seen as a whole, the art of American barbeque makes even the Maastricht Treaty look like a paragon of clear thinking. Nothing is certain or fixed. Even the accepted views on the basic process – that is, indirect cooking of meat by smoke – are not seen as the 'correct' way in some regions, where they insisted that the flavour comes from cooking over a naked flame, hence grilling. Every Que expert has their own secret recipe, their preference for smoking over mesquite chips, say over cherry wood for a slightly different flavour. And regional idiosyncrasies not only abound but dominate. In fact, these numerous differences make up the United States of Barbeque and almost define it.

It's one of those foods like cassoulet that everyone has their own different recipe for, depending on the area, town or person doing the cooking. And it goes without saying that these people always claim their own – or that of their own area – as the best. Although frustrating, this shows a pride that is heartening. The escape from uniformity, the heartfelt belief that your region's way is supreme, an identity created by a certain form of cooking and eating – this is what I came searching for. And here, this is exactly what I find.

Outside the judging barn, a few acres of grass are transformed for the weekend into a miniature city, perched under a fragrant smog of hickory chips, charcoal and the sweet scent of slow-cooking meat – a smell so thick and enticing that it feels possible to grab it from the air in great handfuls, sparking flash floods of saliva in the mouth. Every available inch is squashed full with cooking rigs (ranging from the mini-bar-sized smoker to industrial units capable of cooking up a brace of pigs). Some are surrounded by neat little white picket fences, as if to emphasise the down-home appeal of the cook-off. Others go for a more spartan approach, utilising just the ubiquitous beer cooler that serves as both fridge and impromptu stool.

Wandering around before the competition begins (with the 'No socialising between judge and contestants' rule ringing in my ear), I notice that the competitors all have markedly different approaches to the competition. As some of the pork and beef takes up to 18 hours to cook – and that includes constant basting, mopping and the rest – the previous night has been a long and hard one. Some teams entered into the spirit of the occasion and were slumped over their pits, a pile of empty bottles at their feet.

'We probably partied a little too hard last night,' admits one bleary-eyed team. 'And we had to be woken up because our fire had gone out. But hey, we're here for the fun of it.'

Others avoided all eye-contact with the outside world and sat in conspiratorial huddles around their smoker, eyeing their meat thermometer with all the intensity of surgeons round a flat-lining patient. Having achieved the optimum of five hours' sober sleep in their palatial motor home, they have a steely smugness that floats up with their apple-wood smoke.

Everywhere you looked, there are garish signs advertising past barbeque glories – 'Runner-Up, Whole Hog, Big Pig Jig 2003', screams one. 'Highly Commended, BBQ Sauce, Meat in the Middle

1999', boasts another. Everywhere you look, men of a certain age are crammed into deckchairs, doing what men do around barbeques, swigging beer, poking the embers and talking temperature. Oddly enough, for a method of cooking that is black in origin, the faces are predominantly white and middle class. Once the remit of poor black slaves, professional barbeque is now the sport of their former masters.

The mood is one of controlled frenzy as teams battle to get the fruits of their labour ready in time for the day's judging. Some teams move at a sedate, almost regal pace, their cooking areas oases of calm in the inferno. Others scream Texan-tinged obscenities at each other, desperate to get that brisket just right. And everywhere, hungry tourists and spectators hang around like starving hounds, waiting for a free scrap of meat to be thrown their way. In under an hour, all the fruits of this frantic work will appear before us judges in a white polystyrene box, ready to be munched, judged and scored.

'Remember what I said about pacing,' whispers R.B. as I return from my smoke-scented promenade. 'Look over there.' He points towards a pile of wobbling flesh crammed into dungarees the size of a mess tent. 'Not even that dude can put away all he's given today. If you add it all up, you'd have to munch through nearly 15 lbs of meat. This is the sort of competition that would give your doctor nightmares. So just be careful.'

I hardly have time to contemplate my strategy before the intercom crackles to life.

'Yo, I said yo,' barks a stout man dressed in a white, KCBS polo shirt and perfectly pressed chinos. 'Hey, y'all sit ya asses down now judges. And I mean move.' The chatter dwindles to a murmur as my fellow judges move their way to the tables and sit down, ready for the briefing. With his strut and jarhead cut, he is closer to a Marine drill instructor than official of America's most prestigious barbeque society.

'Are y'all ready to judge?' he shouts.

A quiet murmur answers in the affirmative and we sit with forks and pencils at the ready. Stands are set up around the judging area, where our every move and bite will be scrutinised by a hungry public. My empty stomach begins to wail plaintively as the porky aromas grow more intense. And I'm ready to chew off my own hand in desperate hunger.

As I look around, pen in hand, my fellow judges seem worryingly proficient, covered in pin badges worn like medals with pride – 'Jack 1998', 'Memphis in May 1989'. I've been there, they said, seen, judged and scoffed. I, on the other hand, have nothing save for my name badge with Tom Parker Bowels. The Jack is due to start judging in a few minutes and not really knowing anyone save R.B. I look around the room, trying to put on a pensive face, as if I know what I am doing.

My fellow judges are an eclectic bunch, a mishmash of food writers, restaurant owners, aficionados and local TV stars. Some talk like old friends, having judged many a rib together in their time. Others sign autographs for the crowds that are building up in the seats around the barn. These spectators look hungry and ruthless, as if we were the Christians and they the lions, raring to get their feed. TV weather man Bill Hall is the most popular and his broad face stays smiling, even as the fiftieth person in two minutes shouts, 'What the weather gonna be, Bill?'

'Not too good, guys,' he replies, again and again.

A dreary drizzle mixes with the smoke outside to form a fragrant fog but it does little to dull the excitement. I start talking to Louis Osteen, a well-known South Carolinian chef with oval glasses, bearlike frame and a deep, booming laugh. He carries his bulk well and when he gets especially animated, his floppy hair falls over one eye.

'I'm a loyal Southerner and I believe that the best barbeque is in the South. In fact, I know that. The Southern temperament is the only one in the land suited to slow cooking. The secret is all in how slow and low you cook it.' He brushes an errant strand out of his eyes and goes on. 'The South has given America its best food and writers, as well as the country's only indigenous music, blues, bluegrass and gospel. But hey, they're sitting us down. Have a good day and don't eat too much to start with.'

With that, he trundles off to find his place, leaving me to do the same. I pass another judge, Dustin Elliot, a PRCA bull rider, clad in black from his cowboy boots to his Stetson. Something of a local hero, the crowds lean over the fence to get his autograph, cooing over his boyish good looks. Teenage girls flutter over-made eyes in his direction, giggling every time he glances up. He looks a little bewildered.

Nashville legend Coyote McCloud, rock DJ and heroic imbiber of Jack, looks anything but. Slouched over a mug of black coffee, his bloodshot eyes are hidden behind a pair of mirrored aviators. Looking like the bastard brother of Iggy Pop and Keith Richards, he occasionally breaks into a howl mid-sip. I hear him growl an explanation to a startled onlooker.

'I'm the fucking coyote, man, and today, the coyote's feeling a little tender.'

There are whispers that he has a hip flask stashed away somewhere on his rangy person and as the day progresses, gravity becomes more and more of a problem as he struggles to stay up. Aside from a few raised eyebrows, no one pays him much attention. He mumbles gruffly at anyone who approaches, scrawling the occasional autograph with a cocky flourish.

At the other end of the scale is the legendary Ardie Davies, better known as Remus Powers PhB (Doctor of Barbeque, the ultimate accolade in the BBQ world). A petite man with neatly trimmed beard and black Derby hat perched jauntily on his head, he's the epitome of Southern good manners with a touch of the dandy thrown in. He works the room, doling out advice while happily posing for pictures. Known as the 'Poet Laureate of Q', he wears his authority lightly, eyes twinkling behind big, wire-rimmed moon glasses. His brilliant white apron has three pork bones attached, worn smooth by age and varnished to ensure they stay that way.

I ask the master for some advice. He speaks softly and has a shyness belying his larger-than-life persona, so I move closer to glean every last scrap.

'Judges must be true to their taste buds. Just remember that and you'll be fine.'

I scribble down these Zen-like utterings, the sort of thing Obi Wan would whisper to Luke. Legend has it that he came up with the KCBS oath, scribbled in a moment of inspiration on a scrap of Arthur Bryant paper. He is called upon to deliver the KCBS oath to us all and bids goodbye and good luck. I find my table under the stirring command of Fred Gould, resplendent in black cowboy hat, brass pig buckle and pink piggy braces. He has a passing resemblance to Dennis Hopper, and an intensity of stare that is equally unnerving. But like most of the folk here, this tough, good ole boy exterior is mere cover for the softest of souls.

He is assisted by yet another legend of the KCBS, the glorious Marge Plummer, a straight-talking Southern grand dame with a PhB and a no-nonsense attitude to judging. She's similarly attired, with dangling pig earrings and a denim jacket covered with pin badges of barbeque competitions gone by.

'Remember y'all, no talking during the judging. And start off slow. There's one heck of a lot of meat t'eat.'

Ralph Collins – a gentle ex-TWA pilot who was born in Scotland but now lives in upstate New York – is my neighbour. Modest of tone and manner, he tells me this is his first time. I relax a little. On my other side is journalist Catherine Mayhew, whose wiry frame and school-marm features do little to betray a rapier-like wit. Whenever I falter, a word in my ear from her is enough to set me straight.

The Tannoy crackles to life and we are all asked to stand up. Remus takes to the stage to a round of applause and raises his right hand. 'Now repeat after me … "I do solemnly swear to objectively and subjectively evaluate" … a hundred Southern accents (and one faltering English) murmur the oath back '… "each Barbeque meat that is presented to my eyes, my nose, my hands and my palate." The barn feels like a church in the middle of the Lord's Prayer and some of the judges close their eyes, as if in pious devotion to their Lord.

'I accept my duty to be an official KCBS Certified Judge, so that truth, justice, excellence in barbeque and the American way of life may be strengthened and preserved forever.'

At this point, I pause guiltily. What happens if the visiting UK teams (and there are two, Mad Cow's BBQ and The Major Players, here for the international competition run separately from the main event) spot me swearing away my sovereignty to the former colonies. I look furtively about the room and can't seem to spot them. I mumble the words and we sit, ready for the judging to begin.

There's endless dispute as to the origins of barbeque, most of it of little interest to the non-etymologically obsessed. But 'barbeque' is generally agreed to come from barbacoa, the Arawak for a raised wooden framework of sticks. It was first recorded in Gonzalo Fernandez de Oviedo's (an explorer of the Caribbean) book *De la Historia General y Natural de las Indias*, but was probably in use way before that.

You'll find some fanatics who argue that the word is derived from the French saying 'de barbe à queue' translated as 'from head to tail' and describing the technique of roasting a whole animal. The *Oxford English Dictionary* brushes this aside, however, deciding that 'the alleged French barbe à queue "beard to tail" is absurd conjecture suggested merely by the sound of the word'. Still, no one can quite agree and the argument continues to blaze. Nor can they decide which meat is the original and best.

Although the pig is the classic barbeque beast, there are, of course, variations. Texan barbeque is traditionally brisket (as Texans have traditionally raised beef rather than pork), a tough fatty cut from the front of the cow. Ask any Lone Star boy and they'll swear that brisket is the only true Que. Get over to Owensboro, Kentucky and you'll find that mutton is the meat of choice. You could generalise and say that in the South East, barbeque refers almost exclusively to pork while in the South West, it's almost exclusively beef. As for the Mid West, they use both. But a little generalisation is a dangerous thing in the barbeque world and you'll find plenty of restaurants who buck every rule.

As to the origins of the actual process, the same fierce regional pride abounds. In the South, you would be applauded for saying that the area is the true home of barbeque. Yet utter this again in Kansas City and they'd laugh you out of town. They call themselves the 'capital of barbeque', the city where Wyatt Earp once ruled and Wild Bill Hickock whooped and hollered. Directly north of the South and north-east of the South West, it's the place where Texas brisket meets the pork tradition of the former Confederacy. Once the nation's second-largest meat-packing city (after Chicago), it was perfectly placed for some serious Que.

Legendary joints such as Arthur Bryants and Gates & Sons burn brightly on the national imagination thanks, in part, to the eulogy paid them by Calvin Trillin, a long-time hero of mine. 'Barbeque is a touchy subject all over the country,' he muses in *Alice, Let's Eat*, the third part of his brilliant Tummy Trilogy. 'Some of the regional quibbling on this subject can become ferocious, barbeque specialists being united that the finest barbeque place in the country is Arthur Bryant's of Kansas City.'

This, of course, is a contentious statement and one vehemently denied by locals from other parts of the country. Ex-pat Georgia Harriet Plyler is one. 'Kansas City is full of very nice people, and they simply have no way of knowing that they are wrong about all ideas of barbeque,' she fumes and her husband Phillip is in strong agreement.

'When I read that part about Kansas City in *Alice, Let's Eat*, my heart sank. I happened to be there the next year, and of course made a beeline for Arthur Bryant's. And it was good, just not up there with the gods. I know someday I will meet Calvin Trillin, and will have to have this conversation with him. Very worrying. You do have to remember that beef was the life blood of KC, not pigs, so they are partial to any way of cooking their favourite product.'

But even Trillin admits that no one can agree on what barbeque is. 'Americans argue not just about whose barbeque is second-best' (Bryant's, of course, being first) 'but even about what barbeque is. In the Southwest, for instance, people ordinarily barbeque ribs, but in North Carolina the word is used as a noun only referring to chopped pork that has been flavoured, in a manner of speaking, with a vinegar-based sauce.'

This just about makes sense, but once we enter the Carolinas – to my mind, the fast-beating heart of barbeque country – things start to get seriously complicated. In Lexington, in the west of North Carolina, pork shoulder is cooked over hickory or oak then chopped or sliced and served with slaw and a tomato-based sauce. But on the eastern side of the same state, it's whole hog with a vinegar and pepper-based sauce.

'Though there are myriad variations in the different styles that a local might be willing to spend an afternoon explaining,' muses John

T. Edge in *Southern Belly* – like the tendency of eastern aficionados to offer boiled potatoes dusted with paprika on the side and the western habit of serving a reddish coleslaw shot through with barbeque sauce – 'the novice eater is advised to stick to analysis of meat and sauce when trying to get his geographical bearing.'

Trying to digest these endlessly shifting barbeque boundaries is all but impossible and even experts such as Elie and Edge admit it can get mighty confusing. One truth remains throughout, from Alabama to Virginia. Devotees of whatever meat, method and sauce will all agree on one thing. That theirs is the original and the best, the only true Que.

'In many respects, barbeque is taken as seriously as religion,' writes Stephen Smith in *The Rhetoric of Barbeque: A Southern Rite and Ritual* (Corn Bread Nation 2). 'In fact, the barbeque cults throughout the region often display a hostility to criticism and an intolerance to opposing beliefs that have characterised certain religious groups.'

He's too polite to call them fanatics but that's exactly what they are. Maybe this seemingly simple cooking technique represents something deeper about the American way of life. According to Elie,

> barbeque is a metaphor for American culture in a broad sense, and that it is a more appropriate metaphor than any other American food. Barbeque alone encompasses the high-and lowbrows, the sacred and the profane, the urban and the rural, the learned and the unlettered, the blacks, the browns, the yellows, the reds, and the whites.

In short, the story of barbeque reveals much about the history of the country of America and the people who adore it. It brings families and communities together, binds them in a sense of place and purpose as only truly regional food can. Some are even defined by their style of barbeque, the thing that sets them apart from others. But it goes even deeper than that. A close study of the development of barbeque over the last hundred years gives invaluable and fascinating insight into the history of America itself.

Because despite the dominance of the white middle classes on the competition circuit, this is essentially a food born out of struggle, poverty and bare necessity. 'Whenever pork and people come together, it's a safe assumption that rich people will end up with the hams and the chops and the poor people will end up with the ribs, lips, foots and chitterlings,' says Elie in *Smokestack Lightning*. Barbeque is basically the art of turning the bony, less desirable portions of the pig into something worth chewing. It was almost certainly developed by the poor and abused, a disproportionate number of whom tend to be of African descent. The black population were used as cheap labour and many became pit masters, using the kitchen as the only way to express any sort of freedom or individuality.

'Folks always talk about how black folks are good cooks,' says Lawrence Craig, 'national treasure, a gentleman of the old school', in *Southern Belly*. 'There's a reason for that. Back when I was growing up there were two kinds of jobs black folks could get without being challenged by white folks: cooking and heavy lifting.'

A lot of the pit cooks still are black and the barbeque country of the Deep South was right at the heart of the Civil Rights movement in the Sixties. In those days, it was sweaty, back-breaking work, involving tending an inferno at all hours, wreathed in a choking, sweaty fug of heat and fat. When the hideously long-overdue Civil Rights Act was eventually passed in 1964 – stipulating that any business engaged in interstate commerce could not discriminate on the basis of race – many of the white-owned restaurants were up in arms. Ollie's Barbeque in Birmingham, Alabama, filed suit in the federal court to prevent them having to serve black people. Thankfully, they failed and tales of extraordinary bravery were played out in restaurants across the South.

Aleck's Barbeque Heaven in Atlanta, Georgia, saw the likes of Martin Luther King and Marion Barry, John Lewis and Maynard Jackson come to talk tactics and chew ribs. The L-shaped lunch counter of Woolworths in Greensboro, North Carolina, was where the sit-in movement sparked off, inspiring other peaceful demonstrations across the country. In February 1961, four black youths – Ezell Blair, Joseph McNeill, David Richmond and Franklin McCain – sat down and ordered coffee. A black waitress refused them service, as they were sitting in the 'Whites only' section of the counter. They refused to budge. The white manager, Clarence Harris, didn't call the police and the four men stayed there until the store closed, said good night and promised to return the next morning.

'It was put up or shut up time,' said McCain later. 'We were compelled to take an extra step to do something ... and that "do something", as the world knows, turned out to be the sit-in movement ... the tactic of well-mannered, well-dressed courteous, polite kids just sitting there, well it just left people perplexed.' The next day the four returned, bringing with them 20 others. On Wednesday, there were about 80 students cramming the counter. By Thursday word had spread and more than 100 students squeezed in, along with a few whites. Within a couple of weeks, students in 11 other cities would launch similar protests. It took nearly six months for the Greensboro sit-ins to come to an end, in July, when three black Woolworths staff were served at the previously segregated counter. A year later and the *New York Times* declared that the Greensboro sit-ins were the spark that, combined with 'stand-ins at theatres, kneel-ins at churches and swim-ins at beaches', defined the 'proportions of a national movement'.

The culinary reputation of these tireless pit workers was, and still is, legendary. That's not to say there aren't many fine white-owned and -run barbeque joints. Indeed, at the top of the South (North Carolina), where slavery was much less widespread and the plantations smaller, it was as much a white man's trade as a black man's. But as Trillin points out, 'You could eat at a white-owned barbeque restaurant. But that's kind of like going to a gentile internist. You're not playing with the odds.'

At long last, after what seem liked an interminable time, the judging begins and the first polystyrene boxes are borne into the room to rapturous applause. To my horror, sauces are first, and all have to contain a glug of Jack Daniels. A few splodges of sauce are unlikely to make much of a dent in my raging hunger. They arrive on our judging sheets, one sauce in each of the six boxes. To judge a smudge of viscous liquid is hard enough, especially on its own merits, as they all look equally unappetising. There's precious little aesthetic appeal in barbeque sauce. And your choice of sauce is entirely dependent on your personal taste.

Some, like me, prefer a more vinegary, spicy flavour as opposed to a sweeter one. But being the first category, I'm eager to please and swill each sauce in my mouth as if it were an 82 Lafite. Some are inexpressibly filthy, sweet, garish concoctions that pucker the tongue with artificial unease. A couple taste freshly made and perfectly decent, though I find it hard to get too inspired. On the whole, you'd find better in your local Morrisons. To be fair, with so many regional differences in the sauces, it's a hard task and I just end up giving full marks to the two I like, while dumping the rest with 6 or 7s. The whole point of these sauces is to go with the meat, so perhaps I am being a little harsh. This is hardly the most inspiring beginning to a barbeque feast.

Next up, though, is worse still, the dreaded Cook's Choice or 'Comedy Crapola' as one of the judges puts it. Open to all national and international teams, this wretched section is supposed to highlight the extra skills of the competing chefs – anything is allowed but barbeque. In reality, the dishes are culinary train wrecks, the sort of thing produced in the first week by small Surrey catering colleges. Or the Sunday all-you-can-eat buffet at the Barstow Quality Inn. They all try so desperately hard to be different and sophisticated, with endless garnishes and over-elaborate decorations. But they are hideously out of place in a barbeque contest, like overweight trannies in a Working Men's Club.

'I'm here to judge Que, not fancy food,' complains one judge on my table as the samples are laid out before us.

Another is blunter still. 'If I wanted the Cordon Bleu, I'd fuck off to Paris, France.'

I nod furiously, desperate to get rid of this over-dressed finery and get onto the Que. The sight of a palm-tree made of pineapple and carrot does little for my mood. A dill-infused slab of flabby, dried-up salmon is gut-wrenchingly foul while the less said about the greasy veal vol-au-vent, the better. As the last remains are cleared away, our table bursts into spontaneous applause. A ten-minute break follows, so I go over to sit with R.B. He's equally unhappy with this wretched section.

'Thank God it's over,' he spits. 'I mean, for Christ's sake,' he adds, pointing at an ornately decorated medallion of beef, 'that just ain't right at a Que competition. At least the whole hog's next.' I leave him shaking his head and scamper back to my chair to prepare for whole cooked pig.

As the pork piles up onto my judging sheet – a different sample in each box – I finally feel that the competition is under way. I'm so famished by now that I could devour the hog whole, Obelix style, with the greatest of ease. A ripple of greedy anticipation hangs in the air along with the porky scents and the room suddenly becomes more animated. The watching crowd draw closer, watching every scrap of flesh from plate to mouth with near-hysterical intensity. Like dogs, they unconsciously lick their lips, munching vicariously through our every chew.

'Bring it on,' hollers Ed Roith, another judge and barbeque enthusiast from Kansas. It can be presented 'pulled, sliced or chopped' but flavour and texture is paramount. The first sample is chewy and rubbery, a major blow. Perhaps I have got this all wrong – maybe my tastes are not the same as everyone around me. Is this whole barbeque cult a sham? I have eaten in about a dozen restaurants around Tennessee and all have tasted finer than this apparent crème de la crème. The pork is cheap and flabby, massively undercooked, hideously chewy and appetising as a white bread shit sandwich. It is worse even than the pre-packaged slice we used to get at school, and rather than a smoky savour, it has a tinge of burnt plastic.

This is my first taste of professional circuit Que – supposedly cooked by some of the greatest in the land – and I could have got better at my local BP Mini Mart. Needless to say, I eat both slices in disgust. The next is a little better, a hint of smoke and decent texture. But it is the third sample that epitomises everything I've been dreaming of, a fluffy mound of pulled pork, so soft that it had been wrenched in succulent shards from the cooked pig. A piece of bark (the crusty, outside surface of the pig) may look unattractive to the outsider but this unassuming, blackened piece of skin contains the essence of barbeque, a hint of sauce, a tickle of smoke and a chewy, almost biltong-like consistency.

The table is now totally silent, no sneaky grimaces or silent yawns, just pure, ecstatic concentration. The meat is silken, cosseting and teasing the tongue into a state of rapturous glee. With each grind of the jaw, first the sweetness of the pork is released, then the hickory smoke, both entwined in concupiscent bliss. They complement each other like an old married couple, each egging the other on to greater heights of perfection. We all scribbled furiously, asking for just one more sample. I managed to sneak at least three monstrous mouthfuls from the main box, closing my eyes and letting these flavours dance across my palate. No one dares look at each other (even I am sure this is perfect 9 material) as we hand in our scores. Once we can speak freely again, though, the table explodes in a hubbub of excitement.

'This is why the pig is put on this planet!' exclaims Ralph in an uncharacteristic fit of excitement.

'Evidence that there is a God!' shouts another judge, his mouth stuffed with pork.

The whole table looks like they've been dosed with Ecstasy, with shining, wide eyes and moronic, toothy grins. As expected, we all agree on a perfect 9. All dismiss the first sample as filth, and I relax a little. My taste buds have been true and I start to feel one of the group, rather than the gormless outsider.

This first proper testing gives me a confidence that I'm a worthy member of the KCBS, albeit a rookie one. After this momentous epiphany, the table becomes somehow closer, drawn together in our mutual admiration for the mystery smoker. I can return happy now, having tasted true Que. And despite the frantic edge being taken off my hunger, I am still desperate for more.

Chicken is the next category, and a pretty sordid affair it is too. Much emphasis is put on the smoke taste and soft texture. But the first two are so overcooked that they're mere moments away from carbon, while the next couple seem to have been born in a tar pit and raised on a chemical plant. They have none of the gamey flavour I associate with a decent free-range chicken. I hear whoops of delight on other tables, so the quality is certainly there. We just got unlucky. This is a crushing disappointment, as I have had visions of immaculately cooked free-range fowl, packed with natural flavour and tickled by the smoke below.

The final specimen looks appetising enough, with golden, sticky skin atop a pearly white expanse of flesh. But one bite instantly ruins the illusion as an artificial bitterness and a hint of petrol takes over the tongue, where it stubbornly remains for the next half hour. Only one is anywhere near decent, bursting with juice and gentle smoky flavour. I quickly find the source on the other side of the table and grab a further few chunks, before they disappear off into the crowd (where the remains are thrown to the baying packs). This sample aside, the only plus side of the chicken round is that yesterday I ate chicken unlike any I had tasted before. It even gave my mother's roast chicken – and mine too – some deadly serious competition.

On my last visit to Nashville, I heard wondrous things about Prince's Hot Chicken Shack, a temple to fried chicken in one of the poorer parts of town. But it was closed when I tried to visit, so I went home empty bellied. My other great friend – and long-suffering guide to the city – Ellen, promised a pilgrimage to this legendary restaurant and even managed to rope in the Mayor, Bill Purcell, to join us in our feast. A typically slick and ebullient public servant, he speaks with polished eloquence on most subjects close to the city's heart. But it is his appetite for 'hot chicken' where we find the most common ground, charming as he is, and in him, I have no better mentor.

The British view of fried chicken starts and ends with that slippery, greasy filth called Kentucky Fried Chicken. It sullies the good name of a noble art, a weak and fraudulent pretender to a glorious throne.

'To know about fried chicken, you must have been weaned and

reared on it in the South. Period,' warns James Villiers, the Southern scribe. But not to appreciate it. Just like barbeque, this is a dish which inspires rabid emotions and there is no better place for the rookie to start than Prince's Hot Chicken Shack.

As Ellen and I pull up into a nondescript parking lot a few hundred metres off the main highway, there is nothing to denote a national institution, just a few bland shop fronts with little clue to the business inside. The restaurant is equally anonymous, a small hand-painted sign the only evidence of the Mecca within. Five rickety booths and a serving hatch are its main features, livened up by a tattered poster of the reggae star Beenie Man. On the far wall are some faded, signed photographs of country stars, long ridden off into the sunset.

The Mayor walks in behind us, and with a short introduction ('Welcome to my favourite restaurant in the world!'), sits us down at our table. Despite Prince's simplicity, it is anything but run-down, a thriving restaurant filled with a cross-section of Nashville life. White-collar office workers in their short-sleeved shirts, eating quickly and efficiently so as not to waste a precious second. Factory and construction workers, chomping the portion in two or three bites. Young black families help the children with their chicken, occasionally stealing a golden-hued hunk from a disapproving daughter's plate. They all have one feature in common – a slightly dreamy, cloudy quality to their eyes and an involuntary expression of ecstasy as they bite into the hot, succulent flesh. The smell of the place is all-enveloping, a sharp hit of cayenne pepper mixed with the warm comfort of the sizzling batter.

To order, you walk up to a small, square hole in the back wall and decide between a leg, quarter, half or whole chicken, and white or brown meat. Then you choose your heat, medium, hot or extra hot. Andre Prince, a handsome black lady and great niece of the founding Prince brothers, mans the hatch while keeping a cool eye on the kitchen behind her. I tell her I've come all the way from London to try her chicken. She nods, as if this were nothing out of the ordinary. I then ask, with astonishing presumption, about her secret ingredient, the magic addition that makes her hot chicken the finest in the world. She listens with cocked eyebrow and crossed arms, tapping her fingers on the wood. I tell her, in a very oily way, that her chicken is world famous.

'I know. Now whaddya want?'

The kitchen has little more than a four-ring cooker, where three chattering ladies are hauling the chicken pieces out of the fiery marinade before dredging them in chilli-spiked flour and slipping them into huge black skillets filled with bubbling oil. I look to Ellen.

'Don't y'all be trying the extra hot, mind. It will blow you clean away.' She orders a mild half and goes to sit down. After my experiences with the hot sauce in Albuquerque, I'm slightly cautious. But then I wonder what harm mere cayenne pepper could do to me. It's not even a tenth of the heat of that extract that nearly took me down. What was I thinking in hesitating? This would be a breeze. Extra hot, indeed. Yeah right.

'One quarter chicken, brown and white, extra hot.'

'You sure, honey?' enquires Andre. 'It's real spicy.'

Yup, I smile, and wander back to the table. This will show these lily-tongued Southerners what true British grit is really about.

Ellen greets my order with howls of laughter while the Mayor (who only goes for hot as 'anything more masks the flavour') simply smiles.

'Well, you'll find that extra hot chicken ain't chattin' food,' is all he'll say, before getting back to telling me about West Chester, the whole-hog barbeque capital of Tennessee.

We're just debating the finer points of slaw when the chicken appears. Perched atop two slices of cheap white bread (to soak up the grease), it's topped with a wobbling stack of pickle chips (the ones with the waffle ridges) to counter some of the burn. While Ellen's mild version is a deep golden and the Mayor's a little darker, more scarlet, mine is almost black with cayenne pepper. Miss Prince warns against fizzy drinks, as do Ellen and the Mayor.

'Fire and fizz,' she explains sternly, 'can be fatal to the digestive system,' so I settle for a bottle of fruit punch.

I've certainly never seen a better-looking piece of fried chicken and am almost loath to bite in and ruin the beauty. The smell is so intoxicating, though, that I grab it with both hands, not even noticing the burning of my fingers. As I raise the piece of chicken to my lips, I see the residents of the kitchen stretching their necks to look at the cocky tourist who ordered extra-hot.

The first bite is pure gustatory bliss, the perfect combination of thick, spicy, crunchy crust and exceptionally juicy chicken. I start to chew triumphantly, looking around with a smug grin. Yup, it had a kick but nothing I couldn't handle.

Then the pain starts and hits very, very hard. Visions of that night in the Albuquerque bar flood back and I curse myself for such unthinking arrogance. Being cayenne pepper, the heat builds slowly and gradually. But once it starts, like a tanker of nitro-glycerine careering, without brakes, towards a cobbled street, you realise that it can only end in tears.

First, my lips begin to burn. Then pulse, as if they have been stung by a swarm of hornets. The tongue goes next, as the relentless molten lava reduces this usually active organ to a useless, throbbing wreck. I look up to see Ellen's grinning face fragment into a million splinters as tears flood my eyes. The Mayor, ever the politician, keeps his head down and concentrates on his lunch. He looks up briefly to nod at me, and I stretch a fake smile, spreading still more fire onto the bottom of my nose. The only thing willing me on is pure, pig-headed pride.

Each mouthful becomes more and more painful and numbing until I'm uncertain as to whether I'm swallowing my saliva or just dribbling it out of my mouth. My fruit punch is about as much use as a water pistol on a bush fire, just spreading the agony further down my throat. And the bread, usually so useful in sopping up chilli heat, is so drenched in the scarlet oil that things are made still worse. But on I go, no longer enjoying the torment, just determined to get it down.

Why do I do this to myself? Am I really so simple that I cannot learn from my experiences? You prick, I curse silently, you arrogant, stubborn and vainglorious twat. Any vestige of flavour, texture and enjoyment is long gone, replaced by the relentless, powdery dry heat of the cayenne. Sweat pours down my forehead and drips onto the chicken and all I can see is the top of Ellen's head, shaking with uncontrolled hysteria.

Once again, I reach that moment where my heart is racing so fast, and the natural endorphins in my body so pumped, that I feel myself floating above my numbed body, looking down on the English prat who is sweating so profusely below. Eventually I finish my last bite and fall back in the booth. It is a further five minutes before I can breathe comfortably, let alone talk. The dusty after-burn of cayenne fills my head like the aftermath of a sandstorm, and I vow that next time, it's hot all the way. When I eventually manage to croak out a word, the mayor smiles.

'I told you it wasn't chatting food.'

I blink my assent and am led by the still-grinning Ellen to the car.

Back at The Jack, it's another rest period. I have already eaten a good three pounds' worth of meat, more than three or four times my usual amount. We aren't even halfway yet. R.B. is equally despondent about the quality of the chicken section.

'Yup, ours are pretty damned average too. Too much reliance on the old bottled sauce. Mine are in a different league.'

This is no empty boast. I have eaten his efforts a few nights ago and they were magnificent, with a contrast of textures and flavours that did back-flips across the tongue. At this rate, R.B. would be winning the contest. Our spirits, though, are revived by the next announcement.

'Ladies and gentlemen, take your seats. In two minutes, it's pork ribs time.' A cheer goes up around the barn and you can hardly hear the rest of the spiel. But I just about catch it over the greedy hubbub.

'Now I know y'all love ribs,' the drawling voice warns, 'but keep some room for later. We still have brisket, butt and desserts to go.'

No one pays the blindest piece of attention as the ribs arrive and I thank God for the barriers between judges and audience. They are so close now, straining against the metal, their eyes burning holes of envy into the pork-covered bones.

'Everyone love ribs,' whispers Elaine, with a conspiratorial smile and even this seasoned Que pro admires the burnished racks before her. This is the bit I have been waiting for, what the entire room has been waiting for – the main event, big daddy bastard section.

One of the few things I do remember from yesterday's lesson is what to look for in this category. Under the 'Helpful Guidelines Judging The Four Basic Contest Categories' of the KCBS Official Judges Certification Program is offered the following advice:

Everyone has his or her own idea of what good ribs should be. However, when judging barbequed ribs for a contest, we must take a few factors into consideration other than what we feel may be our favourite rib.

This sounds a little confusing. But it continues:

> We must first determine how well it was cooked. When eating a properly cooked rib, the meat should come off the bone with very little effort and only where you bit into it should the meat be removed. If the meat falls off the entire bone while biting, it is a good indication it is overcooked. When overcooked, the meat has the tendency to be mushy with little or no texture.

Wise words and the only thing they fail to mention (although it was discussed at length during the session) is the red smoke ring. When smoke penetrates the meat, it leaves a reddish tinge on the white flesh. This is a sign of true Que but can be easily faked by unscrupulous contestants using Liquid Smoke. Our job as judges is to spot these mountebanks and flush them out for the fraudulent scoundrels they are.

As I am the rookie, Ed Roith (he of the 'bring it on') turns to me and reiterates the basics. 'The meat should come clean off the bone in one bite, and leave the bone dry as a bone. Now get judging.'

My first bite plops neatly into my mouth. Bliss. With just enough fat to make the mouthful succulent, the smoke creeps along my tongue one way and embraces the pork travelling the other. The sauce adds sticky depth and a hint of spice, the juice trickling down my chin. This is it, I think, as I tuck into the next. This is what I came for, learned for and prepared for. No rib has ever tasted this good before. This is as good as a spoonful of beluga caviar, Giorgio Locatelli's unctuous, sexy truffle risotto. It stands shoulder to shoulder with my mother's roast beef, the J.G. Mellon cheeseburger, the lobster roll at Mary's Fish Camp and the Yellowtail with jalapeno at Nobu.

Before I know it, I am on to the next and the next and the next until my entire being is consumed with snaffling these pork ribs. Some are a little too dry, others flop off their bone with ungracious, indolent ease. They all go down regardless, even when my belly cries for a break. Shut up, you pussy, and take it like a man. It gives a worried rumble in response.

'Man or mouse,' I think as I continue to fill up every available inch.

I undo the top button of my jeans and soldier on. Looking up, I feel the hungry eyes of at least 40 spectators on me, enviously watching my every lick and chew. If I had entered in there, armed only with a rib, I would have been ripped apart. For a second, I consider throwing over a few bones, to watch them scrabble for a morsel. But my Henry VIII fantasies are soon put to an end by the arrival of still more ribs. Officially, we are to try six but I manage double that. Then, in the break, I go on the prowl – well, more like a wobble – for more.

To be fair, cooking for 61 judges is a hit-and-miss affair, even for the most experienced pit master. One lot of ribs may have been nearer to the heat than another, making them over-dry. So one judge might score perfection while another tastes his hugely overcooked. This is the same across the categories (apart from the 'comedy' ones such as chef's choice) so the art of competition barbeque is a fine art, though an imperfect one too. A lot of luck is useful too. But I am a true believer now, bent prostrate and a little uncomfortable in front of the high altar of barbeque.

My hunger had long been sated but greed kicks in like a generator in a power cut as I snaffle anything with a bone. I also begin to understand the sheer masochism of those professional eaters, like Sonya Thomas, who snaffles through 80 chicken nuggets in five minutes, the same lady who managed 161 chicken wings in a mere 12 minutes. She's minute, a mere 105 pounds, with cheekbones sharp enough to cut Spam (six pounds from the can, 12 minutes, by a Richard LeFevre). Under the umbrella of the International Federation of Competitive Eaters, this is classed as a sport and there are prizes of up to $100,000. But these are athletes, in their twisted way, not rank amateurs like me. They eat for sport, and few do it on greed alone.

The next wave is pork shoulder, or Boston Butt. It's not butt at all, just another name for the shoulder.

'Pork shoulder or Boston Butt should be very tender with a definite texture to the meat,' advises my manual. 'It is easily overcooked to get it tender and the judge should make certain in his or her mind that it is not mushy.'

Once again, we are looking for the pink or purple smoke ring but told not to penalise if it wasn't present. Not all methods of smoking show up. By this stage, I'm slowing. I've had to open the second button of my jeans and hardly dare move for fear of flashing my pants. I slouch rather than sit now, and talk becomes onerous. Pork odours envelop my entire being but still I go on. My stomach and I are no longer on speaking turns, and occasionally it sends up a flurry of porky wind to show its displeasure.

Again, entries vary from the sublime to the downright ridiculous and this time, not every sample goes down. But even the very best have lost any real appeal and my palate is shouting out for something green and cold. Is this what the professional eater felt like, reaching the wall?

'We got lemon and lime Cool Aid,' says one judge, when I groan a request for vegetation. He isn't joking either. I become convinced that I have physically filled every space in my body, that any more would cause an overcrowding with catastrophic results.

I burp quietly, to gain crucial room before the brisket arrives. This cut is adored by the Texans and comes from one of the toughest cuts of the cow, the underside chest muscle that spends much of its life supporting the heft of the beast. Usually cooked for about 18–19 hours, all the fat must slowly turn to gelatin making the meat lusciously tender. If there is too much fat remaining, a few points are pulled off. If it takes the best part of an hour to chew up and force down, points off. If you can scrub an iron pan and remove the ground-in dirt, a few more points off. The first check is to hold it and see how easily the slice will pull apart. If it breaks as you stretch and keeps the fine texture, you can be sure of a good mouthful. But over-cooked and it will crumble before it leaves the table.

Once again, the smoke ring looks pretty but as it could have been falsified, it is not subject to a score. I have reached my tipping point now, and gaze down on the meat with undisguised disgust. Yet I can't just get up and say, 'Sorry, folks, for leaving and not judging your hard-cooked brisket. But I'm a gluttonous, belly-worshipping fat fuck who ate more then he could handle.'

So I move through satiation to engorged to plain ill. Even the smell of the barbeque, so wonderful a few hours back, is starting to sicken me. I can hardly look at my fellow judges, let alone the contents of my judging sheet. I reach gingerly down and nibble the brisket. I robotically note my score, and curse for going too fast at the start. The pleasure, anticipation and excitement have long passed. I feel sick to my core.

At least half of the brisket is very good indeed, not that I am in any state to say so. Listless and eager to escape, I need something, anything to move the liquid cement rapidly setting in my stomach. As the last of the brisket is cleared away, I almost cheer. Were it not for the fact that I fear this cheer might be hotly pursued by the regurgi-tated remains of the day's meat. This is it, over, sweet blessed relief.

I have, though, forgotten one last category ... dessert. Now I dislike puddings at the best of times. Life's not long enough to try the best of savoury let alone waste precious time and space on sweet things. I don't mind the occasional treacle tart or chocolate mousse but I'm a man of resolutely savoury tastes. As the rest of the room smack their lips in anticipation, I dab mine in fear.

Being the South, I know I am in for one last push. And I'm not wrong. Huge, intricate creations swim in rivers of toffee sauce, and struggle under mountains of whipped cream and melted chocolate. Peach cobblers, blueberry pies, apple dumplings, fluorescent key lime pies, lemon meringue pies with browned snowy peaks next to sticky pecan pies, peach ice cream and strawberry shortcake ... a roll call of sugary excess, and just thinking about this calorific mess is sickening enough. This is XXX pudding pornography, a lusty smorgasbord of all that is sticky and over-stuffed. In a hungry state of mind, these evocative names alone may have persuaded me to tuck in. But sat like Mr Creosote, hardly able to utter a sentence, less still try a sample of these calorific delights, this is nigh on impossible.

In my fevered, sated imagination they are advancing towards me en masse, a malevolent army of sugary warriors ready to split me open at the belly. As everyone else oooos and ahhhs, I uuur and fwwwr-raward. My all-day eating has been a gross act of unthinking greed and now I'm paying the price. I don't even bother to try the samples before me. I simply can't. I make illegible marks in the box, too sated to even lift my pencil. As the last remains are cleared away, I can't care less who won. I haul my loathsome frame out of the chair and stagger to the fresh air outside. I spot a lonesome bench, and flop onto it, sucking in great draughts of air.

This time I have pushed it too far. I'd make a wretched competitive eater. My head throbs, my stomach churns and every burp is tinged with peril. This is dangerous eating, worse than the chillies or the night on the River Severn. My discomfort is all consuming, and I never want to see food, any food, ever again. Get thee to a nunnery, and be gone.

By the time I waddle back, various jubilant teams are shaking their cups and whooping for joy. They talk of love and barbeque and passion and obsession. I can only think of getting home to bed. I wave half-heartedly at my fellow judges, muttering my goodbyes and thank yous. A few give me a knowing pat on the back, as if to commiserate with me on my first-time splurge. Next time, I promise myself, I'll take it slowly. But for the time being, I just need a long lie down and no mention of pork, pulled, Boston or otherwise. And tomorrow, if I make it through the night, I will start that green leaf diet. Absolutely. Definitely. And no more meat. Ever again.

Two days later, though, my hunger creeps back out from hiding. And thoughts turn once more to Prince's. It's late on Saturday night when I ask the concierge for a cab. He gives me a quizzical look.

'No one goes to that part of town at this time of night. Not even the locals.'

My hunger far outweighs any sense of self preservation so I smile politely and wander around the corner to get a cab.

'Not the place for a white tourist to be at this hour,' says one driver. The next says nothing, just shakes his head and drives off.

In the end, bowed but not defeated, I return to the concierge. For a small fee (50 stinking bucks), he has a friend who will pick it up. Not even this astronomical tag can dent my desperation for another bite of that sweet chicken. An hour later, and a brown paper bag arrives at my room. It is my $60 chicken (the actual food cost just $10) and worth every last cent. The heat is still there, but this time only enough to colour the batter a reddish gold. It dances cheek to cheek with the meat rather than knocking it out flat – the crust crunches, the juices squirt and that slightly dreamy, misty quality floats over my eyes.

John T. Edge rates Prince's as one of his favourite fried-chicken places. In his beautifully formed short work, *Fried Chicken: An American Story*, he writes:

> Speaking of devotion, Prince's hot chicken shack still wins mine, for their four-in-the-morning weekend closing times; for their devotion to gargantuan iron skillets from which emerge some of the savoriest chicken around; for the architectural precision with which they stack a quarter-chicken atop two slices of white bread, crowning the whole affair with a couple or three pickle slices; and for their heavy hand with the pepper wand, their tendency to swab a thigh with enough hot sauce to prod a drunken patron into a stunned semblance of sobriety.

Now John, though Southern to the core, is a white, bespectacled man about the same size as me. If he has no problems going late at night, why should I? I begin to suspect that the taxi drivers cannot be bothered to drive that far. And the concierge and his buddy are out to make a few bucks. I, of course, am the sucker. But the happiest, most sated and tingling-lipped sucker that ever did live.

CHAPTER 5

TOKYO

After returning from Tennessee, I spend a week lying on the sofa, moaning gently. I feel like an anaconda after a particularly large mammalian dinner and vow that I will never again put my gut through such exacting excess. Luckily, Tokyo is my next destination, a place where cool slivers of raw fish replace the acres of barbequed pork. But this stage may well be the most perilous of my journey so far. Because I am off to sample the fugu or puffer fish, a creature so stuffed full with deadly poison that one wrong slice on the chef's behalf can spell an excruciatingly painful end to my tour. Still, even an agonising demise seems marginally more attractive than another mouthful of incinerated chicken.

The professional prognosis is raw, to say the least.

'At best, eating puffer is a game of Russian roulette. Unless you feel that you are a professional fugu connoisseur, leave puffers alone – you will probably live longer.'

As I shuffle through Tokyo's Roponghi district towards a potentially fatal lunch, the stern words of Bruce W. Halstead MD rattle round my head. The previous two hours have been spent with my nose buried in *Dangerous Marine Animals*, Halstead's ghoulishly addictive

1959 opus, and I am ready to believe anything. In among the Stargazers ('may be fatal'), Striated Cone Shells ('death is said to be the result of cardiac failure') and Killer Clams ('drownings have occurred from divers … becoming trapped'), the puffer fish or fugu warrant more attention than most.

Dr Bruce is a man of some import, the Director, World Life Research Institute, no less. And Lieutenant Commander United States Naval Reserve. And Formerly Instructor in Tropical Medicine, Division of Preventative Medicine, US Navy Medical School, Betheda, Maryland. And not just an expert on all of peril in the sea, but a man of admirable directness too.

'It [the puffer fish] makes an excellent poisonous bait for stray cats, but a poor food for humans.' By the sounds of things, the feline population around the Halstead homestead is very much under control. 'Honey, those damned cats are back,' I can imagine him hollering through a thick beard (these naval types are always hirsute). 'Throw out another blower, will you?'

But I do start to question exactly why I am travelling across the globe in search of a fish that could kill me. At this point in time, it seems plain demented. I try to pass it off as yet another search for the ultimate travelling experience, the one I can dine out on for weeks on end. But a niggle at the back of my head tells me that this is my stupidest idea so far.

I know that fugu can be dangerous – why else would it play centre stage in this chapter – but is it mere freak-show food or an integral part of Japan's culinary heritage? As I struggle to make sense of the baffling street map trembling in my hand, last night's whisky excess seeps through every pore. I managed to get steaming drunk, gulping hugely expensive malt and talking bollocks to anyone unfortunate enough to cross my path. My last recollection was crashing some kind of banking party.

Next thing I knew, I awoke surrounded by the detritus of a wasted room service binge. Floppy sashimi sat cloying in the air-conditioned haze next to a half-eaten burger. I felt sick to the skull, and the thought of dicing with death did little for my already-fragile digestion. But I soldiered on, searching impenetrable Japanese script for any clue to my destination.

Ropponghi Hills, home to a thousand ex-pat fleshpots and displeasure domes, looks flaccid in the weak morning sun. At night, there's life of sorts – the wink and leer of neon and cheap paint sees to that. Now, though, the streets are empty, save the odd immaculate street-sweeper, brushing away remains of the previous evening's spillage. 'Sexy Pub–Kiss Me', 'Club Allure' and 'Seventh Heaven' make no effort to live up to their promises, with their shutters tightly drawn to the industrial morn. But with eyes firmly glued to the map, I take a final, hopeful right by 'Club Fairy Tale' and look ahead. A rickety set of wooden steps lead off the street, and into a small door. Over the entrance hangs a stuffed puffer fish, its face frozen in a rictus of startled indignation. I take a deep breath and wobble towards a particularly foolhardy lunch.

There's a hint of the comic about the puffer fish that is at odds with its deadly reputation. You just can't expect this bulbous, long-snouted fish – with its two pairs of Bugs Bunny teeth and Botoxed pout – to cause anything but mirth. They bumble about the seabed, eyes bulging and mouth agape, snuffling for invertebrates and algae. It's only when they're threatened that they furiously suck water into their body, inflating themselves to appear larger, and far less palatable, to any potential predator. But even in this engorged state, they look more like a character in a Miyazaki cartoon than something to be avoided.

My first sighting was equally deflating. Wandering through Tsukiji, Tokyo's legendary fish market, one early morning a few years back, I came across a tank filled with what looked like pot-bellied trout – hardly the stuff of toxic nightmares. With alabaster-tinged portly tummies and tortoiseshell tops, they seemed disappointingly ordinary.

'Ah, fugu,' smiled my Japanese host. He made a short, guttural sound and grabbed his throat. 'Vey poisonous but vey good.'

I had expected a blow-up show, or a flash of piscine menace at the very least, but they just cruised around their bubbling tank, oblivious to all around. I'd seen more menace in a Care Bear.

But when I found out more about the poison contained within their liver, gonads, intestine and skin, my attitude changed markedly. Tetrodotoxin is an immensely powerful neurotoxin, which is tasteless, odourless and totally without antidote. Perfect, then, for taking out suave Double O agents. Assaulted, in *From Russia with Love*, by a boot containing a poison dart, Bond experiences the joy of fugu at first hand.

'Numbness was creeping up Bond's body … Breathing became difficult … Bond pivoted slowly on his heel and crashed headlong to the wine-red floor.'

In the next novel, *Dr No*, the type of poison is revealed. '"It comes from the sex organs of the Japanese globefish," a neurologist told Bond's chief. "It's terrible stuff, and very quick."'

Not all of the species contain the stuff and toxicity varies from fish to fish; there are over 100 species worldwide, with 38 found in Japanese waters alone. But a six-pound Tiger fugu has enough poison to take out at least 32 healthy adults and a lethal dose for one person would easily fit on the head of a pin. Captain James Cook, that tireless transglobal coloniser, nearly met his death rather earlier than planned in 1774 when he snacked on a specimen caught just off New Caledonia.

Luckily for us [he writes in his journal] that only the liver and roe was dressed of which the two Forsters [the expedition's naturalists] and myself did but just taste. About three or four o'clock in the morning we were seized with an extraordinary weakness in all of our limbs attended with a numbness or sensation like to that caused by exposing one's hand or feet to a fire after having been pinched much by frost. I had almost lost the sense of feeling nor could I distinguish between light and heavy bodies, a quart pot full of water and a feather was the same in my hand. We each of us took a vomit and after that a sweat which gave great relief. In the morning one of the pigs which had eaten the entrails was found dead.

He had an exceptionally lucky escape.

The potency of the fugu fluctuates with the seasons, with toxicity highest in the summer spawning season. Very sensibly, the winter months are deemed fugu time, not just for the drop in poison levels but because the fish are far bigger in the colder months and supposedly taste better too. But Dr Halstead is typically frank when describing the poison's effects.

Symptoms of tingling about the lips and tongue and motor in coordination usually develop within 10–45 minutes after ingestion of the fish [a recent report shows that it can take up to 20 hours for the poison to hit]. This tingling may later spread to other parts of the body. In some instances, the numbness may involve the entire body, in which instances the victim may feel as though he were 'floating'.

It gets better.

Excessive salivation, extreme weakness, nausea, vomiting, diarrhoea, abdominal pain may follow. Twitching of the muscles, paralysis, difficulty in swallowing, loss of voice, convulsions and death by respiratory paralysis may ensue. More than 60 per cent of the victims poisoned by this fish die.

In short, it shuts down the entire nervous system, causing a slow and unbelievably painful death. And I am on my way to eat it of my own free will.

At this point, you might be wondering why in God's name people devour the damned thing. Why not leave it to its huffing, puffing and poisoning and go home for a hangover-soothing bowl of ramen noodles? Ever since hearing about it on some long-lost *Blue Peter* report, I had longed to get to Japan and try my luck.

At first, I'd assumed it was as everyday as cornflakes, a regular part of the Japanese diet. These were a race of people who read sex comics and danced in the street, dressed as Elvis. Deadly toxic fish snacks seemed an entirely natural progression. As I grew older, I began to understand Manga and the mannered teenage rebellion of Yoyogi Park. But the lure of fugu never left. Puffer has been an eastern delicacy for many thousands of years, a favourite in ancient China and Korea.

'The taste worth dying for,' wrote the eleventh-century Chinese poet Su Tung-p'o. Puffer bones are often unearthed in Japanese kitchen middens dating back centuries and there are numerous mentions in Japanese historical chronicles of death by fugu. Anyway, it's still a great delicacy in spite of, and perhaps because of, its lethal allure. It's eaten on special occasions, to warm the blood and thrill the palate but everyday tucker, it ain't. Some see it as an aphrodisiac (I've never seen the connection between near-death and sexual kicks), others a Japanese version of Russian roulette.

Donald Richie, esteemed author of *A Taste of Japan*, thinks

its consumption is such a production that consuming fugu becomes a special eating treat, a kind of food happening. And I'd agree. There is a sense of occasion when you go to eat it, heightened by the chance that it could be the last supper. It's also a form of gustatorial conspicuous consumption because fugu is expensive. I suppose you could call it 'event eating'; the chef has an 'off' night and you're curtains.

As is often the case with foods that we know little about, the hype precedes the truth. Since 1949, a complicated system of licensing has been in place, strictly controlled by the Ministry of Health and Welfare. Every fugu chef must pass a series of strict exams before they're even allowed to go near the fish; only licensed chefs are allowed to prepare fugu and the licence belongs to the individual rather than the restaurant he works in. The skill apparently lies in removing the ovaries and liver intact, leaving the slightest trace of poison to gently numb the lips. Many gourmands disagree, arguing that the numbing of the lips is mere urban myth.

I am about to find out the truth the hard way. Each prefecture has a different exam, with Tokyo being one of the most gruelling. I speak to Ken Ichiro Ooe, executive chef at the Park Hyatt's stunning Kozue, and generally held to be one of the country's experts on preparing the fish. Despite our need for a translator to understand what the other is saying, his eyes twinkle when he talks fugu.

'You have to have your licence and two years of experience before you are allowed to prepare fugu. It takes two years to train for the licence, then a further two to work under an experienced chef. So four years in all. There is one paper test then a practical one in which 17 fugus are laid out in front of you, all different species. Each fish has varying amounts of poison in its respective parts, and you must pick out five and prepare them perfectly, under the eye of the examiner.'

Each different prefecture has slightly different tests. In Tokyo, about 1,200 per year try, with a 35–40 per cent pass rate. When you're about to put your life in the hands of a man you've never met, these facts are certainly reassuring. Even better is the news that no one has died in a licensed fugu restaurant for the last 56 years. Well, there is one exception ... there always bloody is.

Fittingly, this was no mere random punter, but a 'national treasure' of a Kabuki actor called Mitsugoro Bando VIII. A leading light in this formalised and very traditional form of Japanese theatre, Bando was a man of insatiable appetites. It was January 1975 and old Mitsugoro had a hankering for the most delectable part of the fugu, the kimo or innards. Included in that was the liver, said to be the finest part of the fish.

Mr Ichiro Ooe had told me how exquisite it tasted, saying he'd tried it many times. 'It has a rich, wonderful taste like foie gras.' Poorly prepared, though, or taken from a fish with high toxic levels, it's lethal. Bando was refused his request a few times but after a while, his demands became so insistent that the chef relented, and prepared four pieces of liver. What can you say to a hungry celebrity who is not used to hearing no? At that point, the chef was probably delighted to shut him up. The other three friends decided – wisely – to give it a miss and Bando demolished every last morsel.

In less than half an hour, though, he was in the throes of the poison. His last words? 'I have eaten the death number.' Granted, it's not exactly up there with Edgar Allen Poe's anguished cry of 'Lord help my poor soul' but in Japan, four is considered unlucky.

Imagine Barbara Windsor being killed by a dodgy oyster and

you'll begin to gather the scale of the scandal. It took a full three years to conclude the court case; the wretched chef was eventually given a suspended eight-year prison sentence and put on two years' probation. There was also an out-of-court settlement of about $150,000.

Understandably, sales of fugu plummeted. 'You get one shot at running a fugu restaurant,' drawls Anthony Bourdain in *A Cook's Tour*. 'One strike and you're out.' Since 1984, it has been illegal to sell the liver, although the truly daring can enjoy it in the Southern prefecture of O-Eta, where it is still allowed.

My more immediate worry is that if there has been one recentish death, there could easily be two. I can see the piece, written 20 years from now, extolling the safety of fugu restaurants. 'After all, only two people have ever died in a licensed restaurant. One was a great kabuki actor who demanded liver. And the other, some foolish British food writer who just got unlucky.'

With this merry thought swimming slowly around my drink-addled brain, I crawl up the steps to the restaurant. It is too late to reconsider, and I have to admit feeling pretty windy. I duck sheepishly into the small doorway and find myself assailed by an instrumental version of 'Can You Feel The Love Tonight'. Please God, I pray, don't make this the last melody to ever fill my ears.

A sixteenth-century haiku I read earlier sprang to mind. 'Last night, fugu with a friend. Today, I helped carry his coffin.' And another joined the chorus, this time penned by Basho, the great seventeenth-century poet. 'I enjoyed fugu yesterday. Luckily nothing has yet occurred.'

Spurred by these happy thoughts, I introduce myself to the waiter. 'Um, Tom Parker from Park Hyatt,' I mumble, in case there is more than one puce-faced gai-jin glutton booked in for lunch that day.

'Fugu, hi,' he asks in a tone suggesting I'm in the wrong place for a burger.

'Yup,' I croak and he leads me to my seat.

By this stage, my hangover has revealed its true, grain-soaked colours; my hands are trembling uncontrollably as my body feels close to breakdown. I ask for the loo, and while in there, do a quick, and concerned, spot check on its cleanliness. All spick and span, I note with huge relief, and loo roll present and correct. This is not the sort of place you want to see a filthy lav.

I heave myself back into the main room, which is small, rectangular and virtually empty. There's certainly no getting away from what the restaurant serves – the blowfish are everywhere, grinning from posters, hanging from the ceiling and leering from silk screens. Real live ones mill about, en masse, in a shallow pond in front of me. In the far corner, a small gathering of men are huddled in close conversation. They barely register my entrance.

I sit down and eye my lunch. They eye me back, then glide off in the opposite direction, portly pashas bored by the view. For the time being, though, they seem spectacularly unconcerned. My waiter comes back, apparently amused by my presence. I get the feeling that I'm as much a novelty here as fugu in a London restaurant.

'Vey dangerous,' he grins, pointing at the fish. 'Much poison,' and feigns an agonising death.

Great, just what I need. I crank up an insincere smile and he points to the fugu-filled water before me.

'You catch?'

For a second, I thought I'd misheard him. 'Catch what?'

At this point, he hands me the most pathetic, impotent rod I've ever seen. A garden gnome would turn his tiny nose up at this limp stick. A single hook dangles off the bamboo pole, to which the waiter attaches a small piece of fish. He hands it to me, and gestures that I should give it a go. Anxious not to seem the fool – and assuming that this is very much part of the fugu experience – I aim at a plump-looking specimen and cast over. It lands with a disconsolate plop on the fish's tail, which then turns around, gulps the food and spits back the hook. My fellow fugu fans stop their murmuring for a moment to watch the gai-jin make an ass of himself. The tourist duly obliges and they return to their huddle.

'Again', my waiter implores, and attaches another piece of fish to the hook. I cast again, this time nearer to a mouth. A fat brute swans over and devours the bait in a bite. I try to hook him as he does so, but am so cack-handed that the entire rod flies over my head and clatters into the corner. A few more tries, and I admit defeat, sweating shame and pure alcohol. Seemingly bored with my less than sterling efforts, the waiter casually grabs a huge net, dips it in the water and hauls out my lunch. I look at him incredulously.

'But what about the rod?' I say pointing to the tiny stick behind me.

'Impossible,' he roars, 'but fun, yes?'

I salvage what little pride I had and nod.

'You want to hold?' To be honest, there's nothing I would rather do less. But in the spirit of picaresque adventure, I agree. The skin is leathery and the fish surprisingly heavy, gasping for air yet still managing to glare at me most unsettlingly. The waiter shouts for his friend, who appears with a Polaroid. He jumps into frame, splays his fingers into the classic Japanese cool pop band pose and captures the moment. It's still sitting here on my desk as I write, a blurred shot of a terrified man holding a very angry fish.

I am in the thick of it now, and there's no chance of escape. I consider making a break for the door but my wobbling legs just aren't up to the challenge. A plateful of fugu skin arrives first, small curls of what looks like white PVC. I pick up the first morsel and gaze at it for a few minutes, trying to build up the courage to take a nibble.

Eventually, I throw it in. The texture is akin to a tap-washer with a slight fishy tang, but it is the ponzu dipping sauce – a mixture of citrus juice and soy sauce – that adds the only excitement.

This certainly isn't a taste worth dying for, although by this stage it is too late. I have passed the point of no return and the fish has entered my body. Every hungover ache, pain and throb suddenly takes on a new significance as I imagine the poison coursing through my veins. I make a mental note of the time, counting down each moment towards my potential doom.

Sashimi follows the skin, cut so thin that you can see the design of the plate below. Great emphasis is put on the presentation of the dish, as it is with so much of Japanese cuisine. It's supposed to resemble a chrysanthemum flower, although the artistry of the chef is not quite up to that – a wilting tulip seemed more accurate. And anyway, who cares about flowers when your doom might be mere moments away? The sashimi is almost as chewy as the skin, and not exactly bursting with flavour. In contrast to the other sashimi I have eaten in Tokyo, it is a massive let-down.

I was always told that once you tasted the freshest sashimi in Tokyo, every other piece of sushi and sashimi you'd ever eaten would wither in comparison. And I always took the advice with a pinch of wasabi. Surely, it couldn't be that much superior. In California, New York or even London, the fish is equally fresh, the chefs just as talented and equally Japanese.

But my first mouthful of truly awesome o-toro sashimi (the fattiest, most expensive part of the belly) was a sensation I'll never forget. Eaten a few years ago in the illustrious surroundings of one of Tokyo's most expensive restaurants, it was as if an entire symphony of sensations had been unleashed upon my tongue; deep, blood red with streaks of white fat, the perfect cube of flesh smelt of foam-flecked waves and melted into my mouth, leaving just a smile plastered across my face. Rich and decadent, the fish also possessed an ethereal lightness that took the breath away. One mouthful of this piscine perfection, the holy alliance of the very finest freshest ingredient prepared with hard-learnt skill, made the whole ten-hour flight worth it. Compared with those tired, fishy flaps that mooch around the conveyor belt at Yo Sushi!, this was not only another league, it was another species altogether.

Anyway, the fugu sashimi is dull and disappointing, with none of the delicacy I have been expecting. Another culinary lie exposed, I think, as my teeth squeak and slip over the plastic flesh. But a thought of my impending demise soon drives out any real gripes, as 15 minutes have now passed since my first taste. My own, clumsy version of a haiku swims around my mind.

First time on the fugu today
Fifteen minutes down
And still not dead

I keep pouting my lips, checking if I can feel even the tiniest tingle … not even a trace. The other aches and pains are a more immediate worry. And when the pins and needles strike a few moments later, I really begin to sweat. This is it, I think, the end. The indignity of it all! I've always imagined going out in some style, perhaps saving a few innocent lives or coming up with some pithy epithet that will live on long after I have turned to dust. But knocked down by a fat fish. How pitifully inglorious. But the feeling passes, thankfully, and before I know it, I'm staring at a bubbling pot of broth called fuguchiri or chiri-nabe.

For those who think that Japanese food is all raw fish and rice, then the huge range of comforting classics can come as a surprise. Nabemono meals are hands-on winter fuel, where you cook the ingredients in a bubbling watery broth. Anything goes from oysters, cod and salmon to chicken, turtle and duck. Quickly cooked, you get texture from crisp vegetables and soft fish, and the broth takes on all their flavours. Sometimes you add rice and noodles at the end.

One of my favourite Japanese dishes is similar, the lyrically named shabu shabu. Here, you take paper-thin slices of intricately marbled beef and drop them, for mere moments, into a donut-shaped receptacle filled with bubbling broth. Once cooked, you can dip your slice in a nutty, sesame-based sauce or the ubiquitous ponzu. The only problem is swapping between the vast cooking chopsticks and the smaller eating ones.

By the time I've finished, it looks like I've slaughtered and sliced a cow on my table. But gai-jins are forgiven most faux pas. The noodles added at the end are the final touch, to be slurped with élan. The fugu version is rather less exciting, though hardly offensive either. First, the waiter drops the nori seaweed in the broth. Then the fish fillets, deathly white, which resemble monkfish. Noodles, tofu and enoki mushrooms all join it in this witches' cauldron. After a couple of minutes, it's all fished out and passed onto my plate. The actual flesh is, yup you've guessed it, entirely lacking in taste. If not exactly the best food I've eaten in Japan, though, it's fairly inoffensive and far preferable to smelly tofu.

I start to sink into my chair a little, relaxing as I believe I've made it. Then I feel a flash of pain, a searing twinge across my brow. Oh Christ, I've tempted fate. My heartbeat reaches a crescendo of terror, the sweat floods out of my body and I wait for the next deadly hit. Nothing. Of course, now it's too late to do anything. But will they sling my body onto the street, or at least allow me the decency of ringing an ambulance first?

As I contemplate my end, I notice another fugu in the pond, a specimen even more rotund than usual, who seems to be watching me with uncharacteristic intensity. I stop my mastication for a moment. Am

I munching on his brother? A child perhaps. Before I establish the full relationship, he turns on his tail and drifts off towards the other side.

OK, by now, I should be dead. Surely Halstead can't be lying. No, I trust the big old bearded American fella. I think I'm OK.

At this point, there is a side-splittingly hilarious trick that can be played by the wacky fugu-fiend. He drops his chopsticks on the ground, as if in the first throes of death. The sound of wood on floor causes total and immediate silence, as the rest of the restaurant turn around to stare. Donald Richie describes the scene.

'After it is discovered that this is a joke, there is good-natured laughter in the dining room and rueful silence in the kitchen.'

Jeremy Beadle, eat your heart out.

The next course, hirezake, is a real speciality and is anything but bland. The fugu fins are toasted then dropped into a cup of hot sake. Nothing had prepared me for the first sip, charred and acrid and tasting exactly like … well, burnt fish fins in booze. But as it runs down my throat, I get a flashing hint of its charms. On a truly cold day, this would certainly kick start the internal heaters. That said, I don't reckon it would set the international cocktail circuit alight. I gamely swallow it, getting ready to make my excuses and leave.

The background music has moved on to a constant loop of the harpsichord version of 'Always On My Mind', and a combination of fear, alcohol sweat and brain-numbing music is starting to take its toll. But the last ordeal is the fugu sosui, which adds rice, egg, spring onion and nori to the remaining cooking broth. It would be soothing comfort food, were it not for the thought of mopping up the poison. It goes down and I half expect flashing lights and fireworks – at the very least, a certificate – in recognition of my stunning survival.

All I do get is a vast bill, around £50, and a charming smile. Perhaps the hangover has delayed my poison reaction but as I stumble out into the winter's afternoon, the sun seems a little sharper, the light a trifle clearer. Despite the minimum risk involved in eating my lunch, I feel that even if I haven't cheated death, I might have succeeded in a cheeky bluff.

A few hours later, and I relate my tale of culinary derring-do (rather smugly) to Mr Ichiro Ooe. He asks what I think of it.

'Not a lot,' I answer, 'I think it's overrated.'

One taste of the blowfish, and suddenly I seem to know it all. He pauses for a second, then starts to talk, his translator enunciating each word for dramatic effect.

'I have eaten fugu more than a thousand times, so much so that I can tell the difference in taste between pretty much every species I've eaten. The great ones have lots of fat, and are superb. You probably need a little more experience before you make a final decision.'

In other words, shut it rookie boy. You know shit. I have just risked my life at some second-rate dive, and now the chef wanted me to try another variety, just for the balance, he says. I have spent the afternoon annoying family and friends by ignoring the nine hours' time difference and boasting of my exceptional bravery – 'Yeah, knocked it out cold and ate every scrap, liver included. Yup, lips tingled and heart stopped for a while but I'm tough, you know. Just battled on and in the end, the poison gave up.'

Knowing my penchant for hyperbole – as well as the fact that it is about five in the morning UK time – the response is more F.U. than fugu. Whatever my tall tale, the thought of eating this damned fish twice is enough to make me weep. Once a year is an understandable extravagance. But twice in a day? I may as well be goosing the Grim Reaper.

* * *

Second time around, the surroundings are rather more palatial, in the Grand Hyatt hotel. By now, I'm fairly blasé about the whole thing, perhaps too much so. The sashimi is infinitely thinner, and although chewy, has a rounded flavour. The plates are certainly more beautiful, the lacquer divine and the presentation more precise.

As I shovel in my final mouthful, though, I panic once more. My lips are numb, tingling and I've only just started. This may be a favourite moment for the true gourmand, but it scares the hell out of me. I wipe my mouth and the feeling spreads. My nose starts to run, and as I wipe it, the side of my nose burns too. Shit, I've done it this time. Text book symptoms. Motor un-coordination must be next.

Oh God, you stupid fool. You twat. I start to apologise to God profusely, apologising for my blasphemous mouth and for being remiss in visiting his house. That is, until one of the chefs notices my wide-eyed panic. He points to the red powder sitting heaped in the ponzu dressing.

'Chilli,' he smiles. 'Burning, no.'

'Oh yes, chilli, of course,' I mutter, glowing as scarlet as the powder before me. I have just spent a week at the Fiery Foods Show and I still can't tell the difference between neurotoxin and capsaicum. It doesn't say much for my palate, although fear makes even the most familiar sensations alien.

The next course consists of a white milky sac of unknown origin.

'What's this?' I ask, rolling it around my mouth. It has a soft texture, creamy and elegant in taste with a slight hint of mackerel.

'Fugu sperm,' comes the reply.

At this point, I'm beyond caring what goes into my mouth, even sperm. The relief of the chilli incident has put the rest of dinner into perspective. This tastes fantastic too. A delicately cooked 'shoulder' of fugu (if a fish can be said to possess a shoulder) is equally fine, sweet and marinated in miso. It's like the difference between a broiler chicken and a proper free-range bird. This feels less like dangerous eating than spoilt feasting and I'm beginning to see fugu's appeal.

The ceremony, presentation and even flavour is rather intoxicating. Even the nabe is superior to lunch, with a more strident flavour. The toasted fin sake, though, is pungent as is its predecessor. I reckon I turned up at the fugu equivalent of KFC this morning, only to find my Prince's Hot Chicken this evening. The experience is so different from lunch that I eventually realise the truth behind the fugu cult. Far from being mere macho eating, it actually embodies the Japanese ideal of ritual, seasonality and presentation to the highest degree. The fact that it is potentially deadly simply heightens the aesthetic appeal.

Despite any preconception to the contrary, the Japanese do not survive on a constant diet of whale meat and endless sushi. Sashimi and sushi are more treat than everyday food but it is true that their appetite for fish is second only to Iceland. And with the mile upon mile of jagged, irregular coastline, fish has always been central to the Japanese diet.

Flicking through the endless cable channels in my hotel room one night, I chance upon a report on the slaying of dolphins up in the North. Sleep is impossible, thanks to a particularly vicious bout of jet-leg that can't be beaten. I am slowly turning loco, squirming and turning and wriggling and moaning, constantly praying for blessed sleep. But the glaring red digits of the bedside clock plod slowly, agonisingly onwards towards dawn. Sweaty feet are my symptoms of extreme jet-lag, and the experience is as discombobulating as it is frustrating. So any new television comes as welcome relief.

It makes grim viewing, nevertheless, as fishermen herd hundreds of the beasts into nets – confusing their sonar by banging sticks – and slaughter them. The sea turns not red but a frothy pink, a festive colour at odds with the massacre that created it. And the noise is sickening, the cries and clicks of these terrified mammals almost childlike. But to the fishermen, these are simply beasts to catch and sell, and they don't have the luxury of anthropomorphisation. When the BBC reporter confronts them, asking if they think their trade is cruel, they reply with a weary, well-rehearsed response.

'We are fishermen and this is our traditional way of life. Why is this any different from any other kind of fishing?'

It certainly shows the difference of opinion between the Japanese and the West when it comes to eating Flipper. But is the killing of dolphins for food any worse than the factory farming of chickens and pigs in Britain? At least the dolphins get to lead natural lives until their death, rather than cooped up in squalid, shit-encrusted barns. And barely a cry is heard when the sleek and beautiful tuna is killed (save from concerned environmentalists, who see stocks dwindling dangerously). Touch a dolphin, though, and all hell breaks loose.

I realise that I will be grappling with a similar problem when I go off to Korea, later in the year, to eat dog. I would rather the dolphin and whale (and dog) wasn't killed for food, but who am I to pass judgement on a group of people who have made a living of it for hundreds of years?

The Japanese do have a taste for pretty much anything piscine and there's little doubt that the Japanese super-trawlers are ruinous towards the environment, and that their appetite for fish far outstrips an ever more precarious supply. But the dolphin and whale huggers over-simplify the problem. And their demonisation of the Japanese can seem simplistic and ill-informed. That said, if the Japanese continue to indiscriminately consume fish at the rampant rate that they do now (and we are not much better), it won't be long before the stocks are decimated for good.

* * *

By the end of my stay, the hotel seem happy to see the back of me. I give most of their residents a series of awkward, greedy questions, wondering where I can go to eat live octopus that still wriggles while you suck its tentacles. Out of season, I am eventually told. Or how about odorigui, small whitebait-like fish that are swallowed alive, squirming in a stock flavoured with vinegar? Out of season. But the food I ate every day was wonderful and no more likely to scare us Westerners than a plate of fish and chips.

We tend to fear what we don't understand, and the image of Tokyo as a neon-bathed nuthouse, where machines blow-dry your ass and used knickers are sold in vending machines, is partly true. As I had been before, I knew exactly what to expect. The mannered politeness, the utter reliability of public services, the utter conformity of the average citizen. But beneath this lies a swirling morass which I can never begin to understand, the pressure of everyday life, the lack of space, the pent-up emotion to which I will never be party.

I once went out with the marketing manager of a major hotel chain, and the evening started off as stiff and formal as could be. A few hours later, we were singing karaoke, drenched in sweat, and stumbling and grasping each other like old friends. He was so wasted that I had to pour him into a taxi at about four o'clock. He literally couldn't walk, and disappeared down the road still singing and swearing and sweating.

The next morning, I saw him and smiled. 'Big night, eh?' I said. 'I'm feeling rough.'

He looked immaculate, despite a mere two hours' sleep, and acted as if we had never met, bowing then turning on his heel and walking away.

When drunk, the Japanese male can be forgiven many things, as if it were a licence to escape the strictures and formality of everyday life. But once work starts again, the mask is raised up and try as you might, the inner person is hidden once more.

There is much in Japanese cuisine that is acceptable to even the most unadventurous eater. Tonkatsu are deep-fried slices of pork served with Worcestershire sauce, a Euro/Asian fusion of belly-filling goodness. Or the Japanese version of Veal Milanese, which is katsudon, deep fried pork cutlets served on a bowl of rice with a fresh egg mixed in.

Kare-raisu or curry rice is another hugely popular dish, appearing some time in the late nineteenth century, where Japanese officials spotted Indian passengers on a French postal ship cooking up what they described as 'aromatic mud'. It didn't really catch on until after the Second World War, when troops were fed it as part of their rations. Now, it is ubiquitous if a little bland compared to the British version.

Tempura is a slightly different variation on our much-loved deep frying while a bowl of rich, fragrant ramen (a Chinese import, like so much Japanese food), thick with succulent pork and deeply flavoured broth, is a lunch of some greatness.

In fact, I'd be far more scared eating in some provincial British towns than taking on everything that Tokyo has to offer. This is a city that worships its food.

As ever, I'm aching to get back, and travel around the entire country, feasting as I go.

My last day there is tinged with regret, first of all for leaving a country whose food I love. But equally, my next stage is Korea and the quest for dog. Somehow, I'd far rather a poisonous fish than a plateful of slowly braised puppy.

I am just over halfway through my journey and I know that the worst is still to come.

CHAPTER 6

KOREA

I like dogs. My first, Eddie, was an irascible Norfolk terrier with a taste for children's digits. Not mine, of course, although a poke while he snored by the Aga was not to be recommended. Eddie had an itchy back and was buried under the mulberry tree behind the old shed. Then there was Willie, a shaggy Lucas terrier who grinned as he wagged his tail. He would bury himself under my covers in the early morning and emerge only to snarl at my father as he tried to wake me up. These were my teenage years and we shared a mutual dislike of dawn.

His best friend, Freddie, is my mother's Jack Russell and a dog of infinite guile and charm. He had little time for my father's impromptu obedience schools, finding all the 'sit' and 'fetch' nonsense beneath him. Instead, he'd stroll off in the opposite direction to cock his leg with studied insolence. He also liked to lay vast turds on the top step of the front door, sneering at the bourgeois pretensions of the other dogs that preferred the privacy of a bush. Willie and Freddie would bugger off together for days, chasing rabbits and following them deep into their warrens. Endless dark, muddy nights were spent with one hand down a hole and the other shaking a tin of biscuits, imploring them to come out. But to no avail and more often than not, the ancient JCB was cranked up to dig them out of some ancient warren.

When my parents got divorced, the dogs went from Butch and Sundance to Ali and Frazier, with endless ripped flesh and snarlingly bloody scraps. In the end, Willie went off with my father and Freddie my mother. Peace was restored but I was wracked with guilt for leaving my dog. He used to sniff my leg disapprovingly when I went to see my dad, catching the scent of his sworn enemy and skulking under the table, hackles raised.

Willie died three years ago and I cried. Like I cried when Harry died, a wise old Labrador with grey beard and foul breath. When his son Rambo hobbled off his mortal coil, I wept too. Freddie is now 19, has one eye (the other had to be removed as the dirt from years of digging finally destroyed it) and is totally deaf. He finds his way around the house by smell, which means cocking his leg everywhere. None of us mind. He still shits on the top step of the front door.

This lengthy personal canine history does have a purpose, in that I hope it proves I'm not some ghoulish animal hater who tears the wings off butterflies and fires crossbow bolts into swans. I do prefer dogs on my knee to on my plate. And I can't say that I am particularly excited by the prospect of travelling all the way to Korea to sup on some canine stew (although the rest of their fiery cuisine is a mouthwatering prospect).

Of all the journeys taken on my culinary adventure, I am dreading this the most. Elsewhere, I have been excited to be getting my teeth into the weird, wonderful and downright disgusting. But nothing, from the threat of casual violence to the decimation of my taste buds, can prepare me for this step of the journey. By this stage, I thought I'd be suitably hardened and able to eat anything that came my way, toughened by the months of perilous munching. But the nearer Korea looms, the more I panic. I forget the ongoing quest for the ortolans (the last email simply read, 'bird flu spreading and our friends look scarce. Hold out little hope now') and my dreams are filled with dog soup.

I thought my feelings on the subject, my rational arguments, were strong enough to overcome my repulsion, the logical telling the emotion exactly where to go. I had little idea, though, of those sentimental ties that make it so hard.

That's because the issue of eating dog is too often clouded in hysteria, misinformation, xenophobia and downright hypocrisy. Forget genocide, global warming and gun crime. If you really want to get the British choking on their toast and marmalade, write a balanced piece on the consumption of dog meat.

I was once told by an editor at a Sunday newspaper that there is more chance of getting an orgy on the cover of the magazine than there was of including a piece in defence of eating dog within. Paedophiles and rapists often get an easier ride than those nefarious foreign devils that gorge on man's best friend. And even the cuddliest grannies get gung-ho at the very thought. Perhaps, though, we should look a little more closely at our own eating habits – the hideous factory farms where pigs and chickens live wretched, squalid lives to provide us with cheap meat – before we rush to condemn the habits of others. There is no more actual risk in eating a well-cooked piece of dog than there is in eating a rump of beef. There are no poisonous glands to cut out, or danger inherent in killing the beast. Anyway, who are we to judge the traditions and culture of a country the majority of us know next to nothing about?

It's not as if the eating of dog is a recent phenomenon. 'Dog meat has been eaten by man through all his history,' writes Calvin W. Schwabe in *Unmentionable Cuisine*, his scholarly tract on all things gruesomely edible. And why not? Dogs provided a cheap and relatively abundant source of meat and our ancestors were not in the slightest bit encumbered by the gooey anthropomorphisation of animals we suffer today. As Schwabe argues:

> British and American abhorrence of dog meat eating … has been so forcefully and insensitively conveyed to other peoples who traditionally obtained badly needed protein from such sources that the practice is being hidden or has even become illegal, as now in Taiwan. What a disservice to mankind to promote one's own irrational hang-ups, particularly concerning so important a matter as food.

Schwabe is able to stand back and observe from an objective distance. Many of us find it impossible. The practice of eating dog is ancient, first recorded (though it almost certainly took place before this) around 500 BC in the Chinese *Li Chi*, a guide to the traditional ritual. That recipe was dog liver, barded in its own fat.

And thinking about it, I'd probably far rather eat the internal organs than the flesh itself. It seems more removed, easier to bolt it down without chewing. Pliny, in his *Natural History* of AD 77, talks at length about the tradition of dog meat and its ritualistic implications.

> The habits of our ancestors lead me to say something else about dogs. The meat of nursing puppies was considered such a pure foodstuff that it was used to appease enemy gods more than any other sacrificial offering. Genita Mana (goddess of childbirth) was honoured with a dog sacrifice, and puppy meat is, even today, served at meals in honour of the deity. We know from the

plays of Plautus [comedy playwright of around 200 BC] that it was eaten a great deal in former times.

When the Mongolians (from where the American Indian originated) sailed across the Bering Sea into what is now North America, they brought dogs with them to fill their bellies. And when the European settlers and explorers set foot in the New World, they counted nearly 20 varieties of dog, most of them raised specially for the table. I wonder if they attached the same significance to rare breeds as we do today with cows, sheep and chickens.

'Say, Attilla, have you tried this fantastic red setter? It's fed on an all-natural diet with lots of space to pant about it. Then it's killed and hung for ten days for maximum flavour. I tell ye, this dog is superb.'

Puppies were far preferred for their plumpness and succulence. Specially fattened on dried fruit (to give a sweet tang to their flesh, just as acorns beautifully scent the flesh of certain pigs), they were hung for added tenderness then marinated in buffalo fat, skewered on sticks and cooked over an open fire. Hernan Cortes, arriving on the shores of Mexico in 1519, found that the Aztecs, under the leadership of Moctezuma, had just two kinds of domesticated livestock – the turkey and the dog (they had pretty much devoured all the wild game in their empire). The latter was 'regarded as a useful but inferior meat' according to Reay Tannahill and a contemporary report of the time said the meats were always served together, 'the turkey meat was put on top and the dog underneath, to make it seem more' (Fr. Bernardino de Sahagun, *Historia general de las cosas de Nueva España*, sixteenth century).

The preferred species was the Mexican hairless dog (the flesh was sufficiently unmuscular to be palatable) and one report written during the time of conquest recorded that a market near what is now Mexico City sold over 400 fattened dogs per week as food. Apparently, every breed tastes different with the poodle more greasy and lamb-like in taste while the St Bernard is rather more beefy. Although I was dreading the thought of eating dog, it was mainly because of the cruel conditions in which they're raised. Or so I told myself.

But breed came into it too. Roast Jack Russell or spit-roast Irish Wolfhound fill me with revulsion but I have no such compassion when it comes to those annoying little fashion accessories that seem put on this earth to yap and shit. I look at a Chihuahua, sniffling and hairless, and feel nothing but disdain. These mutts are just asking to be thrown in the pot.

For all my talk of lofty ideals and a greater tolerance of culinary relativism, I'm just as subjective as anybody else. I just pray that my choice will be neatly chopped up into edible, bite-size chunks like the faceless, vacuum-packed supermarket chicken breast. The link between living beast and steaming soup will have to be distant. So I am a hypocrite. I bang on about the link between living animal and the meat on your plate being crucial, that we accept death as a necessary part of eating meat. Yet faced with a basket of fluffy puppies – and told to choose one for my lunch – I'm certain that I will lack the courage of my convictions.

I delve deep into the bowels of the London Library, searching for evidence that might salve my ragged conscience. The Polynesians have long appreciated the special charms of the dog. Traditionally strangled to conserve blood, the animal would be cooked in an imu or ground oven. Puppies were spatchcocked then grilled over hot coals. Now I realise I'm in full, po-faced historical mode here, but 'spatchcocked' puppy? I've always loved this word, but am more used to applying it to chickens, just before I douse them with lemon and oil and throw them on the barbie. Its original meaning is just a speedy way of splitting and cooking a chicken or game bird by taking out the backbone. But it sounds somehow comical with a puppy, like a fric-assee of Lhasa Apsong.

These Polynesians had a taste for a particular type of terrier and in 1838, W.S.W. Ruschenberger, a ship's surgeon, alighted in the Sandwich Islands (now Hawaii) for a spot of lunch. In his *Voyage Round the World*, he has first-hand experience of a doggy feast:

> Near every place at table was a fine young dog, the flesh of which was declared to be excellent by all who partook of it. To my palate its taste was what I can imagine would result from mingling the flavour of pig and lamb; and I did not hesitate to make my dinner of it, in spite of some qualms at the first mouthful. I must confess, when I reflected that the puppy now trussed up before us, might have been the affectionate and frolicsome companion of some Hawaiian fair – they all have pet pigs or puppies – I felt as if dog eating were only a low grade of cannibalism. What eat poor Ponto?

He goes on to quote a mawkish poem about the dog as 'the firmest friend, / The first to welcome, foremost to defend'. But his sentiment is cut short by a welcome dose of culinary pragmatism:

> However, the edible dog is not one of your common curs, but a dainty animal fed exclusively on vegetables, chiefly taro (a root), in the form of poe (dough), and at the age of 2 years is considered a dish wherewith to regale royalty.

No street mutt this, but the Hawaiian equivalent of Kobe cattle in Japan, the type that are massaged to ensure their fat is evenly spread and played soothing music before drifting off to sleep. For the Aloha dogs, I don't reckon life was all that bad.

One of my favourite books on the subject is Peter Lund Simmonds' exhaustive 1859 tome *The Curiosities of Food (or the Dainties and Delicacies of Different Nations Obtained from the Animal Kingdom)*. In between the chapter on Pachydermata (handy tips on 'Baked elephants' paws' and 'Cutting up the elephant') and the 'fried rattlesnake' of the Reptila section, you'll find a lengthy treatise on dogs in the 'Quadruma' section, placed somewhere between lions and bandicoots.

> In China, the dog is fattened for the table and the flesh of dogs is as much liked by them as mutton is by us. [The] domestic dog of China [...] is uniformly one variety, about the size of a moderate spaniel, of a pale yellow, and occasionally black colour, with coarse bristly hair on the back, sharp upright ears, and peaked head, not unlike a fox's, with a tail curled over the rump.

He gives us little on the actual taste, instead talking of its ubiquity.

> At Canton, the hind quarters of dogs are seen hanging up in the most prominent parts of the shops exposed for sale. They are considered by the Chinese as a most dainty food, and are consumed by both rich and poor.

Even the so-called 'civilised world' enjoyed an occasional bite of canine flesh. In *History of the Oregon Trail* (1844), John Dunn tells the story of a Canadian cook wondering what to prepare on board for an old and dear friend. As the dog was 'a favourite dish among Canadian voyageurs or boatmen', he decides to give his friend a treat. The friend enjoys every last morsel, licking the plate and proclaiming it 'beautiful'. The cook then asks him his thoughts on the meat. The friend contemplates his repast for a moment, then decides on goat.

'Yes,' says the cook, 'you have been eating from a goat with von long tail, that don't like grass and heather.'

The friend is perplexed and asks for further explanation.

'Vy you see,' replies the cook, 'it was my best dog you have dined from.'

I imagine that the chef said this with a beaming smile, waiting for the gratitude to rain down upon his head. But the friend was less than happy.

"The old Boatswain stormed and swore; and then ran as fast as possible to the vessel to get a little rum for his stomach. He vowed that he never again wished to dine with a Canadian cook, or eat pet dogs.'

I was once in Delhi, in some shithole hostel, and ordered a room-service chicken curry. It appeared a few hours later with a vast leg joint that was certainly not avian. I rang the front desk to complain, thinking it might be a cat. And the man at the other end told me to count myself lucky. He himself was very partial to cat and you got far more meat than a measly chicken leg. I should be grateful, if it was indeed a cat, not angry. I rather wish I had tried it but at the time, I was but a sallow youth without a taste for exotic meats.

If a friend cooked up some surprise mutt for me, my feeling would be similar to the unfortunate Canadian. But it shows that the revulsion at eating man's best friend is not a uniquely modern condition. Alexis Soyer, one of the first celebrity chefs of the nineteenth century (he was chef at the Reform Club, advised the British army on food in the Crimea and opened up kitchens in Dublin during the Irish Famine to help the poor), seemed acutely embarrassed to bring up such an indelicate subject in his 1853 history of world food, *The Pantropheon*. He starts cautiously:

We must beg pardon of the reader for informing him that the dog presented a very relishing dish to many nations advanced in culinary science. To them, one of these animals, young, plump, and delicately prepared, appeared excellent food.

He distances himself from such a seemingly barbaric act with his deeply apologetic tone, as if he was held partly responsible for the Greeks' unusual lapse of good taste. He painfully continues:

The Greeks, that people so charming by their seductive folly, their love of the arts, their poetic civilization, and the intelligent spirit of research presiding over their dishes – the Greeks (we grieve to say it) ate dogs and even dared to think them good; the grave Hippocrates himself – the most wise, the least gluttonous, and therefore the most impartial of their physicians was convinced that this quadruped furnished a wholesome and, at the same time, a light food.

Yet even after this short walkies through the dog's culinary history, Korea is still seen as the worst offender of all, a barbarous land where dog flesh makes up the mainstay of their diet and dogs spend their short, miserable lives hiding from the evil dogcatchers. Korea is far from being the only country with a taste for dog, yet in the minds of most British, it's their defining trait. I asked dozens of people for their views on the country and the huge majority mentioned either the 2002 World Cup (where the South Korean giant-slayers rode their skill, luck and determination to the semi-final, vanquishing Poland, Portugal, Italy and Spain on the way) or dog.

The South Korean government occasionally tries to pander to global outrage of this ancient custom by sporadically banning dog restaurants, forcing them to close down. When they put this into action during the 1988 Olympic Games, locals reacted to the news with fury. But it was a token gesture and the moment the hordes of foreign athletes and press had sloped off home, the dog-houses slowly began to reopen and life went back to normal.

The arrival of the 2002 World Cup saw a similar international campaign to bully the Koreans out of eating dog. FIFA President Sepp Blatter bossily announced that the practice was harming the country's international image. Don't worry about the corruption and human rights abuses of other competing countries. Nope, wag your finger at a country for eating a food with which you disagree. As ever, the South Korean government made some soothing noises, the restaurants went quietly but no ban came into place. In reality, the dog is not a staple food in Korea, more of a traditional seasonal speciality. It's seen as an animal of great power. As the dog doesn't sweat (save through its tongue), it is believed to have a huge amount of latent energy locked within its body that, when eaten, is transferred to the consumer.

Summer is the most popular season, as the meat is supposed to stim-ulate you. For an awful moment, I think that it will be impossible to find in the winter (when I arrive in Seoul) but thankfully, a number of restaurants are open throughout the year. Dog is good for the yang (the hot, male part of human nature in contrast to the cool, female yin) and also recommended for liver ailments, malaria and jaundice. In a country where traditional medicines are still very much an accepted part of life, these properties are taken seriously.

But the main attraction is connected with virility, tumescence and aphrodisiac powers.

'One bowl of posintang [dog soup] gives you long-time sexy,' a taxi driver tells me with a toothy grin. 'All night long, no stop, very strong.'

I join in the macho banter, telling him I'm off to eat not just one but two bowls of dog soup.

'Haaa,' he says, 'then double fucky. You the big man.'

I'm not entirely immune to this sort of flattery so nod in a suitably manly way, scratch my balls and even begin to convince myself that this whole trip will be a breeze. I'll go for a big soup and maybe some stew. And got to have the bollocks too, I suppose. Big chat, as usual, and totally different from the imminent reality.

Dog is more popular with men than with women, for obvious reasons, though some indulge. The younger generation is not so keen, often sharing the views of their Western counterparts. The main dog connoisseurs group is middle-aged and older men, going out en masse just as we might go down to the pub.

It's as much a male bonding experience as it is a gastronomic treat and vast quantities of local booze are poured down their throats. I talk to Sid Hardy, the lean, rangy head chef at Seoul's Grand Hyatt who has had many experiences of eating dog meat with his Korean chefs.

'Just make sure you have the soup rather than the braised, as this latter dish has an incredibly strong taste,' he warns. And he admits that it is a little disconcerting to see the wretched dogs in their kennels as he goes out for a pee. I also hear endless tales from other ex-pat chefs across Asia about going to eat posintang.

One immense Swiss man, Markus, passes on a few tips. 'The Korean and Chinese love to watch the foreigner eat the dog and it's a source of huge amusement if you show any discomfort.' He grimaces a little at the memory. 'You must show enthusiasm and respect throughout, and don't look down your nose disapprovingly. Keep whacking down the sojou, a Korean drink that seems a little weak but provides the bastard of all hangovers and if they offer you the balls, then you're truly honoured. Bite down and keep 'em down, that's my advice.'

His words do little to calm a quivering stomach and an increasingly guilty conscience.

I find Seoul a lonely, industrial city, rougher, more raw and alien than other Far Eastern cities I'd been to. It lacks the comforting bustle of Hong Kong and you certainly don't walk around with the childlike awe inspired by Tokyo. As I gaze out from my hotel room over the endless acres of concrete blocks and metal pylons, I feel a very long way from home.

There has been no romantic image of Korea in my head. Unlike Sicily and Laos, two destinations coming up towards the end of my journey, I have given it little thought. Sicily is the home of the Mafia and good food, a place I feel I know and understand intimately despite only having passed through twice. And I see Laos as a hotspot of fading Communist espionage, where MI6 and the CIA still battle for dominance against the long-passed Communist threat. In fact, these two places seem sun-kissed and all-embracing, an escape from the stifling grey of my present destination. I look forward to them, willing on the days where I'd be really travelling.

I have just spent Christmas and New Year with my wife, family and friends. No worrying about flights or hotel checkout times or interesting local cuisine. Christ, even the turkey tastes good when eaten in the middle of my voyage. Usually, I can't stand this bland, ridiculous bird. This year, it is fine, a link to the other 25 or so Christmases I can remember. They never change and this year, I love every ghastly mince pie and paper hat all the more. I have got used to the warm, easy flow of comfortable communal life. Despite my visit to Korea lasting a mere ten days, I am wrenched away from the comfortable rut of everyday existence.

From my bed in Seoul, every memory of my wife and home seems a hundred times sweeter. Even Clarkson, gurning away on BBC

World, can't lift me from my gloom. It isn't that I am surviving in some shack without heat or running water. Far from it: the hotel is a brutally efficient concrete shell, a temple to the executive traveller containing all the piano bars, cable TV and shoe-polishing services any self-respecting computer salesman could dream of. But I couldn't shake off a sense of true isolation, being in a place so alien in every respect. That's not to say Seoul is an ugly city. Charmless, perhaps, but possessed of a mellow beauty too; turning a corner, you'll suddenly happen across a verdant park or winding backstreet that comes as a welcome break to the incessant grey around you.

The Korean people have a reputation for being brusque, dirty, even base. 'We're always forgotten over Japan and China, but our cuisine is rich and varied and we love to eat,' says one charming Korean lady – the widow of a newspaper magnate – who has lived in London for ten years. 'It might seem messy, and the people rude, but it's just our way.'

I find the vast majority of Koreans I meet to be easygoing and ever-helpful. They may lack the fixed smile and ornate subservience of the Japanese, but this, to me, is no bad thing. You never know what seethes behind that immaculate Japanese façade and Koreans tend to be more open. And they are certainly a lot less brusque than your average Londoner.

'It's the forgotten country, a sort of afterthought to China and Japan,' she continues, delighted that I am going out to try the food. 'I'm so delighted that you're going … you'll love it.'

I don't have the heart to tell her I am after a dog. It seems somehow insulting, that thousands of years of her country's culture and history are swept aside in my shallow quest for a taste of mutt.

The traffic in Seoul is brutal. As in so many Asian countries, the rule of the road is simple – size matters. Trucks mow through the streets, hand fixed on horn. They stop for no one. Buses elbow cars to the side and cars jostle motorbikes onto the pavement. Piled high with boxes, these speeding two-wheelers treat the walkway as another lane, not dropping their speed for a moment. The pedestrian is at the bottom of this spewing pile, and crossing a busy road can turn into a terrifying ordeal.

Democracy is a recent arrival to the country, only arriving in 1988. Before then, Koreans were not allowed to travel out of the country at all. And just ten years back, the sprawling view from my hotel room – all steel and concrete – was little more than a motley collection of paddy fields.

I think back to the once-tiny fishing village of Shanghai. A huge American army contingent dominates the Itaewon area below me, in their role as protectors of democracy. The North – a mere 55 km away – is still a constant threat, and tensions are invariably high. The road below my hotel is home to an uninspiring mix of McDonald's, Outback Steakhouses and shabby pizza parlours, a little corner of America on the edge of this great Asian city. Young American soldiers, with the uniform swagger of a resident superpower, throng the bars and burger joints, snacking on Big Macs and Hershey bars, and steering clear of native cuisine. They venture out only to eat, drink or to get the newest Hollywood blockbuster on pirate DVD. The rest of the city is left to its residents.

The Korean cuisine has never caught on in Britain like those of India, China or Thailand. Although there are a smattering of Korean places in the big cities, our immigrant Korean population is relatively small. With its obsession with preserved, fermented vegetables (kimchi or kimchee) and liberal use of garlic and chilli, it lacks the familiar comfort of the curry or the fragrance of Thai cooking. For the less-adventurous eater – or one with a sensitive palate – it seems to offer little and may be a little too brusque for our tender national palate.

But the reality is that Korean cuisine is wide and varied, offering elegant, royal cuisine as well as more earthy peasant fare. You can snack on pancakes (jon) stuffed full with fish, meat and vegetables, fill your belly with hearty stews and cook your own beef in the ever-popular Korean barbeque or bulgogi, perhaps the most famous dish. In the everyday, peasant-inspired cuisine, ingredients are always fresh and the flavours strident. Rice is eaten with everything throughout the year and provides a useful sop for an overdose of chilli. Kimchee is ubiquitous at every Korean table, as essential a part of any eating as salt and pepper is to us.

'Pungency is one of those indispensable tastes in every Korean meal, necessary for stimulating the flow of saliva and the appetite,' writes Lee o-Young in *The Kimchee Cookbook*, and it's certainly hard to escape a whiff of 'controlled spoilage' at any Korean meal. Like the smelly tofu in Shanghai or the natto in Japan, it's an acquired taste although infinitely more palatable.

Just as all the countries in South East Asia use fermented fish sauce to add depth and flavour to their food, Korean cuisine does so with kimchee, soybean sauce, soybean paste and the ever-present chilli paste. To most Europeans (aside from the Germans, who munch their way through mountains of sauerkraut every month), the idea of rotten cabbage is a filthy one. Most of my friends tend to turn up their noses when faced with a slippery pile of kimchee, but the Korean restaurants over here tend not to do justice to the dish. When properly prepared, it tickles the tongue rather than bludgeons it and the soft crunch of the texture is as important as the flavour. There are literally hundreds of different varieties, made from cucumber, lettuce, aubergine, watercress, chive, radish, gourd or turnip, making the best use of seasonal

produce. In the couple of weeks I spent in Seoul, I began to appreciate all the nuances and subtleties of this national dish. Faced with the
prospect of eating it daily, though, I'm a little less keen.

'There's nothing refined about Korean food,' says Sid the chef.
'It's either all boiled up together or all thrown and stir-fried together.'

This is certainly true of the everyday cuisine and the flavours are
bold and brash, angry bovver boys in contrast to Japan's more refined
maiden. But Sid's views are certainly not true of every part of their
cuisine. It's not all palate-stripping heat and pungency and the royal
cuisine is capable of great refinement and subtlety too, as I find at a
dinner with the Hongs.

Mr Hong, a newspaper owner, is away on business but his wife
plays host, alongside their son, Jeongdo, educated in the States.
Buried in the diplomatic area beneath my hotel, their house is all cool,
clean lines and neat minimalism. They are an upper-class Korean
family who embrace the modern without ever forgetting their past.
There is French white wine, silver cutlery and pots of kimchee
fermenting in the garden. Yet one room is kept for the family prayers
and celebrations, with an exquisite paper floor and a chest containing
ritually important items.

As I walk in, I suddenly feel embarrassed at my shabby appearance
(I have managed to dig out a crumpled linen jacket but compared to
Jeongdo's immaculate suit and Mrs Hong's elegant silks, I look like an
incontinent tramp). They are kind and generous hosts and I feel guilty
revelling in their hospitality before ruining it all by asking about dog.
But if I am going to learn anything outside of a book, I have to ask.

When I do eventually get around to it, after much faltering and
spluttering, the tone seems immediately lowered. Yet they are gracious
enough to indulge me. They agree that it is a mainly male delicacy,
although totally classless.

Jeongdo reckons that only about one in five people ate it. 'It's said to stir the blood and invigorate you. The heavy spices are used to disguise the strong tastes,' he says, 'although neither my mother or I eat it, as we're Buddhists.'

I leave it at that.

Dinner is a revelation, classical and restrained. The only nod to Western culture is a flinty Chablis. A light rice porridge comes first, sweet and flavoured with red ginseng (the finest quality) and dates. It tiptoes across the tongue in ballet shoes. Prawns, abalone and bamboo shoot are next, bathed in a pine nut dressing. Again, this is a subtle mixture of textures (the soft and the crunchy) in which every flavour could be tasted separately – refreshing and clean. Then ethereal dumplings, plump pillows stuffed with shards of white crab meat and spring onions. They come with a dipping sauce of Korean soy sauce, lighter and less strident than the Japanese version.

In fact, the only potentially embarrassing moment comes with beef. Served in a searing hot stone container, the meat sizzles as it sits on the table. But as guest of honour, I'm given a chunk of white sinew. This is the choice cut and Jeongdo's favourite comfort food, but as I lift the ball of fibrous, fatty muck to my mouth, my stomach decides it's having none of it and I retch involuntarily. The Hongs seem more embarrassed than me, but try as I might, I can't get it anywhere near my mouth.

Texture is an essential part of every cuisine in the world; how food feels in our mouth is nearly as important as how it actually tastes. The Asians are often said to be obsessed with texture and they certainly appreciate the soft blandness of jellyfish or bird's nest or shark's fin more than we do. These things have no taste, just a rich, gelatinous texture. I can eat the slimy and the slippery with little problem but the gristle knocks me flat.

It's certainly a hangover from childhood, where school mince would be peppered with chunks of the stuff, and they'd squeak around the mouth, rough and inedible. Yet we were forced to eat every scrap on our plate, so this filthy cartilage or unknown body part had to be swallowed. Fat is fine but gristle … gristle is textural overload of the wrong kind, an overwhelming gag inducer that chills me to the bone, Insects, small reptiles, blood and slugs – nothing is a patch on that fearsome moment where your teeth draw back in repulsion from that first uneven bite, the part of the animal that just doesn't want to go quietly.

So seeing it in its purest form, unadorned by flaccid gravy or floury sauce, is for me a vision of hell. The Hongs realise this, smile and say it is not to all tastes. I put it down with a sigh of relief and go to work wrapping the exceptionally tender, fatty beef in lettuce or kimchee (there is white cabbage and radish, both made every autumn). Just as my belly begins to sag into its usual post-prandial position, I realise that there is more to come. 'These are just the appetisers,' explains Mrs Hong.

The Korean main course is always rice and noodles. I have visions of China and Tennessee all over again, yet it turns out to be just cold noodles paddling in a light kimchee broth. On paper, this might sound truly horrific but it has a grace that belies the description. Then just fruit. Aside from the sheer kindness of the Hongs, the dinner is important in that it gives me a taste of another side of the Korean cuisine I probably would have missed. It provides a welcome break from the more earthy flavours and the chance to speak, in English, with someone other than a foreign executive chef.

That's not to say the everyday food is inedible, far from it. These staples are exactly what the belly requires on a cold winter's evening.

Lunch the next day was glorious. Despite the usual difficulties in finding the recommended restaurants (Seoul addresses tend towards the vague and my taxi driver spends 20 minutes matching the symbols on the card to the mind-boggling display of script on signs up buildings), I get to the right place. At least, I assume it is as it specialised in pimimbab, a hearty rice dish and thankfully, there is a picture menu which avoids the usual translation worries.

Once again, I feel hopeless and pathetic at not speaking a word of the language. By now, I am used to it but it does make me feel even more like the short-sighted outsider. The ubiquitous kimchee arrives first, white and fiery, along with a chewy (squid-based, I think) mess that I pick and poke. Then the pimimbab is plonked down on the table, hissing and steaming in its hot, porous stone bowl. Just one glance and you can see this is proper comfort food, the sort of grub devoured by ancient warriors on their way to behead some evil warlord. You add your own spice then mix in a raw egg that cooks into gooey, unctuous strands. The soft rice on top contrasts with the pieces burnt brittle by the heat of the bowl; crisp vegetables add crunch, tender meat chew, and all's held in this fantastically eggy embrace.

For the first time, I actually start to relax and enjoy being in an Asian country 5,000 miles from home. It's the universal power of good food to make the world around you seem more bearable. Chewing away happily, I catch the eye of another Korean diner, doing the same. Ours eyes meet for a moment and we nod in mutual appreciation. In the warm, self-satisfied glow that follows, I almost forget I'm here to see a man about a dog.

Yet that one bowl of crunchy, sticky rice puts me into good spirits for the rest of the day and I potter about the local markets, trying to identify curious medicinal roots while avoiding being knocked down by the pavement Evel Knievels. There's so much bounce in my step on the way to dinner that I almost take off. Bulgogi is another Korean classic, better known here as barbequed beef. I enter what looks like a four-storey barbeque superstore and am immediately engulfed in the sweet scent of sizzling cow.

After lots of pointing and nodding, I'm shown to a table. They're specially adapted, with a coal brazier in the centre, topped by a griddle. Above this is a metal pipe that whisks away the fumes. The waitress is not at all happy to see me, though I never quite work out why. Every time I try to order, she grunts and turns away. She probably has every reason to despise the gawky foreigner in her charge but I soon tire of her spitting rage and try to ingratiate myself with a softer, more friendly face beside her.

Miss Grumpy is having none of it. 'No,' she hisses in perfect English, 'I am your waitress.'

I hardly dare speak again and point gingerly to my choice. She sniffs slightly, as if I had made the wrong choice, only to return moments later with my raw food. The sizzling coals and Miss Grumpy seem well-matched and when my first slice is cooked to old boot, I timidly ask that they leave it rare.

'Um, sorry, would there be any chance of getting it a tiny bit less cooked,' I pleaded, 'you know, a little more bloody.' 'Blood?' she sneers. 'Why you want blood?' 'No, less cooked,' I stutter and make a move to take the beef off the grill. She swats my hand aside. 'No touch,' she snarls and that is that.

You pay according to the quality of your beef (the more fat-marbled, the better). Once it has been cooked (or overcooked), you have a choice of wrappings, from lettuce and cabbage to the slightly aniseed flavour of sesame leaf. Then you have an array of sauces in which to dip your meat and leaf package. The combination of hot meat and cool, crisp lettuce is fundamentally satisfying, especially when the beef is sweet and meltingly tender, tinged with a charcoal crust.

The dinner is far too rushed, even for a person who eats too fast. I try to sit around and read, but this is not encouraged. I am probably being a little harsh on the waitress. She is being bawled at by sweaty groups of boozy businessmen, of whom you would get a glimpse as the sliding door of a private room opened and closed. At the start, they are neat as a church choir, upright and respectable. But my final glimpse sees crumpled shirts, steamed up glasses and three of the ten men passed out on the table. As I left, I looked closely at any colouring on my silver chopsticks. The Koreans still use metal chopsticks, dating back to the days of royalty, when silver chopsticks would tarnish at any sign of poison. It ensured the assassin's hand was tied. Judging by the mood of this waitress, though, the threat was real enough.

The street food, on the other hand, is far less exciting. Insadong is the artistic part of Seoul (or so it says in the guidebook, anyway, and who am I to argue?), divided by a small, winding road that meanders through shops filled with every kind of calligraphy brush, ink and paper. Small stalls line the route, selling hot dogs fried in batter, sweet pastries in the shape of various animals (like waffles), sticky sweets and long, opaque strips of dried cuttlefish and octopus.

One stall catches my attention, a little more shabby than the rest with two steaming pots and a peculiar smell. One pot contains tiny molluscs, snails with a sharp shell, sold by the weight and picked out with a pin. The other contains what looks like a mass of miniature alien eggs, the sort of things that grow up to suck faces and burst out of unsuspecting stomachs. Yellowy brown in colour, they are over an inch long and segmented. I ask the toothless, grinning woman what they are. She hawks, spits and points to a dirty scrap of silk on the next door stall.

It takes a moment or two to realise that they are silk worm pupae, a hugely popular children's snack sold in small paper cups. The old woman takes my money without even looking up and hands me my bugs' eggs. I pick one up; the skin is soft and leathery, the whole thing slightly squashy between the fingers. As I lift up one of these monsters to my mouth, I catch a faint, musty smell. Somewhere between rotting leaves and something more sinister. I throw it in and chew – the casing is tough, holding out for at least four chomps. Then I get through to the centre and wish I never had.

A dirty creamy goo spurts onto my tongue, producing one of the most repellent tastes I have ever experienced. A fetid rottenness, far more strident than even the smelly tofu, engulfs my mouth, spreading its filth to every corner. Every cell in my body is suffused with this festering horror and all I can think of is freshly dug graves. That sense of the everyday hole somehow made awful and repulsive by the thought of a coffin going in. These bugs taste of death. That's the only way I can explain it. The leathery case stays in one piece and the thought of the larvae in my mouth becomes as foul as the taste. The texture is tough and chewy and now rendered obscene. How can a creature that produces something so soft and exquisite, silk, taste so utterly degraded?

I look for a place to safely spit out this disgusting beast and find none. Instead, I carefully regurgitate it onto my hand and throw the monster into the gutter. The goo refuses to budge, coating my teeth and tongue, along with small chunks of the larvae jacket. This unassuming bug had just provided the low point of my journey so far. Insects might seem like one of the more frightening of foods but I have found that most of this disgust comes from long-held preconceptions. So I have only just rid my imagination of the link between insect and disgust when this bastard comes and puts me straight back to square one.

For hours after, I can't rid my mouth of that damp earthy spectre, despite constant dousings with Coke, beer, even vodka. The mere memory still makes me retch. As I creep back past the stall, the woman – who has watched my every stumble with increasing joy – calls out to me. 'You no like,' she cackles before filling her wrinkled palm with at least ten of the buggers and throwing them into her mouth with great gusto. I turn an even pucer shade of pale and rush back towards the relative safety of my hotel.

Alien bugs aside, my eating experiences prove that Korea is far removed from the stereotype of dog smorgasbord. Yet the popular misconception only gets stronger. Thanks, in part, to the rantings of the tabloid press, Korea is a place where 'How much is that doggie in the window' is a precursor to dinner rather than the start of a popular song. We are led to believe that dog-catchers stalk the street with long nails and hooded eyes, scooping up any unwary mutt and stuffing it into a filthy, wriggling bag. Every restaurant will delight, they say, in tricking you into eating sautéed Pekinese's brains, when you just wanted a bowl of chicken.

'Watch what you eat,' warned a friend before I left. 'It's all dog meat. It happened to a friend when he got a Labrador leg in his soup.'

I wasn't entirely sure how this 'friend of a friend' was so certain as to the exact breed but the reaction was far from unique.

My taxi driver to Heathrow had his own take on the subject. 'That's all they live on, them Koreans, dog and rice. Disgusting, they are,' he spluttered, the back of his neck turning crimson with rage. 'Savages! I had a bloke in my cab, right, just where you are now. Chinese, Japanese, Korean, I don't know. All look the bloody same.'

He paused to swear furiously at some poor soul impudent enough to use a zebra crossing, then continued. 'I mean, it's not bloody right is it, that lot eating them dogs.' He seemed convinced that Koreans would go as far as to kidnap your own pets from under your nose, and take them over to their country as hand-luggage. I muttered a few words, suggesting that he might be exaggerating the whole thing just a touch. But by now, he was in full flow.

'Absolutely disgusting. The cruelty of it all makes me sick.' He was quite happy to admit eating cheap pork and chicken. 'Dogs are different, though, man's best friend and all that. Bloody barbarians.'

And it's not just cab drivers who subscribe to this view. Almost all of Britain seems to agree. Their disgust is not directed at the way in which the animal is raised. No, it's about eating our pets. It's like when those nice fluffy seals are clubbed to death by evil foreigners. Yet few could care less about the wholesale slaughter of rattlesnakes, say, or rats. Furry and doe-eyed equals good, while scaly or pink tailed equals evil. Some people won't eat eels because they're too ugly (although not the folk down by the Severn), or rabbits because they used to own one as a pet. Yet they'll happily devour a Dover Sole or a lamb.

Too much of our views on what we should and shouldn't eat is bound up with infantile anthropomorphisation, that animals are somehow more human if they look dinky. And it is this empty rant, rather than any decent argument about animal cruelty, that really defines what is right and wrong to eat in Britain today.

There's a popular urban myth about some European tourists who were travelling around Asia with their dog (quite why they wanted to do that, I don't know, but never let common sense get in the way of a tall tale). In Hong Kong, they went to eat in a highly recommended restaurant and took their dog. (Why? Couldn't he have stayed at the hotel? Most restaurants don't allow dogs.) Anyway, the dog was hungry too and they tried to break through the language barrier to explain this. Was there something in the kitchen he might eat? they asked. Well, you can imagine the outcome. Pooch trots off to the kitchen and comes back beneath a silver salver, roasted whole (not a Chinese technique with the meat, by the way, more Hawaii and Samoan). Cue waterworks and wailing. Different versions of this story have existed for hundreds of years, as this English ditty from the mid-nineteenth century reveals:

> ... he brightened up
> And thought himself in luck
> When close before him what he saw
> Looked something like a duck!
>
> Still cautious grown, but, to be sure,
> His brain he set to rack;
> At length he turned to one behind,
> And pointing, cried 'Quack, quack?'
>
> The Chinese gravely shook his head,
> Next made a reverent bow;
> And then expressed what dish it was,
> By uttering 'Bow-wow-wow'.

Reay Tannahill, in *Food in History*, gives the tall tale short shrift. 'The Chinese being a courteous people, it is unlikely that any guest at a Chinese merchant's table would have been offered red-cooked dog or stir-fried cat, though every European visitor until the end of the nineteenth century went in dread of it.'

And despite all the sensationalist stories, there really is very little chance of being fed a dog nowadays instead of beef or chicken. For one, it's a delicacy and far more expensive than other animals. Why would a restaurateur lose money by giving you dog when you ordered mutton? It's like ordering chicken livers and getting foie gras. In truth, there's more chance of losing a kidney to some cowboy organ dealer (you know, when you accept the drink and wake up 24 hours later with a throbbing pain in your back and a bleeding incision) than ending up with dog surprise. Dogs are kept widely as pets too. Although Asian cultures don't always share our obsession with the cult of the dog, there is absolutely no conflict between owning a dog and enjoying the taste of dog meat. Just as you can have a pet rabbit or pig and appreciate a roast saddle with mustard sauce or a juicy chop, so you can play fetchies with Fido at breakfast before going off to eat one of his brethren for lunch.

My discomfort with the eating of dog lies partly in their status as 'man's best friend'. I can tell myself to strip away the Western hysteria, that it's just another kind of meat, and it still won't make me feel any less nervous or uncomfortable. By now, I have realised that I can't be objective as I do love dogs too much. But I would never condemn any other culture for eating what they wish.

My main problem with the eating of dog – setting aside my emotional nonsense – is related to the manner in which they're raised. Meat eaters have a responsibility to ensure the animals they eat are reared and slaughtered in the most humane manner possible. Chickens should be free to peck and scratch about as is their natural way, roaming the yard, preening and bathing in dust. This not only makes for far better eating but ensures the minimum of stress to the bird.

The broiler hens (those bred for meat), on the other hand, live a short, wretched and squalid life. Artificially hatched, they spend all six weeks of their 'growing' period in vast, windowless sheds. The average broiler house holds 45,000 birds but many have more than

100,000 birds cramped in the dark together. By the time they have reached their optimum size, they have less than 0.5 square foot of floor to themselves and have to fight their way through the feathered mass to reach food and drink. The government has estimated that 6 per cent (or more than 42 million birds per year) die before they reach the end of their growing cycle.

As the barns are not cleaned for the six-week period, the stench of shit and ammonia is suffocating. This often leads to hock burns (caused by exposure of the skin to high levels of ammonia), as well as ammonia burn (an eye condition), chronic respiratory diseases, weakened immune systems and bronchitis. They're bred to grow unnaturally fast and their spindly legs often cannot support the weight of their grossly enlarged breast. Their immune systems suffer, health breaks down and antibiotics are routinely used to control disease.

In the USA, 90 per cent of broiler chickens are so obese that they can no longer walk, instead sitting in a pitiful heap on a filthy floor. After six weeks, they're deemed fit for slaughter (the natural life of a chicken can last as long as ten years) and grabbed by the feet, crammed into crates and driven off to their end. Heart attacks from stress are common, and many birds don't survive the final journey. If the bird is lucky enough to reach the end, it's confronted with a sadistic Heath Robinson method of dispatch. The most common method is to tie their legs to a conveyor belt, head down, and drag them through an electrically charged water bath. This is supposed to stun them before their necks are cut by an automatic knife. But many believe that the process is inefficient, in that a good number of birds are still very much alive and kicking when their main blood vessels are cut. The end result is a fatty, tasteless bird, raised in disgusting conditions and condemned to a slow, painful death. This is the hideous price of those cheap, insipid chicken breasts that infect the supermarket shelf.

The intensively farmed pig's lot is equally wretched, and most are raised in crowded, stinking sheds with only the merest sniff of fresh air. The pig is a highly intelligent and social creature, at its happiest when rooting about in the open air. But the typical breeding female is little more than a piglet machine; a week before her 16-week pregnancy ends, the sow is shut in a farrowing crate, made from metal and concrete. Cooped up in this dingy prison, the animal barely has the room to oink let alone stretch.

Her newborn piglets suckle from a 'creep' or separate section. Supporters claim that this is so the sow doesn't crush her young (which does happen naturally) and so she has little real contact with her young. After three or four weeks (rather than three months or more in organic and proper free-range pig farms), the piglets are wrenched from the vicinity of their mother – which causes all kind of stress. The piglets are moved to indoor concrete pens and pine for their mother's teat, often trying to suckle their brothers and sisters or bite their tails. So the bottom part of the tail is amputated and many of the piglets have their sharp and pointed side teeth clipped to the gum. Fattened on a high-protein diet to ensure the fastest possible growth, they're usually slaughtered around four to seven months, many never having seen the light of day. This process, like that of the chicken, is flawed and many of the beasts are still conscious when they're shackled by their back leg and hoisted towards the cutting of their throats. All because we expect cheap, bland pork.

Proper farming practices – the ones we've used for hundreds of years – are intrinsically linked with a respect for animals and the earth too. And the free-range and organic labels (although there is a lot of leeway in their definition) are not fashion accessories or trends, rather a necessity when choosing your meat. A happy animal will always make better eating than a wretched one yet in a nation of so-called animal lovers, cheap meat is more important than animal welfare.

Yet the dog farms are far crueller than anything experienced in the UK. The organic movements have yet to catch on in this particular trade. You certainly don't get the choice of 'free-range' or 'rare breed'. Not so long ago, the vast majority of dogs that ended up on the Korean or Chinese table were either strays or those nabbed from the street. This still occasionally goes on. One story dominating the headlines in Seoul when I arrive concerns one such missing pooch.

A businessman left his very expensive dog tied outside his office block for a moment while he ran inside to collect a file. When he emerged, the dog was nowhere to be seen. After a huge hunt, the ancient caretaker of the office eventually admitted to kidnapping it, cooking it up and sharing it among four friends (that endeared me to him ... I probably would have snaffled the lot myself). It turned out to be a pricy dinner as the court ordered him to pay back every penny of the dog's worth to the mourning owner.

The Korean Society for the Protection of Animals has numerous incidences of people stealing dogs and selling them for their meat (Seoulsearching.com, an ex-pat website, offers the following advice: 'If you have a large dog with you in Korea, lock it up and keep it inside. It may be stolen, as dog meat is very profitable'). But the majority are raised in farms, both in China and Korea. As you might expect, it's near-impossible to get the location of one, let alone enter its grounds. Try as I might, I am met with blank stares and disinterested shrugs. By all accounts, though, they are places of unimaginable cruelty and suffering. The staff from Seoulsearching.com describe typical conditions observed at a farm just outside Seoul in July 2002:

> Frankly the place was a nasty, stinking mess. Dogs were in hot, dirty and cramped conditions. Fecal matter and urine were running away from the facility. Flies were everywhere. The dogs

smelled bad. They were in poor condition with little or no food, and dirty water. We saw piles of dog fecal matter next to freezers that contained butchered dogs, and other areas that were used for cooking dogs. We saw refrigerated trucks used to transport dog meat to various markets and restaurants. We saw dogs being killed, and dogs barking and crying as other dogs near them were being killed by very slow and primitive means.

These methods of slaughter make for horrific reading. The flesh of the dog is supposed to have properties that boost virility, so the manner of its death is important. Often, the dog is strung up (by the neck or hind legs) and violently beaten – when still alive – so that the dog's whimpering, agonising fear causes an adrenalin rush around its body that is said to increase male virility. It is also believed to tenderise the meat. This process can last anything from a few minutes to an hour, depending on the beliefs and sadism of the executioner. Some older Koreans believe that the more pain suffered by the dog, the bigger the hard-on of its eventual consumer.

Burning and brandings are common too, taking place during the beating, to improve the appearance and flavour (or so they believe). The dog is still very much alive. Slow strangulation by hanging is another method, in full view of the other dogs awaiting a similar fate, as well as electrocutions (via electrodes fixed to the anus and tongue). Sometimes, the poor beasts are skinned alive, as this helps preserve the pelt which can then be sold. If the mutt is very lucky, it might be dispatched with a hammer blow to the skull.

So while I support the eating of dog meat, the means of its production is a lot harder to justify. If this tradition is to continue, perhaps the South Korean government should make and enforce stringent standards to obliterate this wanton cruelty. Yet I am fully aware of the hypocrisy of my predicament. I want to try dog, yet cannot guarantee its provenance in any way. And in eating dog, I will be supporting one of the cruellest farming practices in the world. So I can only hope that by making the plain truth clear, I cannot be accused of glamorising the subject. This is the part of my culinary odyssey I am dreading most and whatever my arguments to the contrary, I know the taste of dog will be a bitter one.

It doesn't excite me in the gastronomic sense either. Every morning, I wake up and decide that today is the day then decide against it and go off in search of more bulgogi or pimimbab. As the days pass, I am filled with a feeling of dreadful anticipation and try to imagine the rest of my year instead, drinking blood-red Sicilian wine with real-life gangsters, risking my life in search of precious shellfish or being persuaded to join MI6 and go spy on Laos. Anything but the damned dog.

'It's just another piece of meat,' I tell myself. 'I'm not exactly dicing with death.' But it hangs over me like a gloomy pall, infecting my everyday greed, and on the eighth morning I decide to get on with it. But finding it isn't as easy as you'd imagine. Even in Seoul, they don't exactly advertise the fact with vast pictures of cuddly canines beaming down from every street corner. I have a few contacts in Seoul and use them relentlessly.

One friend of a friend looks appalled when I ask, as if I had just been caught in flagrante with her grandma.

'I'll ask around,' she tells me through pursed lips. 'But you do know, not all Koreans eat dog. I hope you won't be writing about just dog.'

Of course not, I reassure her. How could someone dedicate an entire chapter to Koreans and dogs? Really. Has she tried it herself, though?

Her face crumples in disgust. 'No, it's horrible. I have a pet dog and would never dream of eating another, however traditional it might be. Among the young, posintang is losing its popularity. But if you want to eat, I'll find it.'

She never comes back. Eventually, after hours on the Internet, I manage to find a traditional establishment. And with heavy heart, set off towards my doggy doom.

My taxi driver, however, is far more supportive. Delighted, in fact. I am off to try one of his favourite dishes, he says. And every two minutes, he turns back and leers through nicotine-tarred stubs. 'Good for strong man. And fuck fuck too.' Just in case I miss his point, he wriggles his crotch, repeating 'fucky fucky' and wheezes happily to himself.

Relieved that he doesn't see me as some sort of monster – and spurred on by a sudden manly thrust – I join in, once again making out that I eat the stuff all day long. What is it about macho chat that brings out the liar in me, as if I'd be somehow less male for not joining in? The lascivious smile apart, he speaks decent English and even suggests a few decent Korean movies to see. I hardly listen. As he drops me off, he beeps his horn and pumps his fist before disappearing into the lunchtime traffic.

I'm left on a cracked piece of pavement in front of some ancient wooden steps. The street is hidden from the main road ten metres away and there is no evidence of a restaurant, let alone one serving dog. I climb the creaking steps slowly, my sense of dread increasing the further I ascend. A cold sweat chills my brow and I realise that this is the last moment to pull out of this ridiculous escapade and return home. I peek around the door, only to see a small, private flat.

Thinking I am in the wrong place, I turn to go just as a small, plump lady comes bustling towards me.

'Posintang?' I stutter.

She nods and I take off my shoes. The only sign of dog here is a couple of pairs of fluffy cartoon dog slippers, sitting neatly in the corner.

I point and give a hollow chortle. She seems unsure how to deal with this nervous foreigner. Am I here to scream abuse or one of the rare ones who actually likes the taste? I can see her trying to work me out, so I try to help, yapping then rubbing my stomach. She looks at me in total bewilderment. By the time I get into the small sitting room, I have almost convinced myself I can manage anything. I'm over-reacting, I say. Now I'm here, I'll try it all.

On one side is a small table, and I sit down beside it and cross my legs. The floor is heated and my heart hammers with anticipation. An advertisement for a red-flecked bowl of soup hangs on the wall. Aside from that, the walls are bare. A television sits in the corner, playing out what seems to be a soap opera set among the accountant community of Seoul. Every time I glance at it, another besuited Korean is waving a finance report in front of some terrified minion. They growl and shout a lot, waving more stock reports and pens. Occasionally a pretty lady comes in to bring tea and they growl some more. And at one point, the boss (well, I assume it's him, as he is the oldest, his hair is gelled in a slick wedge and he has the smartest briefcase) throws a sheaf of paper at his terrified staff.

But just as I am finding out why, my hostess shuffles in again.

'Posintang?' she asks, pointing to the poster on the wall.

So that's what it is.

'Yes please,' I say in my deepest voice and she disappears again, leaving me alone with the business boys once more. I think there's talk of a boardroom coup, as one hair from the boss's wedge comes ungelled and the others shout a lot. But Big Mr Slick stares menacingly at them and slams his briefcase shut. That seems to tell 'em and corporate harmony is restored. It is very, very dull but helps in keeping my mind from the upcoming feast of friends.

The famed soup aside, there is a multitude of ways to prepare the flesh of a dog. Thailand has a dog tartare, minced flesh mixed with a horrible combination of blood, bile and spices as well as dog jerky. The Indonesians and certain African tribes roast it on a spit, while it's stuffed and boiled in Burma, smoked and dried in the Philippines and simmered in wine in Vietnam. This may all sound gruesome but the flesh is treated exactly like that of any other beast. Dog hams are a Chinese delicacy; one European visitor was rather taken, saying that 'one taste led to another, and resulted in a verdict for reason; for in summing up, after a hearty meal, I pronounced the dog ham to be juicy in flavour, well smoked, tender and juicy'.

And this ham is by no means a solely Chinese treat. The great Schwabe claims that the Swiss have a taste for dog ham. His evidence comes from medical reports of trichinosis. *Unmentionable Cuisine* was published in 1979: 'In fact, the only 2 cases of human trichinosis diagnosed in Switzerland in recent years resulted from the patients eating their dog meat too rarely cooked!'

The Swiss also have recipes for dried dog meat flavoured with pepper, salt, black peppercorn, bay, red wine and crushed garlic. Who'd have thought that the land of the cuckoo clock harboured such a dark secret? As to varieties, the Chinese raise breeds such as black-tongued chow especially for food.

'Straight-haired "Chinese dogs" are always eaten in preference to curly-haired "foreign" dogs,' writes Paul Levy in *Out to Lunch*. 'And only puppies are used for the pot.'

A Korean favourite is the Nu-rungi-I or the yellow dog, an intelligent and faithful breed once used to guard houses. They look similar to huskies, with bright eyes and pointed ears. And the St Bernard – the huge mountain dog – is viewed by Chinese dog farmers as a wonder breed, as they are fast-growing, disease-resistant and good breeders.

They're also so placid that they don't bite the breeders, bred as they are to rescue humans in the mountains. If I were to predict a trend in next year's dog-eating stakes, I'd say the St B would be the one to back.

Back in the dog restaurant, the boardroom-based *Coronation Street* is still running when the lady enters the room with my canine lunch. A big, steaming bowl is carefully placed before me and at first sight, looks entirely respectable. I gulp, smile my thanks and she shuffles off, leaving me with Gel Head and the dog. The soup is thick with a vibrant red chilli paste and long strands of brown, finely grained meat. The surface is scattered with shimmering globules of fat, and plump shards of garlic float lazily alongside. The odd leaf of spinach or some other green adds a flash of colour.

This really doesn't look too bad. As I've travelled halfway across the world, the very least I can do is eat the stuff. I grab my chopsticks, grab a strand of meat and throw it into my mouth. The meat is chewy and stringy, but fairly innocuous with a slight gamey tang. It could be cheap beef brisket. You dip it in a chilli and bean paste, then eat. The chilli, garlic and sesame paste obliterate any lasting taste but it really isn't that bad. I'm actually eating dog and if not relishing every bite, I'm doing well.

I start to wonder what I'll have next. How about the bollocks? Should I ask now? Now that really would make a story. I push thoughts of Eddie, Freddie and Willie from my mind and continue to munch the meat. I sit back and take a sip of water, radiating smugness at my culinary bravado. Once again, I've managed to overcome any social aversion, fought through the associations and am taking it like a real man. I push any thoughts of whimpering, strung-up animals to the back of my mind. As I lean over for another bite, I contemplate ringing my mother, just for comedy value.

'Hey, guess what I'm doing?'

… a sigh … 'What?'

'Eating a Freddie and he tastes pretty good. Ha ha ha.'

'Oh Tom!' etc., etc.

But I don't think anyone, least of all my mother, would appreciate being woken at three in the morning to hear about dog stew. I'm just imagining myself bragging about eating dog to friends back home ('Gosh, Tom, you're so brave and daring. I respect you even more than ever') when it hits me – the smell, creeping up my nostrils, winding its way into the fibres of my clothes, taking over my whole sensory self. I can't escape it.

Suddenly the whole room seems infused with this stench. Even Gel Head seems to pause from his corporate bollocks to take a whiff. It's everywhere now. You know when your dog has been out in the rain, possibly down a hole, and he turns up at the door, soaked and wretched? And you bring him into the house and start drying him with that dirty dog towel kept out the back. That is it, the smell of wet dog … wet, dirty, dead dog. No spice, however pungent, could mask this stink.

Every time I reach down to lift out another wisp of flesh, that stench – the stench of violent death – assaults my every sense, negating the chilli and kicking the garlic into touch and, suddenly, there is no glossing over the fact that this is pooch. I feel the ghost of this poor mutt by my feet, not waiting for scraps but staring up with baleful eyes. I try to fight through my attack of conscience, but now a slight nausea begins to creep up around the edges of my long-passed appetite. Every now and again the lady comes in.

'OK?' she beams.

'Yes, yes,' I splutter back, putting my arms into strong man pose to show my appreciation of its virile powers. She is going to wait to watch me eat another bit while I will her to go, trying to repel her with my psychic rays. It doesn't work, so I have to stir the toxic soup, searching for the tiniest shred, dropping it daintily in my mouth and forcing it down, all the while making the suitable lip-smacking noises. This goes on until all the small bits have gone. And all that is left then are the unidentifiable parts, fatty and shameful. The ordeal becomes unbearable. Far from the gloating triumph of a few moments ago, this has become an abject failure.

I have come to Korea with the intention of eating dog and all I can do is nibble at the edge. Suddenly, I hate Seoul and loathe myself for such a stupid endeavour. Travelling to what I have perceived as the outer edges of the culinary wilderness, I'm just not up to the job. How will this play out for the rest of my journey? What is the point of my journey if I can't at least finish what I started? So much for eating dangerously.

At this stage, I am doing little more than pathetically picking at the soup. All this doubt and depression caused by the dog stew below my nose. I push the bowl away, as I can no longer spend a moment more in the room. On the television, the boardroom bores are still locked in gelled conflict, but I have to get out. I holler for the bill, a mess of dog still before me. It's expensive, about 20 quid for a bowl.

'You like?' she asks with a maternal smile for the last time.

I nod numbly and fly down the rickety stairs, almost falling in my haste to escape. The biting Seoul air floods my lungs and I stand for a moment, breathing in, trying to rid myself of that smell. Slowly, my normal senses return. It's dusk, and the streets are jammed with snarling traffic. The petrol fumes seem divine, the burning rubber as sweet as tuberose. Even a whiff of sewer seems somehow innocent in comparison.

But as I start to walk home, a peculiar thing happens. I feel as if a small brazier has ignited in my stomach, sending its heat coursing around the body. I no longer notice the angry cold and I get a spring in my step. It's certainly not chilli heat, as that's a local burn I know all too well. No, this is something spilling out from my stomach and coursing through my veins. As I walk, my ego starts to swell too, engorging into a proud tumescence. I start to imagine a Ready Brek glow emanating from my every pore, and my amble down the road straightens into a strut. My shoulders stand to attention, my chest puffs out and my eyes blaze with machismo.

This is virility, of the sort promised by my taxi driver. The warming of my blood, the confidence bordering on the aggressive, the stirring of my loins. Surely it can't be true. I've discounted all the 'fucky fuck' chat as rubbish, just like any other so-called aphrodisiac. But I have to admit, I certainly feel mighty perky, all the way back to the hotel. I literally shine with confidence and macho charm (and I haven't touched a drop), a feeling that only disappears when I finally go to bed that night. I have since put it down to a delayed shock reaction to that smell. Or even a result of the relief in escaping it. There's no doubt, though, that this cynic did feel an undeniable boost. I suppose I'll never know. One thing is for certain – whatever its powers, I definitely won't be coming back for more.

The next day I leave, not triumphant but bowed and bloody. This has been the low point of my culinary odyssey, hating a meat I knew I would hate. I suppose it is an experience of sorts, but hardly one I could recommend. Did I really expect that I would suddenly convert to dog meat? The whole Korean experience has been rather a dampener on the year. And this eating dangerously lark is becoming more bore than journey of discovery. I have eaten dog, so what? The box is ticked but the experience is unpleasant and it seems somehow ghoulish, against the spirit of the whole journey.

To make matters worse, there is still no sign of the elusive ortolan ('Chances slim but still trying. Hold tight' was the last electronic missive). I miss my wife and only have a couple of days at home (brilliant planning, as I have to come the whole way back again) before flying off to Laos. If this fabled land of ex-spies and exotic foods – the romance of crumbling communism – doesn't live up to my expectations, I may as well pack the whole damned thing in.

CHAPTER 7

LAOS

On the flight back from Korea, somewhere between the silicone implant chicken breast and the latest Jennifer Lopez shitefest, I try to make sense of my Korean experience. Well, about as much as I can after a bottle of red-tinted paint stripper and two Valium 10s. Dog meat is the one food that seems to shock everyone I know, far more than insects or tripe or stinking tofu. These three dishes merely produce a small shudder while the canine provokes outright disgust.

A few months ago, though, before I set off on the journey, things seemed very different. I knew the dog might prove a little tricky to swallow, but believed that once I had set aside my sentimental preconceptions, it would be just another meat soup. Far more terrifying was the prospect of blood soup or giant water beetles in Laos. Yet my experience of the past ten days – most specifically the posintang – was certainly the most unpleasant of my trip so far. Before arriving, I had no romanticised view of Korea or Seoul, so the city neither disappointed nor overwhelmed. It seemed more lonely and desolate, probably because I visited in the depths of winter, so soon after Christmas. Some of the food was excellent and I was always certain I wouldn't go hungry. The regional and national cuisine seemed in rude health, under little threat from the Mac-Typhoon of Americanised fast food.

But still I feel uncomfortable. What has started as a picaresque journey in search of excitement and flavour, an antidote to bland, processed pap, has suddenly taken a turn for the worse. Whereas I was observing on the banks of the Severn or playing around with chillies in New Mexico, this time, my culinary travels have affected me badly. I have deliberately eaten meat produced in the cruellest manner possible, all for a cheap culinary thrill. Would I feel so wretched if it had been a pig or salmon rather than the cuddly dog? Probably not.

Despite all my arguments in favour of eating dog – provided it is properly raised – I feel like a fraud, no better than the person who condemns dog eating while chewing on a Chicken McNugget. In Korea, I became the very person I had so railed against. As the sedative begins to soften the edges of my confusion, I try to think forward to Laos. Here, at least, I'll be the intrepid adventurer, searching out some romantic vision of an age long past.

Typically, my arrival in Laos is an anticlimax. From all the reading I've done on the country – bolstered by travellers' tales – I really felt I'd be travelling once more, living on the edge, watching my back and covering my tracks. The fact that I've never been near the side let alone teetered on the edge is ignored, and I let my clichéd vision of the country wash over me and colour my every thought. If I am really unlucky, I might find myself locked up for a crime I haven't committed, accused of being a Western spy and left to rot for ever. Even if I'm not held up for espionage, I at least expect to fall instantly and madly in love with this little-known South East Asian country, to throw myself into a passionate traveller's embrace and find sun-hardened thrills and exotica in even the most mundane of things.

As one of the few communist countries left in the world, it

promises intrigue, bugged rooms and world-weary CIA agents, talking of the 'good old days' over a cool beer in some shady downtown bar. Even the journey from Bangkok to Vientiane, the capital, seems perilous when described in the *Lonely Planet*.

It's uncertain whether the repackaging of the old Lao Aviation as Lao Airlines [intones the guide ominously] and the leasing of a new Airbus to service some international routes will have any effect on the airline's efficiency and safety ... but many international organisations and Western embassies advise staff not to use the airline.

Yes, I thought as I read this at my desk in London. At long last, some real peril, something far removed from the usual backpacking trail of English menus, Internet access and 24-hour cable. I felt like Norman Lewis or Wilfrid Thesiger setting out into the unknown, armed only with notebook and pen (well, perhaps just a mobile telephone, credit card, travel insurance and laptop computer too). This, I told myself, was true adventure, returning to roots I didn't even know I had. I repeated the *Lonely Planet* quote about the aeroplanes ad infinitum, embellishing it to such an extent that before long, I was regaling friends with tales of night-time landings onto unmarked dirt tracks, the pilot passed out drunk and the propeller held together with just a scrap of Elastoplast. The irony of six guidebooks available on this supposedly 'undiscovered' land was entirely lost upon me.

But the flight into Vientiane could not be more smooth. The plane is clean and modern, the stewardesses slick and the pilots the very model of sober respectability. I look around at my fellow passengers, hoping that I am the sole Western adventurer, aside, perhaps, from the odd 'spook' on 'gardening leave'. Sadly, most would not have looked out of place in a Saga brochure. They sit with their neat hair and crisp trousers and shiny Fodor's Guides, faces set in the benign smile of the affluent, globe-trotting OAP.

What has happened to the pioneers and buccaneers? Obviously long gone in search of a new 'paradise' they can call their own. Which before long will be overrun with the same shiny trappings of Western civilisation as every other spot before. When the landing card is handed out, I fret over what to write in the 'Occupation' section. If I scribble writer or journalist, they might think me a threat. That would be good. A danger, a maverick. I feel a flush of excitement and rebellion. Then panic and put down 'Marketing Executive'. Not that the Laos authorities could care less.

As I climb off the plane, I scan the area for any sign of commie agents, taking covert photographs of the capitalist pigs, ready to shadow our every move around the city. Instead, there is nothing save the beaming face of the stewardess, ushering us into the arrivals hall. The temperature is more Exeter on a late May evening than the torrid humidity of the tropics. Adverts for Orange mobile phones plaster every available space and even the visa process is a hundred times less tortuous than stepping onto American soil (I expected to pay a special 'fine', at the very least, to speed up the process and have a ten-dollar bill neatly tucked into my sweaty palm).

Within two minutes I am through customs and in a taxi on my way into town. I can't see much, save more excitable adverts for the 'very best in telecommunications'. We pass darkened shacks and sleeping tuk-tuk drivers, but it is as if someone had turned off the city at the mains and locked up for the night. Not even a stray dog's bark bothers the silence as we judder towards the centre. The hotel is ugly and executive, and my room basic. But there is hot water, a television, even a hairdryer. I could have been in a Croydon Travelodge.

I collapse on the bed, disappointed. This Laos lark is turning into a bore and I have only been in the country an hour. Expecting some kind of deranged, nymphomaniacal minx, I have ended up with Anthea Turner. The spark just isn't there. With a cursory check around the room for bugs (of the electronic and human kind, though quite how I'd deal with the former, I don't know – and quite why anyone would want to listen to me running a bath and watching BBC World, I don't know either, but it seems the right thing to do), I grab my pad and wander out for my first taste of the Vientiane night.

Until about a year ago, I knew little about Laos. To be totally honest, I thought it was part of Vietnam or Cambodia or even somewhere in the north of Thailand. Now, of course, I roll my eyes indulgently when anyone admits to not having a clue where it is (most thought it a city in Vietnam), and start to lecture the unfortunate individual – in a suitably patronising manner – that Laos is a landlocked country (the only one in South East Asia) about the size of the British Isles, squeezed between Cambodia to the south, Vietnam to the east, Thailand to the west and Myanmar and China to the north. Once a French colony, the Lao People's Democratic Republic is one of the last official communist states in the world, albeit communists who mainly adhere to the Theravadan school of Buddhism. It's also one of Asia's most sparsely populated (and poorest) countries, with a population of just five million people, working out at only 20 people per square kilometre. Compared with the rush-hour condition cramp of neighbouring Vietnam (with 230 people per square kilometre), it's positively empty. At this point, I see the unfortunate recipient of this impromptu history lecture begin to doze and I move on to my next unwilling victim.

My ignorance of Laos turned to near-obsession when a friend, Sam, travelled there two years back, and met a Laotian lady, Sang. They fell in love, got married and now live together in Battersea. Sam would regale me with tales of this quiescent land where life was slow and the food fiery and exotic. The more he told me, the more I realised that this was the perfect destination for the next leg of my journey.

'If you're looking for extreme foods,' he said as Sang brought in a huge plate of laap kai (chicken laap), a fragrant, meaty salad which is the country's national dish, 'you're going to the right place. The Laotians eat anything, from bugs to ant eggs to duck blood soup.'

Sang interrupted. 'It's not that bad. The food is some of the best in the world. It's just that Laos is a poor country and we like to make use of every available ingredient.'

They told of nights drinking Beer Lao with friends, then stopping at the noodle stall to slurp steaming bowls of perfect foe (or noodle soup). This undiscovered cuisine shares many of the characteristics of its better-known neighbours, yet has a soul all of its own. As the evening turns into night, I heard more about raw buffalo meat laap, year-long fermented fish and water beetle sauce. It sounded the perfect place to continue my journey, a place where dangerous foods and communist intrigue walked hand in hand.

As I staggered home, Laos seemed to me the gem of Indo-China, the ultimate Shangri-La for the adventurous eater.

Although it is just past eight when I leave the hotel, the Vientiane evening air is brisk. The blistering hot season is still a few weeks away so days are warm and evenings mild. As I walk through deserted streets, I feel like the sole extra on a carefully reconstructed South East Asian set. The odd tourist strolls past, but even the tuk-tuk drivers have to be approached for a lift. It isn't that they don't want my fare, rather that they are too busy eating and talking, bunched up into each other's seats. Unlike the mercantile fervour of the Thai trader, the Laotians can't even really be bothered to bargain.

I ask how much it is to the restaurant on the banks of the Mekong.
'Twenty dollar,' one replies with a smile.

Seeing it was only a mile away (or so I think), even I realise this is
a touch steep.

'One dollar,' I try.

'Fine, let's go.' He bids farewell to his friends (all grinning at the
huge sum paid out by the gullible tourist) and off we sputter.

As usual, I have hugely miscalculated the distance, the restaurant
being a mere 100 metres from the tuk-tuk stand. We putter down the
main road along the Mekong River, Th Fa Ngum, and I don't see
another soul. Not even a cat. It's like *Village of the Damned* or some
other Fifties sci-fi nonsense, where the inhabitants are whisked away,
leaving the kettles just boiled but nobody in. I think back to the heady
days of the early Seventies, just after the end of the Vietnam War, when
Paul Theroux passed through on *The Great Railway Bazaar*.

'Vientiane is exceptional, but inconvenient,' he writes, his pen
dripping with disdain. 'The brothels are cleaner than the hotels, marijuana is cheaper than pipe tobacco, and opium easier to find than a
cold glass of beer ...'

Nearly every guidebook on the city opens with Theroux's description, then goes on to say, with a tinge of regret, that Vientiane is 'no
longer the illicit pleasure palace it was when Paul Theroux described it'
or how 'Vientiane's once notorious nightlife helped to earn it the name
of Wonderland ... However, the brothels and strip joints vanished
when the old regime fell in the mid-1970s, and the city's night scene is
just now re-emerging after 25 years of puritanical socialism.'

Not that there is any sign of any night scene as I sit down in the
riverside restaurant at a plastic table and order a Beer Laos. Theroux
was there when the city had descended into a Wild West of sex, drugs
and moral decline. The beer arrives, cool, clean and beautifully

balanced. Theroux's cold beer was served in rather less salubrious circumstances than mine.

> When you find the beer at midnight and are sitting quietly, wondering what sort of place this is, the waitress offers to fellate you on the spot, and you still don't know. Your eyes get accustomed to the dark and you see the waitress is naked. Without warning she jumps on to a chair, pokes a cigarette in her vagina and lights it, puffing by contracting her uterine lungs. So many sexual knacks!

The only other guests in the restaurant are an intense-looking group of Frenchmen, softly spoken and well-scrubbed. They murmur in the background, picking at French fries and papaya salads. I look out across the black, swirling eddies of the Mekong. Like the Ganges, Yangtze and Amazon, the Mekong is one of those impossibly exotic rivers that charm you in childhood with their name alone. To be sitting on its banks still gives me a small thrill, even though I see little through the blackness. A garish, glowing beacon of a building (the new Casino, I think), looking more similar to Caesar's Palace than the usual communist concrete, dominates the eyeline on the other side of the bank.

The frog chorus emanating from the bank is loud but struggles to keep up with that most brutal of music styles, the muzak of Andrew Lloyd Webber. His Lordship has much to answer for. As I get lost in the menu, the tinny sound system torments my tender ears with 'Memories' and 'Don't Cry For Me Argentina', played on a wonky Yamaha organ. I move on from Theroux and leaf through the guidebook. Usually, I avoid churches, temples and museums like the plague, the result of having been dragged around too many as a schoolchild.

My guilt at such philistine ways passed long ago, along with paisley shirts and spots. But Vientiane is not a city known for its manifold architectural beauties. Norman Lewis, in his lyrical 1952 book, *A Dragon Apparent*, is straightforward in his view of the place. 'The charm of Vientiane lies in the life and the customs of the people. Unless one is an amateur of pagoda architecture there is little else to be seen.' I think I'm going to get by just fine.

My dinner appears quickly, a succession of small plates served all together. A small wicker basket of sticky rice, a ubiquitous staple throughout the country, arrives with the food. The Laotians are obsessed with this sticky rice, although about a third of their diet is made up of the non-glutinous variety.

'Sticky rice itself almost counts as a piece of tableware,' writes Phia Sing in *Traditional Recipes of Laos* (the greatest Laotian cookbook, and one based on recipes from the Royal Palace in Luang Prabang), 'since it is used both as a "pusher" for bits of food and to sop up liquids ... the person eating will take some sticky rice between the fingers, knead it slightly together and then use it as described above.'

I've always felt fingers are far superior to knife and fork anyway, the feel of the food in one's hands adding to the greedy anticipation.

'Crickets finished,' says my waiter as he opens another beer. 'Very sorry, but come back tomorrow.' I feel a little relieved, as the insect order is the last thing I feel like after 18 hours in a plane. I only order it because it is there and realise there would be plenty of other opportunities for bug munching. The chicken laap is studded with fried garlic, fresh chillies and lettuce. And served with various greenery, some of which resembled ivy. You eat the leaves with the laap, and they added a bitter, slightly astringent taste. The flavour is luscious, undercut with padek, the juice surrounding chunks of fermented fish.

This sauce, similar to the Thai nam pla (or fish sauce), underpins genuine Laotian cuisine. Every household makes their own, leaving the chunks of freshwater fish (mixed with salt water, rice dust and rice husks) to rot away in earthenware pots in the hot sun. The smell is vile, the colour murky and texture sluggish. But the taste is superb.

'Most Westerners baulk at the idea of rotten fish,' writes Natacha Du Pont De Bie in *Ant Egg Soup*, 'but Laotians find it equally repellent that we eat fermented milk with lines of blue mould in it in the form of cheese.'

For most Asians, the idea of Stilton – or indeed most milk products – is revolting. An afternoon spent in Neal's Yard dairy is probably their idea of culinary hell. The laap has a vibrancy that would be near impossible to capture in the Western kitchen; each flavour, from the chicken and chillies through to the herbs, is allowed to sparkle for a moment, show off its flavour and texture, before stepping back and allowing another to take its place. It is very much an ensemble piece, making the salad far more than a sum of its parts. Underlying it all is a charcoal taste, coming from the Laotian tradition of searing garlic, chillies, aubergines and shallots until burnt, then pounding them together and adding them in.

It is the sort of food that creates an involuntary smile of greedy delight, far less sweet than Thai food (the Laotians use little sugar in their cooking). So I attack my salads with gusto, dipping, sipping and chewing. A simple basin full of water sits on the other side of the restaurant. I'm supposed to have washed my hands before I start but hunger overcomes sanitary sense and I dive straight in.

The raw shrimp laap version is stunningly fresh, and I am sure I detect a slight twitch as the plate is set down. Again, pert, simple flavours, all underpinned by the mellow tang of the padek. The crunch of the beansprouts and cucumber and carrot and mint zips over my tongue, teasing the taste buds and widening my smile. Even the Bontempi version of Wings' 'Mull of Kintyre', perhaps the most hateful song of all time, can't dampen my ardour. The country seems to be relaxing and unfurling before my eyes. Or I am, at least.

I slip a little deeper in my chair. My preconceptions of espionage and communist intrigue have been burst the moment I arrived in the airport, but this river view, this joyous food, this laid-back torpor, seemed somehow familiar. I realise that for all my chat, I would be terrified being trailed by police or watched through a camera. The nearest I've ever come to spying is owning the complete set of Bond on DVD and at the first whiff of trouble, I'll be out of the country and blubbing for my mummy. Even in England, I call policemen 'sir' and come over all Uriah Heep in their presence.

But this feeling I have now goes back to something a little deeper, something closer to my over-romantic fictional image of Indo-China, gleaned from Greene rather than Le Carré. The French voices, the sinuous, dark river, the cacophony of frogs … somehow, just sitting in the restaurant, have turned this clichéd vision into something approaching reality.

The final dish is steamed river fish, as succulent and unmuddy as you could hope. With no coastline, the river fish of Laos make up a crucial part of the diet, not just with dishes like this but in the all-important padek too. Alan Davidson, in *Fish and Fish Dishes of Laos*, lists over 70 different species that are found, from the tiny Pa Sieu (or minnow) right up to the mighty Pa Beuk (or giant catfish), an increasingly rare beast that can reach up to three metres in length: 'If you buy a head, as I once did,' warns Davidson with a typically wry grin, 'remember that it may weigh 50 kilos and that you will need to invite 150 guests.'

I mop up the last remnants of my dinner and pay the bill, about 100,000 Lao kip, just over a fiver. As I leave the restaurant, mouth abuzz with chilli and spirits soaring, I hear more McCartney, this time the first awful bars of 'The Frog Chorus' drowning out the soothing croaks of the real thing. Perhaps it is just a sated belly talking but Vientiane seems like a different city on the journey home. No less silent and deserted but comfortable now, and almost familiar.

The next day, my slumber is shattered by the trill of a phone. I pick it up.

'Tom, it's Lucky, Sang's friend. I'm in the lobby. Today, we eat dangerously.'

With a giggle, the line goes dead. I haul myself into a shower, rub the night out of my eyes and take the lift to the lobby. I look around and immediately spot a huge white smile attached to a slim, tiny body. Immaculately dressed in beige jumper and new jeans, her English is far superior to my Laotian. No change there then, and once again, I curse my lack of linguistic skills. Without Lucky, I already know I'd get nowhere. We shake hands and she takes me outside into the heat of the sun.

The city is transformed from the still of night, roads crawling with fume-spewing trucks and Aid-agency SUVs (all neat and shiny and gas guzzling), fighting for space with swarms of tuk-tuks, scooters and sit-up and beg bikes. Tourists step into the dusty streets, blinking like surprised cattle. Policemen relax in the shade while food vendors cook up everything from fresh papaya salad (tam maak-hung) and charcoal-grilled river fish to ping kai (chicken) and baguettes filled with a spicy pork pâté. I have to fight to keep away, but Lucky promises a feast at lunch.

Our conversation is basic and halting. Enough, though, for a short conversation. The rest, I make up with nodding, pointing and making stupid faces. This makes her laugh even more. As we leave town in Lucky's uncle's Datsun, we drive down leafy boulevards and right past Patuxai, a mini-Arc de Triomphe. From a distance, it looks suitably triumphant but as we cruise past, I notice some swirly Laotian flourishes. Palm trees nearby add a surreal effect. The rows of embassies are suitably whitewashed and standing to attention. But a closer look is denied as a phalanx of shiny black cars muscle down the road, the police escort pushing anyone else to the side.

'Government officials,' says Lucky with a shrug. The government buildings themselves are large and vulgar, built in the worst possible taste. Modern and shoddy looking, they're obscenely shiny, coated in gilt and oriental vulgarity. They resemble Thai timeshares, and add little but grotesque profligacy to the landscape. Corrugated iron shacks sit next to crumbling colonial villas, with the usual communist carbuncles staining the landscape with that special brand of grey concrete.

Exiting the city, we pass a sign saying, 'The love of cleanliness is shown in the manners of a civilised people.' A pile of rubbish lies below it. With Whitesnake playing full volume on the radio, the roads get increasingly bumpy and dusty. It's as if the government gave up bothering outside the city limits and we are constantly swerving to avoid enormous potholes.

'The Lao love a party,' explains Lucky as I see the tattered remnants of a local festival. 'Any excuse, Chinese New Year, Western New Year, Christmas, then full-moon festivals, national holidays, whatever. Lots of drinking, eating … we party well.'

She brakes suddenly to let a startled goat pass, then swerves to avoid a gash in the track. We leave a thick, choking trail of dust in our wake, a gesture that's reciprocated by every passing vehicle. The brilliant green iridescence of the paddy fields either side is almost blinding when not blurred by the mantle of dust.

After 20 minutes of bumping and swerving, we cross an imposing iron bridge, and pull up by a curve on the Nam Ngum river. It's deep olive, swirling lazily past. A few fishermen sit on the bank, while rickety bamboo lodges cling to the side. A collection of thatched cottages lead down to wooden pontoons and we climb into a long, narrow room that seems to float upon the water.

'Best restaurant in Vientiane,' Lucky says proudly. 'No tourist here, just Lao.'

It's a weekday, and the Som Ngum restaurant is sleeping.

'At the weekend, you can't move. Very popular with us. I like a lot,' giggles Lucky as I look around. We wash our hands in a bowl in the corner, then settle down at the low table. Thai pop music blares through cheap speakers, the only sound save the odd plop of a fish in the river. The stillness here is as thick and narcotic as opium smoke. The menus arrive and Lucky starts to talk me through.

'You eat everything?'

'Of course,' I reply, my chest swelling up.

'Really, anything?'

'That's what I'm here for.'

'OK.' She rattles off a list of dishes and, occasionally, the waiter will look at me and raise his eyebrow.

'Are you sure?' he seems to be saying.

Lucky ploughs on undeterred.

The rice arrives in baskets, followed by what looks like a plateful of salad, covered with an upturned glass bowl. I reach over to take it off but Lucky stops me.

'Careful, otherwise they go everywhere. Look closer.'

I peer at the bowl, and suddenly realise that something is moving beneath. More to the point, lots of things, all hopping against the glass.

'Live shrimp salad, very fresh.'

So fresh that even lifting the lid a millimetre would see a swarm of these little river shrimp, doing their own crustacean version of the Great Escape. I swoop from above, like a giant troll with a taste for flesh, grabbing a handful of the energetic critters. A few escape, hopping from table to floor but I manage to stuff the majority in my mouth. A lucky minority die instantly, crushed by my molars, but the rest jive about my mouth like living Spacedust. Even the crunch is similar.

But the taste is worth the effort, sweet and tempered by the usual padek, chilli and lime juice. It's not the most practical of salads, and I end up chasing my lunch across the floor. But for freshness, it's unrivalled. It might seem an unnecessarily cruel practice but it's simply a way of ensuring ultimate freshness. In a tropical country, this is plain common sense.

A plate full of exotic-looking plants and leaves appears, as ubiquitous in Laos food as the sticky rice. Aside from the usual lettuce, coriander and mint, there are various leafy fronds that are eaten with the food to add a further dimension of flavour. I can't recognise any of them, and even Lucky is unsure about a few.

'Many eating plants, always changing. Good for flavour though,' she explains as she wraps them into a dainty parcel and throws it in her mouth. While she chews neatly, a bowl of deep-fried something appears. I peer a little closer and they look like golden maggots.

'Baby bee,' says Lucky.

I pick one up, dip it in the chilli sauce and bite. Once again, it's fantastic, a universe away from that hellish silk worm pupa in Korea. Light and crunchy, these bee pupae taste like deep-fried prawns with the slightest hint of honey.

'We eat with beer,' says Lucky and I can see why. It certainly beats dry-roasted peanuts. Squeamish as I am, I can't keep my hands off them. They're as addictive as Pringles, but 100 times as nice. If you closed your eyes and I dropped one onto your tongue, you'd thank me for hours to come. Even the most delicate of constitutions could handle this and, even better, they're wild, natural and very cheap.

By now, the last remaining shrimp have given up any hope of survival and lie gasping their final moments on a deathbed of herbs. Humane person until the end, I put them out of their misery, letting them join their fellow crustaceans in the mass grave of my stomach.

We take a break for a fiery papaya salad, a vivid palate cleanser that whips around the mouth, invigorating and burning at the same time.

'If you come to my country and don't try papaya salad, you can't come back,' warns Lucky. She's an old friend of Sang, both having grown up together. As the relative of a government official, she's relatively privileged. Driving her uncle's car has its advantages too.

'Police don't stop us,' she tells me with a grin. 'Government plates.'

The next dish wipes the smug grin right off my face. At first sight, the grey-green mulch, studded with tiny pieces of chilli, doesn't look too threatening. But emerging from the middle is the front half of an angry-looking beetle, eyes bulging and front legs raised for attack. I pull back, thinking it still alive.

'It's dead, head just for decoration. Water beetle.'

I continue to keep my distance. Having just feasted on live creatures, karma might be coming round to give me a shock. It's a sauce for dipping, Lucky explains, and very popular in the South. I roll a ball of rice in my hand, and dip it in, still eyeing the dead beetle for any sudden, zombie-like resurrection. There's nothing. The taste is strong and slightly acrid, dominating everything else with a hint of nail polish, like the essence of pear drops. This artificial sweetness lingers on the tongue, refusing to budge for anything. It's the nearest I've got so far to an entirely new taste. Although the nail polish gives you a hint, it's so unique as to be unclassifiable. Not horrible, just weird.

I smack my lips but Lucky sees through the charade. She digs in with birdlike elegance. 'Yes, special taste,' she agrees.

Then another salad, dotted with plump, white spheres nestling among the mint, chilli and onion. This time, I spot them immediately. 'Ant egg salad,' I crow triumphantly.

I have been desperate to try these delicacies ever since reading *Ant Egg Soup*. Du Pont De Bie had searched for them ever since seeing them stacked up in a market and only has a taste towards the end of her trip. 'I felt a pang of guilt,' she admits. 'I have always been fascinated with ants, ever since I was a child while on holiday in the South of France ... now I was about to eat them.'

I have no such qualms and spoon a huge hillock into my mouth. The eggs don't really taste of much, save for the very faintest hint of nut. They have a yielding texture which offers a welcome contrast to the endless green leaves of the salad. Having eaten both water beetle and live shrimp, the ant eggs feels almost normal. The usual chilli, padek, lime and herb flavours dominate the mouth but the eggs are surprisingly moreish.

There's a recipe for Mawk Khai Mod (or Ant Eggs Steamed in Banana Leaves) in *Traditional Recipes of Laos* so at some point, they must have been served up to the Kings of Laos.

'In fact,' continues Du Pont De Bie, 'they are full of protein and have been found to contain vitamins B1, B2 and B12 and the trace minerals calcium, phosphorus, iron, selenium, zinc and magnesium. Not bad for something so tiny.'

Although the idea of beetles' guts and hopping crustaceans might seem repellent to us, it's all very much part of the Laotian cuisine. Anything that moves is fair game and the variety of enticing herbs and spices makes any ingredient all the more palatable. For Lucky, and millions of other Laotians, anything that can be gathered from the forest – or bought from the many markets – and doesn't make you ill is a welcome bonus. The ingredients might seems bizarre but to the Lao people, they're anything but.

A few hours into my first day, and I have learnt to shut up about 'extreme' food and just try as much as I could. As the journey progresses, I find myself able to distance myself from what I eat. This failed miserably with the dog but here, it feels entirely natural. Although I am interested in trying out the insects, I never imagined I would actually like their taste. More of a 'very interesting' and tick the box. But here, these are wonderful dishes in their own right. What had seemed so 'dangerous' back in London feels entirely normal, as much as part of the culinary landscape as chillies or chicken. Insects no longer make me squeamish, even less so in China, where they are presented as second-rate tourist attractions rather than as real food.

That doesn't mean to say I'll come home and scour the garden for cockroaches and worms, but these crawly things are just another form of protein, like steak or dog or lamb. This seems an important moment on my journey. Rather than just enduring lunch, so I can say I have done it, I actually begin to appreciate it. Like anything, though, you're not going to love it all. The silk worm pupae are still seared horribly and indelibly onto my palate and the water beetle sauce is more experience than delight. But for the first time, these insects actually become part of an incredibly good lunch.

The aftermath of our lunch feast resembles a tabletop insect holo-caust; a few remaining shrimps, long expired. The odd pupa lost on the floor and only a few white blobs left hiding among the salad. Just as I am leaning back for a post-prandial cigarette, the plates begin to rattle and our small, wooden room starts to shudder. I look over in panic to Lucky, who seems spectacularly unconcerned. After the shud-der, the room begins to move away from the main restaurant, as if torn away by some unseen force. Only 20 feet away from dry land do I realise that this slender, private room is actually a boat with an engine at the back.

When lunch finishes, a driver slips on, fires up the engine and takes us on a spluttering cruise down the river. The banks on either side are thick with luscious vegetation, palm trees and thick plants interspersed with the odd shelter to protect workers from the blazing sun. Cows graze on the banks as I pick at the remains of our lunch and for the first time of the day, there's complete silence. To me, the landscape is so familiar as to be almost everyday. I feel like one of those earlier Sixties hippies, in constant search of spiritual nirvana and the perfect, virgin view. For all I know, the banks have changed hugely in the past few years, but to me, they still seem undefiled by Western eye. Yet there's something more familiar. I know I've seen the scene before but can't think where. Was it in a stoned haze on my gap-year? Probably not.

Then it hits me. 'Nam. *Apocalypse Now. Platoon.* The lush vegetation. The deep brown water. At any moment, I expect a fleet of helicopters to come swooping down, spreading chaos and hot lead in their wake. Never mind that both were filmed in the Philippines, nor that all I can see in this verdurous beauty is a couple of war movies. Once again, the fact is coloured by the fiction. The revelation soon passes and I lie back once more, the thuds of the rotors fading in the distance, as I watch the cows, lazily grazing at the river bank. I feel my eyelids drooping and, lulled by the movement of the boat and the soporific landscape around me, I slip off into a deep and well-fed sleep.

We spend a few hours on the river then climb back onto dry land and into Lucky's car.

'You want to see something different, something really Laotian?' she asks as Scorpion beg to be taken 'to the magic of the moment of the glory nights' (a soft rock classic, as we both agree).

We're on the outskirts of Vientiane, outside a typical country 'evening market' (actually open all day). It's where the local villagers bring and sell whatever they've captured in the surrounding rivers, ponds and forests, the epicentre of a local community. Food is bought and cooked fresh here every day as the majority of households don't have fridges. We pass through the entrance into a wide open space, with concrete floor and hundreds of stalls. Flimsy parasols lean at jaunty angles, protecting traders from the sun. Women sit chattering and bartering behind their own stalls, occasionally brushing the flies off their wares with plastic bags attached to sticks. I'm greeted by a brace of split, dried rats, their faces and fangs caught vividly in the grimace of death.

'These ones no good, too old,' Lucky decides.

I cheer, silently. Deep-fried bugs might be sweet but rat jerky held very little appeal. Lying next door are three squirrels, their little incisors poking from the front of their mouth and their heads all close together, as if deep in the weekly gossip. Their stripy tails hang loose off the table and they look like expensive stuffed toys in the windows of Hamley's.

The fur is soft but nothing compared to the beautiful Jungle Cat that sits, snuggled in a metal bowl. Slightly larger than the average cat, it has a coat that your average couture buyer would kill for; rich, fudgy browns swirled with the creamiest of whites. I smile at its owner, and want to stroke it. It looks so comfortable, on a bed of newspaper and oblivious to all around. But instead of warm fur and a softly beating heart, I feel rigid, lifeless flesh. The body is cold to the touch and I draw my hand back with a shriek.

'It's dead,' I say to Lucky.

'Of course it is. Otherwise it would be back in the jungle.' She shakes her head at my stupidity. 'They're a great delicacy here, but don't take any photos, as a little illegal.'

The owner of this little dead petting farm takes scant notice of us, instead continuing a spirited conversation with her friend next door. There is no real order to speak of, just local storeholders laying out what is good and fresh: piles of tomatoes, fat marrows, bunches of shallot in every shade of purple, four different kinds of aubergine, tamarind pods, bunches of dill, spring onions, nuts, hairy, dried-up strands of buffalo skin (it's soaked then added to laap for extra texture and flavour), baskets of frogs all taking it in turns to attempt a leap to freedom; lizards tied together by their tails like carrots, twitching and pulling each other in every direction; white and brown bunnies, Athena postcard pretty, nibbling merrily at the leaves below. Above them stands their executioner, a wrinkled old lady who's just bought them for tonight's pot. Baskets of shrimp, hopping hither and thither next door to shallow bowls filled with dying, gasping carp. One belly flops pathetically onto the concrete floor and sits, twitching and gaping until picked up and thrown back into its shallow watery grave.

There is no place for sympathy here. Plump toads watch the crowds cautiously, their hooded eyes giving away little. One section is given over to tripe, whole stomachs sitting in piles, ready to be chopped to size. The smell is thick and bitter, the flies brawling and cussing to find a choice spot to land upon. There are endless eels slipping and writhing at the bottom of tubs, enough bugs in baskets to give an etymologist a hard-on, and birds no bigger than a thumb, traditionally eaten whole. I think back to those damned ortolans. How hard can it be to find them in France? We're near the epicentre of bird flu here, yet you can buy them by the sack load. I make a note to hassle my contact further.

Snakes lie limp and useless next to their natural prey, small furry forest rodents that offer no more than a bite of flesh. Some of the stallholders' offerings are pathetically paltry, a pile of weeds, some wretched songbirds and a bowl of teeming locusts. This is the result of their morning haul, and their income depends on it being bought. There's a lively bustle to the market, not raucous and loud but quiet and determined. Most of the fish are kept in minimal water, and the movement of these moribund creatures is slow and halting. The only noise is the quiet chatter of bargaining and the rustle of plastic bags. The police do occasional checks, to ensure that nothing illegal is being sold. But the tip-offs are good and anything faintly endangered disappears for a while, only reappearing when the police are long gone.

One section is entirely devoted to padek, black plastic buckets filled with what looks like chunky sewage. The smell is intense and rotten, yet the longer matured the sauce, the better it is supposed to be. It's ladled out into bags and pots and takes centre stage in the market, as it does in Laotian cooking too. This is the sort of market that would give your average bunny hugger a nervous breakdown, but such is the harsh reality of life in Laos. Lucky admits that this is a little more 'raw' than the average Vientiane market, but not by much. 'This is normal Laos life here.'

For most of the country, existence is hand to mouth. I almost trip over a fugitive eel, slithering through the dust on the road to nowhere. Its bid for freedom is short lived. Lucky says she once saw a tiger cub here, found in the forest and immediately killed and sold. For us, this seems barbaric, with little thought for the future. For the people that eke out a living, it's plain survival. As in China and Japan and Korea, animals are seen as food first and foremost. These people cannot afford to start getting emotionally attached; another beast, another way to make some money and survive another day.

The sheer variety of river fish is incredible, all laid out in fly-blown piles. Lucky assures me that the majority would be gone by sundown.

'This is proper Lao market, country style.' She buys six small silver carp for her dinner, and a bagful of herbs and chillies.

The market is a thrilling glimpse into true Lao cooking, both exciting and a little grotesque. No covering up of the unsightly bits here. For me it is an exotic spectacle. For everyone else, just the usual run to Sainsbury's.

Dinner is at the other end of the culinary spectrum, as I decide to try what is said to be the finest French restaurant in town. The dust and the laid-back chaos of the day have all but disappeared and dusk falls quickly. But the air is alive with the squawks and tweets of thousand upon thousand of noisy, chattering parakeets. As the sun dips down over the Mekong, they all descend to roost on the skeletal radio masts that sit astride the city. Even with the light long gone, they keep up their endless chatter until deep into the night.

Just one day here, and I have already adjusted to the slower pace of life. My usual impatience has turned to a shrug and even the occasional power cuts do little to dampen my growing ardour for the city. Like Lewis said, there's very little to admire in Vientiane but I am smitten. I feel comfortable and well-fed, feeling none of the loneliness of Korea or slight alienation of Japan. Of all the places I've visited so far, it's this messy, sleepy city that's really seduced me.

In the grand and airy Settha Palace Hotel, the dining room is empty but the bar is awash with cashmere-clad, aged affluence. These are the sorts of tourists that every country in the world desires, big spenders yet on the whole well-mannered. The jewellery is discrete and expensive, the scents pungent and the suede Todds loafers worn without socks. They chatter over their martinis, a hybrid of French, English and American, smooth and contented. Dinner is as French as Monsieur Hulot's culottes, exquisitely sweet onion soup, thick with croutons and melted Gruyère cheese. But I can't resist the lure of the Laos again, and revert back to more laap and papaya salad. I creep out of La Belle Epoque, past the groomed ladies and elegant men, and walk back to the hotel.

As Mel Gibson, in *Lethal Weapon*, tells Danny Glover, 'When I was 19, I did a guy in Laos with a rifle shot at a thousand yards in high wind ...' I fall asleep, trying to work out what the hell 'Mad' Martin Riggs was doing all those years back in Laos.

It doesn't take much digging to find out. Gibson's character is the stereotypical burnt-out Vietnam Vet who fought in Special forces. During Vietnam, Laos was supposed to be neutral. Under the Geneva Accord of 1962, it was forbidden to have any foreign military personnel anywhere near the country. Since gaining independence from the French, Laos was split between the military and American-backed Royalist movement, the communist Pathet Lao (helped by the Vietnamese) and the Neutralist Royal Movement, led by Prince Savana Phouma, sitting somewhere in the middle.

Governments (four between 1945 and 1974) and coalitions came and went but it was America's 'Secret War' that caused the most devastating, and abiding, damage in Laos' long and often turbulent history. To help fight the communist threat, CIA agents were disguised as aid workers while the airmen were made to look like civilian flyers. They created this Secret War (kept hidden from the American people) by recruiting the tough, hill-dwelling Hmong in the east to fight the communist North Vietnamese troops and Pathet Lao.

The CIA effort in Laos remains the most expensive paramilitary operation ever conducted by the USA. The North Vietnamese were also breaking the Geneva Accord by occupying Laos and by 1969, there were over 70,000 North Vietnamese personnel deployed there. They invaded the country, rushing down the Ho Chi Minh Trail on their way to the South and the Americans were determined to destroy them, as well as supporting the Laotian government forces fighting a losing battle against the Pathet Lao rebels. This massive air power meant that they didn't have to deploy ground troops and would try to choke the enemy supply lines. So the Americans, as they were not supposed to be anywhere near, could bomb the hell out of the country without fears of disobeying the 'Rules of Engagement'.

The Ravens were a bunch of American pilots who wore no uniform and carried no identification. Their job was to identify targets – under heavy ground fire – and call in air strikes. From 1964 right through until 1973, the Americans flew over 580,000 bombing runs over Laos, one every nine minutes for ten years. This led to more than two million tonnes of ordnance being rained down from the skies, double the amount dropped on the Nazis in World War Two.

Martin Stuart-Fox, author of many books on the country's history, including *A History of Laos*, believes that, 'on a per-capita basis, Laos remains the most heavily bombed nation in the history of warfare'. Cluster bombs (known to the Lao as 'bombies') were particularly favoured, as they could penetrate the jungle canopy and cover a huge area of ground. Eighty million were dropped on Laos, with 10–30 per cent not exploding. That meant that up to 24 million unexploded bombs still remained. Not only did this small, peaceful country endure a virtual black rain of bombs for nine years, but the killing still goes on.

In the last three decades more than 12,000 people, many of them children, have been killed or maimed by bombies or other UXOs (unexploded ordnance). *New York Times* columnist Anthony Lewis wrote that this 'was the most appalling episode of lawless cruelty in American history'. In December 1975, just after America scarpered, taking all its aid with it, the Lao People's Revolutionary Party took over the newly named Lao People's Democratic Republic. The Americans had gone but their bombs remained.

Luang Prabang is the ancient mountain kingdom of Laos sitting 700 metres above sea level. It takes just 20 minutes to reach, flying north from the capital. But the moment I arrive at the tiny airport, I begin to miss the relative bustle of Vientiane. The weather is damp and pallid, the road from airport to town ragged and plastered in cheap signs offering endless adventure trips. It feels like an off-season Alpine village. So much for the earthly paradise adored by French colonials. It is impossible to move at any speed in this town, and everyone is soon overcome by the easy torpor that seems to spike the water. There's the usual hive of Internet cafés, secondhand book-shops, restaurants offering 'Westin cuisin' and the rest of the detritus so necessary to the twenty-first-century traveller. They line the main street, tucked between the temples (or wats) and the rivers (the town sits at the confluence of the Nam Kahn and Mekong rivers), but far from touting their trade, they almost discourage it. The saffron-robed monks mix with well-to-do gay couples, the occasional bewildered hippy (bartering over 2p, just for a change) and plenty of fresh-faced, well-scrubbed gap-year students, moving from temple to temple in a bid to 'do' them all in a day. The locals, for the most part, ignore the impostors.

In just five minutes, I realise the city has changed little since Norman Lewis visited in the Fifties:

> It is built into a tongue of land formed by the confluence with the river of a tributary; a small, somnolent and sanctified Manhattan Island. A main street has turnings down to the river on each side and a pagoda at every few yards, with a glittering roof and doors and pillars carved with a close pattern of gilded and painted designs.

Not just Manhattan, he continues in another article, 'A Festival in Laos', 'but a Manhattan with holy men in yellow in its avenues, with pariah dogs, and garlanded pedicabs carrying somnolent Frenchmen nowhere, and doves in its skies'. He adored the city, waxing about it being

the hometown of the siesta and the Ultima Thule of all French escapists in the Far East. Europeans who come here to live soon acquire a certain, recognisable manner. They develop quiet voices, and gentle, rapt expressions. This is accompanied by the determined insouciance of the New Year's reveller ...

Even the dogs move at their own sedate pace. Life moves as slowly as the Mekong. The tourist is viewed as neither enemy nor walking cash dispenser. We are merely a transitory presence in an ancient royal city, just like the centuries of other transient invaders. The tourists are of a more genteel kind too, predominantly middle class and late to middle age. Even the backpackers have a fresh-faced, scrubbed health, rather than the dope-addled crustiness of Goa, Kathmandu or Ko Phan Ngang. Small children play petanque (boules) on a perfectly kept arena (another French legacy), while coq au vin, onion soup and confit of duck are as much a feature as traditional Laotian food. Day markets line the main road, providing spicy papaya salads, bunches of fresh herbs big enough to stuff a pillow and the usual dazzling array of misshapen tomatoes and chilli.

The meat stalls are thick with fat, black flies and the constant swatting of the owners does little to dissuade them. No one seems to bother, picking up a plastic bag full of fresh blood, a head and a big slab of liver. The meat is predominantly water-buffalo. Everywhere, people are eating and gossiping, dipping their sticky rice into endless soups and salads. A few tourists sit on makeshift tables, grinning self-consciously and trying not to choke as the chilli is thrown in with a liberal ease. I smile knowingly at them, but I don't know where my smugness comes from. I'm one of them, the well-dressed tourist with money to spend. In the eyes of the Laos, we're all the same.

The people of Luang Prabang have long been known for their easy-going approach to life.

'All down the main street, which runs between the hill and the river, the ladies sit behind their baskets, flirting with the men, who cruise up and down with apparently not much else to do' was the reaction of H. Warrington Smyth, British national and 'loyal servant of HM King Chulalongkorn' of Thailand. He had made it up the Mekong at the end of the nineteenth century in search of gemstones (his book is straightforwardly titled *Exploring for Gemstones on the Upper Mekong*). 'What with the attractions of the music, their love and battle songs, and perhaps other things, the Laos of Luang Prabang keep late hours, and are late to turn out.'

His tome is gentle but cannot hide the slight Victorian concern he feels for such a happily indolent race. But central to a basic under-standing of Laos is the Buddhist view of money and work. Norman Lewis explains:

> It is considered ill-bred and irreligious in Laos to work more than is necessary. The father of a family cultivates an amount of land, estimated, by a bonze [or Buddhist priest] who is expert in such matter, to be sufficient for his requirement. If there are six members of the family, six standard, equal sized portions will be cultivated.

Necessary work will be completed, leaving all the more time to sit around, talk and eat. It sounds the very pinnacle of civilisation to me. But in Luang Prabang, the wats and bonzes are central to life, both for the gaping tourists and the respectful locals. There are 66 wats in the city, and you'll often be walking down some back-street, turn and come face to face with some ornate wall or gold-plated roof. The city is on UNESCO's world heritage list, and thus protected. But you immediately get the feeling this is a work-ing religious centre, rather than an attraction kept on life support for the benefit of the foreigners.

One thing I do notice, above the occasional hoot of the tuk-tuk horn, is a complete absence of birds. Not a cheep or even a whistle, save from the tiny songbirds sold at the entrance to the temples. Kept in miniscule bamboo cages, they are for tourists to buy and set free, thus salving their conscience. Of course, the birds all fly back to the same tree once liberated, where they are recaptured for the next gullible bunch that comes walking along.

I take a left off the main street and descend a slight hill to be met with my first sight of the Luang Prabang Mekong. It is fast approach-ing the dry season and the river is low, sluggish and muddy. Piles of rubbish sit beneath fluttering flags of drying laundry and a few long, heavy cargo boats cruise downstream. Half a dozen elongated passen-ger boats sit hauled up on the mud, their sailors huddled over a bowl of foe (the Laos version of the Vietnamese Pho noodle soup). Bursts of Thai pop drift downriver, tangled up with the strangulated crow of the local cockerel and the incongruous lament of a solitary harmonica.

I find a restaurant perched above the steep bank and decide to stop for lunch. The cuisine of Luang Prabang is different from that in the rest of the country, more refined and regal as befits its status as the royal and holy city. Locals say that the food is more special and fussy, traditional and long established. More wealth meant a surfeit of meat and complicated dishes. Luang Prabang is the gastronomic centre of

Laos and proud of it. The 34 wats and the bonzes who live in most of them are central to the culture and food of the region.

Every morning, the monks and novices walk a specified path through the old section of the city. And the locals (and tourists, of course) line the streets, filling the monks' bowls with sticky rice, fruit, biscuits and other treats. The monks get to eat and the donor accrues merit for himself, his family and his ancestors. On special Buddhist days, the poor put their bowls alongside those of the monks and when the monks' bowls are full, they put the rest into the empty bowls. So everyone is fed. Huge vats of foe are cooked up and distributed to the temples. And eating is very much a communal affair, as much bought from the market stalls that dot the streets as cooked at home. There are no kitchens as we know them, rather small clay vessels, filled with wood, the pot put on top.

Khai Paen, a dried river moss and Luang Prabang speciality, doesn't sound like much. But it's highly addictive. It's cleaned, dried out in thin sheets then sprinkled with sesame seeds before being deep fried. Similar to the seaweed so beloved by Chinese restaurants, it's served with a tangy tamarind sauce. Phak nam is a type of watercress particular to the area and comes as the star of Luang Prabang salad, a mixture of eggs, peanuts, coriander, dill, mint and lettuce, all drenched in a garlicky, eggy dressing. For me, it is too rich, too heavy and bland. The highlight is a Laotian sausage, crisp and perfectly porky, served with a pungent chilli shrimp paste. The fresh crunch of the vegetables and the fatty rich-ness of the sausage are well tempered by the punchy dressing. The fish larp is different here too, pounded into a soft paste rather than roughly chopped. And the steamed fish comes in the form of an eggy omelette, delicately flavoured with coconut and chilli. Soft and elegant, it is true royal food.

As I wander home, the sun has risen to its height and the feeling is one of blissful torpor. Saffron-clad monks sit in the cool shade of temple porticos, chattering quietly while the tuk-tuk drivers stretch out in the back of their cabs for a sleep, or play a very slow game of cards. Motorbikes bearing perfectly elegant Laotian ladies cruise by; they perch on the back in side-saddle, shaded from the sun under dainty umbrellas. The only people on the streets now are red-faced tourists. At one point, the stillness is broken by a funeral procession. A tuk-tuk bearing a coffin is followed by a flotilla of bikes, motorbikes, scooters and more tuk-tuks, crammed with relatives.

The mood is merry. The city seems content with its dusted, faded glory, the old temples with their dulled gold and weather-beaten reds. The French colonial villas have the same attitude, with cracked walls, crumbling facades and smudged-white paint. They wear their dilapidation like a favourite old coat. I walk behind a pair of English couples, immaculate in their pressed slacks, white socks and polished leather shoes. They must be around 70 but aside from a little gentle moaning ('Gerald, you will tell our waiter tonight that we don't like it spicy. It does so disagree with my stomach') and bossing ('George, you do know that you shouldn't eat all of the lemongrass ... it's there for decoration'), they're keen to lap up every last detail of this unspectacular spectacle. A barrel-shaped, sun-ravaged German with fisherman's pants and a thick neck argues gutturally over the price of Internet access and we all purse our lips. The Laotians just shrug and go back to their slumber.

After spending the afternoon in bed (I usually can't so much as close an eye after lunch) in a deep and vivid sleep, I pull on some clothes and get ready for the trudge back into town. Night has fallen and, with it, the temperature. Dressed against the elements in jumper and jeans, I make my way towards the Apsara, a boutique hotel in the centre of town owned by a contact given to me by Sam called Ivan Scholte. I'm particularly bad at contacts in foreign lands, feeling myself an unwelcome imposition at the best of times. I pretend it's because I'm self-conscious but know full well the main reason is laziness and boredom. I'd rather eat by myself than talk crap with someone who doesn't really want to see me over some awkward dinner. The problem is that locals or local ex-pats are always the best source of real information, unless you want to slavishly follow the well-trodden guide book path. I felt immediately relaxed with Lucky, but that's because our silences were comfortable. With silence sorted, there's little worry about the rest. But I have no idea what to expect of Ivan, nor he of me.

The restaurant overlooks the Namh Khan and is open to the street. The place is already full and I ask the barman for Ivan.

'Um, it's me,' says a voice behind me and I turn to see a tall, bespectacled man dressed like an off-duty city banker. He's good looking, in cashmere V-neck and stripy shirt, with impeccable manners, an easy charm and piercing blue eyes. I am put immediately at ease by his manner.

'Now what would you like to drink? A glass of wine, yes? Wonderful.' He pours out a glass of Chablis and as I glug it back, he starts to talk. 'I've been looking for a hotel in South East Asia for years,' he says, one eye on the new guests coming in. 'Vietnam seemed too much trouble, what with being ripped off at every juncture. Then I came to Laos and fell in love. Up here in Luang Prabang, there's a limited capacity for aeroplanes coming in, so the tourism cannot become rapacious.'

He looks down at my now empty glass. 'Right, time to fill that up.' He pours a generous slug. 'Here, most people are politically apathetic and happy to get on with what they want to. There's still some man left over here from the French days, though I'm not sure how truthful his endless stories are. They seem somewhat embellished. He's probably an accountant from Lyon. Now let's eat. Where's Charlotte?'

As he says that, a small, blonde woman with flustered hair and a bag full of cameras comes rushing in.

'Sorry I'm late,' she trills, 'you know how it is.' She's another ex-pat, a journalist and photographer and based in Thailand. 'Ivan and I are old friends,' she explains.

As we sit down, Ivan tells me the story of his pet civet cat. 'Well, I used to have one anyway. Was very fond of it actually. Lived in a huge cage outside my house. Very sweet, was given to me by an employee of my girlfriend, who found it orphaned. Of course, let it loose in the house and it used to go a bit crazy, jumping everywhere and shitting in the bath ... by the way, you're out of wine. Here, have some more.'

The warm fuzz of alcohol spreads thorough my veins and I ask where the civet cat is now.

'Well, you see that's the thing,' he replies with an embarrassed shrug. 'My neighbours nicked it and ate it. I found a hole in the cage and no sign of the cat. Bastards. I tried to start a rumour that it had had SARS, just to give the fuckers indigestion. Anyway, there we go. What a wretched end, though. Ah, here's the jaew bong, a local speciality. Dried buffalo skin mixed with red chillies, garlic and shallots, a sauce for dipping dried beef or vegetables into. The skin gives a good crunch at first, as well as a chewy texture. The shallots and garlic are burnt, to give that real smoky Laotian taste. Tastes better than it sounds.'

It's rich, and the skin chewy, eaten with thin slices of air-dried meat. Raw buffalo larp follows quickly, the meat hand-chopped and mixed with roasted rice powder for crunch and flavour. The nam paa-dek (the juice surrounding the padek) adds body and depth, the mint and other herbs zip. Quite superb again, and embellished with a few chewy slices of buffalo skin. Then Say-uwaa, buffalo blood sausage which is just like a black pudding, only more spicy and herby. It has an earthy flavour, flecked with herbs.

The rest of the evening descends into a white wine haze, as course after course, fish, meat, appear on the table and I leave late into the night, having bored everyone stupid, no doubt, wobbling back home with the promise to meet Charlotte first thing at Phousi market.

It's typical that the nights I get to bed early and wake bright eyed and all that are invariably the days when I have little to do. And when I get steaming drunk, it's guaranteed that I'll have not just an early start but the prospect of something appalling to put in my mouth too. It happened in Japan and is certain to happen again before my journey is over.

Today is no exception. I arrive with heavy head, unable even to force down black coffee. Charlotte, who didn't drink last night, is a little more enthusiastic to see the dawn. She bounces in, explaining that we're going to be taken around by Ruth, the Australian owner of a local restaurant and cooking school. Markets are always the best place to get a taste of everyday Laos life. This is similar to the night market I've seen with Lucky, only it sells every kind of item, edible or not.

We meet Ruth in the market's car park. She has cropped, grey hair, Pat Butcher dangling earrings and a throaty Australian boom. The morning is cool enough to see your breath but at this moment, the less I see of my own breath, the better. She tells us the market was opened just two years ago.

'In the mid-Nineties medication was strictly limited. I had to bring back malaria drugs from abroad as no one had enough.'

She first came to Laos in 1974, when her uncle was the Australian Ambassador. 'It was a very different place then,' is all she will say.

We pass the usual muddles of tamarinds and chillies, and pyramids of the sticky, hairy strips of dried buffalo skin and strips of dried buffalo liver to chew, like biltong.

'They're big on innards here, don't waste a bloody thing,' she shouts. 'One thing you must understand is the Lao love sweet, bitter and sour, sometimes in the same dish.'

She thunders on through, greeting locals and pointing out every ingredient. Then she stops. 'My parents were killed up here in Luang Prabang, so everyone was afraid to let me come up.' She stares into the air for a moment.

Charlotte and I look to the ground, not sure what to say. This powerful comment hangs in the air for a moment before she plucks it away and moves on.

'The Lao have no past tense or no future tense. They live in the now so there is no real written history of the country.'

She points out the carrots, broccoli and cauliflower brought over by the French. Her voice booms across the market, but the locals have heard it all before. They barely look up.

She picks up a hunk of wood. 'The Lao use wood in their cooking, as they love texture as well as taste. They take the bark off, chop it up and add to dishes. It's the only place I know in the world where wood is used in bloody food.'

I make a note to seek some out. I ask about the ant eggs, expecting her to congratulate me on my daring.

'What? Very few Lao actually eat the bloody things. I reckon it's some bloody Western fixation.'

I retreat behind Charlotte, suitably chastised.

'But they will eat anything that crawls, jumps or flies. Just not too many ant eggs about, I reckon.'

She strides on through the market. 'Ah, padek.'

The stench is thick and fetid, like open sewers in the heat of the sun. She grabs a ladle and starts stirring a black plastic bowl filled with a thick, diarrhoea-like liquid.

'Here, have a sniff,' says Ruth, thrusting it under my nose.

I move surprisingly fast in the circumstances, bolting to the relative safety of the vegetable section. One more second in that grotesque fug, and the contents of my stomach would be splattered over the floor. I take a couple of deep breaths, swallowing back down the saliva that has flooded my mouth.

'You alright?' asks Charlotte.

'Yup,' I mumble, wishing the tour was at an end and that I was back, tucked up in bed with a cool breeze playing over my sweating forehead.

The soothing greens of the limes, chillies, green beans and cabbages abruptly give way to the raw meat section, where the warm stink of recent death turns the air into a visceral sludge. The usual swarms of flies are in attendance, nonchalantly swatted off with long switches. Chunks of coagulated blood sit in quivering piles, next to the usual display of innards, heads and the rest. Ruth picks a turkey, still warm after its recent death.

'This is a legacy from the Americans. They used to bring them in for Thanksgiving and they've sort of stayed here.'

Great, they annihilate the country with their bombs and leave the blandest bird in existence as a memento. How kind. The market has the same quiet activity shared by the whole country, and everyone seems to be chewing or snacking on some delicacy or other.

'The Lao have food in their mouths from the moment they wake up to the moment they go to bed. They eat street food, at home, whenever they're hungry … it's a great grazing country.'

As if on cue, a gaggle of women flutter by, chewing on thick strips of buffalo skin.

I manage to avoid tasting a piece of grilled lizard (I know I should but *you* try eating Kermit's cousin when debilitated by a wretched hangover) by staring intently at bags of disposable pens, piled high next to cheap make-up and state-of-the-art rice cookers.

'It's the women who are the big drinkers in Lao, not the men,' says Ruth pointedly, catching a whiff of the neat alcohol pouring from my pores. 'It's the women who run the show too. They inherit the property, they do the trading, they're the money makers. They also eat far more chilli than the men, and will happily sit eating Tom Thumb chillies by the handful.'

I think back to the raucous group of ladies I pass every time I leave my guesthouse to go into town. As I amble past, they burst into well-oiled hysterics, asking my name and offering me a shot of whatever they're drinking. Petrified, I smile and hurry on. Ivan also told me about the 'ladies who lunch' at one of his favourite feu stalls.

'It's best to get there before three, otherwise they're legless. They can really put it away. The men are pussies in comparison.'

None of this chat does my hangover any good and the fish section, with its flapping, suffocating creatures, adds just another odour to an already raddled palette.

'Fish has got so expensive these days,' explains Ruth. 'The rivers just aren't rising any more. You might have this idea of everyone in Laos subsisting on fish but that's simply not true. The Hmong diet is just steamed rice with boiled veg. Or steamed rice with fried veg with some padek. Many people still live at subsistence level here. In 1995, there were no books, pens, deodorant, shampoo, medicine …. Nothing. Laos is changing fast. Now come, let's get back home.'

I breathe a heartfelt sigh of relief as we leave the sights and smells of the Laotian morning market. Under other, more clear-headed circumstances, I'd have revelled in every moment. Today, I just want my bed.

We drive back to the centre of Luang Prabang and sit in the colonial cool of Ruth's restaurant. Her brusque facade drops a little as she talks of her Laotian family.

'Every Laotian who lived through the Sixties and Seventies has seen horror beyond belief. The Hidden War was an atrocity, no families escaped. During the Communist time, many Laotian women were taken from their homes to serve as prostitutes.'

She breaks off to greet one of her chefs. 'And then there was the bombing. The bombers left the North Thai base every six minutes and if they didn't find their target, they just dropped their load anywhere over the country. The bombs are still everywhere. And I've seen the destruction these bombie bombs leave. There's nothing much left after being blown away by one of these.'

Her steely gaze hardens, and she stops, lost in angry contemplation. 'Of course, the Americans still deny it ever happened. They set up the whole drugs thing. The CIA used drug money to finance the fight against communism. Anyway, that's a whole different story. Now, back to the food.'

It seems a little trite to be talking of sauces and textures after what we've just heard. But in Laos, the pleasure taken in eating seems to salve the memories of the past. The collective experience that is eating together might help deal with the collective hell they've all been through. But then, as Ruth tells us, there is only the concept of the present, no past or future. Which makes the enjoyment of the moment all the more important.

Ruth clears her throat and launches into a well-rehearsed patter. 'It's all about taste and texture, sweet, sour, bitter. It's a drier form of cooking than Thai, and less sweet. And the heat comes from adding chillies and pastes, rather than everything being super-spicy from the start.'

I ask her about the larp.

'Well, I wouldn't touch raw larp in a restaurant, unless you've watched it being prepared. They're delicious but you have to be careful.'

I tell her about the buffalo one I ate the night before.

'Well, you'd certainly know about it by now if it was dodgy. Where did you eat it? Ah, the Apsara. That's fine.'

The lunchtime rush has started (well, a few more scooters whizz past) while Ruth tells us how Luang Prabang has changed.

'Ten years ago, there were five trucks, three cars and 60 motorbikes. Everything was run down and there were two hotels and two guesthouses. Now look at it.'

As if on cue, a phalanx of well-dressed Germans clip by. Ruth has to get back into the kitchen but before we go, I ask if she knows Oliver Bandesman. All my contacts in Laos have suggested that I meet him. He is said to know the country intimately, with a reputation for the rather eccentric. The atmosphere changes abruptly. Any warmth is driven away and her eyes set into a stare while her mouth puckers with disgust.

'I have no contact with that man. And I suggest you do the same.'

No amount of prying will get Ruth to tell me more. It just makes me all the keener to find him.

'Oh, don't worry about that,' says Charlotte as we go off for lunch with Ivan at one of his favourite noodle houses. 'Oliver is very, well, let's say flamboyant. I only met him this morning, but he's utterly charming. A true character. I saw him first in the airport, speaking immaculate Laos to a policeman, a Jack Russell sitting at his feet. Very elegant, mid-fifties, and speaks seven languages too. There's nothing he doesn't know about the country. He's got a beautiful shop just up the road. We'll go and see him later.'

I've already built him up into some sort of Conradian figure, pursuing a life of aesthetic perfection, reading ancient Laotian poetry while being gently fanned by beautiful young cherubs. It's going back to my fictionalised Indo-China, back to boozy journalists and pampered pashas too afraid to return to the real world. And Luang Prabang, although civilised, is far removed from the real world. Like every isolated outpost, it's bound to have its share of the more colourful figures, escaping from I don't know what.

After a bumpy tuk-tuk ride uptown, we find the familiar, slender shape of Ivan hunched over a bowl of feu. Madame Nom's is little more than a rattan roadside shack with plastic tables and chairs. Geese squawk outside, occasionally waddling in to pick at any scraps dropped on the floor. A mynah bird guards the entrance, mimicking the sound of a starting scooter. Occasionally, he breaks into a pitch-perfect rendition of the deep, phlegmatic hawking of his mistress. At the back is a small kitchen with a large vat of brown bubbling stock. The family sit glued to a Thai version of *Big Break*, breaking into hysterical giggles as another trick shot is pulled off. The floor is dirty and wooden and the walls plastered with calendars featuring pouting Thai pop princesses and shyly smiling Laotian ladies. There are pictures of the family too, and a piece of dried honeycomb takes pride of position. We sit down next to Ivan, who admits to feeling a little ropy too.

'Anyway, this feu will clear any lingering hangover. I eat it every day. I've tried every place in town but this is the best, with the finest stock and the freshest noodles.'

Charlotte has to rush off again on some photographic mission, but Ivan orders – in his perfect, English-accented Lao – another bowl of the same, for me. In under a minute, a huge, steaming, invitingly brown bowl of water buffalo feu is dumped before me. The smell is intense and inviting. Alongside the usual foliage of fresh basil, spring onions, coriander, mint and unidentified leaves are a bottle of fish sauce, two types of fresh chilli (the small, ferocious, sharp scuds and the more elongated, fresher-tasting ones in yellows and light greens), chilli paste, sugar and a Maggi-type seasoning. You customise your soup to taste.

I load my bowl with the herbs, then a splodge of the chilli paste. It takes on a reddish hue and the fumes bring a tear to my eye. Then a handful of fresh chillies, a dash of fish sauce and a drop of lime. If only all food was this much fun. Nothing, though, prepares me for the meaty intensity of the broth; the flavour is rich and strident, first a hint of mint, then the crunch of spring onion then the warmth of the chilli. The fish sauce deepens the taste, the lime lifts it up.

I have to stop here and take stock. I take another sip and another, and a mouthful of noodles. It's true. This is not only the best soup I have ever tasted but possibly the finest dish of the trip so far. Compared to this dirt-cheap feu, even the finest o-toro sashimi pales into insignificance. It brings a tear to my eye, seriously, and that's not just the chilli. I want to stand on the table and praise the good Lord, thanking him for my good fortune. This is comfort food eaten in a shack a long way from home, the sort of experience that you never want to end. Everything seems born to come together in my bowl. The noodles are superb, fresh and slippery while the meat provides tender shards of deep meatiness.

We slurp in silence, not wanting to waste one precious drop. If I drop dead now, my face falling splat into this bowl of soup, I'd die happy. Actually, forget what I said about this 'possibly' being the best food of the journey. It's the winner by a mile. A simple, roadside staple, with no fuss or fawning waiters, just the essence of South East Asia in a bowl. OK, so feu's a Vietnamese import but in this incarnation, it's totally Laotian.

'The soup has to be good,' says Ivan, pushing away his empty bowl. 'Everyone here has a strong opinion of food, their favourite places and the ones to avoid. If the quality's bad, no one will come.'

We seem to have lost our collective palate in Britain, despite the huge popularity of TV chefs and glossy cookbooks. We are happy to just put up with the mediocre to avoid a fuss. Or perhaps a great swathe of people doesn't even know what a good broth tastes like. They're so benumbed by the over-salted pap of the ready meal that they no longer can tell good from bad. If I could bring this feu on a road show, take it around and let people see how simple good food has to be – no garnis, flounces, foams or millefeuille – I'm certain that they would turn their back on tasteless rubbish.

Looking around the room, I see dreamy smiles everywhere. They're all locals but every sip is savoured and adored as much as the first. Ten minutes later and my hangover has evaporated. What started off as a wretched day has turned into something special, all thanks to a 30p bowl of noodles.

Filled with the joys of life and good soup, I go back to find Oliver. In my mind, he's a link with the old Indo-China of my imagination, a colonial relic who should be dressed in a silk suit, cooled beneath a vast rattan fan. At his feet would be local lovers and servants, there for his every need. To me, Oliver seems the civil servant who never left. And I can't wait to meet him, ready to sit back and hear a raft of old stories about the good old days. His shop and house is a typical two-storeyed, wooden colonial building, with a long wooden balcony on the second floor. I walk in and ask a European-looking man if Oliver is in. He motions upstairs. I slip off my shoes, and creak up a wonky, steep set of wooden stairs.

'Oliver?' I whisper, to no response. I clear my throat. 'Oliver?'

'Hello,' comes the response, in rich, guttural German baroque. 'Come outside,' the voice says.

I go through the room, covered with pictures of 1930s aeroplanes. Piles of books and magazines sit neatly stacked in all the corners. Oliver's stretched out on the balcony, his face swarthy, handsome and well-lived in. His skin is deeply tanned, to match the bass of his voice, his hair Daz white, and piercing, brilliant blue eyes look me up and down. He looks nothing like I imagined yet fits his role to perfection. Behind him, an 18- or 19-year-old lolls indolently, coquettishly picking his nails. While Oliver is in an old T-shirt and jeans, the boy is immaculately attired in pressed chinos, crisp Oxford shirt and shiny shoes, a Laotian vision of the preppy ideal. I smile at him but he looks away.

'Welcome,' says Oliver, his eyes boring through my skull. 'You must be Tom. You're the man who has come here to, how shall I put it, eat dangerously. Well, you've come to the right place. Now, start off at Mali. Her catfish eggs are superb. Beautiful.'

It's as if he has known me all of his life. He has a natural charm and elegance, a self-confidence that immediately puts me at ease. He gesticulates wildly then smacks his lips.

'Guide Michelin gives stars. Oliver hangs real stars. You'll see them there, still outside the restaurant.'

His manner is direct and disarming, his tone straight but passionate. He doesn't waste words, rather relishes every one that emits from his broad mouth. He often speaks of himself in the third person, a useful affectation of ego or insanity. But with Oliver, it seems entirely natural. A natural, expansive storyteller, you get the feeling that he's told every tale a million times. But his sheer charm and presence make you feel as if you are hearing it for the first time. He's very different from the ex-pats with their 'quiet voices and gentle, rapt expressions' that Lewis came across.

'I've been here for nine years. I came in front of the current carpetbaggers.' He says the last word with evident distaste. 'It's

Chinese New Year tonight, so it's all a little frantic. You know how the Lao love a party. Having said that, where are my dogs?'

He stands up and looks over to check on three Jack Russells, stretched out comatose in the dust below.

'OK, they're fine. Can't be too careful though. Right, first off go to Mali, have the catfish eggs fermented in the ground. And the Or Lam, the beef stew with the wood. You chew the wood to get a taste of the jungle.' It's the same thing that Ruth told me about this morning. 'Now, I've got to go, a minister is coming up for Vientiane and I want to show him a piece of land I've bought over the river, to create a garden and protect it from the developers. You must see it tomorrow. Come after lunch and we'll visit. It will blow you away.'

He stretches and gives a loud yawn. 'I'm really frantic at the moment.' He fixes me with those glacial eyes, then winks. 'Can't you see?'

Behind him, the teenager continues to clean his nails.

I can't help liking Oliver. He may not be exactly what I expected but he offers a very decent alternative, right down to his local lovers. Passion and energy radiate out of him, and it is impossible not to be pulled in. I understand why Ruth thought so little of him. He seems a love or hate figure, with precious little middle ground. We arrive at Mali where the eponymous owner greets Ivan like a long-lost son. The restaurant is busy and typically basic, a scruffy wooden building on a main road similar to the noodle place. There's a smattering of Western tourists (it's Author's Choice in the *Lonely Planet*, the three Michelin stars of the backpacker world) mixed in with Lao families and the atmosphere is one of contented chatter.

As usual, most of the family are glued around the television, where Chelsea play Everton on a wet, cold January evening in West London. The theme to *An Officer and a Gentleman* plays on a loop in the background, though I can only see two of Oliver's three stars. Perhaps he's taken one away.

Ivan orders some Laung Prabang specialities, including the fermented fish eggs. The menu is long and translated into rudimentary English. The 'minced ripe meat' sounds particularly alluring, along with the 'grinded crap peper sauce'. But I'm desperate to try the wood stew (or bon waan – the wood is actually sa-khan, a woody stem) and fish out a chunk the moment it arrives. It's soggy, like chewing on waterlogged pine and has a strange flavour, midway between resin and spice. It numbs the tongue and makes it tingle, similar to the Sichuan pepper I ate in China. That classic Laotian taste of charring undercuts the stew, and big clumps of dill add their anise fragrance. The wood does little on its own and I spit it out. In the context of the chicken stew, though, it adds another interesting note.

'It is an acquired taste,' admits Ivan. 'But I'm rather fond of it now.'

We plough our way through the usual larps (the duck one is superb) and Jee Sin Lod (grilled dried beef) with more Jaew bong. As is the tradition in all of Laos, the dishes are served at the same time, so you pick your way through different plates. The famed fish eggs have the strong, fermented flavour that you would expect, a real sucker punch to the palate. One bite is enough, though.

Dinner sprawls on for a few hours, as dish after dish appears on the table. Eventually, we all roll home, past the shuttered huts and moonlit paddy fields. Chinese New Year is at full tilt, and music blares out from every direction, along with hoots of laughter and sporadic fireworks. The partying goes on late into the night and I fall asleep to the sounds of 'Doe, a Deer' and 'Twinkle Twinkle Little Star' melded together into some bonkers, speeded-up hardcore anthem.

After another lunch of shimmering feu, I go back to meet with

Oliver. I jump to avoid the Jack Russells strutting down the main street and take it as a sign he's about.

'Ah, now where did we finish yesterday?' he says by way of greeting as I climb up the stairs. There's no sign of Oliver's young friend.

'Oh yes. It was all very different nine years ago. When I arrived, the Lao were just blinking themselves awake, hungry ghosts. They had endured 30 years of famine. Before the commies took over, Luang Prabang was a royal city. Just the royals, their retainers and monks. Deeply civilised and cultured. Not opulent, for Laos is not a rich country. But a place of culture and learning and fine food. When the commies came, they were all chased away or escaped. Most of the monks ran away too, along with the rest of the ruling class. The whole landowning class upped and left. Then the Lao farmers arrived. So when I arrived, it was a town of ghosts.'

He stops talking and, as if on cue, the air is suddenly filled with the sound of drums. Apparently this happens every day at four but being out of town (or, more likely, asleep), this is a first for me. It's 4 pm, a call to the peasants working in the paddies, telling them it's two hours until dark comes and they better start thinking about coming home. It's still used to this day. The town comes alive for a few moments, and it's just possible to imagine the city in its heyday. Oliver's house is opposite a temple and if you ignore the small group of Japanese clicking away, we could be 100 years back. He settles a little deeper in his chair, and wiggles his large, shoeless feet.

'I was born in Asia, Bangkok, and I grew up there. Bangkok in the Forties was like it is now. The tallest building was only five storeys. But here, I'm trying to revive already-dead handicrafts, the old art of making paper, like the stars you saw. Tourism pays for the refurbishment of the old houses, for the resurrection of the Royal Dance Troupe.'

The colonial gone to grass, Kurtz without the power issues. He talks with his hands and grips you with his stare. He has the feel of a slightly mad visionary, the unsettling glare of the true zealot, although he is never anything but eloquent and lucid.

'I'm also dedicated to replanting all the teak forest here. The French stripped the land of their rosewood and teak and floated it down the Mekong, to sell at great expense. Over there, where I'm going to take you, is one of my teak forests. They call me Mr Teak.'

There's nothing false or boastful about his conversation, despite how it sounds, and you cannot help but be caught up in the big gestures and grand ideas. If he'd told me he was building a spaceship out of rice noodles, I would have believed him. A conservationist at heart, he operates for love, not money. Or so he tells me. Perhaps he is hoodwinking me into some grand scheme, a brilliant huckster looking for a cheap buck. Somehow, I doubt it. All he wants to do is share his vision for the future of Laos, not profit from it. His house is fairly basic, and his lifestyle spartan.

His past saw him travelling the world, and he obviously once had deep pockets. There are still shades of the jetset about him, his tailored shirts and suede loafers. He lived in Italy for years, and some Italian friends of his that I met said he was the most gifted chef they had ever met.

'Now I have everything I need though. I don't even miss the taste of pesto or Parmesan. I am completely at home here now.'

And despite all the stories and whispers of this enigmatic man, you believe in him because he wants you to. As you would expect from such a magnetic figure, he's outspoken on any subject you care to choose. But he's particularly scathing about the Western-run aid agencies.

'Look around, look at all these big, shiny four by fours.' Both Vientiane and Laos are overrun with them, purring through the streets or sitting outside the houses of government officials. 'They're the basic unit of corruption. Everyone wants one and the aid agencies hand them out like sweets.'

They are indeed, everywhere, these blacked-out, air-conditioned bubbles that shelter the soft skins and polished nails of the West's new invading army. Once, we sent soldiers. Now, it's aid workers. Most are beyond reproach, I'm sure, upright and moral men and women who want to do their bit to help. But it's impossible to operate without a little oiling of the cogs. And those four by fours are as much proof as you need.

'The other problem here now is Yaba,' continues Oliver, 'that super-strong speed pill. It's endemic here now, and criminally addictive. It's a cheap kick that is costing lives all over Asia. Drink is a problem too, nearly on Polish or Russian levels. And the women are the worst. I remember when big piles of marijuana were sold in the markets, used to add a nice kick to soups. It has a good flavour and effect and was used as a herb. Of course, the commies banned it. Too much fun. But at most Lao parties, they'll usually be some "giggly" soup about. OK, time to go.'

We climb down and the dogs awake, trotting at his heels as we stride towards the river. 'Let's get some beers,' he cries. 'Nothing better than Beer Lao and the sunset.'

Suitably armed, we clamber into a long, narrow boat and skim across the muddy waters of the Mekong.

We alight on the other side, climbing a roughly hewn path carved through the thick vegetation of the river's precipitous banks. In a rough clearing, about 30 or so spindly saplings wave in the breeze.

'It will take a lot of work, but this is my land. No one can touch it. Now follow me. We climb again, this time to a small hut built into the hill. I look back over Luang Prabang, and find myself unable to tear my eyes from this awesome vista. The temples' golden roofs glow in the waning sun. The city seems so comfortable, so perfectly suited to the lazy bends of the rivers.

The only jarring sight is the three ugly, Meccano-like radio towers that blink their red lights into the fading day. But even these do little to detract from this tranquil beauty. My eyes are soothed and a feeling of well-being washes over my entire body.

'Incredible, no?' he smiles.

I nod, dumbstruck. This is it, my Indo-China wet dream. For once, the fiction has become reality and delights rather than disappoints. We settle back on the wooden platform and watch the sun sink down. The city sits shrouded in the smoke of a thousand fires, as the smell of cooking wafts over the river towards us. The silhouettes of the temples start to grow fuzzy as the golden light disappears behind the hills. The tuk-tuks whiz about in the distance like ants, and the whole scene makes perfect sense. Every moving thing fits into a pre-ordained scheme of perfect harmony.

'I was the first European visitor to the Thai Islands, you know.'

Even the conversation fits, the old Asia hands' stories of a region untouched by tourism or dollars or four by fours.

'My father was a successful businessman and we travelled across from the mainland on a rattan boat. We got off at Phuket, and I wandered off, looking at these stunning empty beaches.' He pauses, his eyes lost in memories and takes a swig of beer. '"Where have you been?" he asked when I turned up late for dinner. He couldn't abide lateness. "The beaches," I said. I was 14 and it was 1949. "We should buy some land now, Papa," I begged, "with the money we have now in our pockets." My father was cross. "All you think about is beaches. The money is in diesel engines, not beaches." Twenty years after that, even my dad had to admit he got that very, very wrong.'

I'm still transfixed by the vista, intoxicated by the fantastic green of the trees, the jagged outline of the mountains behind, the sinuous charm of the rivers, the glittering gold of the temple roof. For the few remaining minutes of the day, we sit in silence, lost in the lazy beauty of this magical land. Words seem unnecessary and clunky and for ten minutes, I'm with the French colonials who believed that this place truly was the last earthly paradise.

For the first time on my journey, I've fallen in love. Not just the food or the people but the country as a whole. This, for me, is my Xanadu and for one romantic moment, I imagine giving it all up, and coming here with my wife to spend the rest of our days in sybaritic exile. At the back of my head, reality indulges me for a while, leaving me to wallow in indulgent dreams. Then kicks back in once more. That's all it is, it says. Enjoy it then return to the real world. Night falls and we reluctantly climb back down to the boat. The dogs greet us again on the opposite shore and Oliver strides off into the dark.

'Come back any time, Tom,' he shouts back, his white hair the only visible part of his body. 'I'll always be here.'

My last dinner is back at Mali, although this time I am alone. Ivan and Charlotte have gone down to Vientiane for the launch of Ivan's elegant, Laotian girlfriend Lamphoune's new store. We are to meet up the next night.

Arriving there by tuk-tuk, I have agreed with the driver a 3,000 kip price that even my impaired arithmetic can work out is too much. But as we arrive, the driver changes it to dollars. I give him the original fare and storm off, awash with guilt and self-loathing. Never mind that he has tried to pull a fast one on me – I feel like every tourist I despise, quibbling over a couple of quid that means nothing to me. I know I am right but I feel so wretched that I run back, pushing another 4,000 into his hand and apologise. He looks bemused but smiles anyway, and I enter the restaurant, still seething with anger and guilt.

The place is packed and the waitress's attention hard to get. I sit with my neck craned, desperate to catch her eye. But every time I come close, her attention is grabbed by someone else. I realise that I'm actually up against another tourist with shaved head and huge nose, and dressed in a Che Guevara T-shirt. We catch each other's eyes for a split second and from then on, it's war. He emus his neck up and down, lifting his hand to grab her attention and when she doesn't see it, changes the gesture into scratching his head. When he thinks no one's watching again, up goes the hand, flapping slightly then down again when spotted by anyone else apart from the waitress.

By now, the rich young locals in their Dunlop jackets and shiny Nike trainers have arrived on their shiny Yamaha scooters and crowd around the communal hot pot tables. They have no such problem with the waitress and get served immediately. Eventually, there's a breakthrough and I grab the waitress, pouring out my order in a garbled rush. I look and smirk at Che Gonk triumphantly. He scowls and then gets up and walks towards me. Christ, he's either going to hit me or far worse, try to talk to me. I put my head down until all I see are his sandals and baggy travellers trousers getting closer and closer. He reaches my table (I'm studying the fish sauce bottle with a fierce intensity) and I give up. I'm cornered. But he carries on past me and I realise, to my joy, that's he's just off to the loo.

As if reading the situation, Neil Diamond breaks into a triumphant 'Caroline' on the stereo and my beer arrives. I get some padek juice with boiled vegetables. The stink is inhuman but the taste divine, salty, sharp and hot. Then more river moss. Tourism has many down sides but the revival of a long-forgotten cuisine is a good thing.

As a farewell to Luang Prabang, I order the pure fermented dish, the muk pha-dek, light steamed. The fish has been gently rotting in its bowl in the sun for months and I expect something rotten. Instead, it's soft, subtle and mild, a salty aftertaste the only hint of power. Again, the smell is fairly fierce. The 'little birds' are just that, black and sticky with long, elegant beaks like a quail.

'Eat it all,' says the waiter and I bite off the top part of the body. The small bones snap between my teeth, before a bitter goo spills out from some cavity or other. One half is quite enough. I think of those damned, elusive ortolans once more. There has been silence for a few days now, and things look bleak.

This is my last night in a city that charms you into moving at its own gentle pace. It is so far removed from any other city, remote yet civilised, sleepy yet possessed with an electric undercurrent. As I finish off the last drops of the second Beer Lao, I realise that I could easily get used to this life. No wonder those French colonials were so enamoured by Luang Prabang.

I am sad to leave but arriving back in Vientiane, I feel one step closer to home and Sara. Despite my love of Laos, I am missing my wife. I check back into the Laos Plaza and, the next morning, meet up with Lucky again. She is smart as ever and says she is taking me for one last, true Laotian treat. We climb back into the car – with the usual pounding, soft-rock soundtrack – and drive out of the city.

'Where are we going?' I ask.

'You'll see,' grins Lucky. 'Very Laotian place, near Thai border.'

The city passes by, then we are on the smooth road towards the Friendship Bridge and the Thai border. About five kilometres past the turning, we pull off the road and into a car park. The restaurant is made from concrete and corrugated iron, the modern version of Luang Prabang's wooden shacks. The place is packed; on one table, ten soldiers knock back beers and noisily tackle their noodle soup. Next door, sober-suited government officials sit in silence, nodding obediently as the leader lectures. A group of women giggle together on a lunch out.

'This place famous for cow stomach, I come here every week,' says Lucky, ordering with practised ease. 'If there's too much, I take home for the fridge as stomach keeps well.'

As usual, the kitchen is little more than two Lao stoves, one with stock, the other charring ingredients. Next door, a woman cuts fresh rice noodles (100 kilos are sold per day), chopping then throwing them into boiling water. To her left is a long wooden table, dripping with blood and metre-long lengths of tripe. Thick, creamy yellow and honeycombed, it's chopped and served up with astonishing speed. The flies are very much in evidence but they barely have time to settle on a piece before it's thrown into a soup or salad. The first dish arrives, and Lucky's eyes gleam.

'Soft raw innards salad ... proper Lao food.'

The tripe is the honeycombed part, just given a brief wash then chopped and thrown in with lettuce, coriander, mint, lime juice, roasted shallots, padek and chillies. By this stage, even raw tripe couldn't scare me too much so I smile and dig in. The texture is more rubbery than ever when uncooked, with a slight beefy taste. But my teeth make little headway on the slippery piece of tummy going round and round my mouth, so the Pepsi has to come in and wash it down. I'm not going to offend Lucky by spitting it out (and I have banged on, stupidly, about how much I love tripe) yet there is no way I am going to finish this pungent pile of offal. The smooth tripe (or rumen) is like raw meaty calamari. It flits about the mouth but can be swallowed.

Less digestible (and remember tripe is very indigestible unless cooked for a long time) are the bits with the tiny fingers on, looking like one of those novelty 'French ticklers' with all the nobbly bits. I fuel up on sticky rice, taking fistfuls then swamping a tiny piece of stomach in the starchy mass. The chilli and padek make it more bearable but my jaw is getting tired. A slightly dodgy tummy is not exactly helping my progress but Lucky tells me how popular this 'inside larp' is in Laos. The various greens served with the larp take away the bitter tang of the offal but enough is enough. I push the plate away, saying I want to leave room for the next course.

'Everybody loves it,' she beams. 'Especially my daughter.'

The feu comes next, shimmering and thick with still more tripe. By now, I've seen enough buffalo stomach to last me a lifetime, but concentrate on slurping the fresh noodles, and picking up a few squares of meat along the way. I start to notice other choice bits of offal too, a chunk of liver, a slice of spleen and a few slippery pieces I dare not identify. I douse the soup with enough padek and chilli sauce to sink a ship and plough on. Lucky, who is under five foot and no more than six or seven stone, has already finished three times what I have picked at.

Even with the sauces and the noodles and the bitter leaves (that look a little like samphire) and the red leaves (which have an acidic, lemony flavour) I can still feel every bumpy nodule on my tongue. Some bits behave and go down my throat in one while others loiter around my mouth like truculent teenagers. I dip the fresh chillies in a punchy prawn chilli paste, bite one in half and immediately regret it. I may have been in Laos for over a week, but my chilli tolerance is still pretty low. The broth is nowhere near as good as in Luang Prabang but the noodles are light and perfectly slippery.

After a few minutes, I drop the charade and stop eating. Lucky doesn't seem the slightest bit offended. She just asks the waiter to pack it up and we get back in the car. I can't help but sigh with relief. Lucky has taken me to sample the best of real Lao food, things that might seem repellent to us but are utterly normal to them. Nothing was so disgusting that I couldn't give it a go, though I was sad to miss the cold duck blood soup. I just couldn't find it anywhere. But I've come and I've tasted and I've walked away, alive and enamoured with the country. I found a thriving food culture, every mouthful fresh and exciting. I might give the soft innards salad a rest for a while but I'd prefer it over the bland ubiquity of a supermarket ready meal anyway.

Lucky drops me back at the hotel and we say goodbye. 'You coming back?' she asks. Oh yes.

I spend my last night in Laos at the opening of Lamphoune's new shop. She's Laos's version of Terence Conran, blessed with immaculate taste and an ever-growing empire of shops selling antiques, silks and clothes. Her family fled Laos when she was young and she grew up in France, where they still spend half the year. I stumble over unpaved roads to reach the most incongruous sight – a shiny, glass-fronted shop lit up like a film première. A half-interested crowd watch the mix of Lao and Europeans sipping Chablis while models sashay down stairs in Lamphoune's new collection. I could be at any party in the world, sitting inside this slick, up-market Habitat in the middle of Vientiane.

As the last few models file past, I realise that this is the face of the new Laos. Shaking off its wretched past, parts of Laos are looking to the future. Although the vast majority live only in the present, like Ruth said, the outside world is keen to come in. I only hope that the traditions and cuisine do not disappear in the rush. As I stumble back through the broken, unlit streets, I think of Theroux's last views on the country:

> Laos, a riverbank, had been overrun and ransacked; it was one
> of America's expensive practical jokes, a motiveless place where
> nothing was made, everything imported; a kingdom with

baffling pretensions to Frenchness. What was surprising was that it existed at all, and the more I thought of it, the more it seemed like a lower form of life, like the cross-eyed planarian or squashy amoeba, the sort of creature that can't die even when it is cut to ribbons.

When he passed through, Laos had been raped and ransacked by years of bombing and American intervention and French occupation. Now, though, I hope it's a different story. If Theroux came back again, I'm absolutely certain he would change his mind.

CHAPTER 8

SPAIN

It was the picture that started it – one man tensed against the elements. He stands at the edge of a rock, looking out to sea. The Atlantic seethes at his knees and his face is set in measured anxiety. Around his waist are a mesh bag and rope, to ensure he doesn't slip into the swirling sea. There is absolutely no room for error here. In his hands are two poles, one attached to a sharp metal blade. He's waiting, his body tense, waiting for that one chance when the waves relent and he can chisel off his precious harvest.

When I first saw the photograph, buried deep within the weighty *Culinaria Spain*, it looked like a vision from another age, a depiction of an old way of life long passed. The colours are muted and grey, more suited to the pages of a *Time Life* series from the Sixties than a shiny tome from the twenty-first century. This is no fanciful reconstruction of an ancient art, but a depiction of the everyday struggle of *percebeiros*, the Galician fishermen who risk their lives to feed Spain's appetite for *percebes*, or goose neck barnacle.

The stakes are high, but so are the rewards. These shellfish grow only on the outer edges of limestone crags, often miles out to sea and pummelled by the Atlantic waves. The art of the *percebeiro* lies not only in split-second timing and the sure-footedness of a mountain goat, but a deep-felt respect for the sea too. It's an incredibly dangerous job, claiming casualties every year but I want to get out there and see it for myself, maybe even give it a go. Never mind that I know nothing of the sea; my fishing skills are laughable, and my nautical prowess non-existent. The problem, though, lies not only in finding these famed *percebeiros* but in actually convincing them to let this land-lubbing liability anywhere near their boat.

I've been looking forward to this part of the journey for a while. Rather than facing the endless slog that is long-haul travel, this is mercifully close, a mere two hours from home. And I'll also be travelling with two old friends, which makes the trip into more of a merry jaunt than some of the previous adventures. In the week or so spent in England after getting back from Laos, I've bored anyone foolish enough to listen on the joys of this little-known country. I'm certain that my wife is close to throttling me after hearing tales of Oliver or live shrimp salad for the ninetieth time in an hour. I am like one of those wild-eyed missionaries, preaching the Laotian gospel to anyone who will listen.

But I can't deny that the country has had a huge effect on me. It certainly calmed me down for a bit but the Luang Prabang pace of life is not easy to uphold in London. Within a few days I am back to my impatient, self-obsessed self but no other destination on the journey so far has affected me so strongly. A place where my preconceived fictional notions were not destroyed by the reality, rather enhanced.

My romantic vision of Laos was all the more attractive for having visited it. Spain offers a different sort of excitement, the chance to prove my manly prowess as I battle wind and waves to harvest what many Iberians see as the ultimate in shellfish delight.

Barely known over here, the *percebes* is an odd, prehistoric-looking beast. Its finger-sized tube of scaly skin ends with a hard white, claw-like talon. Imagine an elephant's leg and foot, reduce by a few thousand times and you have the *percebes*. If you scrunch up your eyes tight enough, it does slightly resemble a young gosling – or at least its neck and head – struggling out if its shell (hence goose neck). But despite being one of the stars of the Spanish seafood firmament, it's not a pretty creature, lacking the sensuous curves of the oyster or the neat good looks of the scallop.

The first time you set eyes upon this curious creature, you could be forgiven for thinking it some long-forgotten fossil, the shellfish version of the coelacanth. Raquel Welch might have snacked on them while washing her bearskin bikini. Actually a crustacean rather than a mollusc, the *percebes* commands huge prices across the country as its gathering is so fraught and unpredictable. The only time the fishermen can get anywhere near these groups of *percebes* is during the new and full moon, when tides are low and the jagged rocks that guard the coastline are exposed. Even then, the waves are fierce and the currents raging.

In winter, conditions can be so bad that the *percebeiros* will be stuck in harbour for months, unable to get near their favourite patch. And the price shoots up accordingly, right up to 160 euros per kilo. But the Spanish and Portuguese are right to covet them as they are superb. You boil them up, pinch the outer skin and twist it off to reveal a long pink stalk of flesh. This is the edible flesh. The taste and texture are glorious, 'among the most delicate morsels the sea has to offer' in the opinion of Teresa Barrenechea in *The Cuisine of Spain*.

Even Alan Davison, a man not given to effusive hyperbole, admits, in his piscine classic *North Atlantic Seafood*, that 'the exquisitely strong taste of the sea was, to use a cliché with accuracy, a real revelation.'

My first taste of this sweet shellfish was as a child in Spain. We used to go and stay with parents' friends in the hills above Granada and the *percebes* would be eaten before lunch as a tapa, along with machego, almonds and jamon. They were also a source of great amusement thanks to their limp, phallic appearance and my sister christened them 'pink willies'. The name has stuck ever since. As we grew up and the family holidays stopped, so did our annual *percebes* feast. And although they remained a delectable morsel of childhood memory, it was at least 15 years until I saw their alien forms again.

If it hadn't been for an old friend, the *percebes* might have faded from the memory altogether. But when Eddie Hart – alongside his brother Sam – opened up Fino restaurant three years ago in Charlotte Street, London, our paths were fated to cross once more. Fino arrived on the scene to a fanfare of praise, delight and heady reviews. Here, at last, was a Spanish restaurant that believed first and foremost in the impeccable quality and freshness of its ingredients. The brothers had grown up in Majorca and had spent much of their adult life living in Madrid and Barcelona. They were – and still are – evangelical, obsessive even, about finding the very freshest shrimp, the sweetest anchovies, the nuttiest Jamon Iberico de Bellota.

Eddie is the younger of the two, the more talkative and immediately outgoing. At any party, you will usually find him at the centre of a merry group, singing Spanish love ballads in his deep baritone, punctuated with the occasional forward roll. After a couple of sherries, Eddie is not impartial to a spot of light gymnastics on the pub floor. Sam, who is married with two children, is a little more reserved, at least until you get to know him. Both are true gentlemen, kind and generous. They also know more about Spanish food and wine than anyone I know, and manage to combine their charm with a hard-nosed professional edge. If this is starting to sound like an extended

PR puff, I'm sorry. But Fino easily lives up to any hyperbole. And Eddie and Sam are the perfect companions on my quest for *percebes*.

There are few people you can sit down and talk with about the idiosyncrasies of different kinds of ham or langoustine or razor clam. But with these two, I have easily met my match. They spent six months perfecting their tortilla so that the potatoes are just crispy and the egg oozes from the middle. And their Jamon croquetas took eight months until they had reached that perfect balance of unctuous and just set. Forget tired old octopus swimming in a torrent of oil, or patatas bravas covered in ketchup. This is better than most Spanish food in Spain.

Three years later, and the place is still packed and Sam and Eddie have yet to lose one iota of the passion, dedication and hard work that makes the restaurant such a success. But one afternoon, about two years ago, Eddie called me. They'd just managed to get hold of a shipment of *percebes* which were selling out fast. If I wanted to get a taste, I had to come in quick. I had no idea what he was talking about, until he explained that they were the dinosaur feet.

'Ah, the pink willies,' I cried.

'I suppose you could call them that,' came the slightly startled reply. And within four hours, Eddie, trencherman Seb (once I told him, not even an armed militia could have got in his way) and I were attacking a pile of *percebes*, their juices squirting across our clothes as we picked, twisted and pulled our way towards the sweet flesh within. The shellfish were devoured in moments, the last of the consignment. I asked why he didn't have them on the menu more often and Eddie said that the origins were rather shady. One month, a kilo might come in with the regular order of wet fish but there was little clue as to their origin. He was trying to find out more but his enquiries usually came to nothing. Then he went into their tiny, windowless office and pulled out

Culinaria Spain. I was transfixed by the drama of the photograph and even more enthused when I read about the perils of gathering them.

'We have to go out,' I slurred to Eddie. We had already made light work of a couple of bottles of Manzanilla and everything seemed possible.

'Fuck off,' said Seb, with his usual delicacy. 'Why would they want you making their life any more dangerous?'

Eddie gave an almost imperceptible nod, far too polite to agree that Seb was right.

We stumbled off into the night but Eddie promised to look further. For two years though, neither he nor Sam had heard a peep. Their supplier had gone to ground and it looked as if *percebes* would be little more than an occasional annual treat.

But for the last year, as I had greedily traversed the globe, Eddie tried every approach. The fish markets, his Spanish octopus suppliers, even the Spanish embassy. For months on end, we'd hear things looked promising, then silence. Not a squeak. Then another call would arrive, saying it all looked good followed by one saying it was all off.

This to-ing and fro-ing went on for weeks and the process began to seem all too familiar. I still hadn't heard any more about the ortolans and my contact, like Eddie's fishermen, had gone dead. I began to despair at the thought of missing out on this, perhaps the most nostalgic part of the whole trip.

Eddie, as ever, was stoic. 'Fingers crossed and all that. I just have a feeling it will be OK.'

Another two weeks passed and time was running out. Then the call.

'Tom, Eduardo here, we have *percebes*, I repeat we have *percebes*.'

I whooped, flying out of my chair and knocking a can of Coke flying across my desk.

'We spoke to one of our wine suppliers, Terras Gauda, in Galicia, and they know someone who knows someone who might be able to help. No guarantees, but if we can get to La Guarda in the north-west of Spain in the next week, then there's a chance of seeing it all happen. But remember, nothing is certain. We might have to get there and wing it. But it's our only lead.'

After professing my undying love, I cancelled everything and booked my passage to Vigo. The phone rang again. It was Eddie.

'More good news. We've just got our first lot in again for years. See you at eight.'

My other line was beeping, with Seb's name flashing up. There was no way he was going to miss out either. Three hours later, and the three of us were back, messing up our clothes and feasting on *percebes* once more. The book lay open before us, the photo seeming larger, brighter and suddenly more tangible.

'Goose neck barnacles force the Galicians into a waiting game,' says the first line. And any other would-be fisherman too.

I fly to Madrid with Sam, early one Sunday morning. Eddie is already in Spain, having flown over a few days before to meet an old friend, Fernando. The brothers have a new book out and are keen for Fernando to cast his eye over it.

'What did he think?' asks Sam as we queue for the plane to Vigo.

'Hardly looked at it. Opened one page, grunted and threw it to one side. I think he was offended by two English boys daring to open a Spanish restaurant in England and writing a book on it. His way is the only way and thank God he didn't look too close. He probably would have told us every recipe was wrong.'

An hour later, we land in Vigo, home to Europe's biggest fishing fleet. Its fish market is reported to be the second largest in the world, after Tsukiji in Tokyo, and it lies at the heart of the Spanish fishing culture. As we drive out of the city and south down the coast, we're stunned by the cheap, artificial desecration of the sweeping coastline. It's some of the most horrible architecture I've ever seen – cheap, Swiss-style chalets with bright terracotta roofs. They look like Woolworth's-designed ski-lodges, cheap toy town huts that even the goblins would ignore.

The landscape itself is rugged and green, like the west coast of Ireland. All share the Atlantic extremes, the cool mists, fierce winds and constant rain. Yet today, the sky is a deep blue and as we drive down the coast, our nostrils fill with that clean, bracing but unmistakable scent of the Atlantic. The road winds past more of these garish seaside homes, their facades dead set on wrecking any natural charm. The shore is lined with ragged rocks, crowded with fishermen, amateurs on a Sunday, casting out in the hope of catching something good for dinner.

But when we arrive in A Guarda, a small fishing port that sits above the Rio Mino's entry to the Atlantic (Portugal is just over on the other side), our hearts sink further still. Looking up from the port, we see a hideous higgledy-piggledy mess of gaudy, modern houses, clinging to the hills on either side of the harbour. It's an entire town-ful of brutal buildings, crossly elbowing each other out of the way.

Our hotel is in what looks like the oldest building in town, a former monastery whose thick walls offer protection from the horrors outside. But despite our initial shock, the harbour is packed with couples and families, sat along the promenade, chewing and spitting pippas or sunflower seeds.

'It's the Sunday sport around here,' says Sam as we crunch through the empty shells.

The last thing to pass our lips was some fairly grubby tapas in Madrid airport, so Sam and Eddie walk from bar to bar, studying the menu intently. 'The menu is important. But even more, you want a crowd of people in there,' says Eddie. 'That's the best way.'

The shops on the seafront are a curious mixture of the touristic and the necessary. One manages to combine them all, offering souvenirs, knives, fishing rods and reels, bait boxes and pharmaceutical supplies. We eventually settle on a fairly nondescript bar on the corner, with tables outside and a small crowd within. It's little more than a cheap dockside retreat, but there are over 40 tapas listed. We ask for a plateful of *percebes*, determined to start on a good note.

The waiter shakes his head. 'Not possible. The waves were high last week, and the fishermen couldn't go out. Maybe later this week.'

Even the waiter knows the state of this market. I suddenly worry that we might be cutting it a little fine. Stupidly optimistic, we had allowed three mornings in A Guarda, reckoning that we'd probably fish for two out of three. But looking out, beyond the 50-metre seawall that guards the harbour, the Atlantic looks foamy and forbidding. I wouldn't want to venture out in a liner, let alone a four-man pontoon. We have come expecting everything to be perfect and ready for us – a sort of fishy theme park adventure – yet here we were, the night before, without having even met our contact.

Things are looking pretty dire. Well, at least until the tapas arrives. Queen scallops on a tiny shell, sweet, succulent and everything a well-brought-up shellfish should be. Then Galician octopus, soft and pliant ('double sucker', notes Sam, nodding with approval. 'Much better texture and flavour'). The fat crystals of sea salt add welcome crunch.

Out at sea, a fishing boat honks and the gulls squawk still louder. We order another bottle of the crisp local wine, made from the Albarino grape, and the whole expedition gets bathed in a boozy glow. We stretch, sink lower into our chairs and start to think that this isn't so bad a place to spend a Sunday night after all.

'I don't think you'd ever come here for a holiday in a million years,' says Eddie.

We nod.

'But to be fair, this is a working town.'

It gets about two paragraphs in the *Lonely Planet*. But most of the space is taken up saying how nice it is elsewhere: 'the treat here is to head 4km up from the town to Monte de Santa Trega'. The town is right out on the north-western extreme of Spain. In the Middle Ages, many believed that this spot was the end of the world. Looking at the modern town planning, many might still agree.

Eddie and I are keen to pile the table high with more tapas but Sam advises caution.

'Pace is everything,' he says quietly. 'A few here, a few there. We're in no hurry.'

As the sun starts to set, our initial hatred of the town softens into a mild dislike.

'And you certainly can't fault the food or drink,' says Eddie.

We move on to the next bar, where another equally impressive array of tapas arrives.

Then Sam's phone rings. He talks seriously in Spanish for a few moments then puts it down.

'What?' I ask.

Eddie edges closer. 'Is it on?'

He smiles. 'We're to meet Marcus, our contact, here in ten minutes. And he will be with one of the *percebeiros*. Fingers crossed.'

There's nothing left to do save eat another mouthful of octopus, take another swig of wine and pray to Virgin del Carmen, the patron saint of the fishermen.

* * *

Galicia is a long way removed from the dry, dusty heat of the South. It's actually unlike anywhere in the country I've ever been, far closer to the climate and landscape of Northern Europe.

'Galicia has always been a place apart,' writes Elizabeth Luard in *The Food of Spain and Portugal*. This is because Galician roots are largely Celtic and the influence of the Moors minimal. There's no sign of the saffron or ornate arches that are so prevalent in the rest of Spain and they even have their own language, *gallego*, which is widely spoken.

'I cannot understand a bloody word,' admits Sam as we try to eavesdrop on a gabbled conversation next door. 'It has nothing to do with Spanish, an entirely different root.'

The coastline is 700 miles long, rugged and windswept, and the shellfish better than anywhere else in the country. Inland, the region is heavily forested, with barren hills, endless eucalyptus forests (the trees are not indigenous, rather favoured for their quick and straight growth) and hilly, scattered with some of Spain's finest vineyards. The remains of a Celtic village sit up by Monte de Santa Traga, little more than a collection of old stone huts. The view over the sea is actually far more interesting than these antique ruins, but their presence further reinforces the feeling that this area is different from the rest of the country, the Galicians more isolated and a breed apart.

It's certainly one of the poorer regions, with farming and fishing still the traditional means of employment. Many Galicians have been forced to leave their land and look for other work abroad. Yet in spite of this – or more likely, because of it – the culture of eating and drinking is strong. The churning Atlantic Ocean provides plenty of oxygen for the plankton, which in turn attracts the bigger fish. There are over 80 different types of saltwater fish caught from these shores (or further out, trawled by industrial-sized super-boats).

Shellfish is particularly abundant, with scallops, six different varieties of prawn, brown crabs, spider crabs, mitten crabs, langoustines, lobster, oysters, sea urchins and a huge variety of clams. And the *percebes*, of course, the finest of them all. Then there are the magnificent eels from the rivers, trout, carp, and the lamprey with its circle of sinister teeth. A meal is never complete without some kind of *empanadas*, a wheat flour pie filled with everything from pork and beef to tuna, cockles, scallops, vegetables and sardines. And sweet ones too for pudding, cut into squares and eaten with gusto. Like the pasty in Cornwall, these are supremely practical foods robust enough for the fishermen to slip into their pockets, ready for the hard day ahead.

As the pastures are so lush, the area is also famed for its beef and the milk makes *tetilla* (or tit) cheese, loved by the locals though not so adored by us. It's on the bland side, more rubber Cheddar than unforgettable fromage. Their white grape, the Albarino, makes a majestic white wine, the perfect match for this food, crisp with a hint of fruit. And then Orujo, the local grappa made from the grape skins and a spirit that played far too prominent a role in our time there. This abundance of marine life, of milk, beef, wine and pies, made me think that even if the *percebes* never turned up, the trip would not be a total waste of time.

Marcus is our contact with the fishermen, a local agent for the Terras Gauda wine. I had expected someone middle-aged and serious but instead, he's young, slick, and clad head to toe in the most shimmering of tracksuits. He fiddles with his telephone incessantly. My Spanish is fundamental, to say the least, but we chatter idly while, on the television, torrential rain washes out a Real Madrid game. A small terracotta bowl of chickpeas arrives with my tenth glass of wine, alongside chunks of chorizo and a few squares of tripe. But this has been slow cooked for hours, as tripe should be, until melting, then mixed into a creamy sauce. I eat it in two mouthfuls and we wait for the fishermen.

The barman asks me why I'm here in A Guarda. I tell him we want to fish for *percebes*.

'Que?' he asks again, as if he didn't quite believe me.

I tell him again.

'No,' he cries and lets out a howl of laughter. Then he proceeds to tell the rest of the bar, who momentarily take their eyes off the sodden screen to hoot with delight. The antics of these three stupid Englishmen are far more amusing than the *Galacticos* sitting, bored and wet, in their dug out.

'You come all the way over from England to fish for *percebes*,' he asks us all, his eyes damp with tears. 'You're fucking mad. Mad!' He blows his nose. 'You know how dangerous it all is. Well, I'll tell you one thing. If this wind keeps up, that book, that ...' he points at my notepad, '... might get a little wet.'

He wanders off again, still shaking his head, making sure that any new customer is quickly informed of our foolhardy mission. Having made quick work of a good few bottles of the white, spirits are high. Eddie has half the bar enthralled with some tale involving Yerbas (a Majorcan speciality) and dancing, I think, or maybe a forward roll. Whatever it is, his bushy eyebrows dance around his forehead like disco caterpillars as he holds his audience in rapt attention.

I look for Sam, who is talking intently to a young, good-looking man dressed in T-shirt and tracksuit bottoms. His hair is shaved, save a half-dozen short dreadlocks that hang like a valance from the back of his head. And his eyes are light blue but warm and his arms adorned with leather bracelets. I assume he's the local party boy, looking more like trance party crusty than anything else. I keep an eye out for the usual dog on string. Eddie and I wobble over.

'Meet Celli, this is the poor man stupid enough to take us out.'

He smiles and we shake hands.

'At the moment, we're all smiling,' he says with one eyebrow raised. 'Tomorrow, it might be different.' He has an easy confidence that immediately puts us at ease, and a sort of unspoken gravitas and sharp mind that makes you want to impress him. In his hands, I think, the words swirling around my head like brandy in a glass, I feel safe.

But for all his skills on the water, finding dinner is a rather different matter. It takes us about half an hour, driving wildly in the dark, before we literally crash into the sign for the restaurant. Celli has never heard of it. The room, when we eventually arrive, is all rough-hewn stone and crisp white napkins. As the wine is ordered, Celli tells us about A Guarda. Before the sea-wall was built, the waves would come off the ocean and come crashing into houses with immense force.

'You have no idea how big that swell gets in winter. The *paseo* [promenade] where you sat outside was only made three years ago. Before that, there was just a small wall between us and the sea. It can be pretty hairy out there,' he says with pragmatic understatement.

From what little I remember the next morning, the food was good, but a little modern perhaps for our first night. There was a sea-urchin pancake, rich and luscious, then langoustines, wriggling fresh. A lamprey *empanada* was less subtle, the flesh assertively fishy and almost overwhelming.

'Well,' says Sam after wiping his mouth, 'now I've tried lamprey, I'll never have to do it again.'

Then, as usual, my notes descend into an elliptical scrawl, and all I can decipher is 'fuck that tastes like beef', 'this is posh food' and 'why do we say all shellfish taste like sea ... have drunk sea and not good ...'

Celli eats slowly, not wasting air with empty chat, nodding slightly when a dish is good. Every time we steal one of his cigarettes, we thank him effusively. Eventually, it's too much.

'Stop saying thank you. You are all welcome to my cigarettes now, we have eaten together. Just take them.' This is neither curt nor bad-tempered, just a straightforward statement of fact. With Celli, there is no bullshit or small talk. And everything he does say is as honed as it is direct. The only thing I record that is truly legible are his parting words.

'See you tomorrow at 5.45. Tonight, you're all so polite. Tomorrow, if we go out, I'll really hear you swear.'

By now, I should have learnt my lesson. I know I've said this again and again, in Tokyo and in Luang Prabang, but I just never learn. Once more, I wake for an important morning, only to be maimed by the leftovers of last night's excess. I can try to excuse it by claiming we were overcome by the exuberance of arriving somewhere new, but these arguments do little to cut the mustard.

And this morning, we are all suffering for our sins. It's 5.30 and a shower does nothing to ease my pain, nor does it wash away the dregs rolling around my body. As the minutes pass, the intensity of my hangover increases. Sam and Eddie look equally shaky and silent, and we troop down to the harbour without a word being uttered. Even viewed through aching eyes, though, the town looks far better at dawn, a time of silhouettes rather than full-frontal views.

The sun starts to climb up behind the hill and, for a second, you could even call it beautiful. There's no sign of Celli but across the harbour, a group of six men huddle together, shooting the occasional glance over to us. We're a conspicuous trio as it is, not helped by Eddie's loud tweed Edwardian poacher's jacket.

'Well, at least they won't mistake us for tax men,' says Sam.

Piles of lobster, crab and octopus pots lay stacked up along the wall. Half an hour passes, and there's still no sign of Celli. The harbour water is as flat as a puddle and we reckon (great mariners that we are) that all is OK. Then we peer out and over the 40-foot seawall, where the Atlantic waves crash ferociously.

'I think the point of a harbour,' notes Sam, 'is to keep it calm within when the waves are raging outside.'

But looking at the white-caps over the horizon, I begin to pray secretly that we won't have to face them today. I don't think my belly could take it. Celli eventually arrives, dressed in full wetsuit and hiking boots with a thick sweatshirt over the top. If we're going out, we're woefully underdressed. I'm in jeans, trainers and a jumper and even Eddie's Edwardian delight looks of little use this far from the drives of Norfolk.

Celli lights up a cigarette and confers with his fellow fishermen. Another half hour passes, and still no decision. More men appear, in different versions of Celli's uniform, and they smoke some more, cough and talk. By now, the sun's light is almost at full power. A van drives up, screeches to a halt. We can't see in but Celli tells us it's his brother, the big boss. He'll have one more scout, looking beyond the seawall before the final decision is made.

At this point, I'm past caring and so tired that I would swap a bed for anything, even the whole reason of my journey. Celli shows us his fishermen's shed, reeking of oil and old fish. Wetsuits and sou'westers hang from shelves packed with polystyrene boxes, nets, plastic cases and tattered old bags. A big freezer takes up the back wall, filled with pre-hooked sardines as bait for the conger eels. The floor is wet, covered with ropes and buckets and rusty hooks. And a couple of small, shiny anchors attached to a harness. I pick one up and it's surprisingly heavy.

'For the boat?' I ask.

'No,' says Celli, 'for anchoring us to the rocks while we gather.'

The news doesn't exactly improve my mood. And the smell in there is so intense that I can only stand it in hits of 30 seconds before I rush out, gasping for salty air.

The brother's car appears again and Celli bends down to the window, shaking his head. He looks over at us and we know it's not going to happen.

'Too dangerous,' he says with a shrug. 'But there's room for one of you helping me haul up the octopus pots.'

Sam and I look to the ground, shuffling our feet. As hoped, Eddie accepts and while he helps Celli push a rowing boat down in the sea, Sam and I trudge off back to bed.

The life of the *percebeiros* is an erratic one, long periods of waiting around, frustrated by the elements, followed by frantic periods of non-stop activity. All are licensed, either to the shore or the sea. The shore collector is not allowed to venture out to sea and vice versa. The sea *percebes* are more highly prized, as all that seething water gives more food for them and thus more size and flavour. But it is far more dangerous. The fishing (or gathering) is strictly licensed by the government, with a 3,000 euro fine if you're caught collecting them without this licence. These new rules were put in place five years ago, to ensure the long-term survival of the species.

There are also limits as to how many days the fishermen can go out. For the sea *percebeiros*, natural conditions dictate they only collect in the new and full moons, when tides are lowest and the best hunting grounds exposed. But by law, they may only go out a maximum of 12 to 15 days per month. And on those days, they are allowed six kilos per person per day ('a generous amount,' admits Celli). But it is rare when the fishermen get a full haul. Winter is the most dangerous season, with seas being so rough that they might not be able to go out for three months. Yet the rewards are great, scarcity building up the price. Their work is usually done by 9 pm, leaving the rest of the day to drag up the octopus pots (Celli had about 60 in the bay) and clean the *percebes*. So boredom is common, as are tense mornings where your livelihood looks increasingly precarious. It might seem an unenviable life but every single fisherman we spoke to would have it no other way.

Later on, walking up the hill towards the market, we bump into Celli's mother, a short handsome lady with dark blonde hair and strong views on everything. Eddie and Celli are still out at sea, gathering the pots. A famed *empanada* cook, she is fiercely proud of the Galician cuisine.

'The King of Spain demands the best,' she announces as we sit in the mid-morning sun, 'but even the king doesn't eat as well as us Galicians.' She then launches into a passionate explanation of how she makes her *empanadas*, and what she puts in. 'Everything that's good, from clams to scallops and clams to tuna and lamprey and vegetable and chorizo. There is no limit.' She pauses. 'Sorry, I talk too much.'

She has four sons. Alejandro, the older brother we glimpsed earlier, and Celli are the *percebes* men. Another is out at sea at the moment, chasing swordfish.

'He stays on board for three months, travelling far and wide. They freeze the fish on board. My fourth is a teacher. My husband was a *percebeiros*, and his father before him. They work right up to 65, longer if they're more fit. Ah, here's Celli.'

We look up to see Celli and Eddie hauling their catch up the hill. Eddie looks a little green.

'We sat on the boat,' Eddie explains, lighting a cigarette, 'and Celli attached the rope connecting his pots to a winch. They were hauled in, one by one, and I not only had to pull out the octopus but bash 'em on the head too.' His face looks pained. 'I didn't mind them twisting their tentacles around my arm. It actually felt rather nice. But their eyes as I tried to kill them. So human and baleful I felt rather guilty. Still, we got seven of the buggers and a few bits and pieces too.'

I look into the bucket where the brown bodies, limp and shiny, swill around. The eyes do look remarkably poignant, like the deep brown eyes of a cow.

'I'll take those to market later,' announces Celli's mum.

Even in a town of this size, the fresh market is of huge importance. It's a two-storey purpose-built block, with permanent stalls. And despite being a Monday morning, there's fat-lipped hake, brute-ugly monkfish (stomach slashed to reveal the all-important liver), glittering sardines, limp piles of octopus and turbot as long as my leg. Upstairs are the butchers and greengrocers. Even for a slow day, this range of seafood is staggering. The first boats of the week went out this morning and everything we see was caught less than five hours previously.

Even so, Celli is suspicious. 'Mondays are never as good. We'll come back tomorrow.'

Lunch is in Bitadona, a smart restaurant on the seafront. A tank sits by the entrance, filled with angry lobster, three different kinds of crabs and two of shrimp. I sit, transfixed before it, watching the lobsters eye each other up, their claws bound to prevent any carnage. We're the first to arrive. Sitting at the table, I begin to panic that we'll never even get near the *percebes*, save eating them. I've seen the rocks they're gathered on (from the top of the hill with one of those telescopes that cost a euro to use), I've eaten them, talked about them, even seen sharpened the tool with which they're removed.

As to the gathering ... it looks a lot less hopeful. Eddie looks remarkably well on his minimum of sleep but Sam and I are rather more subdued. It's only after the second glass of wine that I start to feel complete again. Alejandro, Celli's brother, comes in and introduces himself. He's smaller than Celli, but broader, his face the sort of deep brown that footballers' wives could only dream of, natural and perfectly suited to the face. His hair is slightly receding and his face is round with a delicate, slightly upturned nose. He smiles rarely and, like his brother, rarely wastes a word. He watches the three of us intently, as if uncertain of our motives. He's not entirely sure as to what we're up to and occasionally squints as he stares, as if checking to see that we're real.

'You're too white,' he says to me, 'too long indoors. A bowlful of local stew will add some colour to your face.' He then explains why *percebes* always come with a piece of the rock attached to them. 'The restaurants like it as it gives the shellfish a longer life. When that bit of rock is cut off, they start to bleed and lose liquid. Which is why we always leave a little chunk on when preparing.'

This uncharacteristic outburst over, he goes back to chewing on his bread. I tell him that I heard the shells were dried and used as a lucky charm. His face breaks into a smile for the first time.

'The Celts might have worn them, just as they did the scallop shell. But not now. The Romans thought them an aphrodisiac, because they looked like pink dicks. I'll show you where their g-spot is later. I don't need it any more, I have two kids.'

The table erupts and although the dig is good natured, my face turns the same colour as the freshly boiled shrimp before me. This dose of public humiliation, though, seems to soften his attitude and his whole demeanour changes. Instead of glaring, he grins. The prawns are striped crimson and white, fat, plump and addictive. No sauce is needed to blunt their just-boiled taste. The taste of a truly fresh prawn is so different from that of the frozen as to be an entirely different creature.

Then the *percebes* appear, like a dinosaur spare-part depot. They steam gently ('bring seawater to the boil, throw them in and once it gets back to the boil, ready to eat') and the less adept among us (well, the Brits) are tied into cotton bibs. As you piece their skin, the juices have a habit of squirting around the room with huge force. Davidson talks about an old La Coruna cookery book, *La Cocina Practica*, which 'tells you just to boil the barnacles briefly in salted water, but adds a lengthy injunction to use a large napkin, covering your whole chest when eating them. (In fact, if the pinch-and-open technique is carefully executed, the risk of juices squirting about is small.)'

But try as I might, I can't control this gushing, phallic beast which I suddenly realise resembles an erect circumcised cock. You tear away the tumescence to get at the limp pink inside. No wonder the Romans went so crazy for them. I'm certain that the Chinese have yet to set eyes on them, otherwise that really could spell disaster. A million impotent elders would leap on the shellfish and that would be the end of it. These *percebes* are fresher than I've ever tasted before, despite not coming in that morning. Fulsomely flavoured yet not quite as assertive as an oyster; the flesh is firm and tender. You pick them up in clumps, undressing each tube one by one, before throwing the spent containers into the pile below.

Despite the fact that we've only known Celli for 24 hours and his brother for just two, they welcome us with a generosity and kindness that are entirely undeserved. Although the people I've met in Korea or Gloucester have gone out of their way to be hospitable, these Galicians take it to another level. We feel, after just a few hours of eating and drinking together, that we have known them for years. The Galicians have a reputation for hospitality to strangers yet this is way beyond any expected stereotype. This is pure good spiritedness, with nothing expected in return.

Every time we try to pay for drink or dinner, they scowl, pushing us away. In the end, we have to use stealth to get to the owner, slipping a credit card and making him swear to use it. The rest of lunch is the usual Galician fish and octopus, so fresh that no embellishment is needed. Crab croquettes melt in a puff of béchamel, hake cheeks (actually the jowls) are fantastically fishy in the best possible way and still more of the Albarino poured down.

By the time we are finished, it is almost dark and yet more sleep beckons. We take to our beds unnaturally early, praying for better luck the next day.

I feel a little better this morning, for obvious reasons, although the sea looks equally nauseous. Today, we really have to get out there. This time, Alejandro and Celli are waiting, leaning up against nets piled up like just-cooked vermicelli.

I ask Alejandro what he reckons. He gives a full-body shrug. So we hang around like yesterday, watching dawn work her facelift magic on the town, turning it briefly from modern carbuncle to maritime idyll. We try to convince each other it's looking better today, suddenly pretending to some seafaring knowledge and giving endless chat about wave height and flow. Of course, we have no idea as to what we're talking about. But it fills the time and gives us hope. I heard that two *percebes* fishermen were killed last week, not far down the coast. But this doesn't seem the best time to bring it up. God knows what taboos I'll be trampling on by talking of death at this time of the morning. More likely, seeing how sensible and intelligent they are, they'll tell me I am talking shit.

I get the feeling that today might be more positive, the way the nets are pulled out a little further, and Celli sharpens their weapons, sparks flying, on an electric sander. By the time he's finished, the steel could slice sashimi. They fish different patches every time they venture out, leaving the *percebes* to grow before harvesting again. It's in their interest to keep stock levels healthy and no one knows more about the state of the sea than them. The sun is now up and Alejandro's face looks grim.

'Rough out today,' he says and my stomach lurches. Celli suggests we might go and watch the shore fishermen gathering but it's hardly the same. It's like watching the kids fool about on the nursery slopes while the real men cut swathes through the off-piste powder. Anyway, I am rather expecting to have a go myself, take part in a few minutes of extreme fishing.

For the next hour, there's plenty more 'beard-scratching' (as Sam calls it), as more and more fishermen turn up, clad in full wetsuits, heavy boots and thick jumpers.

'We could go and check out your underwater larder,' suggests Eddie, referring to the cage in the harbour where crabs and shrimp are stored alive, until there are enough to sell. This really is a last resort, but while we continue to wait, we start taking photos of Alejandro as he goes about his morning chores. The rest of the fishermen take the piss.

'Ooohh, you're so international,' coos one.

Alejandro brushes off the jeers but when I ask him if there is any chance of us joining in – i.e. actually getting out onto the rock – his broad face hardens into an incredulous scowl.

'Are you fucking joking?' he roars. 'In this job, you have to use your head. People die, but only fools and amateurs. We respect the sea and we don't die. Pah, really, you think I'd risk your lives and mine in letting you anywhere near.'

He spits and shakes his head. 'Really!' Like all of his fellow fishermen, the jokes and clowning-about stops as they get nearer the water. Another fisherman passes to prepare his boat.

'This time of the year is nothing compared to winter. Then, it's warmer in the sea, with your wetsuit, than out …'

Alejandro continues to glare out to sea. He talks to a few more people then turns to us. 'OK, we go. It is safe.'

The relief is immense. Even if I won't be fishing, at least I can actually watch. The harbour suddenly comes alive; boats are dragged down to the water and pushed down the slippery, seaweed-coated slope into the sea. Our boat contains just Alejandro, Celli and Jose, a chisel-jawed teenager. But the other, rival crew contains six more salty types. There's 'Catweazle', five foot high and hidden under a bush of matted hair. And Joerges, an old-timer with sad eyes and jowls like Deputy Dawg. Dressed in their mish-mash get-up, they look, from a distance, like Tudor courtiers, all thin legs and bulky tops.

I manage to land on my ass, despite being told to watch my footing, but in minutes, the harbour is receding behind us as we fly over five-foot waves towards our goal. The boat has two motors, essential in case one breaks down while the boat is buzzing around the rock. Being left with no engine would spell disaster, as it's the boat driver – in this case Alejandro – who runs the whole show, deciding when it is safe to get on and off the rock as well as hollering out warnings of especially huge waves.

The floor of the boat is covered in sun-baked starfish, unwanted detritus from the octopus pots. The waves are far more impressive face to face, immense swells into whose troughs we disappear. From the shore, they looked like little breakers but once among them, you realise quite how powerful they actually are. We speed towards a slippery, jagged island, about 500 m from the shore and no bigger than a tennis court.

As we approach, Celli and Jose move to the front of the boat, bodies tensed and eyes bright. Alejandro plays the boat like a master, watching the waves crash into the rocks and choosing his moment carefully. Every muscle is strained in anticipation. He guns the engine forward, just metres away from the rocks, then draws back, judging the risk too great. He's like a great rider, teasing his steed forward, pulling it back. We sit, transfixed. One mistake, and we'll all be firewood. The other boat draws alongside, moving backwards and forwards, and up and down on the swell. Then they jump, a gazelle-like leap onto a flat section of rock. The only flat section there is. And the other four do the same.

Suddenly, the rock is swarming with half a dozen fluorescent ants, scurrying over the surface, wedging themselves into cracks, and chipping frantically at the rock. They deposit their booty into a mesh bag, tied around their waists. And they keep a constant eye on the waves, ducking as monsters crash in. They disappear under the foam for a moment then appear again, dripping wet and looking for the next spot. In particularly dangerous spots, they use ropes and anchors to secure themselves more tightly. Alejandro, meanwhile, is stroking the engine back and forth, watching every wave and member of his boat intently. If someone goes in, he has to be ready to grab them before they're pummelled to death. Any time he spots a vicious-looking set, he hollers to the rock. They wave back in acknowledgement, bracing themselves for impact.

Sitting in the boat starts off as fun, but the continual up and down movement, like a huge soggy rollercoaster, soon gets my sea legs wobbling. Regardless of age, all the men are fleet of foot, crouching, leaping and skipping across the slippery rock.

'This time of year, it's certainly not worth risking your life for the *percebes*,' shouts Alejandro, struggling to make himself heard over the waves. 'The prices just aren't high enough. At Christmas, we take a few more risks. So this is a relatively safe spot.'

As another seven-foot bastard crashes down upon the fishermen, I don't even want to think about what a bad day means. This is every bit as thrilling and dangerous as I imagined (although I didn't factor in the sea sickness). Quite how I believed I'd be taking part, I don't know. It's scary enough bobbing in the boat. Alejandro can't disguise his excitement and admits he is a little disappointed not to be there on the rocks.

'It's a very addictive profession,' he says with a rueful glance. 'You always spy the best, the fattest in the roughest, most dangerous place. And you just have to get it. Look.'

He points to Celli who is almost hanging off the side, frantically chipping away at the base of the rocks. He has about five seconds before the next wave crashes in, but makes it with milliseconds to go, leaping up to higher ground and bracing as it erupts. Although the two boats are rivals, there's enormous camaraderie between them all, each looking out for the other's back. Alejandro gives the driver of the rival boat a lift back to his craft (he's left it tied on a moving pulley system) and they work harmoniously together. Alejandro checks his watch and realises that the two hours before the end of low tide is imminent. He shouts out 'ten minutes' to the rock and prepares to pick up his crew.

By now, the ants have slowed down, their net bags bulging with booty. Every time a truly giant wave appears, they all scamper to higher ground, wait for the sets to pass then go to the edges once more. One false move, one misjudged step, and you're in the middle of that green and white seething cauldron at the foot of the rocks.

'Remember that the *percebes* don't escape, so we never take any unnecessary risks,' says Alejandro, his eyes on the rock at all times. 'If it is too dangerous, we wait. But the younger guys, they are more impulsive and have no fear. I was like that once. But you learn. A life for *percebes*. It's just not worth it.'

All the time, while I get greener and greener, trying to stare at a horizon that only reappears at the peak of a wave, Alejandro is working the boat once more, effortlessly reacting to silent, imperceptible changes in current and flow.

When the moment is exactly right, Alejandro shoots in and Celli and Jose jump and smash back into the boat. They've got two kilos each and their faces are ablaze with adrenalin. With just a few minutes to go, Alejandro guides them onto the next set of rocks, where they jump off and start again. We're now up against the clock, as high tide is starting to rush back in, making the currents stronger and waves more dangerous. I try a raw *percebes*, softer than cooked and infinitely more salty.

'They taste of the Atlantic, nothing more,' says Alejandro. He curses. 'Sitting here watching is like being the footballer on the bench. I want to be out there.' He looks longingly at the rock, then decides it is time to get them in and head home. He hollers, waving his arms.

Celli and Jose time their run alongside Alejandro, and as he flies in, they hurl themselves on board. Their eyes are gleaming and their breath short, excitement pumping through their veins. These are the super-elite of fishermen, highly skilled in their tiny world of rock and sea. But more than that, they relish every moment. As Alejandro said, it's an addiction as much as anything else, man against nature, but this time with decent rewards. They certainly fish for the money, but also for the sheer joy of doing what they love. There's little doubt as to the peril they put themselves in. But their passion for their sport is overwhelming.

Once back on shore (much to my pasty relief), the brothers' mother and father come down to help them sort (into different sizes) and clean the catch. Their father is small and stocky, but with the same quiet dignity and confidence of his sons. They scrape off any barnacles and baby mussels with a sharp clasp knife, then throw them into different boxes depending on size. It's a long and boring job, but friends drop by for a chat, grab a knife and start into the soothing routine of scraping and cutting. Their mother chatters while the seagulls argue and bicker overhead, waiting for the occasional scrap.

In a next-door boat, a conger fisherman guts his slippery catch. A cigarette hangs out of his mouth, as he slits these monsters – still very much alive and teeth gleaming – down the belly, pulling out the guts and reclaiming a vicious hook. Some are six foot long, as thick as a man's thigh and capable of taking off a hand. But he treats them as if they were mere anchovies, occasionally jumping out the way if a jaw comes too close.

We walk back to our hotel and drive up to Monte de Santa Trega, where we look back over the rocks this morning. From this height, they look like small brown scars on a green body and the waves look no larger than ripples. Despite not getting onto the rock, the fishing was as thrilling as I had expected. Going out this morning was a sobering experience, a way of life so alien to my soft, unworked hands. To say that the experience has lived up to the *Culinaria Spain* hype sounds trite, yet that picture was entirely real, not faked for some eager photographer. More than the fishing, though, it is meeting Celli and Alejandro that has made the whole trip so memorable.

Over lunch with the brothers and Jose, the talk goes back to *percebes*. Between mouthfuls of scrambled egg with sea urchin (natural bedfellows), they describe how *percebes* can grow as large as shot glasses, and the bigger they are, the more they're worth.

'But as you know,' smiles Celli, 'those big fuckers make it as hard as possible for us to find them.'

I ask how the shellfish feed.

'Look,' says Alejandro, picking up a *percebes* from a nearby plate. 'The nail-like hoof at the end opens and all these thin strands (they look like wet silk) filter all the goodness out of the water. The base of the stem clamps onto the rock. At this time of year, they're not quite at their best.'

I ask him which he thinks are the best in the world.

'The Galician, of course!'

Although they're popular in Spain and Portugal – and grow right down the Atlantic coast to Africa – here, they say, are best.

'What about Morocco?' Eddie asks.

'Pah.' All three laugh. 'Like shit!'

At 4.30 pm every week day, the *percebes* are sold – along with every other fish – in a large concrete bunker in the middle of the harbour. An electronic scoreboard dominates one wall, with a price in euros. This is known as a 'Dutch' auction, where the price drops and people bid per lot with handheld electronic buttons. So the first person to buy today, at 30 euros per kilo, gets to choose whatever he or she wants. The highest prices allow the most perfect – and largest – fish. The centre of the room contains boxes in rows, filled with *percebes*, octopus, dogfish, sole, sea bass, all in every shape and size. You also buy the box with a 4 kilo minimum spend.

Prospective buyers, from large-scale fish wholesalers to smaller fish stall owners to housewives looking for something for dinner, prod and sniff the fish. Spectators jostle for position behind the barriers, whispering conspiratorially to each other. 'Did you see her? Paid far too much for those bass,' and 'Look at that halibut. Isn't it beautiful.'

As the price drops, the prime fish disappear and the smaller fish remain, idling about like last picked for the team. The *percebes* go first, then a magnificent 6 kilo bass (Eddie says that the best Spanish restaurants need the most perfect fillets, hence their happiness to spend more on a huge fish). So why are some fish worth 30 euros per kilo while another of the same species is just 8 euros? Mainly, it's because size matters. But everyone here is looking for the best deal there is, waiting until the last second to bid before someone else gets in.

The stout matrons with thick ankles and slippers are mean bargainers, coming in at the bottom end to pick up a case of monkfish or a couple of gurnard for the best possible price. The price stops every 50 centimes or so, while the successful vendor wanders among the lots and picks his or her favourite. At 25 euros, no one is going to buy octopus or dog fish, so all the turbot and sea bass disappear first (most are still alive and there is no fishy smell at all in the room).

Although vendors are happy to pay top whack for big fish, the more average-sized don't move until the price has halved, while in England, all fish, no matter what size or fresh state it's in, go for a set price (i.e. £10 per kilo of haddock); this Dutch system rewards the bigger fish and the best quality. The huge sea bass get 30 euros per kilo, while the small, normal-sized one just 10. Every single person in here knows more about fish than I will ever learn and it was an exhilarating experience, similar to the Tokyo tuna auction but somehow more exciting.

At around the 11 kilo mark, the locals start circling. A heavy-set old lady, in a thick black and white dress, moves in and claims a few monkfish.

'It's for her shop around the corner,' whispers Celli. He is not allowed to buy, as a fisherman, and you have to be registered before you can bid.

'Imagine if we had this every day in London,' Sam says to Eddie. Their eyes glaze over. 'This makes Billingsgate look like a bring and buy sale.'

The first octopus is sold off at 4.30 euros, to a thickly mousta-chioed restaurateur who comes back again to grab some smaller versions at 4.10. The whole process is highly theatrical, lots of poking, smelling and chin scratching. The last monkfish sells at a mere 2.95 euros per kilo ('Too much head,' reckons Sam) while the first skate to go is sold at 2.55 euros. The congers rank even lower, pulling in 1.60 per kilo and now a brace of tough old bags shuffle through the tiddlers and soup stuff. A perfectly respectable skate goes for 1.10 euros ('It's the worst time of year for skate now,' whispers Celli) and a tiny dogfish with sandpaper skin gets 0.46. Last of all are the Marajota, the bony blue fish, which struggle over the line at 0.42.

'Ah, the sweet smell of capitalism in action,' sighs Sam. 'The market dictates the price, right before our eyes. If the fish isn't up to it, it's almost given away.'

The room is now empty, save the boxes of bought fish, now having shovels of shaved ice thrown over them to keep them cool.

I ask Celli how much he got for his *percebes*.

'Twenty-nine euros. OK. Not bad. We miss a few days, and the price goes up.'

Leaving the next day, we are weighed down with boxes of *empanadas* freshly cooked by Celli's mother, local *orujo* decanted into old wine bottles and a kilo of fresh *percevas*, packed carefully into a coolbag and covered with ice. We try to pay for the shellfish, but the men's faces are so fierce in their refusal that we step back.

'How about a contribution to the church,' offers Eddie.

Silence. They will not take a penny.

I hug Celli goodbye but Alejandro is more guarded, a firm hand-shake. It takes longer than three days to get that close to him, though he smiles and clasps our hands. It is almost a tearful farewell.

'You'll be back,' says Alejandro as we get into the car.

And as we drive away, waving frantically, the town suddenly seems a vision of beauty.

'How could we have ever thought it ugly?' says Eddie as he digs into an *empanada*.

'No idea,' says Sam. 'We all got it wrong.'

Our final ordeal is British customs as we aren't entirely sure as to what we are allowed to bring in. We certainly aren't going to risk our treasure by asking so we check them in and wish them well. As we pick up the bag the other end, our hearts skip ten beats at the sight of 30 policemen, armed to the teeth, with Alsatians straining at the bit.

'I think this might be somewhat of an overreaction,' says Sam as we pass. But they are there to welcome a particularly boisterous group of American rappers, rather than three windy Brits.

As we divide up our spoils, I am desperate to get home. 'It is unlikely that the reader will have to cook these barnacles,' writes Alan Davidson but for the first time, I am happy to prove him wrong.

At home, my wife awaits her first taste of *percebes*. I arrive and put a huge pot on the boil, heavily salted. Sara peers at the *percebes* with a bemused smile.

'You went all that way for these?' she asks.

'Just wait until you try them,' I reply.

Twenty minutes later and we're sat cross-legged on the floor, a pile of empty bodies to our side.

'Pretty damned good,' she admits. 'But are they really worth risking your life for?'

I take another bite of sweet flesh. 'It's a well-calculated risk. And these men have a pretty good grasp of the odds.'

She shrugs. 'Pretty damned good,' she says and reaches out for another.

CHAPTER 9

SICILY

The last journey of my year promises to be the most exciting, though not necessarily through culinary derring-do. After two days spent back at home (and these brief respites are becoming more and more attractive), it is time to head off to the southern extreme of Italy, and an island that, in some ways, seems hardly connected with the mainland.

The Sicilian cuisine is refreshingly free of the truly exotic. There is little chance of drinking snake bile wine in the shadow of Etna or munching on water beetles in the narrow, twisting back-streets of Palermo. Well, unless I am to capture the snake of Laurence's poem, drinking from his stone trough in the 'deep, strange-scented shade of the great dark carob tree ... on the day of Sicilian July, with Etna smoking'.

I expect the usual tussle with offal but by now I am entirely unfazed by whatever the ruminants can hurl at me. Tripe has just become another everyday food, although I still prefer it long cooked and covered in sauce. But the real danger from this leg of the journey will come not from the contents of my plate, but from my dining companions themselves. Well, so I hope. Thanks to the 'connections' of an old friend, Luca (half English, half Sicilian, all man), I am hoping to break bread with the Mafiosi in Sicily, stir tomato sauce with the capos and bond manfully over endless glasses of robust red wine. We might even swap tips on slicing garlic.

They will have nothing to fear from my presence, of course, as I am well-versed in the ways of *omertà*. I have seen both *Godfathers* more times than I can remember and know Lampedusa's *Leopard* (book and film) intimately. I have even sat through Cimino's turgid *The Sicilian* with the wooden Christopher Lambert, which is not an experience I'd want to repeat. All this, I feel, more than qualifies me to sit at their table. More than that, I think I understand Sicily, the tumultuous history entwined with the struggle of the peasants. I have certainly read enough books on the subject. Never mind that I have only passed through it a few times, can barely mutter a word of the language and hardly understand my own neighbourhood let alone an island on the outer extremes of Europe. On this part of the journey, I expect to be welcomed wholeheartedly into the warm, manly hug of the Sicilian Mafiosi.

If, during the course of my visit, some of my burly companions slope off to town, muttering about 'an old friend to visit', I will turn a seasoned blind eye. I have visions of outdoor country feasts and criminally strong coffee. If I am really lucky, I may even get an invitation to a 'family' wedding, although I do worry that my envelope of cash may appear a little anorexic in comparison with the pot-bellied packages of my fellow guests.

But my long-time fascination with the Mafia will stand me in good stead. Despite the endless, devastating Mafia wars that have scarred Sicily for a century, despite the innocent bystanders murdered, the families destroyed, the relentless climate of fear and brutality, the inherent corruption, extortion and terror wrought by these over-romanticised villains, I am entirely unable to disassociate the truth from the fiction. I choose to believe the Hollywood hype, all that talk of honour, loyalty and fraternity.

This was the 'dangerous' romance of the old movies, from Jimmy Cagney in *Scarface* to Warren Beatty in *Bonnie and Clyde*. In this alternative, rose-tinted world, violence was beautiful and balletic, lovingly filmed in slow motion. These heroes were just making a living, any way they could. And the Sicilian Mafia are the same, everyday folk who just happen to be pretty handy with a shooter. They walk old grannies across busy roads and idolise their mammas. Sure, sometimes things get a little rough but they have a code – no women and children, no priests – that they stick to at all costs. And hell, do they know their food. As I talk over my trip with Luca, I imagine we've walked right into the hot beating heart of the Sicilian Mafiosi.

Luca just smiles and shrugs his broad shoulders. 'Let's take it as it comes,' he says. 'Who knows, we might get lucky. But whatever happens, we'll eat like kings.'

In retrospect, I'm not sure why I believed the Mafia would throw open its ranks to a pale Englishman with a pot belly and a notebook. Much of my confidence stemmed from Luca, a man who seemed to make the impossible everyday. I had met him 15 years ago, through an old girlfriend who was his cousin. He bounded into the house, laden down with presents, thick black hair slicked back and skin bronzed by the Aeolian sun. Although half English, he emanated a macho, Southern Italian charm that scared and excited me in equal measure. But his more pressing concern was one of embarrassment. He hadn't brought anything for me.

'Such bad manners,' he kept muttering. 'You must excuse me.'

I had never met him before and he had no reason even to know

I would be there. But his overwhelming charm made it seem genuine (which it was) rather than over-the-top showboating. We became good friends and since then I had spent every year at his family's hotel on Lipari, the largest of the Aeolian islands, just above Sicily. It was, and still is, one of the places where I feel at my happiest and most secure. You wake to the distant hum of the Messina hydrofoil. And from your bed, you can see it disappearing like a white dot into a brilliantly blue horizon. The food is as good as anywhere on earth, the fish freshly hauled from the unimaginable depths of this sunken volcanic range, the caper berries just plucked from the side of the road. Tomatoes were unparalleled in their sweetness, while sea urchins were bought for a few lira from street urchins who made the diving their trade.

Being so close to Sicily, I never stopped asking Luca endless boring questions about the Mafia. 'Were there any here … what do they look like?'

He bore my onslaught with good grace, as did his parents, Hermione and Marco.

'This is the far South,' Marco used to say, his elegant Roman face dappled by the light from the pool. 'You learn to avoid these things, to not get involved. I have had a hotel here for 40 years and I've mostly managed to avoid any trouble.'

I pressed him for more, just a juicy little anecdote, an extortion dressed as a polite request. He just smiled. I thought he was being closed and enigmatic, but I now know that he was simply bored rigid by the same old questions. It is possible, he seemed to say, to live near Sicily, without being a part of the Mafia, or at least under their protection. He was more interested in running his business than answering asinine questions.

Luca was more forthcoming. Although a few inches under six

foot, Luca has a boxer's build and the swaggering roll of a prize bull. His smile is wide and features kind, and his generosity and loyalty legendary. His temper was fierce, like the spewings of Stromboli, and equally unpredictable and short lived too.

'As a child, growing up here,' he told me between bites of arancini (deep-fried rice balls) down in a portside bar, 'I knew nothing about the Mafia. Then I watched *The Godfather* at school in England and became obsessed. My father didn't like it at all, told me to push that stupid rubbish from my mind. But I was a naughty teenager, and wanted to know more. I remember asking my grandfather where one could sign up for the Mafia. He told me it was a club I wouldn't want to join. Which made me all the more fascinated.'

So when Luca started to tell me about a man known simply as 'The Fisherman', I almost choked on a mouthful of rice. Small, and unassuming, he, like many other of the islanders, ran a fish stall near the harbour. Occasionally, we dropped by for a coffee in the morning. My Italian is basic so I could only pick up the odd snippet. No surprises there, then. The only exceptional feature were his eyes, gimlet-like and cold.

'The Fisherman,' Luca said in a whisper, 'was exiled from Sicily to Lipari, where he was said to be one of the main henchmen of one of the biggest families. Everyone knows who he is, but he is treated with the greatest respect. He's not a man to fuck with.'

I wasn't going to argue. Next time we went for our coffee, I studied him more closely. His hands were hard-worn, and his accent thick. The only visible sign of wealth was a heavy gold crucifix around his neck, although this was far from unusual in a Catholic country. I looked for some sort of sign, some hidden badge, but found nothing. He was courteous and modest yet the memory of the eyes stuck with me. How many people had looked deep into their depths, pleading for their lives? I had no idea but found the whole experience incredibly exciting.

'We'll meet his sister first,' Luca said, 'in Catania. Then we'll move across to Palermo and see some real action. But the food ... my God, it's amazing.' He closed his eyes for a moment, chewing involuntarily on thin air.

'Sicilian cookery is living history, its gastronomy born out of serial rape,' writes Clarissa Hyman in her *Cucina Siciliana*. This kicked-about island has suffered two thousand years of occupation, as well as endless earthquakes (on 28 December 1908 a massive one destroyed the north-eastern city of Messina, killing over 100,000 people) and the ever-smoking threat of Etna. Yet it's lapped by three seas teeming with fish, blessed (in parts) with a fertile volcanic soil and watched over by the blazing fury of an African sun. This relentless heat gives Sicilian fruit and vegetables an intensity of flavour and vibrancy of colour that is almost unequalled anywhere in the world. If you planted a euro coin in the ground, you wouldn't be surprised if it flourished and grew into a 100 euro note. Yet parts of the island have long been wracked with pitiful poverty, where everyday existence is a grinding struggle. In Sicily, abundant bounty and bare subsistence are never far removed.

Many of the world's great civilisations passed through and conquered the island, unable to resist its fertile (and strategically important) allure. The Greeks arrived around 750 BC, founding Syracuse and providing a base for the cuisine. The scent of the wild flowers was so heady that it put the hunting dogs off their prey. They brought with them their taste for fresh fish, fish soups and simple vegetable dishes, introducing honey (or a taste for it), wine, almonds, olives and ricotta. Around 211 BC, the Romans barged in, cultivating wheat, grain and pulses. Then the Vandals came from Northern Africa (only a step away), the Ostrogoths and the Byzantines.

The Saracens were the next owners (North African Berbers and Spanish Moslems) in AD 827, bringing with them innovative irrigation systems, aubergines, sugar cane, spinach, bitter oranges, rice, apricots, pasta, spices, sultanas and tuna traps. They taught the Sicilians how to dry fruit, make sorbets from Etna's snow, as well as leaving a taste for cuscus, spit-roasting and deep frying. They encouraged people to raise sheep and goats and commercialised the citrus production. Next in were the Normans at the end of the eleventh century, bringing with them a flavour of the North; preserved cod, involtini (stuffed meat or fish rolls) and adding blue-eyed children to the already swirling gene pool.

It was thanks to King Roger II that the first mention of pasta in Italy appears. He had sent an Arab geographer to explore the islands, where he reports that:

> To the west of Termini lies the town of Trabia, a most pleasing site, rich in perennial waters and in mills, with a fertile plain and vast farms, where they manufacture vermicelli in such great quantity as to supply both the towns of Calabria and those of the Muslim and the Christian territories as well ...

He called the vermicelli itriya, an Arabic word for strings of flour and water. The Normans were succeeded by Peter of Aragon in 1282 and for the next four centuries (with the occasional respite), Sicily was under Spanish rule. They, too, plundered the island for Spanish coffers, treating the majority of Sicilians like curs. But they brought with them – and left behind – peppers, tomatoes, potatoes, chocolate and squash from the New World, as well as a taste for sweet and sour flavours.

At its height, the ostentation and finery of Sicilian Baroque made Palermo one of the culinary capitals of the world. Well, for the rich, anyway. While the moneyed classes feasted on the French-influenced likes of pheasant pâtés, puff pastries and expensive flourishes (known as Cucina Baronale, mainly based on Arab and Spanish cooking and still eaten today in Palermo), the less fortunate ate what they could. Under the Greeks and Romans, it was little more than gruel. For the peasants in later times, eating consisted of whatever they could find, the Cucina Povera: bread, tomatoes, a few herbs.

So the cuisine still runs from the basic – a bread soup floured with bay – right up to the complex extravagance of the creamy cassata. But somehow, Sicilian food is united by the power of its flavours.

'In Sicily,' writes Hyman, 'the flavours seem more powerful, hotter, spicier, sweeter, their simplicity elevated by the sheer quality of natural produce that thrives under the southern sun. Not just flavour: colours, scent and size seem exaggerated and intensified.'

But it's not a place understood by other Italians. Those in the North have long looked down on their far Southern neighbours. 'Sicily is, to say the least, baffling to Italians from other regions,' writes Luigi Barzini in *From Caesar to the Mafia*.

To understand and govern the inhabitants, cater to their needs, and solve some of their fundamental problems have proven almost impossible tasks at all times. The attempt was made, with little success, by Greeks, Romans, Byzantines, Arabs, Normans, French, Neapolitans, Piedmontese, and the US Army. Even Sicilians have seldom shown themselves capable of coping with the intricate mechanisms of their own life, certainly not the Mafia which does not always manage to run things as smoothly in its domain, which is Western Sicily, as its opponents think.

> The reason why Sicily is ungovernable is that the inhabitants
> have long ago learned to distrust and neutralise all written laws
> (alien laws in particular) and to govern themselves in their own
> rough home-made fashion …

I, of course, knew all this from my cinematic Mafia studies. And when we do arrive there, I expect the island to show its soul within moments.

Italy has always been a place of comfort, one of the twin pillars of my culinary upbringing. I spent the first 12 summers of my life in Ischia, a small island just off Naples. We would travel out, en masse, braving the high-speed chase of the Neapolitan cab ride, the often tumultuous (and vomit-splattered) hydrofoil crossing and the shaky disembarkation onto the island.

Lunch was the high point of the day, a long trestle table laid out with deep-fried courgettes, plump mussels, tiny silver anchovies in oil and soft squid rings sharp with lemon. And then the ultimate Spaghetti Bolognese (from far up North but childish tastes are impervious to regional idiosyncrasies), then hunks of meat, their surface seared black from the coals. And fresh fish, shiny and winking, quickly grilled and impossibly sweet.

In between annoying the resident Germans (my grandfather, a war hero, would sternly tell us to behave but with a twinkle in his eye), we'd gorge on pistachio and chocolate ice-cream, smearing it over our faces and T-shirts. Then wander down to the harbour, where our parents would drink Americanos and we would share a Coke. My father and uncle would wear dodgy striped jackets and Panama hats, the Englishman abroad circa 1910.

We'd all blub when it was time to leave, and the only prospect that awaited us at home was the interminable slog of the Michaelmas term. But Italian food was as familiar as toast and Marmite and shepherd's pie, comfort food rather than frightening exotica. But now, 20 years later, I am back in the country I love most, almost spoiling for a fight.

Yet Sicily is different, somehow more exotic, far removed even from Naples and Reggio Calabria. The accent is harsher and the sun more intense. More than that, it doesn't really feel like Italy at all, and seems miles away from the gentle memories of my youth. Italy always seemed a place of safety, surrounded by family and familiar tastes. The trip to Sicily is different, though. I'm not just going in search of shady fellows and fabulous fish. I am keen to prove that the films and books are right. Laos has almost lived up to my imaginary vision and I am pretty certain that Sicily will too.

Spring is in full gush when we arrive in Catania, the sun starting to take on the fury of summer and the citrus trees heavy with fruit. But Etna still wears her mantle of snow, apparently the first time for 12 years. The Sicilians talk a lot about unusual events and sinister omens but this is just blamed on the less prosaic vagaries of global warming. It is impossible to ignore this full-on thrust of spring, and the greasy memories of the BA sandwich are wiped from our memories in moments.

'Right,' says Luca as he swerves to avoid a car travelling in the wrong direction, 'we're going to meet with Carmela first. She's the sister of The Fisherman and keeps an eye on things when he's away.'

Five minutes, and we're already off to meet a *Sopranos* character. This is exactly how I imagined the place to be. Luca seems immediately at ease, slipping back into native mode and driving as if he had never left; red lights become mere advisory signals, pavements are treated as slip roads and the horn should never stay silent for more than a moment.

'Now remember, don't mention the M word. Be normal but say nothing.'

I nod, dumbly. We draw up to a shabby-looking bread store and just before we get out, Luca tells me why The Fisherman had been exiled.

'Someone had acted in a dishonourable way to his sister, Carmela. So he had to kill the man. He did it in broad daylight in Catania, walked up and shot him in the face. Despite being at a crowded lunch, no one, of course, saw anything. But they managed to nail him somehow.'

At the very least, I've expected a glittering facade and a few dodgy-looking young men moping about outside. This is no different from the local bakery. A small woman walks out, her body lean but her face tired. I expected big blonde hair, clunking gold jewellery and perfectly manicured nails. Instead, she's disappointingly normal with a neat brown bob and a minimum of make-up.

'Luca,' she purrs, both syllables thick with smoky depth. '*Come va?*' She opens the door, hauls him out and hugs him. 'Mamma Mia, ten years. Now, all grown up.'

Luca blushes, as if in the embrace of an embarrassing older aunt.

She turns to me. 'Tomas, *sì?*' I nod, 'Ciao,' and she pulls me into her scented clasp.

Aged around 40, she has slightly crooked teeth and deep brown eyes. Every time she smiles, the corners of her eyes wrinkle and soften her features. '*Vuoi mangiare, sì?*' I nod eagerly. This is one of the few Italian words that needs no translation.

Ten minutes later, and my knuckles are as white as my face. Red lights, zebra crossings, give-ways … all ignored with a cackle. Even Luca starts to look a little worried as she shoots over a two-lane highway, scattering cars in her wake. Not that he will admit it. Since arriving, his chest seems more prominent and strut more pronounced.

319

His Sicilian side is bustling and pushing its way past the more demure English demeanour.

Carmela, on the other hand, is sweating bravado out of every pore, hurtling down the streets like someone who suffers absolutely no consequences from her actions. Neither police nor private citizen seems to faze her as she cuts a swathe through downtown Catania. I try to take in the scenery but spend more times with my eyes tightly closed and my right foot pumping an imaginary brake. When we eventually arrive at the restaurant, I almost weep with relief. Pull yourself together, I tell myself. I'm within touching distance of the Mafia and acting like a frightened maiden. I compose myself and follow them into the restaurant.

The highlight of lunch is a pile of tiny sardines, resembling elvers with their long, sinuous bodies. The taste is soft, and subtly fishy, though Carmela pronounces them too old.

'In last night, not this morning. Not perfect.'

Luca nods in agreement. I look for some sign of Mafioso recognition. Why aren't the waiters fawning over our every bite, or offering special delicacies from the kitchen, courtesy of the chef? Goddammit, where's the respect? I study Carmela more closely as she chatters with Luca. Her eyes are soft and a liquid doe-like hazel. Yet if you look close enough, you catch the glint of steel hidden behind. You see it when she complains about the fish, or talks to Luca about the past ten years.

For all her verve and bravado, there's a sadness too. Not immediately perceptible but manifested in the occasional lost glance into the distance or quiet, plaintive sigh. That aside, there's certainly nothing to mark her apart from the women in the restaurant. Her clothes might be a little more revealing; her tummy is lean and bare, yet no longer blessed with the firmness of the thirties. And her pink top plummets rather alarmingly. She's attractive though, despite an inglorious face and features. She and Luca talk fast, not bothering to translate. I pick up a few snatches of family chat but am so delighted to be eating in Sicily that I give up eavesdropping after a few moments and devote myself fully to the simple pleasures of truly fresh fish.

'Jesus, buddy,' says Luca after we've left lunch. He wipes his brow and widens his eyes. 'Since I last saw her, everything has changed. Then, she had four brothers, all apparently part of the organisation. Now, she just told me with barely a flicker, one is dead, killed by the police. Another is in jail. The third, The Fisherman, has gone on the run and is in hiding. And the fourth, in hospital.'

Why, I ask, gunshot wound to the neck?

'No, he ate too much. Too fucking fat!'

But Luca says this is happening all over the island, where the war against organised crime is being stepped up and, in many cases, the women run the show through brute necessity. To me, Carmela seems so normal, grabbing bread and pasta to take home, gossiping with her friends and moaning about the freshness of the fish. And as much as I want to, I can't quite believe that she is so deeply involved.

'Let's just say she knows where the bodies are buried and keeps the brothers' interests alive. And leave it at that. Remember, nothing is what it seems here and as much emphasis is put not on what is said, but what is left unspoken.'

I begin to realise I simply don't have the first clue about how this island works. Only a niggling doubt, but my smug self-confidence begins to teeter. What seems so glorious and primal on luscious widescreen is rendered ugly by real life. Back at home, I was convinced that I would be documenting the relationship between the food and the Mafia. But the more I think about it, the more uncomfortable I feel.

Carmela is nothing like her fictional counterpart and the destruction of her family was anything but thrilling. I think back to my reasons for not visiting Afghanistan or Iraq in search of trite foodie treats. Am I being hypocritical, then, in coming to Sicily? People are being murdered and families ripped apart. I try to swat this irritant from my mind but it refuses to budge. Just a bit of time, I think, and the guilt will disappear.

Catania is a city that sits in the shade of Etna, its buildings crafted from the dark grey volcanic rock. You cannot escape its brooding presence, although the Piazza del Duomo is wide and elegant, with a stone elephant sat bang in the centre.

Luca's itinerary for our stay is brutally busy and all-encompassing. He's determined that I see the island from every angle and drink in every opinion. The Sicilian air seems to have transformed him from city ghost to gambolling satyr. In London, he rushed about, trying to fit 40 meetings into one day, barely able to move without two telephones glued to his ear. He was a whirlwind there, taking hours to calm down and break away from his business talk.

But here, the lines drop off his brow and his shoulders droop comfortably. His chest is still held out, proud, but his talk has slowed and his walk too. Tonight, he wants me to meet an old Sicilian Duke, one of the remnants of the old, aristocratic Sicily of *The Leopard*. He lives a few miles out of Catania, behind a thick, ancient wall, the remnants of a once-mighty estate.

'My ancestors had a direct line back to William the Conqueror's brother,' says the Duke as we enter his drawing room. His skin is smooth and tanned, mirrored by an immaculately soft beige cashmere jumper. His white hair seems all the brighter in contrast. We sit surrounded by an entire armoury of rifles, pistols, knives and ammunition. Hunting prints clutter the wall, fighting for space with faded leopard skins; there are yellowing cases and stools made from elephant's feet. I assume the weapons are inactive until I see a range of modern handguns that would scare Charlton Heston stiff. Every available inch is filled with cases containing still more knives and guns, yet, oddly, the impression you get is homely and old-world, an island of calm in an ocean of conflict. But God save the poor fool who tries to break in here.

Despite being in his late seventies, his blue eyes still burn fierce and proud. The floors are covered in good Kilim rugs and the furniture is grand, old and heavy. I get the feeling of faded wealth, not penury, but all the possessions of an age long past stuffed into one last room. It is at once grand and sad.

'What you have to remember is that the Honourable Society, those people who many say are the same as the Mafia, had nothing to do with the Mob.' He spits out the last two words as if they were gnats on his tongue. 'The Honourable Society have long been part of Sicily, they were the law-keepers, the top of the hierarchy, just like English sheriffs. It was only when the American criminal mafia re-integrated themselves, after the Second World War, that the Mafia as we know it began. America sneezed and we caught the cold. It was a bastardisation of the Honourable Society.'

I had always assumed that the Mafia and the Honourable Society were broadly the same organisation, under a different name. And that the latter was simply a more evolved version of the former.

'Look,' the Duke seethed, getting more and more animated, 'they always say that Salvatore Giuliano [a Sicilian bandit who fought for the poor of Sicily and was betrayed and murdered by his cousin in 1950] was a Mafioso. Was he hell! He was a man of great courage, a man who wanted to pull Sicily out of the dark ages.' The Duke's nose flares as his hands flail crossly. 'The area he lived was one of the poorest in Sicily, and he stole from the rich to give to the poor. He wanted no relationship with the Mafia, and was killed because of it.'

By now it's getting late, and the Duke is still not entirely sure why we're here. He has told his stories and we have drunk them in along with his wine. I am starting to understand that I really know nothing, a rare Socratic moment of clarity. The Duke tries to explain it in the most basic terms he has to hand.

'When the Irish and Sicilians first started emigrating to the USA, the Irish had the natural advantage.' He pauses for a sip of wine. 'They spoke the language. The Sicilians were hard working and intelligent but had to learn a new language. So they had to get organised and fight the Irish stranglehold. Which they did. They started to exploit prohibition via corrupt politicians and policemen. They gained in strength until after the Second World War; they were actually helping the Allies take over Sicily.'

He looks straight into my eyes and catches a flicker of uncertainty. I think he realises there's little point discussing history, however basic, without giving me a little background.

'We Sicilians have always had a tradition of revenge. If someone slights the family, it is not only necessary but imperative.' He pauses again. I know about this vendetta thing. You know, I'll burn down your house and piss on the ashes sort of thing. But the real vendetta is more deep rooted than mere male big chat. Norman Lewis, in *The Honoured Society*, talks of the Sicilian tradition of 'vendetta':

... ancient, tragic games whose rules were established perhaps before their ancestors reached the shores of the Mediterranean ... The poor man's only shield was the Mafia and the vendetta. Justice was not to be come by, but the association of men of honour, silent, persistent and inflexible, could at least exact a bloody retribution for the loss of a wife or daughter, or the burning down of a house ... It was in the school of the vendetta, too, that the traditional character of the Mafioso was formed. The common man, a victim of absolute power, had to learn to stomach insult or injury with apparent indifference so that vengeance could be delayed until the opportunity for its consummation presented itself.

Lewis met a Sicilian man, D'Agostino, in a Naples prison, while on army duty there in 1944. He had committed five brutal 'honour' killings and Lewis asked whether he would commit those crimes again, given another chance.

'Surely you don't imagine I had any choice, one way or the other? Honour's honour and a vendetta's a vendetta. You might say that destiny put its big fat thumb in my neck and squashed me like a beetle.' The warders nodded their sympathy and their agreement. That was the way it was.

The Duke is getting weary and we prepare to leave. As we say good-bye, he takes my arm.

'When the Honourable Society ran things, if you were caught stealing, you were told off by the Capo. It was a great honour to be told by the big man and you respected him. So you fell into line. But protection of your family is at the heart of everything in Sicilian society. You cannot lose face and there are ritualised ways of dealing with things. You don't just go and kill your enemy. There are ways.'

His grip tightens. 'Remember the Honourable Society looked after the peasants, they administered the common law. The Mafia are just a bunch of over-romanticised thugs.' It is as if he can see right into my brain. I am one of those deluded fools who has always 'over-romanticised' their every move. The niggle I felt early is slowly turning to a full-blown itch.

I leave the house more confused than when I entered. If this fabled Honourable Society was so noble and upright, how could it not be connected with the Mafia, the sort who ruled over the land, extracting tributes and 'taxes' from all that moved under them? I did see that the tradition of '*omertà*' and 'honour killings' was Sicilian rather than that of the Mafia. It is an island that has spent the majority of its existence under occupation, so a powerful group of local men administering their own, more understandable laws could seem appealing to the impotent peasants.

Lewis talks at length about the 'Honoured Society'. Before World War I, he describes the rise of Calogero Vizzini, one of the first great 'dons' of the modern age.

It was probably at this point that Calogero was invited to become a member of the 'Honoured Society'. By the very nature of that association – the most secret, the most powerful and most abiding of all secret societies – the fact that one is a member can never be admitted. At the most a Mafioso may allow himself to be described as 'a man of respect', or 'a friend of the friends', or accept – as did Calogero Vizzini at the age of 25 – the title of Ziu, meaning uncle.

But I remain unclear as to why so many Sicilians still talk of the 'Honoured Society' with such reverence when behind all the ritual and secrecy, it is another criminal organisation.

Of course, I wanted to quiz Carmela too, but there is no chance of that. As we drive back, I notice every street is plastered with anti-Mafia posters. Reading these exhortations to rise up and break the criminal stranglehold, the *copollas* (the traditional flat hats), *luparas* and riotous country feasts seem a long way off. We meet up again with Carmela, to go together and see the Catania fishing port. But we arrive early, at about 10.30, so the place is empty. That means another 20 minutes of travelling through the city with my eyes closed.

Carmela seems blessed with the ability to stop her car within a flea's pube of the one in front. Anyone who questions her driving (and there are many) is met with a flurry of throaty insults. Luca earlier explained that although she might be very much part of the organisation ('with the Mafia, you are never sure,' he warned cryptically), it wasn't as a capo or even a lieutenant. Her brothers had all been the workers ('think Pussy rather than Paulie'), the middle of the chain grafters. They 'looked after' things.

The plus side of our drive is that my Italian vocabulary gains some useful, if mainly scatological, additions. But the relief when we park (well, drive up onto the pavement, Sicilian style) is huge. As we get out, an ancient, cadaverous wreck of a man hobbles over and asks for a euro. His breath reeks of old tobacco and rotten teeth. I expect them to walk on, but both cough up.

'This way,' Luca says, 'the car is safe.'

'But Carmela's here,' I whisper. 'Shouldn't there be some respect or something?'

'It's a different area here and the boss of this area makes sure that an eye is kept on all cars that pay the toll. It is neither legal nor illegal, just the way it happens here.'

From car parking to car bombing, the Mafia doesn't miss a trick.

We stop for a drink in the old town, behind the university. The streets are packed, thanks to Italy's strict anti-smoking laws. Even in the heart of Sicily, these rules are obeyed. We buy a beer, sit outside, and watch the young crowds go by, enveloped in a fug of weed. Everyone is smoking and if they're not smoking, skinning up. Customised cars glide slowly past, so all can admire their shiny alloys and thundering bass. Rich, northern-looking students, clad in Barbours and cashmere, stand next to the local wide boys, hoodies up and barely visible through the acrid smoke. Across the street, local spivs all in black and festooned with gold, whisper and watch the women pass. The mood is calm and unhurried. If this were England, there'd be a fight in moments.

'People only fight here for a good reason,' says Carmela. 'It's not the sort of place to pick a fight,' she adds ominously. By now, she's swaying slightly.

'Italian women can't drink,' says Luca. 'And she's had five beers.'

Still, she insists on driving but first, we stop for a snack. We pull up to a chrome-plated trailer, parked at the side of the road. It's like a mobile kebab van, only bigger, with a long charcoal grill and a selection of food that would put Fortnum's to shame. Rather than a grotty, scrofulous doner and a deep-fried saveloy, there are fresh steaks, sausages, Veal Milanese, artichoke hearts, Russian Salad, sun-dried tomatoes, chips slathered with mayonnaise and marinated anchovies. The whole trailer gleams like a freshly polished Buick. My sausage sandwich is perfect booze food, richly porky with a touch of fennel. This is a rare late-night snack I won't regret the next morning. If I ever make it that far.

Carmela falls back into the car, grinding the gears before shooting off into the night. We are headed for Aci Trezza, a small town outside Catania. Carmela has decided that the main market is boring, but this is where the action is. We arrive in a deserted car park just past one. Everything is still, save a few lorries parked around the perimeter. The only noise is Carmela who is now singing and trying to get us to join in. Her drunkenness is mainly good-natured, though she occasionally bellows at us for no apparent reason. That steel, so well hidden at lunch, is rather more exposed now. A lorry cabin sometimes flares up, as a cigarette is lit. There's a feeling of pregnant anticipation, like the start of a rave where everything's there save the power. A skeletal cat stalks the edges.

'Isn't that dodgy,' asks Luca, 'a thin cat at the fish market? Not the best of signs.'

By now, Carmela has climbed out of the back and is being sick behind the car. We pretend not to notice. We wait and wait, not entirely sure if we've come to the right place. It's not as if our guide is fully alert.

'When this all kicks off, they say it's amazing,' says Luca, ever hopeful.

My pathetic reserves of patience have long departed and I really couldn't care less.

'All the fish is sold within a matter of minutes, a feeding frenzy of bartering and borrowing.' Luca pauses, as another few lorries pull up and take their place. 'Any second now,' he promises.

Carmela crawls back into the car and slumps in the back. And we continue to wait. Another hour passes, accompanied by a gentle snore from the back. To keep awake, we pace the perimeter, peering into the cabins to see the sleeping occupants, their woolly hats pulled over their eyes. We wander into the local café where swarthy-looking folk gulp tar-like Espresso. We order two. They're thick, hot and bitter. Luca is dressed in his shirt and jacket and despite his Sicilian accent, he looks out of place.

As for me, I look as if I've stumbled from another world. My face is pasty, even for an Anglo-Saxon, and my Italian accent is more Home Counties peep rather than Sicilian drawl.

A fat, Jean Reno lookalike with bulging eyes and filthy plaid shirt stares intently at us. We look away. Luca asks the barman when the market starts.

He looks at his friends, then shrugs. 'What market?'

We walk out again. 'You're trembling, buddy,' says Luca.

Wet as I am, my knees are knocking at the strength of the coffee rather than sheer fear and I worry that I'll never sleep again. Still more vans and trucks are rolling in, but there is no sign of anything else, no fish laid out or money exchanged.

Carmela wakes up briefly to answer the phone. She grunts a few times, then throws it down. 'Most of the deals have been done tonight on the way over the island,' she slurs. 'My friend had a whole load of anchovies to bring and sell, but someone else found out and offered to buy the lot from him halfway. They did the deal in a local petrol station.' Then she slumps down again and begins to snore.

We wait another half an hour before giving up and driving home.

The next day, Carmela rings us. 'You idiots. At 4.00, it apparently all went mad, every kind of fish under the sun. No patience.'

I don't think that she remembered even being there.

The following day, we meet up with Nunzio, a Catanian local who is to drive us across Sicily.

'I don't trust myself,' mutters Luca. 'And we need someone who knows the place properly.'

Nunzio reminds me of a prep school master, with tweed jacket and neat moustache. His eyes are slightly magnified by his bright round glasses and his voice is low and dulcet. I immediately feel safe in his hands.

The morning is crisp enough to break off and drizzle with oil. Etna has her head in the cloud, snow down to her waist. The lemon trees are groaning with fruit, and flash by in a Technicolor blur. Prickly pears, their thick, platelike leaves covered in spikes, huddle on the edge of the road while the occasional orange grove breaks the yellow mass. Now and again, I catch sight of the sea, foam-flecked and angry. But then the pine forests close in again and it disappears from sight.

As if there isn't enough yellow, vivid buttercups crowd the verge, dazzling the eyes until the sheer intensity of colour forces you to blink and stare ahead. We pass Taormina, clinging precariously to the side of a rock, while the odd ruined watchtower stares mournfully out to sea. A non-stop procession of towns hug the shore and as we climb up, way above the coast, wispy fronds of wild fennel scent the air and wave us on our way. The white almond blossom looks like fresh snow; pure and white.

This orgy of spring is so intense that it hurts. Not for Sicily the odd clump of daffodils or demure blossom. This is a relentless, full-frontal assault on the senses, the emergence of a primal force that is more goat-hoofed satyr than the first cuckoo in spring.

A few hours later, having passed through the centre of the island – a place of green, rolling hills, windswept moors and the occasional ruined farmhouse or Norman castle – we reach the outskirts of Palermo. On the radio, there's a piece about a local woman who pretended she was an anti-Mafia judge. She blacked out her car windows and attached a blue siren to her car and received endless freebies, from long lunches to holidays abroad. In Sicily, these officials are held in high regard. The scam was only revealed when she applied for a massive loan (using her fake official credentials). But although most are rightly venerated (it's a dangerous job), there are individuals who see themselves as above the law and therefore entitled to a free ride.

'My father respects them,' says Luca, 'but refuses to give them all totally free board. The hotel would go bust otherwise.'

We arrive just before dinner and although the city is dark, its air is perfumed with a thousand different feasts. The night starts off quietly, meeting up with two of Luca's friends, Roberto and Alessandro, at a trattoria hidden away in a less salubrious part of town. We fight through gangs of teenagers posing moodily on scooters and stallholders selling off the remnants of their stock. The atmosphere is not menacing, exactly, more wary and closed. We stick out like Parmesan on a bowl of lobster linguine, and Luca tells me this is still a traditional, Mafia-controlled area.

It's a relief when we get inside to the restaurant, a simple room with fish packed on ice near the entrance. The bustle is warm and enticing, and the place packed with what looks like a mixture of locals, lawyers (well, sharp suited anyway) and that special kind of affluent Italian who seems born into a pastel cashmere jumper and sockless loafers.

Roberto and Alessandro are both Sicilian, the former working for a bank, and the latter an organic farmer with a small estate outside Palermo. They are keen to show me real Palermo food, 'not some bullshit tourist place with *Godfather* posters on the wall'.

I remember the first few courses well enough; ethereal panelle, deep-fried chickpea fritters that melt hotly on the tongue.

Luca manages about ten. 'They're my favourite food,' he tells me, as if I hadn't noticed.

Then a whole boiled octopus, dumped on the table, red and livid. I chew gamely through a tentacle or two, even sucking out the black gunk inside the brain. But with no salt, oil or anything else, I eat more out of politeness than anything else.

'It's frozen, not fresh,' whispers Luca as I embark on my third rubber band. 'Which is not always a bad thing but this is bad quality.'

I can also just about recollect the next two courses, although the local wine was flowing liberally. The first was a taglioni with prawns and fresh fish roe. My only notes are spidery 'stunning' followed by a quote from Alessandro: 'This is a treat, something you give to someone you owe a favour.'

I put a mass of ticks next to this, so assume he was right. Then there was a typically Sicilian dish involving long-cut macaroni with anchovies, pine nuts and sultanas. The rest of my notes, like the rest of the evening, are a write-off. Just like the night of the hot sauce in New Mexico and numerous other occasions in the past year where I got too pissed to speak any sense, let alone write it.

After an endless succession of bars, we end up in a crumbling palazzo in what I am told is the birthday party for an Olympic wind-surfer. I wish I could entertain you with stories of Palermo by night but just two things remain; the women seem awesomely beautiful, lithe, poised and proud.

And next day I suffer from one of the worst hangovers of my entire journey, a force ten bowel-breaking, head-cracking, stomach-churning bastard that is usually only treatable by two days in bed in a darkened room. It is less hangover and more pure alcohol poisoning, and certainly not the best state in which to go off for a morning's eating around Palermo's markets.

You may be feeling a slight twinge of déjà vu here. Once again, I manage to scupper all chances of a civilised morning by overdoing it the night before. You may have thought that, after Albuquerque, Tokyo and Luang Prabang, an intelligent sort of person might have learnt his lesson. I'll leave you to draw your own conclusions.

The Mercato di Ballaro is less famous than the Vucciria, but, according to our hosts, far more typical.

'Too many Chinese there,' said one local when asked about it. 'This is still mainly used by locals.'

It's one of the oldest markets in Sicily, tucked away in a labyrinthine warren of streets. Our guide is Guido Agnello, president of the Fondazione Palazzo Intelligente in Palermo, entrepreneur, aesthete and expert on all things Sicilian. Dressed in olive corduroy, he has snowy white hair down to his shoulders, and a perfectly trimmed beard and moustache. Thin and angular, he looks like Roy Strong played by Johnny Depp. Luca's mother told me he was known for being the best-looking man in Sicily in his youth but he is entirely unselfconscious and lacking in any vanity. He has a patrician air but without that slight supercilious arrogance. Studious, highly intelligent and passionate about the regeneration of Sicily, he is as much at ease with the aristocracy as with the stall-holders. Everyone seems to know him and, wherever we walk, a chorus of 'Ciao Guido' follows us.

I am barely even able to walk, so wracked am I by the excess of last night. Every fishy smell, every butchered beast makes me retch and even the most innocuous of sights – a pile of glowing lemons or box of gnarled tomatoes – causes unsettling lurches in my belly. Luca doesn't seem as badly punished as me and, as usual, his immaculately brushed hair and spotless jacket give him an air of respectability that I can only envy.

But even in my weakened state, I feel that stepping through these narrow streets is like entering another era. Even the precarious piles of counterfeit DVDs and CDs do little to break the old-world atmosphere. Shops and stalls line the winding streets, and the din of the salesmen is deafening. The defining feature of pretty much every part of my journey has been the markets. This one seemed rather less extreme, in that I can't spot the usual menagerie of endangered creatures, as in Laos. It is less ordered than Tsukiji in Tokyo and much more noisy. And less dour and alien than Seoul (well, at least I can recognise everything and there is no sign of dog).

But all the markets I have visited over the past year share the same basic vision; flavour, quality and freshness are valued above appearance. Seasonality and locally produced are not trendy buzzwords but pure common sense. Buying from nearby farmers not only reduces costs but ensures that the produce is of the finest standard.

Despite the superficial differences – the piles of chillies and galangal in Laos, the fugu and cod sperm in Japan, the sinister herbs in Korea, the *percebes* in Spain and the bugs in Beijing – a decent market is the same the world over. Although a few intrepid tourists do wander about, this is a working market, a place where locals buy their daily bread.

The first stall is filled with the fruit of spring's loins, fresh peas, tiny pods of broad beans (this is only March), gleaming aubergines, piles of fennel, different varieties of tomato, and citrus fruit in its every guise. Behind it, a modest, bespectacled man, clad in a dirty white overall, greets Guido. He looks more like an accountant than vegetable seller but they kiss and we move on.

'That man,' whispers Guido as we walk away, 'is the big man in this area, the capo of the market. Everyone answers to him.'

I look back in surprise, and he nods at me. Hardly the Marlon Brando of popular legend. My hangover has become markedly worse in the last few minutes and I feel as if even the slightest taste will be too much. I can't really appreciate the market as all I can think of is getting back to the cool shade of my bedroom. Nothing else matters. I make all the right noises – 'umm' when a basket of body-popping shrimp are lifted to my nose; 'ahh' as a trayful of quivering, bloody liver is proffered for our inspection – although the sight of any food is pretty unbearable.

Everywhere, the banter of the market hangs heavy in the air. Heavily stubbled men hack up a swordfish, its mouth open in outrage and sword pointed towards heaven. A messy queue forms, and each chunk is wrapped in paper, then a cheap plastic bag. All I can concentrate on, though, is keeping the contents of my stomach from meeting the street.

'Come,' smiles Guido, 'I'll show you a proper Sicilian breakfast.'

We duck off the street into a high-ceilinged bolt-hole.

'Welcome to Taverna Azzura.' Pictures of the Virgin Mary mingle with giant wooden vats of wine while in the far corner, huge metal stills stand ready to unleash their toxic load. A long bar is set up along one side and the market traders crowd it, sipping passito (a sweet wine from Zibibbo), tearing off hunks of fresh bread and spreading them with anchovies or tiny sardines or anything else they have picked up in the stalls outside. It is 8 o'clock in the morning.

Guido gets a few glasses and hands one to me. 'You must try this. It's fantastic, even at this hour of the morning.'

I smile, weakly, and look to Luca. He grins back and takes a huge swig.

I, on the other hand, can't go too close for fear of embarrassment. I take a pretend sip that doesn't fool Guido.

'Maybe a little early, eh?'

I nod and we go out once more into the scrum. An old man hobbles across the main thoroughfare, his body gnarled and his face severe. The market erupts when they see him, jeering and shouting, and he tries to move faster. The children run past him, pulling his clothes. I look away in embarrassment and next time I turn, he has been swallowed up by the crowds.

We take a turn into an even more crooked street, and find ourselves at the heart of the market.

'Not even the police come this far, even now,' say Guido. 'It's off-limits. Fifteen years ago, even I wouldn't come near. Palermo has changed a lot since then, mainly for the good.'

A butcher's stall is festooned with skinned goat's heads, ghoulish and pathetic at the same time. With no eyelids, their eyes seem to follow your every move. I spy a pile of tripe, catch its gamey tang and scuttle on, sick at the thought despite my new-found fondness. That Galician dish was superb and the Italians have a number of wonderful ways. But even the mildest, softest piece of offal seems more extreme now than a cauldron full of dogs.

Fish stalls creak under the weight of the produce, gleaming in the early morning sun. The area around their stands is already awash in a stream of melted ice. Small sharks share space with thick blocks of salt cod, seemingly stiffened by starch. We're getting towards the end now, and I almost weep with relief. Even the water isn't going down well and alcohol seeps noxiously from my every pore, making me sicker still.

But just as I'm about to escape, Guido calls me over for one last treat.

'Now this is a feature in every town all over Sicily.' He gestures to a small shop on his left. 'It's the *tripperia*, the tripe shop. Come.'

I try my utmost to wriggle out, citing all sorts of pathetic excuses. It's as if I'm being dragged to a bloody death in the Colosseum. But Guido is insistent.

'You want to see the real Sicily. Well, this is a good place to start.'

As I walk in, my senses are mauled by a horribly familiar pong.

The room smells cheesy and off, with hints of hot, rotten meat. It's suffocating too, close and fetid, and every breath is a nauseous ordeal. An ominous-looking vat bubbles in the corner, with a two-ring gas cooker next door. On top of the gas are two open pots, one filled with what looks like tripe under cheese and breadcrumbs. And the other, a tripe and tomato stew. I don't even want to know what's contained in the closed vat.

A pile of white plates wait expectantly alongside the cooker. Close by is a long marble counter where two old men chew slowly on their tripe, paying little attention to our entry. I gag and try to step out of this Boschean vision of intestinal hell, smiling at the old crone behind the pan. I'm nearly there, edging towards the door. And just as I'm about to gasp my first breath of sweet, tripe-free air, Luca calls me back. He is standing in front of Guido and his face is set in a manic grin.

'Hey buddy, you love tripe. Why are you leaving? Come, Guido, let's get Tom a bowl. He's starving. He's so English and polite, far too embarrassed to ask himself.'

What Guido can't see is Luca's eyes, streaming with tears of delight. He composes himself just long enough to make sure I have the real thing.

'Not those yummy stews,' he says, trying to keep the glee from his voice (and failing), 'I mean the real thing. The plain boiled tripe, au naturel.'

At this point, I would have gladly slipped Luca into a pair of concrete boots. And smiled as he sank to the bottom of the harbour for an extended piscine siesta.

'Cunt,' I mouth at him, all the time trying to look composed. I'm too ill to be truly angry but seethe impotently all the same.

'Sorry buddy, missed that. Oh, he wants a good plateful. Has to keep that belly round. He loves it so much.'

The crone cackles (actually, I'm sure she did nothing of the kind – in fact, she's probably a respectable, good-looking, middle-aged lady; at this point, though, she is the witch behind this bitches' brew), opens the fearsome cauldron and spoons out a grisly mess. She plonks it down on the top and it seems as if every eye in the room is turned onto me.

I look down at the torrid mass of off-white strips, my sweat dripping in and adding a salty tang. Some of the tripe resembles morel mushrooms; or body parts of an alien race with a taste for human flesh. My mouth starts to flood with saliva, a sure sign that the rest is close behind. My body is now soaked with boozy sweat, my head pounds and my stomach warns me to back off. I pick up the smallest strand, a brown and bobbly monstrosity and drop it in. I know the taste. I know the texture. I know I'm going to puke. I screw up my eyes and chew feverishly, willing myself to swallow and escape. The offal releases its stinking juices into my mouth.

'Very smelly and very good,' I hear the crone shriek.

At last, I force it down and without even pausing, sprint outside. I look frantically around. Despite this being a maze of backstreets, there is no quiet corner in which to unload the contents of my belly. I choke, gasp and slowly, very slowly, the real world comes rushing back in. The mass armies marching up my throat retreat and my honour is saved. I take deep draughts of the air, still shaking and blinking through the tears to see Luca bent double, grasping a wall for support.

For one blissful moment, I believe the hangover has finally got him too and he's feeling my agony. But as I look closer, I realise that he's wracked with laughter, not pain. Never has the idea of vendetta seemed so sweet.

That's not to say I feel any better as we walk towards lunch. I am ignoring Luca and striding ahead, trying to regain a modicum of respect. We pass a pile of scooter parts laid out on a rug.

'All stolen,' says Guido.

As I watch, two burly men wrench apart a machine that seems in perfect condition.

'As I said, this is not a police area. Everything is run by the local boss.' The coyly titled 'mixed meat' is sold in bags from the backs of scooters. You pay your money and it's like a meaty 'Lucky Dip'. I pass by quickly.

'The city was crumbling and the place was infested with criminals, real lowlifes. Orlando cleared it all up with culture,' explains Guido, wiping his glasses with a pristine white handkerchief.

Leoluca Orlando looms large on every corner in this city. He was Mayor of Palermo from 1993 to 2000. At the start, Palermo was suffocating under the vice-like grip of the Mafia and recovering from the ruinously corrupt rule of Vito Ciancimino, a man who transformed Palermo into a concrete wasteland as he handed out building contracts to his Mafioso buddies. He was later arrested, making him the first Italian politician to be found guilty of membership of the Mafia. Although only Mayor for two months, it was his five years as Councillor for Public Works that saw the city's Green Belt destroyed, along with many of its most beautiful villas.

But Leoluca was different, the first official to take on the Mafia and for the next seven years, he denounced them and began to transform the city. He became a hero of the people, a man who could do no wrong. This period was known as the 'Palermo Spring' and was the time when the city was reborn, and its residents could walk the streets again without fear. At the heart of his campaign was his removal of all the city contracts owned by the Mafia. He aimed to cut off their wealth, and pretty much succeeded.

His wide, handsome face smiles out from every street corner, as his current campaign is running for Prodi's 'Democrat' party. There is little doubt of his achievements and his bravery (he still has to travel everywhere with armed guards) but I have heard whisperings that no man is that powerful in Sicily without the 'right' connections. And some say that he was born into a 'well-connected' family of Mafiosi. As others consistently say, nothing is ever what it seems, even the saviour of Palermo. There may be a chance, Luca said, of meeting him tomorrow.

'But who knows?' he says.

'Orlando embarked upon a policy of restoring old buildings,' continues Guido, his white locks fluttering in the breeze, 'and organising festivals, opening up old places and getting people into areas like this. So if there was a festival, a panino man might appear, and a man with beers and water. And slowly, the life came back. Look at it now. Tourists everywhere, old buildings restored. It's an incredible change from the dark days. Ah, here we are.'

He stops at a fruit and vegetable stall and we walk through a door in the wall into a tiny kitchen with a few tables. As is usual, there are three deep freezes, two gas burners and empty beer bottles everywhere. We are in the middle of La Kalsa area, perhaps the poorest and most notorious of Palermo's neighbourhoods. It was once an Arabic part of town and the area even has its own impenetrable dialect within the Palermo dialect within the Sicilian. Although in the middle of a restoration project, one can easily imagine it 50 years back. The buildings lean on each other, as if passing long-kept secrets.

'In the old days,' explains Guido, 'this is where Mafiosi who were wanted by the law would eat. They would slip in through the fruit stall into this hidden room.'

Nowadays, a door has been built in the side and you can walk onto the street. But although the area has changed, it doesn't seem that the room's inhabitants have. A group of men sit huddled around the plastic table, playing cards and drinking wine from cheap tumblers. They are fishermen mainly, their faces beaten into deep furrows by the winter storms and summer heat. They look as if they've just tumbled out of Mafia central casting, with a collection of ragged scars, toothless leers and scuffed leather jackets. At last, a rare match for my Hollywood preconceptions.

I momentarily forget my hangover, so thrilled am I that one cliché, at least, turns out to be true. Of course, they probably have nothing to do with any criminal organisation but my fervent and usually patronising imagination sees otherwise. A tiny, toothless man greets Guido with a grunt of joy.

'This is Monkey,' says Guido, 'one of the greatest free-divers Sicily has ever seen. He's called Monkey because he eats whatever he likes. Well, he eats anything.'

Monkey gives a gummy grin. 'He could get the finest sea urchins from the black depths of the ocean.'

His woolly cap is pulled low over his forehead and his foot is in plaster. He waves a crutch towards an outdoor table and we all sit down. A big bottle of Pepsi is set down at the table and for the first time, I breathe a sigh of relief. But the contents of my glass do not match the bottle's label. It's red wine, hidden in the bottle to avoid any annoying taxes. The proprietor, a fat man with a face like a side of ham, throws down a boiled meat salad to start and a plate of peppery radishes with a pile of salt. The boiled meat looks good but I'm still suffering.

I pick at the tomatoes and anchovies, and drop the rest into the mouth of the mongrel at my feet. The table is cleared for a platter of swordfish in the Palermo style, which usually means covered with breadcrumbs. The Sicilians love their bread and will travel miles to their favourite baker.

Monkey starts to tell a joke so long and drawn-out that even Guido looks a little bored. It's about a man and a baby, as far as I can gather, asking directions in a train station. But he tells the joke with every inch of his body, leering and grinning and crying and waving, and pointing and screaming, all in about ten different voices. I can't keep my eyes off him and in him seems the essence of Sicily; the noise, the theatre, the pride and the hidden jokes. Then I realise that I'm up to my old tricks once more, generalising without having the slightest clue as to what I'm describing. And go back to wishing I were in bed.

I curse myself – for the fiftieth and final time, thank God – for last night's excess as a plate of golden fried calamari appears in front of us. I manage a mouthful here, one there. But I'm missing out on a traditional, no-nonsense Palermo feast, eaten in the street yards away from an old Mafia hideout. Even an armful of broad beans, thrown in the middle and eaten raw with salt, as tiny as a baby's fingernail and sweet as can be, does little to break my fast. The spring sun peeps out once more from the clouds and bathes us in its rays. Instead of joy, I just worry about being burnt. The occasional roar or shout comes from the men indoors.

Like everything I've seen in the city so far – the party in the palazzo, the secret room, the tiny bars, the unspoken rules – Palermo is a city that hides behind walls and inscrutable expressions, a place no foreigner (and by that I mean Italians too) will ever come close to understanding. But picking at fresh broad beans in a trattoria without menu or even name, I allow myself the thought that at least I might have had the slightest whiff of a city that rarely shows its face.

After lunch, we're joined by Riccardo, Guido's brother and blessed with the same thick locks of white-grey hair. He is broader than his brother, but his good looks are more casual and less sculpted. He wants to take us up to Monreale, a few miles above the city, and as much as I want my bed, we agree. I hate churches at the best of times, but this cathedral is something else, predominantly Norman but unquestionably Byzantine in influence.

Riccardo is in charge of converting an old monastery next door into a fully fledged museum, but today he has a more pressing matter – bread. The best, he says, in Sicily, and therefore the world. It's dense and chewy but lingers wonderfully on the palate.

'It keeps for a week too,' he says as we rip off chunks. 'Taste the beauty.' He tells me of a book he once wrote, called *Poor Food But Good* (it loses something in translation, I think).

'It was in the Eighties and the whole island was in an awful state, an economic slump. I blame it all on Ciancimino, the most corrupt bastard that ever lived. It was he who destroyed so much of the city's beauty, and the slump was because of him.' He bit off another lump of bread and chewed angrily. 'I remember,' he says suddenly, quite out of the blue, 'one spring 30 years back.' His eyes are magnified by his glasses, giving him an owlish look, and he seems lost in the recollection.

'I was eating with the big boss, the capo, out in the countryside near here.' I dare not ask why. 'We have some of this bread, fresh broad beans, pecorino, and it's a perfect spring day.' He pauses for effect. 'The capo eats the beans then the cheese then takes a long draught of cool local wine, straight from the clay jar. He drinks deep, smiles and a dribble of wine runs down the side of his face. He was a big man, and he looked at me as he wiped away the wine. He said, "I could happily die now. But there's not even anyone to kill me."

'Now don't take the story the wrong way. But it was a glorious spring day like this one and this powerful man was so moved by the simple beauty of fresh, seasonal food that he wanted to die. Fantastico, eh?'

It's as romantic a tale as I've heard told here, despite being told about a known killer. If Mario Puzo had got wind of it, no doubt it would have appeared in his trashy classic and added still more fuel to my fervent imagination. But the story is as true as it is memorable and seems so typically Sicilian that it could almost work as an epitaph for half the people I've met so far. The light is fading as we drive back into Palermo and Riccardo is in full flow about food, namely the dish he thinks is most typical of Sicily.

'Of course, sardines cooked in a special way. Sarde a Beccafico from Palermo, named after the bird that pecks the figs and is good to eat. But they were too expensive for the poor, so they made this dish, with pine nuts, and currants and orange juice, to make them look similar. They put the tails of the sardine up in the air, just like the plump bird. This is the true cooking of Sicily, made from whatever is cheap and available.'

I see Luca ostensibly nod then shake his head towards me. When it comes to food, only one way is the best – the cook's own.

We pass an advert for a new Renault car, with a stereotyped mobster grinning out, all gold and cigars. He holds a baby in his arms, dressed in the same gangster garb. 'The family that renews itself' runs the tagline.

'Ten years ago,' Luca says, 'no one would have found this funny.'

Riccardo agrees. 'The city is safer now, filled with civic pride. In the old days, my mother wouldn't let us near. Of course, we crept in but it was scary, truly threatening. It all changed when Falcone [the famous anti-mafia judge blown up just outside Palermo in 1992] was murdered. Ever since the power of the Mafia was hit by Leoluca, and the people decided they'd had enough, it all changed. In 1992, there were tanks in Palermo and the army everywhere, a big purge to clean out the Mafia. The people had had enough and took to the streets. The police got one of the big boys, Toto Riina, but they have still not got Bernardo Provenzano, the *capo di tutti capi*.'

A few weeks later, when I was back in England, Provenzano was eventually captured in a shepherd's hut in the mountains near

Corleone. He had been on the run for 43 years, living the life of a hermit. He was finally caught when the police tracked his laundry – pants, vest and socks – to his final rural hideout. He was living in the way of the old Mafiosi – a pot of chicory simmered on the stove and the freezer was full of bread.

In this respect, the most powerful man in the Sicilian Mafia was identical to the likes of Don Vito and the rest of the old-school 'Honourable Society'. And was nearer to a monk than to the garish excess of *The Godfather* and their American ilk. As Piero Grasso, Italy's chief anti-Mafia prosecutor, said at the time of his arrest, Provenzano had made a conscious choice to live like this.

'It was the most in line with his peasant origins, best suited to an outlaw and also an example of "Mafia ethics" for other Mafiosi. He was setting an example.'

That evening, we have a drink with Professore Gaetano Basile, a renowned writer and food historian. Wise and white bearded, he tells us that the Ballaro Market is 1,100 years old, the name coming from *al-ballarath*, an Arabic word meaning 'market of mirrors'. He has hardly sat down before he launches into a passionate exposition of Sicilian cuisine.

'It was only in 1852 when the tomato was first used by the aristocrats in Sicily. Actually, the first recorded use was in Pasta alla Norma, the famous dish.'

He pauses to take a sip of wine. 'It looks like Etna, with the lava as tomato sauce, rocks as aubergine and the snow as salted ricotta.'

This being Sicily, this is far from the only explanation as to its invention. The most popular is that it was named after Sicilian composer Bellini's *Norma*, an opera so adored that a dish was created in its memory. Another version is that the dish was 'as good as Norma', hence the name. And the least exciting – but most probable

– was that '*norma*' means standard, using as it does the staple ingredients of the island. But he gave me little time to linger.

'Up until 1852, just the rich ate tomatoes. All the nobles had cooks and they kept detailed records of what was eaten, as well as a shopping list. I believe, though, that the tomato has done tremendous damage to Sicilian cuisine.'

I look over at Luca, whose eyes widen in quiet disagreement. That sort of chat could get you shot in Naples.

'And another thing. It's always said that the Arabs invented cassata [a ruinously rich concoction of marzipan, sponge, sweetened ricotta and candied fruit] but it was actually a Sicilian dish, first seen around 1887. Anyway, the Arabs never had candied fruit. They say the word came from *qas'ah*, Arabic for a large, steep-sided bowl used to mould the cake. That's rubbish.' His eyes blaze as he rights this scurrilous wrong. 'It comes from *cacio*, meaning cheese.'

I nod, desperately trying to keep up and trying to pretend I actually like this sickly confection. And as learned as he is, I start to fade away, dreaming of molten puddles of mozzarella on top of fresh tomato sauce and a thin, charred pizza base.

An hour or so later, we arrive at the pizza place recommended by Luca's friends. It's packed with people attacking chariot wheels of blistered dough, the tomato sauce so fine that it marches up the nose, making every hair stand to attention. So when one of the waitresses laughs at our request for a table ('Try booking three weeks in advance next time') I almost collapse in despair. We limp out, assailed on all sides by these visions of pizza perfection, and for a few minutes, we sit in silence.

'Life must go on buddy,' says Luca as he clasps my shoulders. 'Be strong.'

I nod stoically and we find a table in a local trattoria, eating a decent, but unmemorable, Spaghetti alla Norma, all the while gazing longingly through the window at the lotus eaters over the road. At the end, the owner, Biondo, appears, pulls up a chair and starts to talk. He has a huge, greying Afro of black hair that bobs around as he chatters. In comparison to this electrified, unkempt barnet, his moustache is thin and immaculately trimmed. Like the fisherman at lunch, he manages to talk using every part of his body; feet, ankles, fingers, shoulders, even hair. Rather than talking with us, he shouts at us, telling us stories of how dangerous Palermo used to be. ('I still carry a gun at night. No fucker's going to nick my takings.')

He then moves on to tales of the Mafia. Everyone I've met in Sicily has their own story and experience, so firmly are they ensconced in everyday life. But only a few are happy to talk openly. Probably not so much from fear any more, as boredom. Biondo has no such qualms and launches into his greatest hits. He seems to enjoy my wide-eyed fascination, each story getting more and more extreme. No one, though, paints them as heroes. Or portrays the bleak days in Palermo, in the Seventies and Eighties, as anything other than horrific. To the average person, the Mafia are everyday problems to be avoided at all costs.

'One night, in my old restaurant, back when things were really bad,' his hair bounces in time to his wildly gesticulating arms, 'a very smart man came in and booked the whole restaurant for his friends. Of course, we all pay our *pizzo* [meaning bird's beak, taste or bung] and pray they stayed away. You knew he was Mafioso, but he ordered lobsters and crabs and beef and cassata and oysters and endless bottles of Champagne.

'"This," he told me, "must be a dinner fit for a king."

'So we spent days preparing all this and the night came and the expensive cars drew out and everyone came in. Then, last of all was a small old man, the capo. He looked around and sat down and I was just about to start the food when I was told to wait. The capo called me over and asked for a piece of boiled fish.

'"I am a simple man," he said, "of simple tastes."

'I was amazed, with all this luxury waiting ready to be served. But we got him his fish, and a slice of apple. And for half an hour, he ate alone. Then he thanked me and left. This was a member of the old school, the Honourable Society who do not flaunt their cash. The second he had left, though, we were told to serve the food and these men feasted like Romans, drinking and shouting. Then at two on the dot, someone clapped his hands and the room went quiet and they all filed out like well-behaved school children. Whatever you say, they used to have discipline.'

Luca asked if there was ever a problem in their paying.

'Paying? Of course! One time, about six men came in and ate about a million lires' worth of food and wine. This was a small restaurant, so being who they were, I offered a generous discount, for old friends. I realised I had said the wrong thing and the table went quiet. One said that a million lire of damage to the restaurant tonight would be the least of my problems, until one man I half knew saved my skin. He told them that I was joking and of course they shouldn't pay. For one moment, everyone stared. Then burst into laughter. They liked the food, so left plenty of money in the end. But I learnt never to demand again.'

The niggle that turned to an itch has grown into something close to guilt. Here I am, approaching this part of the trip like some ghoulish ambulance chaser, looking to glamorise murderers. The old Mafia may have had perfect manners but that didn't stop them from being responsible for extortion and murder. The longer I spend here, the quicker their ill-earned lustre starts to peel away.

* * *

On the way back, Nunzio hears us talking about Biondo and quietly asks if we knew of Don Calo. Calogero Vizzini was one of the legends of the Honoured Society, a man of 'refined and imaginative criminality', Mayor of the town of Villalba, honorary colonel in the US army and the most powerful, wily and cunning Mafia chief in the whole of Sicily. Large and bulky, he spoke in a thick Sicilian dialect, dressed in shirtsleeves and braces and was the man who helped the American Allied forces arrive in Sicily in 1943.

He typified the old school Mafia, the skewed patriarchal figure that inspired both fear and respect.

> No Mafioso sees himself as a criminal [writes Lewis], and the Mafia has always been the enemy of petty crime ... the organisation demands blind obedience from its members, but will defend them in return through thick and thin ... The capo-Mafia [i.e. Calo] considers himself a lawgiver, concerned with the welfare of his people, and prides himself on watching over the advancement of deserving juniors in the organisation with the assiduousness of the master of novices of a religious order. In his own eyes, he never steals from the community, but can see no objection to exploiting his power over men to enrich himself ... he is self-righteous and full of justifications.

Yet even Lewis has a grudging respect for Don Calo, so quick-witted and politically adept was he in his dealings. And many Sicilians still believe that he was the last of the old breed, the Honoured Society that disappeared with the arrival of undisciplined American mobsters, with their drug dealing, disrespect and conspicuous wealth.

'He was a gentleman,' says Nunzio, and I'm sure I catch a nostalgic smile flickering across his face. 'It was 1971 and I was a bus driver.

We would leave Palermo at 5 am and get into Catania by about 9 pm. The roads were poor and the going slow.' The journey now takes about three hours. 'My bus was filled with German tourists and just before I left, an old man shuffled up to me, well dressed but unshowy, and asked for a lift. I had space and invited him on. About 30 km out of Palermo, he asked if we could stop. Sure, I thought, and let him off. He thanked me and climbed into a waiting car and drove off.'

He coughs deeply, dislodging a glob that he spits out the window. 'A little later, we stop for breakfast, there's about 25 of us. We all eat and drink and when I go to pay, they'll hear nothing of it.' He shakes his head. 'I try again and they say no so I put it down to some random act of kindness and drive off. But I make the journey every single week and every time, even with the bus full, we are not allowed to pay a lira. One time, I ask about the local wine, hoping to buy a bottle and take it home to Catania. Within minutes, a 10-litre barrel is loaded on the bus. So at this stage, I think enough. I ask the owners why we never pay, why the wine, why everything.'

He takes one last, deep wheeze from his cigarette and throws it out of the car. 'So the man says, "Some time ago, you gave a lift to an old man. You don't know who it was, but I'll tell you. It was Don Calo. Because you acted so kindly to him, you could turn up here with five buses and you'd still never have to pay."'

Nunzio shook his head at the memory. 'Three years later in Taormina, I met a Sicilian American just in from New York. He said to me, "Tonight, four kids are coming from Palermo. You need to pick them up and bring them back here." I realised that this was something serious, so asked why he'd chosen me, I was young and inexperienced. The man replied, "Because you gave a lift to someone and didn't breathe a word. You are the right sort of guy. Just do it." So I did and that was the last dealings I had with them.' Later on Luca told me that was payback time.

We're nearly at the hotel now.

'It's different now,' he says. 'When Don Calo died, there was a change in Sicily. Everything got vicious. There was no respect or control. Don Calo's death saw the end of the Honoured Society and the start of drugs. In the old days, when you were weak and poor, you would ask them for help and they might ask you for a favour in return. It's not the Honourable Society any more, just ruthless thugs. Now, even a handshake means nothing.'

Of course, Honourable Society or not, Don Calo and many before him were adamant that the peasant should be kept under the yoke, crushing any notion of trade unions or the right to work their own soil. For all the talk of help and protection, it was the old Honourable Society that was utterly ruthless in ensuring the ancient status quo of Sicily (a few feudal landlords and Mafia men running a vast number of peasants with no rights or land of their own). They would kill anyone who opposed them, opening fire on groups of peasants and ruling by fear. One man tried in the Forties, Placido Rozzotto, the son of a Mafioso himself. He attempted to unite and organise the peasants to stand up and use their collective might to break the tyranny. It nearly worked.

But one night, in 1948, Rozzotto went off for a stroll. And never came back. The remains of his body were found deep in a 90-foot ravine outside Corleone and the killers were acquitted thanks to the usual lack of evidence. But these oppressors made sure that no petty crime took place and anyone who overstepped the mark was destroyed. They were powerful and vicious oppressors but men who believed that their own brand of ancient order, of *omertà* and vendetta and control of the poor, was far superior to any new-fangled communist rubbish emanating from the government in Rome.

The next morning, we are supposed to drive south from Palermo to join a sardine-fishing trip. But the weather is too rough and instead we drive to Castellammare del Golfo, an old fishing town which was once the most notorious town on the island for Mafia bloodshed. The writer Gavin Maxwell claimed that in the Fifties, 80 per cent of the male population had served time in prison, while one in three had committed murder.

Today, the most violent thing for miles is the incessant screech of the seagulls and it has the air of Bude at the start of the summer season. The town is also famous for a kind of pasta, Busiati, fresh and rolled along the stem of a grain so it coils. The bread is flat, so fishermen can carry loaves easily under their arm as they wander through the early-morning streets. Palermo and the surrounding area are so obsessed with fresh bread that you can even buy it fresh on a Sunday.

'Even with a fever,' says Luca biting into a piece of the bread, 'the people will wake up to crawl out of bed and get their fresh bread. People in Catania tease the Palermo lot about their obsession with bread. The breadcrumbs are an essential part of the cooking of this area.'

Even within Sicily, the regional identities are well defined. Quite aside from the culinary quirks (*cuscusu* in Trapani, for example) of each region, the social characteristics are sharp.

'In Palermo,' says Luca, 'people are known to be much harder. Palermo is seen as closed and institutional, show-offs who can be arrogant. Whereas in Catania, everyone is more open and works harder.'

The fact that Luca is a Catanian (well, from Lipari but almost the same) may account for his bias but I have heard the same repeated over and over again. As for the cooking, it's not just a question of each region and town or even village. Like the rest of Italy, different houses will claim that their speciality is that much better than the one next door, that much more delicious and authentic.

We stop off in the village of Scopello for a Pane Cunzatu, a popular sandwich that they claim as their own invention. There are different versions nearby but the key is the use of cheap ingredients. They take a loaf of long, flat bread, split it and drizzle with oil, sprinkled with salt, pepper, chunks of tomato, anchovies and pecorino cheese. Other towns might add olives but here, this is heresy. The result is Sicily in a sandwich – punchy, salty and robust. The tomatoes are sweet, tempering the aggressive salt of the anchovies, while the cheese adds its lactic weight and hints of oregano lift it all up. Made with second-rate ingredients, it would be near inedible. Here, though, you couldn't consider eating anything else. It's as much a part of the landscape as the old tuna-tinning factory lying empty by the shore below.

Of course, a mere sandwich does little to feed our hunger and an hour or so later, we are sitting on the seafront of Mondello. Four kilometres out of Palermo, this is where the city escapes the searing summer heat and the rich have traditionally owned second houses. The streets are thronged with Sicilians, wandering from one cup of coffee to another gelato. No one seems without food for very long although the obesity is nothing compared to America.

We're in Da Calogero, a place started in 1932 as a shack on the shorefront specialising in sea urchins. They still sell these prickly beasts by the thousand and even now, two men sit at the front, just by the street, their sole job to crack them open (they wear a heavy glove on their right hand) and send them over to the hungry masses.

The owner, Angelo, is a well-fed mountain of a man with a long white ponytail, drooping moustache and voice as deep as the Tyrrhenian Sea. One rumble from him brings platters of tender octopus, locally caught and served with oil and lemon. Then fasolari, a clam only found in this area, with bright red meat, a tough texture and marked flavour. One is quite enough. The whelk-like mucconi (so called because they look like lips) taste of lukewarm seawater but have good texture. The mussels are exquisite, plump, orange blobs of perfectly sweet flesh while the sea-snails, Sciacca, wallow in a rich tomato sauce.

Best of all are the urchins, as close to a taste of subtle perfection as I know. They're much softer here than in Japan, and less fishy. Each creature only bears up enough food for half a spoonful but their flavour make even the finest Colchester native seem brash and unwieldy. Eating these from the shell is like prostrating yourself on the altar of pure oral pleasure.

Luca is bellowed at by Angelo for putting a drop of lemon on the reddy-orange inside but takes little notice.

'Bollocks to that. In Lipari, we eat with lemon. In the days before refrigeration, it was supposed to disinfect the flesh. It brings out the flavour, rather than drowning.'

A long and loud argument ensues, which ends with Angelo storming off, muttering darkly, while Luca swears under his breath. Luca does admit that his father is a purist like Angelo. I still think the lemon cossets rather than overwhelms but keep my mouth firmly shut. In England, I can bang on all day about the lemon or Tabasco on oysters debate (I'm with both, but in minute quantities). Here, I'm well out of my depth. The sea urchin pasta is more decadent still, intensely smooth and rounded, a fiesta of overexcited hyperbole. It's like the warm, scented breath of a mermaid, more evocative than strident, each bite giving just a far-off whisper of the sea. The ingredients are so fresh as to need little embellishment and Luca is still amazed at the vibrancy of the new Sicily.

'It's like a new person,' he says between bites, 'and I hardly recognise it from 15 years ago. Well, apart from the Palermo people. They still think they know best.'

That afternoon, we fester in the unmoving traffic on the way to Bagheria, a seventeenth- and eighteenth-century aristocratic summer retreat now connected to Palermo in an unbroken sprawl of suburbs. Still more markets line the road, from official-looking stalls to men flogging homemade bread from the back of a van. Luca wants me to meet a priest who has taken on the Mafia and started to reopen long dormant estates, using men fresh out of prison and drug addiction to farm the soil. I expect to meet him in some quiet backstreet church and am amazed as we drive into the Villa Palagonia, or 'villa of the monsters', a masterpiece of Sicilian Baroque.

'I'm afraid you can't see many of the monsters,' admits Padre Salvatore Lo Bue, 'as the lights are broken.' But peering through the gloom, I can make out dragons and soldiers, gods and unidentifiable beasts scattering the lush gardens. The villa was built by Ferdinand, Prince of Palagonia, a hideous hunchback bitter at his beautiful wife's endless infidelities. The statues were supposed to caricature all of these lovers and the roof of the ballroom was originally entirely covered in mirrors, so he could watch the movements of his wife. Now, they are old and cracked but you can still get a taste of the ornate opulence that once thrived within.

As we walk through to Padre Salvatore's private quarters, we pass a tortoiseshell cabinet stuffed full with buddhas. This is no ordinary Catholic priest. He is about 50, dressed in a well-cut suit with a white silk polo neck, more Armani than Ave Maria. He has large round glasses and neat, short grey hair. But this is a man of quiet, intense authority. His clothes might be sharp but his passion and dedication quite extraordinary. We sit down and a tray of rich Sicilian cakes arrive, and a jug of freshly squeezed orange juice. He offers the cakes around ('Any time you go into a Sicilian house, you'll be offered these cakes,' Luca told me afterwards) and once everyone is munching, he starts to talk.

'I've been working with recovering drug addicts since 1983. There's a huge unemployment problem in Sicily but, for ex-addicts, it was even harder to find work. They would finish their community work but always be labelled "druggies" and "ex-cons" so couldn't get any kind of job. Most didn't even have a primary school education so it was a Catch-22 situation. No diploma, no work.'

He stops to take a small bite from what looks like a dollop of pure cream. He licks his lips carefully and continues.

'So my solution was to get them to work on the land. It's not an attractive profession for kids but if something else was attached, it would be of more interest. All the lands and estates confiscated from the Mafia were lying abandoned and no one dared to enter them. For obvious reasons.' He looks at me and smiles.

'"The Mafia had all of this property because of you," I told the kids. "They got fat and rich on your addiction." So if they had the courage of going in, working and sleeping at these estates, it was like being cleansed of their past.'

The tray of cakes is proffered again and I take another sticky concoction, so as not to appear rude. I manage to drop it down the front of my jacket but the Padre proffers a cloth, waits for me to spread the stain all over my chest, then carries on.

'At the start, everyone said we were crazy. To produce olive oil and fruits and peppers from this Mafia land. But then they started to realise that we had created something special. This wasn't just an ideal, the products were fantastic too. The only problem was that no one would offer us a penny of financial support. We ran courses, "A course towards legality", to help the ex-addicts get going. The government used to give us about €50,000 per year to help, which wasn't much anyway. But when we asked for extra funds to help these courses, they even stopped the €50,000. Then in 2005, they came back and offered €500 per year. It was an insult and, of course, I didn't take it. They have so much money, yet they give nothing.'

For the first time that night, the priest raises his voice a little.

'When the ex-cons and drug addicts leave prison and go to the town hall for work, they're sent straight to us. But we don't get a whisper of help.'

We sit in this high-ceilinged room, all staring intently at the priest. No one speaks and the only noise is the occasional clink of ice in the orange juice. This is the first time I've heard someone bucking the trend (although Orlando did; I've yet to meet him) and fighting for the rights of the twenty-first-century peasants, the drug addicts held in the Mafia's grasp. He is a remarkably brave man, and fully aware of the risks he is taking. Yet he is so enthused that it is impossible not to be inspired by his scheme. And you get the feeling that if the Mayor even lifted a finger to help, his life wouldn't be worth living for much longer.

I ask if there have been any repercussions from the Mafia. The cakes do another round and a cat mewls outside. It's now totally dark outside.

'Well, since the start, we have planted more than 4,000 new olive trees, and we do everything from the planting to the harvesting. But in 1999, the night before we moved into a new property, a tractor was burnt in the main hall of the house. And 260 olive trees were cut down with chainsaws. It was the ex-owners, making their displeasure clear. The *carabinieri* even have phone calls recorded, with the Mafia kids telling each other they wish they had more chainsaws so they could finish the job.'

He shrugs. 'But the *carabinieri* will do nothing. For the same reason, the town halls do nothing. However good a cause that they might believe it is, the Mafia are still strong here. So far, I've sold two houses, three cars and another house in Palermo just to finance it all. It is worth every penny.'

He gives me a bottle of the olive oil, a symbol of all that he has fought for. It's organic, called 'Libera Terra' or 'Free Land' for obvious reasons. And the top of the label proudly bears the words, '*Dalle terre confiscate alla Mafia*'. 'From land confiscated from the Mafia.'

This oil is not only well made (grassy, with an intensely peppery finish) but offers a way out for ex-prisoners. And it does so by breaking the taboo and taking on the might of the Mafia. As we get ready to leave, the Padre tells me about the town itself.

'Bagheria is not only a town of seventeenth-century aristocracy and artists. It's always been one of the lungs of the Mafia. In 1981, five people were killed on the streets on Christmas morning, from a drive-by shooting. And that's just one incident. A few years ago Mannoia, the 'chemist' of the Mafia, had all the women in his family gunned down. This would have never happened in the old days. A local senator was killed recently, and a minister too. They even killed the head of police here. The Mafia are still very much in our midst but I am against them and I want the world to know. You tell your readers. And I've just sold 200 bottles of our oil to Tokyo, so it's really starting to take off. This oil will just get better and better.'

What he doesn't actually say is the danger he faces himself. The robes of priesthood are no longer a shield against the bullets of the Mafia. And neither is his faith. As the small figure disappears back into the black garden, overrun with statues, I feel more awful still for thinking the Mafia anything but a cancer across the face of this island.

* * *

We drive back to Palermo in silence. Eventually, Nunzio speaks.

'These are people who are not scared,' he says quietly. 'This is true bravery. I know how dangerous it is for a man like him to do what he does. This lot have no problem with killing noisy priests.'

Half an hour later, and we are back in the city. But Luca receives a last-minute phone call and suddenly it looks like our dinner with Leoluca Orlando is on. Before dinner, though, there is one last thing I have to try – *milza*, a Palermo street classic. Sliced veal spleen is grilled then mixed with lemon juice, salt and pepper and eaten in a soft bun. The taste is strong and the texture a little chewy but overall it is robust and beautifully beefy. The contrast of soft bun and chopped gland is superb, despite sounding foul. It is exactly as street food should be – fresh, hot and packed with flavour.

I eat mine *schiettu* or *nubile* which means plain but it can be topped with fresh ricotta and grated caciocavallo to become *maritatu* or 'married'. Even for me, this is a taste combination too much. I wipe a dribble of spleen juice from my cheek as Luca eats the last of his golden panelle (by now, he has admitted an out-of-control addiction to these chickpea fritters) and we drive to a palazzo in the centre of Palermo, where Leoluca Orlando will be awaiting us.

Actually, we will be waiting for him, as he is famously tardy. But with a never-ending supply of snacks to keep us going until dinner, no one is complaining.

'To eat properly in Sicily, you have to eat in a private house.' We are sitting in the palatial splendour of Antonio's family palazzo. Like most of Palermo, the entrance looked unassuming, dull from the outside, its face turned inwards. In the day, the door is almost hidden behind a vegetable stall. But once you get through the thick walls, you enter into an old-fashioned world of heavy furniture, silk walls and ageless privilege.

'Every 20 km, the food changes in Sicily and if you go from Trapani to Catania, you'll find a world of difference. Have another arancino.' Antonio pushed the tray towards me.

These deep-fried rice balls, known as 'little oranges', are ubiquitous in Sicily and this one was filled with a rich ragu. They are fresh from the oil, hot and soft. Luca, meanwhile, is making light work of his fiftieth panelle of the day.

'Leoluca is coming later, but he's always late. He's campaigning all day, as the elections are just around the corner.'

His cousin, Riccardo, comes in. Half English and half Italian, he is slim and immaculately dressed in a fusion of Euro chic and Savile Row sharp. He starts to explain about Orlando.

'In 1993, Orlando came to power in Palermo on the anti-Mafia ticket. For the first time in history, the working classes erupted and rose up, wanting to get rid of the Mafia after the murder of Judge Falcone, the great anti-Mafia judge You have to remember how brutal this murder was. They used half a tonne of TNT to blow up the road and his wife and three bodyguards were also killed. So the anti-Mafia feeling was passionate and Orlando rode that wave into power, becoming so popular with the people as to become untouchable, even by the Mafia.'

At this point, there is a commotion outside and I feel the man even before he enters the room. The doors fling open and Orlando strides in, with a well-combed mass of black hair, thick eyebrows, his rugged face touched at the edges with a slight jowliness.

'Sorry I'm late,' he growls, 'but I've been working for 25 hours. I've just got back from a 4,000 person meeting in Catania, then another meeting after that.'

Like all politicians, he cannot resist the theatrical and within moments, we're all clear as to who should be the centre of attention.

But it doesn't matter, as it is almost expected. And his natural charm disarms too much cynicism. He's dressed in striped shirt, soft cashmere jumper, Tod's shoes and smells beautiful. Dinner is a feast, pasta with artichokes and baby broad beans with fresh ricotta, a mouthful of Sicilian spring. We chatter about Sicily, while Orlando is locked deep in conversation with another guest, a fellow, but more junior, politician. Then there's fusilli in tomato sauce, wrapped in smoky aubergine, but as Orlando finishes his food, and sits up ready to address the table, we all go quiet. It is as if the main attraction has turned up – he is an adored if controversial figure in Sicily – and we all sit in silence, waiting for him to start to speak.

He looks around the table, catching all of our eyes, and then begins his oration. 'The main problem with Sicily is that we don't speak the language of today and think the old way. It's not corruption or the Mafia.' He takes a deep draught of wine then stares deep into my eyes. 'I studied philosophy and I try to promote the pride of identity. Leoluca is the saint of Corleone. My grandfather was born in the office of the Mayor of Corleone. The town hall is the former palace of my family. I am Sicilian and I cannot change my identity. I'm proud of it and I have to fight against other Sicilians perverting this identity. When we talk of the Sicilian Mafia, we talk of an identity based in criminality.'

He chews on a biscuit and carries on. 'Family perverted into a criminal group, fellowship into allegiance and honour into shame.'

These words are as smooth and burnished as a sea-worn pebble and I realised this is a well-practised spiel. But it was impossible to take one's eyes off him and he reeled us all in, hooking us like wide-eyed tuna from the depths of the sea.

'We won against the old, traditional Mafia. Today, it does not control the minds of the people as it once did. I'm not saying that the

Mafia doesn't exist. But just as the old Mafia perverted traditional values, the new Mafia still perverts identity. Freedom without respect for the rules is a perversion of the rules. I try to teach a respect for the law and Sicily rather than respect for the Mafia.'

We're getting deep into sound-bite land here and I'm still trying to eat my swordfish and scribble down notes. But there's no doubting the power of his argument. His tone is steady although you sometimes cannot help feeling that this line is well-used. When he starts upon the story of Falcone, though, things get more personal.

'In 1992, after the killing of Falcone and Borsellino [an anti-Mafia colleague of Falcone's, killed by a car-bomb along with five of his police guards], people took to the streets, building a human chain. Normal people were disgusted by the violence, their protectors had been murdered. They killed the good kings and went too far. In Sicily, we have never killed the king. The Mafia bosses made a huge mistake. Those two were noble men and the Mafia killed a king on an island where good kings aren't killed. When the women read about Orlando,' he says of himself in the third person, 'saying *he* will be next, the women said Orlando was not alone. The people are with him.'

Normally, talking about oneself in the third person is an advanced sign of megalomania, or at least rampant egomania, but Orlando's speech and story are compelling. By now, everyone has stopped eating to pay homage to the king of this table.

'The Mafia can kill one man, a hundred men,' he cries, his voice getting more emotive, 'but not thousands of women and children. After the killing of the judges, a powerful Mafia boss decided to get rid of me. But I had the heart and the soul of the people. I had married the Falcones, old friends of mine.'

He trails off and sits lost in thought for a moment, then goes on, on a different tack. 'Normally, organised crime is against and outside the church, outside and against the state. The Mafia is against and inside both those. I want to make them common criminals, nothing more, to strip away their identity. I lived with my wife and daughter in a tiny flat in Palermo, with just four chairs. We had no one for lunch or dinner, no family or friends. It was just too dangerous to be put together with them.'

For the first time, the seasoned mask slips away for a second. But only for a moment. The politician kicks back in. 'My strength comes from speaking to poor people. They believe in me. When my daughter was eight, she asked why people who respected the law lived so badly, and those outside of it were so happy. It's all about changing perceptions of the Mafia in Sicily.'

By now, dinner has stretched deep into the night and the cassata has long been cleared away. But Orlando continues regardless.

'When I was 20 years old, I went to Heidelberg in Germany. Friends would ask me where I came from. Italy, I'd say. Where? The South. Where? they'd push. Sicily. Ah, they'd say, Mafia.'

I remember back to my first meeting with Luca and squirm.

'At that point my life changed. I could go on being embarrassed and living in the Sicilian grey area – my parents and millions of other Sicilians never mentioned the Mafia, just said to keep quiet and forget – or I could be proud of my country. Normality is the goal of modern Sicily. To fight against the normal criminal, the police are enough. But to fight against their identity, they are not sufficient. Zero tolerance does not work against something entrenched in society.'

He pauses so we can digest his words.

'The real problem with Sicily is that we live in the eternal present, the past does not exist, the future does not exist. In the last few years, a film has been made about my time as Mayor of Palermo. "I'll play me," I said.'

I giggle and try to hide it as a sneeze. Leoluca may be charming and inspirational but, by God, his ego could fill the Teatro Massimo.

'"No," they said, you were never a mere mayor, but the clock-maker. You gave Sicilians respect for the past, present, tomorrow." And in the movie, I played the clockmaker.'

There is little doubt as to Orlando's achievements: he corralled the anti-Mafia sentiments into a cohesive whole, using the power of the common people to push forward his much-needed reforms. He made people proud of their Sicilian heritage once more, proud of their city. Yet most people I speak to are not whole-hearted in their support. And like everything else on this island, nothing is to be taken at face value. Many see him as a political opportunist, a chancer who picks the right time to ride into power. A few actually hate him, saying you don't hold that sort of power in Palermo without the right connections. On the whole, the voices of dissent are the cosmopolitan middle classes. The view of the vast majority of stallholders, farmers and shop owners is one of unanimous praise. And whatever they may say, my opinion of the man is based on three hours in his company. I certainly like and respect him. But he is still a slick politician and at this moment, I feel like a spectator at one of those interminable Castro rallies.

'Another problem is the cliché of the Mafia,' he says, suddenly seeming to tire. This is the very cliché that drew me here in the beginning, the basis for a chapter in a book on eating dangerously. I blush, feeling like a shallow fraud.

'When Brando died, a journalist rang me up and asked me for my views. I said he was a wonderful actor and *The Godfather* a wonderful film. But both were tragedies for Sicilians, they made out that Sicily was all about the Mafia. *The Leopard* too. Great book, fantastic film, but it is how everyone sees Sicily. The land of *The Godfather* and *The Leopard*.'

I'm convinced he's worked me out. Jesus, a week ago I really did believe I knew it all. I confused the beauty of Coppola's vision, the perfection of Lampedusa's prose, for the truth.

'The two best-known pieces of art about Sicily are for us,' he goes on, 'the two tragedies. We are victims of our own cliché. But it's looking up. In Corleone last year, there were many robberies. And I rang up the Chief of Police and said, "Congratulations, you have normal robberies." It used to be one of the safest places in the world. But I'm so happy it has normal crimes again. It shows the Mafia power is waning.'

He looks at his watch. 'I must go. I have an election to fight.' He gets up, smooths down his hair and strides out.

Even five minutes after he's left, his presence still looms large. Whatever you feel about his ego and chatter, Orlando is one of the architects of the new Sicily and, because of that, a positive force, at least to this outsider. I leave the island chastened and a little embarrassed. Just over a week ago, I was blissfully unaware of my ignorance. I really believed the hoary old stereotype, another hack in search of romanticised violence, codes of honour and corrupt politicians.

By the time I leave, though, I am utterly confused. The surface has been barely scratched and that convenient black and white – the moral and historical certainty of those endless books and movies – is revealed to be a million different shades of grey. The Mafia is a whole lot less interesting by the end, too, less glamorous and a lot more depressing; common criminals disguised by the finery of family, duty and honour. Whether or not the 'Honoured Society' were that much better than the modern-day mob, I don't know. The likes of the Duke and Nunzio certainly thought so. And my views of this era of Don Calo have simply been gleaned from the eloquent pens of Lewis and Lampedusa.

What I am certain of is a new optimism on the island, be it in the regeneration of previously decrepit areas, a tangible civic pride or simply the rise in tourism. These are the only real truths of my visit, that and the sheer diversity of the Sicilian cuisine. In fact, the only real danger of this final leg of the tour are my hackneyed, outdated preconceptions of the island.

And, I suppose, the perils of mixing boiled offal with a humdinger of a hangover.

EPILOGUE

I sat idle for the first few days back at home, not entirely sure what to do with myself. Sicily had seen the end of my journey and in one way, I was relieved it was all over. No more boredom and Jennifer Lopez movies while cruising over Russia. No more jetlag or communication problems or unsuitable hangovers in visceral foreign markets. I could sink back into my comfortable rut, chewing on roast chicken with my wife while glued to *24* and reruns of *I'm Alan Partridge*.

But after a week, I began to question the relevance of the whole endeavour. Was there any point to this picaresque, greedy tour? Twelve months, four continents, 20,000 air miles and two inches on my waist. For what? When I started, I wasn't really sure what I would find. I knew this wouldn't be some quest with a neat, pat ending and a Jerry Springer-style monologue to tie up any loose ends. If my first aim was to find an alternative to the increased dumbing down of our national palate, I had succeeded. My palate had been teased, tantalised, befouled, astounded, thrilled, delighted and disgusted. Rarely bored though, in the way one of those supermarket meals can only do.

The regional cuisines were thriving, not through some middle-class obsession with artisanal, organic produce (although that was certainly present in Santa Fe) but because the food culture in China, Japan, Korea and almost everywhere else I visited was thriving. The only place I didn't get to try exactly what I wanted was in England, with the elvers. But as a food writer, I cannot but be heartened by the rise in committed small producers who still care about flavour over the fast buck. I realise I'm the middle-class bore I've just mentioned, but there was good reason for not eating elvers. They were simply too precious a commodity now to waste on local bellies.

The British food culture still has a long way to go. Ready meals and processed foods are consumed in ever-increasing amounts, but there is hope. Good, fresh food for all is the aim and I remain positive that one day, we might become a nation where food is a matter of national debate, not just on BBC2 and Channel 4 but in the streets, shop fronts and sitting rooms. I dream of the day where each village has a total belief in the inherent superiority of their own regional recipes, just like in Spain or China or Sicily. The wheels are turning in the right direction, albeit slowly.

My only regret (save drinking excessively at the wrong moments) was missing out on the ortolans. My contact went dead, disappearing in a puff of bird flu panic. This ultimate gem of French gastronomy seemed fascinating but my failure in finding a specimen was almost as important as crunching upon its bones. It proved, beyond all our wildly different views of what is and isn't disgusting and dangerous – my friend's pea, Dougie's banana – that food is still inherently dangerous. That everything we eat has the potential to be deadly, whether by choking, poisoning or passing on a bird flu we know little about.

Think of beef and BSE, eggs and salmonella, the potentially carcinogenic Sudan 1 and its infiltration into our food chain. Even the most basic foods can become a threat to health when handled without due care. Nothing I tried was truly dangerous. The tripe got less bad as I got used to it (well, save the really plain flaps of stomach) and the insects, snakes and other varied creeping and slithering things were sometimes interesting, but never life-threatening. And I'd happily eat those ant eggs again and again. The fugu could have induced a slow and agonising death but the odds were heavily stacked in my favour. If I had prepared it myself, then the peril would have been more real.

But even the most squirm-inducing dishes – the stinking tofu, the filthy silkworm pupae and raw tripe – were just foods that I didn't enjoy. Like cottage cheese, nut roasts and turkey rissoles. Take away my upbringing and preconceptions and they're all just food, fuel for survival. Yet I proved myself a hypocrite even with this theory, as I was simply unable to separate my love of dogs from the logic of it being just another piece of meat. The method of its production is unspeakably cruel but it was a lifetime of sentimental baggage that loomed equally large. I tried to be clinical, put aside all these childish aversions. And in Seoul, I failed. Despite my pompous soundings to the contrary, I met my limit there.

The importance of knowing exactly what we put in our mouths is paramount. Asia and much of Europe do not share our obsession with hiding the origins of steak in neatly vacuum-packed trays. A wild snake, freshly caught and skinned (and preferably not some hideously rare specimen), is far superior to the broiler chicken. The more we learn about the source of our food, the better. It is this knowledge and understanding that lessen food's inherent risk. In Britain, locally produced food has become a rallying call and righteous cause. And in a country that lost its culinary way some time after the First World War, this is a positive movement. But in the rest of the world, local food is plain common sense; the link between beast and plate is never hidden, rather celebrated in all its gory glory.

I also learnt that my capacity for sweeping generalisation and twee stereotype was vast, with entire continents being judged before I had actually visited them. If anything, this year showed me how pitifully little I really knew. If I broadened my stubbornly narrow mind by just one millimetre, then it was a success. Most of all, though, this year of so-called eating dangerously proved that regionalised cooking and cuisine are still very much alive. McDonald's and its ilk get ever more powerful but the joys of home-cooked and comfort food burn more fiercely still. With a few exceptions (in Japan and Korea), I kept away from the haute cuisine and cheffy flourishes. I wanted a real taste of the country I was in. Whether or not I succeeded is up to you. But far from putting me off the more exotic reaches of our worldwide suste- nance, this year actually made me crave them all the more.

BIBLIOGRAPHY

GENERAL
A Cook's Tour, Anthony Bourdain (Bloomsbury, London, 2001)
Strange Foods, Jerry Hopkins (Periplus Editions, Hong Kong, 1999)
The Curiosities of Food, Peter Lund Simmons (Ten Speed Press, Berkeley, 2001)
The Oxford Companion to Food, Edited by Alan Davidson (OUP, Oxford, 1999)
Unmentionable Cuisine, Calvin W. Schwabe (The University Press of Virginia, Charlottesville, Virginia, 1979)

ELVERS
A Book of Food, P. Morton Shand (Jonathan Cape, London, 1927)
A Taste of the West Country, Theodora Fitzgibbon (Pan, London, 1972)
Consider the Eel, Richard Schweid (University of North Carolina Press, North Carolina, 2002)
Cornucopia, Paul Richardson (Little, Brown, London, 2000)
English Food, Jane Grigson (Macmillan, London, 1974)
Food in England, Dorothy Hartley (Little, Brown, London, 1999)
Good Things in England, Florence White (Jonathan Cape, London, 1932)
The Naturalist on the Thames, C.J. Cornish (Blackie & Son, London, 1905)
The Shell Country Book, Geoffrey Grigson (Phoenix House, London, 1962)

NEW MEXICO
Green Chile Bible, Edited by *Albuquerque Tribune* (Clear Light, Santa Fe, New Mexico, 1993)
Hot Peppers, Richard Schweid (Madrona Publishers, Seattle, Washington, 1987)
Red Chile Bible, Kathleen Hansel and Audrey Jenkins (Clear Light, Santa Fe, New Mexico, 1998)
The Book of Eels, Tom Fort (HarperCollins, London, 2002)
The Chile Chronicles, Carmella Padilla (Museum of New Mexico Press, Santa Fe, New Mexico, 1997)
The Chile Pepper Encyclopedia, Dave DeWitt (William Morrow, New York, 1999)
The Feast of Santa Fe, Huntley Dent (Fireside, New Jersey, 1993)
The Fiery Cuisines, Dave DeWitt and Nancy Gerlach (Ten Speed Press, Berkeley, California, 1995)
The Hot Book of Chillies, David Floyd (New Holland, London, 2006)
The Spicy Food Lover's Bible, Dave DeWitt and Nancy Gerlach (Stewart, Tabori and Chang, New York, 2005)

CHINA
China Diary, Stephen Spender (Thames and Hudson, London, 1982)
Revolutionary Chinese Cookbook, Fuchsia Dunlop (Ebury Press, London, 2006)
Sichuan Cookery, Fuchsia Dunlop (Penguin, London, 2001)
The Food of China, E.N. Anderson (Yale University Press, New Haven, 1988)

NASHVILLE
Alice, Let's Eat, Calvin Trillin (Random House, New York, 1978)
American Fried, Calvin Trillin (Doubleday, New York, 1974)

Barbeque America, Rick Browne and Jack Bettridge (Time-Life Books, Virginia, 1999)
Cornbread Nation 2, by Lolis Eric Elie (University of North Carolina Press, North Carolina, 2004)
Finger Lickin' Good, Paul Levy (Chatto and Windus, London, 1990)
Fried Chicken, John T. Edge (G.P. Putnam's Sons, New York, 2004)
North Carolina Barbeque, Bob Garner (John F. Blair, North Carolina, 1996)
Smokestack Lightning, Lolis Eric Elie (North Point Press, New York, 1996)
Southern Belly, John T. Edge (Hill Street Press, Athens, Georgia, 2000)
Southern Food, John Egerton (University of North Carolina Press, North Carolina 1993)
Third Helpings, Calvin Trillin (Ticknor and Fields, New York, 1983)

TOKYO
A Dictionary of Japanese Food, Richard Hosking (Tuttle Publishing, Boston, Maryland, 1996)
A Taste of Japan, Donald Richie (Kodansha International, 1985)
Dangerous Marine Animals, Bruce W. Halstead MD (Cornell Maritime Press, Cambridge, Maryland, 1959)
Food of Japan, Shirley Booth (Grub Street, London, 2000)
Japanese Cookery: A Simple Art, Shizuo Tsuji (Kodansha International, 1980)

KOREA
History of the Oregon Trail, John Dunn (unknown, 1844)
The Kimchee Cookbook, Kim Man-Jo, Lee Kyou-Tae, Lee O-Young (Periplus Editions, Hong Kong, 1999)
The Korean Kitchen, Copeland Marks (Chronicle Books, San Francisco, 1993)
The Pantropheon, Alexis Soyer (Simpkin Marshall & Co., London, 1853)
Voyage Round the World, W.S.W. Ruschenberger (unknown, 1838)

LAOS
A Dragon Apparent, Norman Lewis (Jonathan Cape, London, 1951)
A History of Laos, Martin Stuart-Fox (Cambridge University Press, Cambridge and Melbourne, 1997)
Ant Egg Soup, Natacha Du Pont De Bie (Sceptre, London, 2004)
Fish and Fish Dishes of Laos, Alan Davidson (Prospect Books, Totnes, 2003)
Notes of a Journey on the Upper Mekong, Siam, H. Warrington Smyth (John Murray, 1895)
The Great Railway Bazaar, Paul Theroux (Penguin, New York, 1975)
The Ravens, Christopher Robbins (Bantam Press, London, 1988)
Traditional Recipes of Laos, Phia Sing (Prospect Books, Totnes, 1995)

SPAIN
Culinaria Spain, Marion Trutter (Konemann, 1999)
Modern Spanish Cooking, Sam and Eddie Hart (Quadrille, London, 2006)
North Atlantic Seafood, Alan Davidson (Prospect Books, Totnes, 2003)
The Cuisine of Spain, Teresa Barrenechea (Ten Speed Press, Berkeley, 2005)
The Food of Spain and Portugal, Elizabeth Luard (Kyle Cathie, London, 2004)

SICILY
Cucina Siciliana, Clarissa Hyman (Conran Octopus, London, 2002)
From Caesar to the Mafia – Luigi Barzini (The Library Press, New York, 1971)
Sicilian Food, Mary Taylor Simeti (Grub Street, London, 1999)
The Honoured Society, Norman Lewis (Eland Books, London, 2003)